# BOLINGBROKE AND HIS CIRCLE

*Harvard Political Studies*

PUBLISHED UNDER THE DIRECTION
OF THE DEPARTMENT OF GOVERNMENT
IN HARVARD UNIVERSITY

# BOLINGBROKE

## AND HIS CIRCLE

*The Politics of Nostalgia in the Age of Walpole*

---

ISAAC KRAMNICK

HARVARD UNIVERSITY PRESS

*Cambridge, Massachusetts*

1968

The frontispiece in this book is a portrait
of Lord Bolingbroke by an unknown artist.
It is reproduced with the permission
of the National Portrait Gallery,
London.

*To Miriam*

# Preface

Behind this study lie two questions. Why is Bolingbroke, known primarily as a rationalist philosopher of the Enlightenment, so worshipped by English conservatives who are themselves, since Burke, so set against what the Enlightenment represents in political, social, and religious thought? The second question relates to Bolingbroke's public life. How does one explain the intense animosity between Bolingbroke and Walpole which provides the energy for English political life between 1725 and 1740? Is it mere vindictiveness, ambition, jealousy, or the inevitable reflex of the "outsider" against the "insider"? Or is it, as the late Victorian writers thought, their falling out at Eton which forever fated them to be protagonists?

These questions are not unrelated. In order to understand Bolingbroke's appeal to later Tories, I think that one must first come to terms with the nature of the opposition of Bolingbroke and his circle to Walpole. Examining the published writings of the period, the grand public statements, helps somewhat to understand the dynamics of this great feud. But it is necessary to go beyond this to the less obvious world of public and private debate. Pamphlets and the weekly newspapers were the political platforms of Augustan politics; it is here that the great opposition takes on flesh and blood. It is here, then, that one discovers that the concern of Bolingbroke's circle with corruption goes far beyond the mere person and political practice of Walpole. Bolingbroke's obsession with Walpole and the personification in him of cultural, social, and political corruption is, we are usually told, a rationalization of mere spite. But there is much more than just this. Bolingbroke could as easily have said, as Nietzsche did in *Ecce Homo,* "I never attack persons; I only avail myself of the person as a strong magnifying glass with which one can render visible a general but creeping calamity which it is otherwise hard to get hold of."

It is Bolingbroke the critic of a corrupt and venal society who has so appealed to the English Tories. They are not concerned with Bolingbroke the philosopher. If they care about religion they are apt to dismiss the Enlightenment Bolingbroke as an aberration explained by his sojourn in France. What really matters and what enshrines Bolingbroke in the Tory Pantheon are his political writings and career, in which he rejects the new age of liberal individualism and the introduction of financial capitalism into English society and politics.

Much of what Bolingbroke and his circle wrote about in their poetry, pamphlets, and papers was an inaccurate assessment of the England they knew and a poor prediction of the future. Much of their attack was unfair to Walpole. In terms of my own political position Bolingbroke's message also involves values and beliefs no more appealing than those he questioned. This study is, then, by no means another in the long line of conservative apologia for Bolingbroke. But evaluation and criticism is not my principal concern. My immediate task in this book is to make the rather novel claim that Bolingbroke and his circle did have something significant to say about English politics and society. Some of Bolingbroke's errors have been exposed by Peter M. G. Dickson in his recent study, *The Financial Revolution in England, 1688-1756* (New York: St. Martins, 1967). I regret that my study of Bolingbroke was already in the hands of the publisher when for the first time I had access to Dickson's superb study. Although I wish I had had the benefit of it, I feel obliged to let my own work stand. I am heartened by the fact that my much less extensive investigation into economic history is fundamentally in agreement with Dickson's masterfully researched findings.

This study began several years ago as a doctoral dissertation at Harvard University. During the intervening years I have accumulated many debts to scholars who freely offered advice and criticism. In the initial period of my research at the British Museum and before my ideas took shape, many English authorities on the politics and history of the period talked with me about Bolingbroke. Many of them may not even remember the hour or two or more spent with this particular visiting American, but I have always cherished their kindness and assistance. At various stages in the life of the manuscript it has been read and criticized by John Dunn, then visiting Harvard and now at Kings College, Cambridge; by Judith Shklar, Harvey Mansfield, Jr., Carl J. Friedrich, and Samuel H. Beer; all of Harvard. J. G. A. Pocock of Washington University at St. Louis and Michael Walzer of Harvard both read and gave advice on parts of the manuscript. George Nadel of the Warburg Institute and Bernard Bailyn of Harvard University were particularly helpful to me and throughout the preparation of the study have persistently championed my efforts, providing support that often lightened my work and worries. I hope that in some way the finished product reflects the many cogent criticisms and the continuous sage advice offered by all these scholars.

I also want to thank the institutions that have made my research and writing possible. Research in England was funded by a grant from the Social Science Research Council in its program for legal and political philosophy, now sadly defunct. The transition from dissertation to manuscript was facilitated by a generous summer grant from Harvard University. The typing of the manuscript was financed through a grant from Brandeis University. For important clerical assistance I want also to thank Cornelia Cummings, Linda Giardina and Judith Fleischer.

I must also acknowledge the kindness of the editors of *History and Theory* and the *Political Science Quarterly* for permitting me to use in this book parts of articles that originally appeared in their pages.

There remain three people to whom I am particularly grateful. My wife, Miriam, has helped in all stages of the preparation of this book. Moreover, whatever of value there may be in my excursions into the world of literature is owed in great part to her keen understanding of Augustan letters. Within a broader context I would also like to thank Stanley Hoffmann of Harvard who played a decisive role in shaping my intellectual development and Judith Shklar of Harvard who has, not only in the preparation of this book but over the years, provided guidance, encouragement, and friendship. That this book has been written is the best acknowledgment of my debt to them.

Waltham, Massachusetts                                Isaac Kramnick
August 22, 1967

# Contents

## Contents

# BOLINGBROKE AND HIS CIRCLE

For the new England, or the present state of things
caused by the Revolution, as far exceeds the
old, as light does darkness, as liberty does
slavery; or as happiness does misery.

—*The London Journal*, 8 August 1730


[Rome] who had been the envy, as well as the
mistress of nations, fell to be an object of
their scorn, or of their pity. . . . Into such
a state . . . as miserable as this, will the
people of Britain fall, and deserve to fall.

—LORD BOLINGBROKE,
*A Dissertation Upon Parties,* 1735

# Introduction: Bolingbroke, Political Thought, and the Augustan Age

"Who now reads Bolingbroke, who ever read him through?" The answer to Burke's famous query is that many have, and many still do. Those who have sought to understand Bolingbroke's writings have usually emphasized their biographical and psychological roots. It is traditional to analyze his writings against the background of his controversial personality and his meteoric and somewhat scandal-ridden career. Since he was vain, deceitful, conniving, irreligious, traitorous, and immoral, his ideas must be useless. Such a suspect personality and such an opportunistic career could hardly produce any ideas of value. Robert Walpole himself established this expedient method of dismissing Bolingbroke's ideas. He answered Bolingbroke's attack on the Septennial Act in 1734 with a counterattack on the thinker and not the ideas. How could anyone listen, Walpole asked, to the ideas of such an "anti-Minister,"

who thinks himself a person of so great and extensive parts, and of so many eminent qualifications that he looks upon himself as the only person in the kingdom capable to conduct the public affairs of the nation . . . (a man) void of all faith and honour, and betraying every master he has ever served . . . Can there be imagined a greater disgrace to human nature than such a wretch as this?[1]

Similarly, in the nineteenth century, Whig scholars rejected Bolingbroke's ideas less for their intrinsic content than for his alleged lack of principles, moral, political, or religious. Thomas Macaulay cautioned against paying heed to Bolingbroke for he was self-seeking and treacherous: "a brilliant knave."[2] John Morley, Walpole's Victorian biographer, wrote of Bolingbroke that "in every part he was a consummate posture master . . . Of all the characters in our history, Bolingbroke must be pronounced to be most of a charlatan.

Of all the writing in our literature, his is the hollowest, the flashiest, the most insincere."[3] Leslie Stephen dismissed Bolingbroke's political thought because it was merely "a transparent covering for personal hostilities." He was a rake and an intriguer, a "representative of the current insincerity of the time."[4]

More recent scholarship continues a similar pattern. His principles, writes C. G. Robertson, can be discounted, for they were determined by his insatiable ambition for power and were colored by his treacherous and lying life.[5] A recent chronicler of the eighteenth-century Commonwealthman and his ideas, Caroline Robbins, avoids Bolingbroke, not because his opinions exclude him from her study, but because he is far too devious and unprincipled to be worthy of attention. He is an opportunist, whose writings and journal merit no consideration.[6] J. H. Plumb, the definitive biographer of Walpole, cautions against dwelling too much on the ideas of Walpole's chief opponent for reasoned thought was not Bolingbroke's forte. His personality is the key, Plumb suggests, that unlocks the true Bolingbroke. Fate had been unkind to Bolingbroke. "He could not forbear to cheat; there was a twist, a bias in his nature, that drew him irresistibly to duplicity. The secret game and intrigue were his métier."[7] But the most sweeping of the biographical interpretations of Bolingbroke's ideas is to be found in recent writings on the period by the disciples of Sir Lewis Namier. Implicit in their method is the denial of any significance to Bolingbroke's thought other than as a reflection of the period in his career when he was an outsider seeking office.

There have been, to be sure, some who have avoided the biographical and the psychological, and have offered formal and intrinsic interpretations of Bolingbroke's opinions. In recent years scholars have found in close readings of Bolingbroke's texts the origins of the idea of nonparty government, the first articulation of the theory of legitimate opposition, and the ideas in reaction to which Burke was led to his theory of the legitimacy and necessity of party.[8] Others have seen Bolingbroke's political views as the source of Montesquieu's theory of the separation of powers, as an early contribution to the theory of constitutionalism, and, finally, as a repudiation of Machiavelli's immoral political thought.[9]

What has not been done in trying to understand Bolingbroke's writings, however, is to look at them from a fourth perspective, their social context. Although I shall not enter here into the intricate methodological problems inherent in the concept of ideology,[10] it should be apparent that inquiry along the lines of what Marx called ideology, the relationship of material existence and ideas, is essential to an understanding of Bolingbroke's writings. Such an inquiry need not serve the same polemical purposes as it did for Marx who, to show that they were tools of class warfare "unmasked" the real social roots of ideas and "exposed" their hidden class character. More appropriate for our purposes is inquiry along the lines suggested by Mannheim's adaptation of Marx. The political views of Bolingbroke can be seen as products of his social existence, of his position in the group life of Augustan England, in terms both of economic class and occupational group. Bolingbroke's writings should be seen as examples of what Karl Mannheim calls a "style of thought,"[11] in this case characteristic of certain social groups, that is, the nobility and the gentry. This "style of thought" informs his political ideas and firmly roots them in the social, economic, and political position and interests of the groups that he represents, which in turn are the social carriers of these ideas. It is, of course, not novel to suggest that a writer's opinions on society and politics are shaped by his preferences or interests. In the eighteenth century Walpole accused Bolingbroke of this very thing, and in the twentieth century, Namier's students repeat the charge. What has to be noted, however, is that Bolingbroke's ideas illuminate more than partisan political preferences.

Underlying the formal terms of Bolingbroke's political philosophy and his discussion of the English Constitution is an attitude critical toward his age and its socioeconomic developments. His primary concern is with developments in the social order that affect the political world. Since he is seldom read in these terms, however, Bolingbroke has always seemed an enigma for the historian of political thought. His thought appears elusive and idiosyncratic; he doesn't seem to fit. Appearing after the seventeenth-century giants Hobbes and Locke, and before Hume, Burke, and the theoretically productive era of George III, he is mentioned casually as one proceeds to the less puzzling era of the Industrial Revolution and the new England. But considering his thought as an outgrowth of special conditions in Augustan England makes Bolingbroke less of an anomaly. His career and writings are a comment on and a reaction to the economic, social, and political changes that occurred in England in the first part of the eighteenth century. His period is overshadowed by the social developments that preceded it in the seventeenth century, which lie behind the thought of Harrington, Hobbes, and Locke, and by the era of industrialism and the rise of middle-class liberalism that followed, which so interests the student of Burke and English radicalism. The Augustan period, however, was not lacking in social developments. Revolutionary social change was an important part of the fabric of its society and had a correspondingly important impact on political institutions. The financial revolution of the Augustan years with its growth and development of banking, credit, and capital facilities, was an indispensable prerequisite for the Industrial Revolution conventionally dated from the middle of the century. Bolingbroke regarded these changes as the root of that corruption which he described as pervading English society. Walpole and his Robinocracy, the term coined by the Opposition to describe Sir Robert's regime, were the glaring symbols of a corruption that, to Bolingbroke, involved much more than mere jobbing, pensioning, and buying of commoners; in a broader sense, it signified the disorder and chaos brought to the traditional political and social world by money and financial innovations. To Bolingbroke, Walpole's political corruption was the symbol of a much larger corrupt society; a society quickly leaving behind an older and purer aristocratic ideal. The financial revolution of 1690-1740 was, then, the most meaningful social experience in the lives of Bolingbroke and the others in his circle, like Pope and Swift, who shared his "style of thought"; it informs all their writings on politics and society, and it feeds their gloom, their satire, and their indignation. They saw an aristocratic social and political order being undermined by money and new financial institutions and they didn't like it.

Two reactions to this socioeconomic experience characterized Augustan England. Some accepted the new order, to some extent sponsoring it, even while basing their political power upon it. Walpole and his establishment Whigs wholeheartedly endorsed the new age and Defoe sang its praises. Another group, typified by Bolingbroke, rejected the new England and lamented the demise of what they considered to have been the traditional political and social structure firmly entrenched since the days of the Tudors.

However, recent political studies of Augustan England assign little significance to this ideological division and suggest that ideas, including socially conditioned ideas, played no role in the political life of these years.[12] The opposition party, it is contended, was made up simply of the "outs": independent Tories, dissident Whigs, small merchants and traders. Whatever program the opposition might offer, such as limitation of the executive through Place Bill and Triennial Parliaments, was meaningless because the purpose of the opposition is assumed to have been simply to rally the gentry and small merchants, and hold them together by appealing to their political prejudices. No group or party, argue John Brooke, Lucy Sutherland, and Archibald Foord, really intended to implement these doubtful political principles. What the opposition said was not important; all that mattered was what they did and who they were. The opposition, this interpretation suggests, was not held together by any set of ideas; it was only an alliance of groups in a similar strategic position, outside the government. Like Rockingham Whigs in opposition later in the century, Bolingbroke's opposition, it is contended, had no base in ideas, no policy, no ideology, no set of principles. The element of ideas, in Sutherland's words, is "meaningless."[13]

This book will suggest an alternative interpretation of Bolingbroke's program of opposition. It contends that the opposition was also based upon political ideas and principles and not merely the common interest of the outsider. Far from being meaningless, the opposition was held together by a particular set of ideas. It had an image of an ideal political order and of the threat to this order which it felt had arisen in England since the Glorious Revolution. The Walpole government and the Bolingbroke opposition represent, then, two different sets of ideas about society, government, and economics.[14] But this claim, central to the argument of this book, should not be misunderstood as an endorsement of the one and an indictment of the other. If it appears that Walpole's side tends to be represented here as the evil and Bolingbroke's as the virtuous it must be noted that this is Bolingbroke's interpretation and not the author's. The old order sought by Bolingbroke in his nostalgic flight from the political and economic innovations of his day was a dream which could not suffice for this new age. Walpole and his world represented an essential step on the path to a stable and modern British economy and polity. The task of this book, however, is neither to praise Bolingbroke's views, nor condemn Walpole's, but simply to put forth the claim that Bolingbroke had views that can be constructed into a meaningful and coherent whole. The validity and value of this whole is another question and, by and large, doubts are indicated. Nor does the book tend that much to assail Bolingbroke with the clear divergence between his writings on virtuous government and his own less than virtuous actions. This has been done adequately already. So adequately, in fact, that few have ever thought that his writings had any worthwhile content. That Bolingbroke was a double-dealing opportunist even in his old age should not preclude an effort to understand and appreciate his writings on politics.

But the division between Walpole's government and Bolingbroke's opposition was more than simply ideological; the two camps were also divided by a totally different conception of the nature of politics. To the minds of Bolingbroke, Swift, and Pope, Walpole perfected a politics of administration and manipulation that contributed generously to the total degradation of public life. Politics for Bolingbroke's circle was supposed to be played out in an elaborate theater where the style of the performance was almost more significant than the deeds done. In order to perform the governmental roles of statecraft properly, one had to be properly bred. Walpole's administration had instead, they felt, perfected politics as an acquired skill, one of conciliating interests and manipulating men, mean talents that stripped the glory and the gloss from politics. The image Bolingbroke preferred shines through the many classical allusions found in his and opposition writings. With theatrical gravity, noble gentlemen stand before the people and win support by virtue of their eloquence and the compelling aesthetic force of their rhetoric, whereas in his own age Bolingbroke felt that politics consisted of sordid and undramatic management and behind-the-scenes manipulation of interests and ambitions. With the stability Walpole brought to England he introduced politics as administration, and Bolingbroke's reaction to this development parallels his fascination with Elizabeth and her age. Not only could he regard her reign as the last example of a unified, strong, and sturdy England, but also as the last time that the English

Court acted as a court should, the last time national life was headed by a unique fusion of aesthetic and political experience. He considered her age as a time when virtuosity, glitter, and dazzling personal force were set upon a sharply delineated stage and when the fate of England and Europe was worked out in public by a group of brilliant players around one central and most brilliant player. Now all one had was the sad spectacle of the Georgian Court, a public performance totally lacking in aesthetic appeal.

As much, then, as Bolingbroke was concerned with the substantive problems of the drift of public policy and the development of public finance, he was also concerned with the procedural dimension of politics, its style and how it was carried on—how men acted in the political arena. Style, he believed, was very much related to the nature of man. Men of breeding and family knew best the refinements of public performance. The degeneration of politics in Walpole's regime was, he felt, intimately related to the changed nature of the players, to the rise in public prominence of moneyed men. Bolingbroke's conservatism was not simply social and economic, then, but also stylistic and aesthetic. He reacted not only against a change of policy, but also against the personnel and methods by which the change had been brought about.[15] His own career and public performance as politician, writer, and philosopher were a testimony to his different conception of the art of politics. As comfortable in a French salon or *academie des lettres* as in the House of Commons, he wrote learned disquisitions on philosophy, religion, and the study of history with as much ease as he penned his political pamphlets and supervised his weekly journal. His many years in France and his literary and scholarly connections there and in England left him irrevocably estranged from Walpole's world and helped account for the permanent suspicion with which he was regarded by most Englishmen. But not so by Pope and Swift! They and the rest of Bolingbroke's circle were irresistibly drawn to his side in their common lament that such truly great men as Bolingbroke should be prevented from governing England while, as they conceived it, dunces shaped her course, bringing her to the reign of dullness and "universal darkness."

# I

## The "Anti-Minister": The Political Career and Writings of Lord Bolingbroke

At the appropriate age of twenty-one Bolingbroke took his place as one of England's governors when his grandfather vacated the family borough in 1700, and young Henry St. John became Member of Parliament for Wooten Basset in Wiltshire.[1] In his *Letter to Sir William Windham*, written in 1717, Bolingbroke cynically described the Commons. "You know the nature of that assembly—they grow like hounds, fond of the man who shows them game, and by whose halloo they are used to be encouraged."[2] Bolingbroke and another new member of the Parliament in 1701, Robert Walpole, would show the Commons much game in the course of their careers.

Bolingbroke's meteoric rise to prominence is indicated by Robert Harley's choice of him to play an important role in the passage through Commons of two significant pieces of legislation: the Act of Settlement in 1701, which Bolingbroke prepared and introduced along with Sir Charles Hedges, Secretary of State; and the notorious Occasional Conformity Act, which Bolingbroke along with William Bromley, an M.P. for Oxford University, introduced into the Commons in 1702. High office was his early reward. He had deftly cultivated Harley, realizing that his future lay in his hands, and Harley, taken into the government in 1704 as Secretary of State, secured the Secretaryship of War for his twenty-six-year-old protégé.[3] His career suffered a setback, however, when after 1706 Marlborough and Godolphin began placing in the Ministry increasing numbers of the once-disgraced Whig Junto. By 1708 the Whigs had taken over completely. The Tories, it seemed, talked too loudly and eagerly of peace. Harley and Bolingbroke were replaced.

8

Sacheverell and the events of 1710 brought Harley and Boling-broke back to power. In the *Letter to Sir William Windham* Boling-broke reviewed the objectives of the new Tory government, which included first the material considerations of private and party interest.

We came to court in the same dispositions as all parties have done . . . to have the government of the state in our hands; our principal views were the conservation of this power, great employments to ourselves, and great opportunities of rewarding those who had helped to raise us, and of hurting those who stood in opposition to us.[4]

There were other objectives of a less material nature, "which had for their object the public good of the nation, at least what we took to be such." These included the end of the war, an attack on the moneyed power, and the defense of the church. While in power, Bolingbroke also sought to implement exclusive single party govern-ment. He tried to break the Whigs with as much zeal as Walpole would later try to break the Tories. The great proponent of coalition government under Walpole was himself the author of an earlier most thoroughgoing notion of single party hegemony.

The view, therefore, of those amongst us who thought in this manner, was to improve the queen's favor, to break the body of the Whigs, to render their supports useless to them, and to fill the employments of the kingdom down to the meanest with Tories.[5]

The principal policy objective of the Tory government that ruled from 1710 to 1714 was a quick end to the war with France. Boling-broke's party had cooled to the war ever since 1706, when, after the Battle of Ramilies, the Spanish Netherlands had been cleared of Louis' troops and the French were driven from Italy. The object of the war, the containment of Louis XIV and French power, had been secured as far as the Tories were concerned. But the Dutch, the Emperor, and Marlborough wanted more. The French must be driven from Spain. "No peace without Spain" became the Whig cry. But the patience of the country esquires was exhausted. Tory opposition to the war became a political outlet for their grievances against what the Tory writers called "the modern Whigs." The modern Whig with his war and his new financial order was under-mining the country. Land taxes, national debt, the Bank, the moneyed corporation, stockjobbers, the Dutch-Emperor alliance, redcoats trudging through foreign lands—all were sponsored and defended by the "modern Whig."

Behind Bolingbroke's efforts to end the war lay attitudes that he maintained throughout his life. His preoccupation with socio-economic change determined his performance in office in the same way that it informed his activity and writings in the remaining years of his career. He was a critic of what he considered a new England a full decade before the Walpole era, and he continued a critic in the decade after the Great Man's fall. The campaign against Marlborough's war introduces the thread of continuity that runs through Bolingbroke's entire career. The war and the new moneyed order that subsidized and supported it were, he thought, bringing destruction to the landed gentry and subverting the traditional constitutional and hierarchical structure of society. In his *Letter to Sir William Windham*, Bolingbroke described his attitudes of 1710-1714.

We looked on the political principles which had generally prevailed in our government from the Revolution in 1688 to be destructive of our true interest, to have mingled us too much in the affairs of the continent, to tend to the impoverishing of our people, and to the loosening of the bonds of our constitution in church and state. We supposed the Tory party to be the bulk of the landed interest, and to have no contrary influence blended into its composition. We supposed the Whigs . . . to lean for support on the presbyterians and the other sectarians, on the bank and the other corporations, on the Dutch and the other allies.[6]

His party's intention, wrote Bolingbroke, was to restrain the influence exercised by the Bank, the East India Company, and "in general the moneyed interest," over the legislature. "The country gentlemen were vexed, put to great expenses and even baffled by them in their elections; and among the members of every Parliament numbers were immediately or indirectly under their influence." The most frightening result of the war, he contended, "was the prodigious inequality between the condition of the moneyed men and of the rest of the nation." The landed gentry, he reports, had borne the entire load of the national expenses while the money men, who were adding nothing to the common stock but thriving by the war and its financing, "contributed not one bit to its charge."[7]

To further the objectives of peace the new Tory government

engaged in a vast propaganda effort. It had at its service the pen of Jonathan Swift, who had left forever his early Whig affiliations. The long friendship between Swift and Bolingbroke began with their work on Swift's Tory journal, *The Examiner*. Dr. Francis Atterbury, Matthew Prior, and Bolingbroke wrote the earlier numbers of the weekly, but from November 1710 to July 1711 it was entirely a creation of Swift.[8] With biting satire and vicious invective *The Examiner* drove home three points: the war only enriched the money men and caused suffering to the landed; England contributed too much to a war that served only the ambitions and interests of the Dutch and the Emperor; and the great and revered Marlborough and other Whig leaders made fortunes by corrupt manipulation of the war's management. Swift isolated the money men, the allies, and the Whig leaders as the war party, a theme he repeated in his immensely successful pamphlet of 1711, *The Conduct of the Allies*.[9]

The use by Harley and Bolingbroke of pamphlets and newspapers as platforms from which to influence public opinion marked an important step in the broadening of political awareness and interest beyond the traditionally small group of Court and Parliamentary players. The expiration of the Licensing Act in 1694 had given pamphleteers freedom to issue anything that could not be suppressed as seditious or as libelous, and the political community was itself enlarged by the increase in literacy associated with the early growth of the middle class.[10] In the four years of violent partisan strife between 1711 and 1715 the merchants or writers could read in their coffee houses the pamphlets and newspapers of Addison, Steele, Defoe, Swift, and lesser luminaries of Grub Street.[11]

At the same time the Tories sought to organize intellectual support. In the summer of 1711, Bolingbroke founded the Brothers Club for men of wit, learning, and breeding. There would be no drunkenness or extravagance here as in the Whig Kit-Cat Club. "Improvements of friendship and encouragement of letters are to be the two great ends of the society."[12] This aristocratic and intellectual circle, which included Swift, Arbuthnot, and Bolingbroke, was soon joined by two young poets, Alexander Pope and John Gay. Out of the Brothers Club developed the Scriblerus Club and from its members eventually came the satires of *Gulliver's Travels, The*

*Dunciad,* and *The Beggar's Opera.* For the next thirty years this group of wits and satirists, committed to scourging the follies from mankind, directed their offensive against the corruptions of the new England. Like Bolingbroke, they feared the passing of the traditional society upon which their aristocratic cultural ideal was based.

Bolingbroke's great achievement in these years was his negotiation of the Treaty of Utrecht, signed in April 1713. It secured final passage only by action which set constitutional precedent binding to the present day. In December 1712 Swift jubilantly wrote to Stella of this dramatic development.

I have broken open my letter, and love it into the bargain, to let you know that we are all safe: The Queen has made no less than twelve lords to have a majority . . . She is awakened at last . . . We are all extremely happy.[13]

Bolingbroke was unsuccessful in a lesser known aspect of the Treaty, however, for Parliament rejected part of it, a commercial agreement with France, that had been close to his heart. This effort places Bolingbroke in the Tory free-trade tradition which antedates that of Adam Smith and the Whigs.[14] His arguments were not economic and involved no critique of mercantilism. Bolingbroke's desire for freer trade was politically motivated and a striking anticipation of the nineteenth-century arguments of free-trade liberals like Richard Cobden. In a letter to Prior in which he describes the Whig opposition to the commercial treaty, Bolingbroke relates his hopes for the agreement.

This is calculated to hinder those prejudices, which our people have been possessed with against France, but which began now to wear off, from being extinguished; and so not to keep up the strangeness between the two nations, and not to preserve such a temper of mind, in our own people, as may dispose them, upon every slight occasion, to a dispute with France. Now the most effectual way of preventing this, is certainly an open and advantageous commerce between the two kingdoms. Nothing unites like interest; and when once our people have felt the sweet of carrying on a trade to France, under reasonable regulations, the artifices of Whiggism will have the less effect amongst them.[15]

Bolingbroke's most significant and enduring legislative contribution during these years of Tory government, other than the great treaty, was his sponsorship of the Landed Qualification Bill of 1711, a measure the Tories had sought since 1696. Their bill of 1711, though easily circumvented, sat on the statute books until the reign of Victoria. It stipulated that no man could sit in the Commons as a Knight of the Shire unless he had six hundred pounds annual value of land, or, if he represented a borough, three hundred pounds. Bolingbroke championed the Bill in the Commons and revealed the extent of his anxiety over the potential political effects of the contemporary economic revolution by his argument. The diarist Peter Wentworth has preserved Bolingbroke's speech to Parliament.

Mr. St. John's speech was pretty remarkable on the qualifying Bill for in setting out how necessary this Bill was to be enacted, he gave some touches upon the late management, as that we might see a time when the money'd men might bid fair to keep out of that House all the landed men, and he had heard of societys of them that joined stocks to bring in members, and such a thing might be as an administration within an administration, a junto, and these money'd men might arise to such a pitch of assurance as to oppose the crown and advice in matters that did not belong to them.[16]

The Tory government came to an abrupt end in the events of 1714. Harley and Bolingbroke split, Harley resigning and Bolingbroke assuming the *de facto* position of first minister. Anne lay on her deathbed, and the hopeful prospects of Bolingbroke's future lay with her remaining power to make appointments. Perhaps it was the long memory of the irreverent, rakish Bolingbroke that determined her failing mind; the prudish Queen, as Swift had called her, chose not to leave the kingdom to the dubious management of her libertine Secretary of State, Bolingbroke. She gave the staff instead to Shrewsbury, a Hanoverian. The Queen died on August 1. By the end of the month Shrewsbury had been replaced by Townshend. On September 18 George I landed in England.

On March 26, 1715, Bolingbroke fled from England to Paris, where he joined the forces of the Stuart Pretender. Robert Walpole immediately moved his impeachment, a motion that was carried without a single dissenting vote. Bolingbroke was declared a permanent exile and stripped of his title and estate.

Bolingbroke's hasty flight has given rise to a great deal of scholarly speculation. Some consider it tantamount to a confession of longstanding Jacobite connections, as the Whigs charged; others attribute it to a natural reflex of fear at the prospect of Walpole and Whig vengeance. Bolingbroke contended in his *Letter to Sir William Windham* that he had never previously plotted with St. Germain and that his flight was dictated by his conviction that a Whig inquisition would try him for high treason on the basis of the Treaty of Utrecht. He claimed that his flight to the Pretender was not prompted by loyalty to the Stuart line, but merely by the prospect of a reign by the Pretender that would better serve the Tory party interest. If James could be persuaded to convert to Protestantism, Bolingbroke reasoned, the Tories would enjoy more preference than under the Hanoverians.[17] But whatever may have been its initial inspiration, Bolingbroke's Jacobite interlude is really neither that enigmatic nor that surprising. Gentry discontent and resentment were filling the Jacobite ranks with countless recruits seeking a return to the past, desperate recruits attracted by the nostalgia and romanticism of the Pretender's cause.[18] As an articulate spokesman for these interests, and as leading critic of the new order, it was in a way fitting that Bolingbroke devoted a year of his career to this most enticing dream for putting the past back on its throne.

Bolingbroke's years in France were more than simply a romantic adventure, however. These were the years in which he turned wholeheartedly to the study of history and philosophy; the years in which he met and befriended Voltaire and Montesquieu; the years in which he produced his earliest learned discourses; and the years that solidified his role as one of the important links between French and English ideas at the beginning of the Enlightenment.[19]

Bolingbroke's first published essay on politics was written two years after his arrival in France. His *Letter to Sir William Windham* was part of his effort to obtain a pardon and to be reinstated in England. Through the British envoy to France, the Earl of Stair, he had already begun the long and arduous process of securing his return to England. In letters to Stair, Bolingbroke ever prone to duplicity, offered his services to the new monarch while renouncing his previous party and Jacobite behavior. "In the plan which I have formed for the rest of my life I shall have no regard to either party." He offered even more in payment for a pardon; he would "quell the spirit which gives encouragement to all the Jacobite prospects." Having gone far, he cheerfully went farther. If he were allowed to return, he would "break ye opposition to ye King and increase ye number of those who write in an affectionate submission to his government."[20] The long *Letter*, written to convince his Tory friend of the need for purging the party of all vestiges of Jacobitism, concludes with a ringing denunciation of the Pretender.

If the Pretender was restored, we might most probably, lose our religion and liberty by the bigotry of the prince and the corruption of the people. We should have no chance of preserving them, but by an entire change of the whole frame of our government, or by another revolution. What Reasonable man would voluntarily reduce himself to the necessity of making an option among such melancholy alternatives.[21]

The King seemed pleased enough by this performance. By November 1717 it was known in London that Bolingbroke was under the King's protection.[22] His chances for a full pardon were enhanced in 1718 when Walpole and Townshend went into opposition leaving Sunderland and Stanhope at the head of the government. Stanhope, an old drinking friend of Bolingbroke's, cultivated him as part of his effort to solidify his power over Walpole, hoping Bolingbroke could bring the loyal Tories to his ministry. In 1718-1719 Stanhope repeatedly consulted Bolingbroke in Paris on foreign policy and Bolingbroke offered what little prestige he had to the support of Stanhope's Peerage Bill.[23] The Bill was defeated through Walpole's efforts, and so, too, were Bolingbroke's chances for immediate pardon. The deluge after the bursting of the South Sea Bubble in 1720 made Robert Walpole first minister, and the prospect of Bolingbroke's reinstatement dimmed. Walpole remembered keenly his own humiliation of 1712 when Bolingbroke had him sent to the Tower. Now in council Walpole was heard to say, "May his attainder never be reversed, and may his crimes never be forgotten."[24]

While in France, Bolingbroke moved in the highest social and intellectual circles. He knew the aging Henri de Boulainvilliers and the youthful Voltaire.[25] He cultivated the French Newtonians through his philosophical mentor, Levesque de Pouilly. The English mathematician and secretary to the Royal Society, Brook Taylor, "expositor of Newton's sublime philosophy to foreign nations," was a frequent visitor at Bolingbroke's country home at La Source.[26] As Pouilly introduced Bolingbroke to the study of philosophy that led to his later essays on natural religion and epistemology, so the Abbé Joseph Alary initiated Bolingbroke into the mysteries of historiography and the French school of scepticism and pyrrhonism that would lead to Bolingbroke's famous *Letters on the Study and Use of History*.[27]

Bolingbroke's social and intellectual life in France merged comfortably in the sophistication of the salon and at the pleasant pastoral retreat of La Source; more formally it took shape at meetings of the Club de l'Entresol, which, in the words of Robert Shackleton, was "one of the most interesting organizations in the whole of the French eighteenth century."[28] What little information remains of this club is contained in the memoirs of one of its members, René Louis de Voyer, the Marquis d'Argenson.[29] A large number of the Entresol's members, including Montesquieu, were of the nobility, both of the sword and the robe. Their interests were thus clearly those of the Parlements. Indeed the head of the Parlement de Paris paid tribute to the Entresol by demanding that it admit his son-in-law to membership. The membership in the Entresol of the Chevalier Ramsay, whose pietist and fundamental religious views seem so out of place in this freethinking circle is now more comprehensible. This disciple of Fénelon had himself contributed to *la thèse nobilaire* by his popularization of Fénelon in 1721 with his *Essai Philosophique sur le Gouvernement Civil*. D'Argenson was the only notable exception to the Entresolists' *nobilist* tendencies.[30]

The Entresol was part of the intellectual ferment sweeping the French aristocracy in the early eighteenth century and played an important role in this development by providing an intellectual arena for the high nobility of the Paris region. It is this aristocratic sentiment that was the abiding political influence Bolingbroke derived from his French sojourn. Boulainvilliers and his ideas were significant in this respect as they were prevalent in all the circles in which Bolingbroke moved. *La thèse nobilaire* with its glorification of a feudal past, its aristocratic and antibourgeois bias, its preoccupation with decentralization, balance, and intermediary powers, provided a frame of reference in which Bolingbroke could analyze his own society. Bolingbroke paid specific debt to this French influence in *The Craftsman* and in his political writings, when he referred to Boulainvilliers' gothicism or commented favorably upon the political and Gallican aspirations of the Parlements. Its influence however, was much more fundamental and informed his entire political outlook.

The years in which the erring English statesman was rusticated to France were far from stagnant. Bolingbroke, a scintillating and urbane courtier, moved easily through the more prestigious Parisian salons and aristocratic country chateaux. He collected about him a coterie of distinguished and learned men from whom he could learn much and to whom he was able and willing to impart much. When he returned to England, his friends hardly knew him, for in France he had become a grave philosopher quite above trifling. Pope, impressed with the new Bolingbroke, wrote to Swift, "Lord Bolingbroke is the most improved mind since you saw him, that ever was improved without shifting into a new body, or being."[31]

### OPPOSITION AND *The Craftsman*

Bolingbroke returned to England in 1725 only after Walpole saw to it that he could never take his seat in the House of Lords or even hold public office. Walpole would bow to pressure to have his old adversary returned, if he must, but he meant to render Bolingbroke as impotent as possible, intending no challenge to his own control and management of Parliament. By this maneuver, Walpole determined the course of English political life for the next fifteen years. An extraparliamentary opposition with Bolingbroke at its center would be the focus of the opposition to his rule.

Dawley, Bolingbroke's country home, became after 1726 the favorite retreat for distinguished aristocrats and intellectuals, much as La Source had been in France. Once again the Brothers Club and the Scriblerus wits assembled, augmented by new and younger aristocratic patrons. There could have been few more impressive gatherings than those housed by Dawley: Bolingbroke, Alexander Pope, Jonathan Swift, Dr. Arbuthnot, John Gay, Lord Chesterfield, and William and Daniel Pulteney.[32] Walpole had ignored the advice of the third Earl of Shaftesbury, who had written in 1710, "'tis no small advantage even in an absolute government for a ministry to have wit on their side, and engage the men of merit in this kind to be their well wishers and friends."[33] Perhaps no minister in English history would be so virulently and consistently assaulted by intellectuals as Walpole was in the years 1726-1728, during which time Bolingbroke's *Craftsman,* Swift's *Gulliver's Travels,* Gay's

*Beggar's Opera,* and Pope's *Dunciad* appeared, all of which works were, at least in part, intent upon maligning Walpole and his system. Walpole had had only token opposition since his accession to power in 1721, but with Bolingbroke's return and the appearance on December 5, 1726, of the Opposition newspaper, *The Craftsman,* the great assault on his rule began, with Bolingbroke leading the charge.[34] A pamphleteer described the mood on the eve of battle.

> All hands were employed and engines set to work, manuscripts were circulated, the press loaded, coffee house talkers, table wits, and bottle companions had their instructions given them.[35]

*The Craftsman* wrote of itself: "These papers will survive as long as the English language, and convey the character of the Times in which they were written, to the latest generations." One week later, Walpole's *London Journal* ridiculed this claim and added that "so far from descending to the latest generations, this generation will neither buy nor read them."[36] *The Craftsman's* prediction was far from correct, but *The London Journal* also erred in its claim. Walpole's contemporaries did buy and read *The Craftsman.* A complete picture of Bolingbroke's social and political thought is impossible without intensive study of his newspaper, not only because in its pages first appeared two of his most important works—*Remarks on the History of England* and *A Dissertation upon Parties*—but also because of the leading role played by the newspaper and journal as platforms for political ideas in the Walpole era. The fierce struggle between Walpole and the Opposition filled the pockets of Grub Street hacks and printers during the ten years the newspapers and pamphlets of the Opposition battled with those subsidized and distributed by Walpole.

A writer in one of Walpole's papers of the 1730's described his paper's activity: "We have in the course of seven or eight years, drained all the topics of government and fought thro' all the weapons of a ministerial war."[37] That such conflict was waged by newspapers rather than arms, strategems, or the Tower, reflected the profound stability that Walpole had brought to English politics. It also reflected a broadening of public opinion which had become a matter of consequence in political life because of the increasingly larger and literate middle class. Moreover, Bolingbroke's unique nonparliamentary position made the use of the press the more imperative, thus contributing to its importance as a political factor. Even so, the new political community could take its political philosophy only in small doses to be swallowed in one sitting at the coffee house. Nor, for that matter, were the disgruntled gentry and lesser merchants eager to read lengthy and complex essays on the origins of the state. Vituperation and anger were what appealed to the reading public, and the political ideas of the period are found in newspapers and pamphlets rather than in sermons or philosophical treatises.

Estimates of *The Craftsman's* circulation vary. Oliver Goldsmith would have it that *The Craftsman* sold more rapidly than even *The Spectator*. Samuel Johnson's estimate was equally high.

> It was more read and attended to than any political paper ever published, on account of the assistance given to it by some of the most illustrious and important characters of the nation. It is said 10,000 of that paper have been sold in one day.[38]

On the other hand Laurence Hanson, student of the newspaper in the early eighteenth century, estimates *The Craftsman's* circulation at some 500 compared with 12,500 for the most popular weekly of the period, Walpole's *London Journal*.[39] The Walpole papers at the Cambridge University Library put *The Craftsman's* circulation at 1,250 copies per week.[40] Whatever its circulation, its impact was decisive. "It raised the whole tone of political controversy in the press, for the criticisms which it made were both pungent and well informed."[41] It also served to raise the prestige of the press, with such influential and well-born people as Bolingbroke and William Pulteney participating closely in its work.

*The Craftsman* excelled in a form of barbed wit and biting satire that fed the appetites of its reading public on one individual as the object of all its villification and ridicule, on one who was not known for his good humor nor particularly fond of this kind of satire. "Walpole hated it, hated it furiously and bitterly."[42] The first number of the paper explained its name. The purpose of the venture, wrote its fictional editor, Caleb d'Anvers, was to expose corruption and craft in all professions.[43] The mysteries of state and political craft were the most mischievous of these corruptions, and the paper dedicated itself to unraveling and exposing the dark secrets of political craft.[44] Such a task was not easy, for the public might not listen to these ministrations of truth. Bolingbroke had written Swift in 1721 of such doubts. "This monstrous beast has passions to be moved, but not reason to be appealed to, . . . Plain truth will influence half a score men at most in a nation or an age, while mystery will lead millions by the nose."[45] Still week after week *The Craftsman* villified Walpole and the corruption which, it assumed, pervaded the entire social order.

*The Craftsman's* favorite weapon was the most effective in the Augustan arsenal, satire. An angry Member of Parliament described how the paper's writers "shot their poison in the dark and scattered it under allegories in vile libels."[46] Walpole's system was depicted as a unique form of government, the Robinocracy or Robinarchy. In a "Persian Letter," *The Craftsman* of October 18, 1729, has Usbeck, a traveler to England, writing home of this strange form of government, made up of three orders: monarchy, aristocracy, and democracy, in which all three are dependent upon the Robinarch, or chief ruler, who, although legally a minister and creature of the Prince, is "in reality a sovereign, as despotic, arbitrary a sovereign as this part of the world affords." The Robinarch and his associates come from plebian stock and have few estates, yet "he rules by Money, the root of all evils, and founds his iniquitous dominion in the corruption of the people." The Robinarch secures to his will the deputies in the assembly as well as the Prince. In the past this may have been a difficult task, but modern Robinarchs are skillful in encouraging luxury and extravagance, which, together with the disbursement of honors, titles, preferment, and pensions, help make the Robinarch's task an easier one.[47]

In Swift, Bolingbroke had a master from whom to learn the technique of satire, and *The Craftsman* shows that the lesson was well learned. Bolingbroke's belief in the decline of the distinctions between the two parties is argued in terms much like Swift's depiction of the Big Endians and the Little Endians in *Gulliver's Travels*. *The Craftsman* described the two parties in England on one occasion as the Knotists and the anti-Knotists, on another as the Noodles and the Numseuls.[48] Satire in general and in Swift's art in particular, derives much of its impact through the play of size and significance, in making small things large, large things small, irrelevant things important, and important things trivial; thus the relative importance of men, represented in *Gulliver,* is dramatized by opposing Gulliver to miniature Lilliputians and towering Brobdingnagians. Interestingly enough, *The Craftsman's* characterization of Walpole frequently used the imagery of monsters and giants with perhaps the bitterest example of this occurring on July 22, 1727, when the paper gave the details of a famous monster on exhibit in Westminster.

The Body of this creature covered at least an acre of Ground, was part colored, and seemed to be swelled and bloated, as if full of corruption. He had claws like an harpy, his wings resembled Parchment, and he had above 500 mouths and as many tongues; from whence he took the name of Polyglott . . . As ostriches eat iron, his favorite diet was gold and silver. He would carry a prodigious weight. I have known above 200,000 men ride at once upon his back . . . He could make more than three hundred of his tongues at once, lick his feet, or any other part about him.[49]

Elsewhere, *The Craftsman* pictured Walpole as a giant from whom hung huge bank bills, exchequer notes, lottery tickets, and tallies, but only a small bag of money. How better to describe the new economy based on vast paper credit and little real money? Walpole is also "the greatest monster of power and wickedness, that ever infected the face of the earth."

In another number, he is the Leviathan—not a water animal—but a "great, voracious land-fish whom we call a wicked minister," and there is even an essay devoted to that "gigantic evil minister Goliath." *The Craftsman's* satire also finds Walpole the grasping insect and the "noxious caterpillar."[50] In depicting Walpole in terms of such monstrosity and deformity the Opposition suggested the extent to which his political sins threatened his position as *homo sapiens* in the chain of created being.

Walpole was even occasionally the butt of some of *The Craftsman's* advertisements. Running through the first four years of the paper were advertisements for Dr. King's "golden specific" guaranteed to cure any one of many problems. So miraculous was this remedy that as one testimonial tells, a gentleman who opposed the government and claimed England was a horrible country, took the cure, and is now content and convinced that the people of England live under the best of governments.[51]

Another favorite technique of Augustan ridicule and satire was the historical comparison, for which once again Swift was the model satirist. In *The Examiner,* he had written:

I have therefore since thought of another expedient, frequently practiced with great safety and success by satirical writers; which is, that of looking into history for some character bearing a resemblance to the person we would describe and with it the absolute power of altering, adding or suppressing what circumstances we please.[52]

*The Craftsman* abounds in this form of satire; countless essays are directed against corrupt and despotic ministers of the past, Roman, Russian, French, and English; English history in particular was combed for any evil minister who could be used for thinly disguised comparisons with Walpole. The two most often enlisted were Cardinal Wolsey and James I's minister, Buckingham, whose careers were continually shaken from their historical mothballs and dramatized, with due emphasis placed on their obscure birth and low education and on the exorbitant wealth they acquired in office that enabled them to raise families of parts, to build palaces, and to offend the nobility. If, on the other hand, a disguise for criticism of Walpole's corrupt financial dealings in Commons were needed, the career of the Earl of Danby was used.[53]

On two occasions *The Craftsman* approached true satiric grandeur in its war on Walpole. The first is definitely attributable to Bolingbroke, and appeared in his published works as "The First Vision of Camilick."[54] *The Craftsman* reprinted the dream of one Camilick, a Persian prophet, who dreamed of a large and magnificent hall, empty except at one end where a king sat beneath a canopy which supported a sacred parchment. The nobles of the country entered and, with the king, bowed down before the sacred constitution. Another and larger assembly dressed in lesser finery followed and offered adoration to the covenant. While the two gatherings and the king joined in a chorus of imprecation on any who would lay hands on the parchment, there suddenly burst into the hall a portly man of plain face and plain clothes who held in his hand a purse of gold. The ruffian sneered and looked disdainfully at all his betters who, seeing him, turned from the sacred covenant and fell before him.

He trod over their backs, without any ceremony, and marched directly up to the throne. He opened his purse of gold which he took out in handfuls and scattered amongst the assembly. While the greater part were engaged in scrambling for these pieces, he seized, to my inexpressible surprise, without the least fear, upon the sacred parchment itself. He rumpled it rudely up, and crammed it into his pocket. Some of the people began to murmur. He threw more gold and they were pacified. No sooner was the parchment taken away, but in an instant I saw half the august assembly in chains.

When, finally, his purse was empty, the intruder fell to the ground powerless. Having no gold, his power left him and the parchment rose once again to the exalted place, all chains were dropped, and the nation was once again free with its constitution inviolate.

Five years later, in an article which cannot be assigned definitely to Bolingbroke although its condemnation of the new age certainly bears his influence, *The Craftsman* told of another vision.[55] In a dream d'Anvers, the fictional editor, found himself in a pleasant and fruitful island where a happy and prosperous people lived in freedom. The countryside abounded with produce and the cities were rich in skilled artisans and honest traders. The island's government was stable and free. "The constitution of her government was so happily mixed and balanced that it was the mutual interest of the Prince and the people to support it." Liberty and plenty filled the happy Commonwealth. But suddenly, a tree shot up, and grew so high that its head was lost in the clouds and its branches darkened the land.

I saw it put forth a vast quantity of beautiful Fruit which glittered like burnished gold, and hung in large clusters on every bough. I now perceived it to be the Tree of Corruption, which bears a very near resemblance to the Tree of Knowledge, in the Garden of Eden, for whoever tasted the fruit of it, lost his integrity and fell, like Adam, from the state of innocence.

The fruits bore inscriptions such as "East India," "Bank contracts," "South Sea," "Differentials," "Patents," "Credit," "Stocks" and other terms characteristic of the new order. Perched in the middle of the tree was a fat man who plucked down the golden apples and tossed them to the crowd below. The tree and its fruit poisoned everything in sight. As the blight spread and covered the entire land, the farms would not produce, the artisan went hungry, the merchant laid up his ships, and "a general scene of poverty discovered itself amongst all ranks of the people, and nothing was to be heard through the whole land but piercing lamentations and agonies of despair"—nothing, that is, but the gluttonous laughter of those scampering in and around the tree and eating of its financial fruits.

*The Craftsman's* satirical pose could be dropped when less incriminating criticism was offered. Week after week it criticized particular aspects of Walpole's rule, the standing army, stockjobbers, the land tax, and high interest rates. It contained sober condemnation of the placemen and pensioners sitting in Parliament. At the same time it repeatedly asserted that the two parties had changed their nature and had ceased to bear their old characteristics. Another preoccupation of its pages was criticizing what it called the new dependence of Parliament upon the executive and the new powerful position of a "prime minister." In 1727 and again in 1729 it warned against the possible use of the Sinking Fund by corrupt ministers for purposes other than those intended by Parliament,[56] a prediction rendered accurate in 1733.

In one area of domestic politics *The Craftsman* could rightfully claim great success, the defeat of Walpole's excise scheme in 1732-1733. It claimed "the defeat of it hath been acknowledged to be owing, in a great measure, to our writings." From October 1732 until April 1733, when Walpole withdrew the proposal, virtually every *Craftsman* was devoted to an attack on the measure. It roused the gentry by reminding them of Locke's pessimistic insight that all taxes inevitably hit the landed, so that although the excise might place duties on wine and tobacco, inevitably land would suffer. In addition, the paper conjured up images of vast armies of office holders needed to enforce the excise. The passions of the City were stirred by descriptions of excise agents breaking into houses and shops destroying distilleries and ruining small merchants, and, added to this, were stories of arbitrary proceedings and fines levied by excise commissioners. So aroused was public opinion, so flooded was Parliament with petitions, that Walpole was forced to withdraw the measure.[57]

### HISTORY AND PARTIES

Two of Bolingbroke's major political works, his history of England and his essay on parties first appeared in the weekly pages of *The Craftsman*. Twenty-four essays in 1730 and 1731 make up what later would be published as *Remarks on the History of England.*[58] Bolingbroke began the first issue of this long discussion of English history by citing Machiavelli's plea that nations and governments return to their first principles in order to maintain their health and prolong their lives. The purpose of the essays, Bolingbroke suggested, was to help revive the spirit of liberty and recall the minds of men to the true notions of the British Constitution. In Bolingbroke's history, according to Herbert Butterfield the first important "Whig" history, the dynamics were provided by the interplay of two "spirits," one of liberty and one of faction.[59] The former embodied the national interest while the latter embodied individual and partisan interest. Bolingbroke saw the development of English history as a Manichaean struggle between these good and evil forces. The spirit of liberty was represented in the mixed constitution whose parts were so balanced that no one part depended on the other, while the spirit of faction was embodied in any threat against this ideal constitutional structure.

The spirit of liberty first emerged in England's Saxon past, and persisted through the middle ages, unaffected by the Norman Conquest. From the Conquest to the Civil War various monarchs and their reigns gave substance to one spirit or the other. The evil monarchs who gave succor to the ever-lurking spirit of faction included Richard II, Henry VI, VII, and, of course, James I and Charles I. The patrons of the spirit of liberty included Edward III and Henry V. Henry VIII began as a partisan of liberty, but under the evil influence of his corrupt and upstart minister, Wolsey, he developed into the most evil of all England's monarchs. The greatest of all patrons of liberty was, of course, Elizabeth.

In his *Remarks on the History of England,* Bolingbroke dated the rise of the Commons' strength from its acquisition of land and power during the reigns of Henry VII and Henry VIII. The Civil War resulted from James' and Charles' failure to recognize that the Commons already, under the Tudors, had acquired the power of a rank equal to that of the House of Lords and the Crown in the constitutional balance. The principal villain behind the upheavals of the seventeenth century was James, who served the sinister purposes of the spirit of faction. To be sure, he shared some of his guilt with others. "Churchmen and royalists attacked the constitution. Puritans and commonwealthmen and above all a motley race of precise knaves and enthusiastic madmen ruined it."[60] The *History* ends with the events of 1640.

The intent of the *History* is overtly partisan, as its entrance into the world in the form of weekly essays in *The Craftsman* attests. There are countless allusions to Walpole in its references to corrupt and scheming ministers seeking to end the independence of Parliament and ruin the balance of the constitution, the essence of liberty. It points often to the absence of a standing army in reigns of liberty and the association of a standing army with reigns of the spirit of faction. "Standing armies like swords can ruin the constitutions they mean to protect."[61] In his *History* Bolingbroke is clearly out to out-Whig Walpole's Whigs. The *History* had one most significant repercussion; it touched off a debate that raged for ten years in the party press and pamphlet literature, in which Walpole and Bolingbroke refought the historiographic battles of the seventeenth century.

*A Dissertation upon Parties* also appeared first in *The Craftsman* during the winters of 1733 and 1734. The work was first published in its entirety in 1735, and within the next four years went through five editions and a French translation.[62] The tone of the *Dissertation* is much sharper and more reckless than any of Bolingbroke's previous nonsatirical writings, a demonstration of the confidence doubtless born of the successful excise campaign. What is ostensibly a discussion of parties in this work is really a continuation of the earlier *History of England* bringing it from the Restoration to the 1730's. According to Bolingbroke, the intent of the work was to destroy the odious distinctions and obsolete party labels which persisted long after their actual elimination by the Glorious Revolution. It was necessary, on the contrary, to show that Englishmen really agreed on the issues which had formerly divided Whig and Tory, to accomplish which the *Dissertation* begins by tracing the development of party labels and differences in the Exclusion Crisis. Even at that time, Bolingbroke implies, when the Whigs sought to exclude the future James II from succession to the throne, the differences were based more on exaggerated fears of possible republicanism or royalism than on overt acts. In any case, the cooperation involved in the Glorious Revolution effectively ended party distinctions and whatever party conflict followed was more in the pursuit of power than of principle.

Bolingbroke's attitude to the Glorious Revolution as revealed in the *Dissertation* is essential to an understanding of his reaction to his own age and to subsequent Whig attitudes. The Revolution, Bolingbroke claimed, did not alter the constitution but merely renewed it and restored it to its original principles of liberty, born in the Saxon past.[63] The promise of the Revolution had never been fulfilled, however, and the perfection of the constitution never actually achieved. Elections had not been free, nor had the independence and frequency of Parliament been maintained. The mixed and balanced government had been destroyed. The Septennial Act, for example, contradicted the Revolution's goal of frequent parliaments, and standing armies were too reminiscent of Stuart despotism.

Since the Revolution, the distinction between Whig and Tory had disappeared, but in its place the *Dissertation* cites the rise of new divisions. There were those who were angry with the government but who wished to keep the constitution—Bolingbroke's position. There were those who were averse to both the constitution and the government—a small number of Jacobites and republicans. Finally, there were those attached to the government who were, in fact, enemies of the constitution—Walpole and his group. The second group was unimportant. The first and third Bolingbroke labels country and court, or constitutionalists and anti-constitutionalists. In rhetoric anticipatory of Burke's, Bolingbroke described the sacred constitution which he saw Walpole and his anti-constitutionalists bent upon destroying.

That noble fabric, the pride of Britain, the envy of her neighbors raised by the labor of so many centuries, repaired at the expense of so many millions and cemented by such a profusion of blood; that noble Fabric, I say, which was able to resist the united efforts of so many races of giants, may be demolished by a race of pigmies.[64]

Echoes of Swift are heard once again when Bolingbroke describes the anti-constitutionalists as insects of the earth, "and like other insects, though sprung from dirt, and the vilest of animal kind, they can nibble, gnaw and poison, and if they are suffered to multiply and work on, they can lay the most fruitful country to waste."[65] It was not Walpole alone, however, whom Bolingbroke blamed for the failure of the post-Revolutionary years. The economic developments of the past forty-five years were, in his opinion, primarily responsible.

*The Craftsman's* weekly essays on parties in 1734 highlight the overriding theme of Bolingbroke's Opposition. Since the Glorious Revolution, Bolingbroke contends, the means of influencing by money and governing by corruption had increased phenomenally. Changes in the structure and management of the public revenue had wrought fundamental constitutional changes. Like a Pandora's box, the Revolution and its new financial order had spread corruption and evil over Britain. Taxes had increased, as had officers of the revenue who claimed power over men of superior rank. A spirit of rapine, venality, fraud, corruption, luxury, and avarice had overtaken the land since 1688. "The establishment of the public funds on the credit of those taxes produces greater mischief than the taxes themselves, not only by the increase of corruption and the power of the crown, but by the effect it has on the spirit of the nation, our manners, our morals."[66] Since the introduction of this new order, Bolingbroke contends, millions toiled for the handful who were proprietors of the funds. A revolution had taken place in the nature and holding of property which, once diffused among the many thousands, he now saw flowing into the pockets of the few, while stockjobbing and other mysterious arts of the new economic order further upset the traditional social and political order of society. Good Harringtonian that he was, he noted how power inevitably followed the new configuration of property. The heart of Bolingbroke's political analysis is found in the short utterance with which he summarizes these post-Revolutionary developments in the *Dissertation.* "THE POWER OF MONEY AS THE WORLD IS NOW CONSTITUTED IS REAL POWER." This was not the case in the seventeenth century, for "it was prerogative, not money, which had like to have destroyed our liberties then."[67] The meaning of the essay is clear; Bolingbroke's constitutionalists reject the post-Revolutionary social and economic order and Walpole's anti-constitutionalists accept it, indeed build their rule upon it.

Several of Bolingbroke's other published writings originated in *The Craftsman. A Collection of Political Tracts by the Author of a Dissertation upon Parties* appeared in London in 1748, bringing together many of Bolingbroke's more interesting contributions to *The Craftsman.* Some of the numbers in the *Tracts* are not published in Bolingbroke's collected works.[68] Most of these numbers contain familiar arguments, but one, "On the Policy of the

Athenians" deserves mention as a tour de force of the Swift-Bolingbroke method of historical satire. For three consecutive Saturdays, Bolingbroke sustained a critique of Pericles, who, it was clear to all, was Walpole. Pericles is described subverting the Athenian constitution and destroying Athens. He screened corrupt men and spread bribes and jobs in the assembly. He fostered luxury with public money. Bolingbroke even extended the comparison to include Pericles' corrupting the Athenian assembly with a species of secret service money, and refusing to allow anyone to look at the books of his administration. Meanwhile, poets and wits warned the polis against Pericles, but they were never heeded.[69] This history might not have impressed the Abbé Alary, but if nothing else, it helps to illustrate the nature of the political dialogue in Augustan England. One week later, there appeared in both Walpole's *London Journal* and *Daily Courant* a defense of Pericles![70]

The publication in *The Craftsman* of *A Dissertation upon Parties* marked the high point of Bolingbroke's insolence with impunity. Walpole had had enough. This was made quite clear by Walpole's reaction to the Opposition effort to repeal the Septennial Act. *The Craftsman* had put great stress on the need to repeal this law, which had been imposed in 1717 as a temporary expedient in reaction to the Jacobite invasion. It argued that the people needed frequent opportunities to call their representatives to account for the trust given them and to approve or disapprove their conduct by electing or turning them out. On one occasion, *The Craftsman* described this as the proper procedure by which one obtained a desirable rotation of office holders "which is the very essence of Harrington's *Oceana*."[71] The Opposition motion came to a vote in Commons in 1734.[72] The proponents proved how a seven-year tenure increased the potential for bribery and corruption while the government responded with equal certainty that long tenure contributed to independence. The debate was a dull one until the appointed hour when the Great Man, Walpole, rose to speak. His attack on the Opposition's Triennial Bill was prefaced by a scathing indictment of Bolingbroke. If, during the past decade, Walpole had smoldered under the scorn Bolingbroke heaped upon him, the moment had come for Robin to show his fire. If there were any doubt that Bolingbroke was the principal figure of the Opposition and *The Craftsman*, there could be no more after Walpole's speech. He ridiculed Bolingbroke as an "anti-Minister" who placed such an inflated judgment upon himself that he thought he alone could conduct the affairs of the nation. "Can there be imagined a greater disgrace to human nature than such a wretch as this?"[73] Bolingbroke, sensing the liability he had become for the Opposition, laid down his pen and once again fled the country.

Shortly after arriving in France, he wrote a letter of defeat and resignation but Bolingbroke could never really withdraw and end his career. A letter, written to his nephew in December 1735, which anticipates his *Idea of a Patriot King* suggests that he had not yet tired of exposing those he considered men of craft.

Whatever happens it will be a comfort to me that I have had the opportunity before my death of contributing to revive the spirit of the Constitution in Britain . . . The Victim may be saved, even tho', the same butcherly Priests should continue to administer our political Rites, or who knows? a zealous high priest may arise, and these priests of Baal may be hewed to pieces.[74]

### PATRIOTS AND KINGS

In France Bolingbroke settled at Chanteloup, where he renewed acquaintance with his old circle and the Comte de Matignon, the Comte d'Argeville, the Marquis d'Argenson, and M. de Silhouette. He wrote Windham, the parliamentary chief of the Tories, that he had finished with political life. He would now, he resolved, turn his energy wholly to scholarship.[75]

As the months passed, however, his letters to Windham indicate that Bolingbroke could not leave off his preoccupation with English politics. It was not only Walpole, he wrote, but the entire set of economic and political innovations since 1688 that were the cause of England's disorders. It is Windham's task, Bolingbroke wrote, "to hinder the consequences of the Revolution from destroying that constitution which the Revolution was meant to improve and perpetuate." Bolingbroke linked his earlier Jacobite experience with this antipathy to the world of the modern Whigs. "I once thought there was another remedy to this fatal evil, a remedy which might . . . radically cure the distemper, but perhaps I was mistaken." Reading Bolingbroke's letters to Windham, one notices the consistency that characterized Bolingbroke's thought. A letter of 1737 repeats the theme first examined under Queen Anne in

1710 and repeated again as late as 1749 in Bolingbroke's last piece of written work.

You say that the monopoly of money in a few hands discloses itself manifestly. Is not power engrossed in a few hands as well as wealth? Whilst you have weak princes on the throne, some cabal or other will draw the whole wealth of the nation and the whole power of the state to itself . . . These are the fruits of those principles . . . that a number of men who called themselves Whigs . . . began to plant almost half a century ago, and have continued to plant and to propagate ever since.[76]

In France, Bolingbroke wrote *A Letter on the Spirit of Patriotism*, which, although written in 1736, was not published until 1749 when it appeared with *The Idea of a Patriot King*.[77] Bolingbroke had already unsuccessfully prodded the Commons to restore the traditional constitutional order in his *Remarks on the History of England* and *Dissertation upon Parties*. Later he would turn to the heir to the throne with the hopes that a Patriot King would return to the glorious era of Elizabeth. In the *Letter on the Spirit of Patriotism* he placed his hopes on the nobility, calling upon them to resist the new England. There are, he declares at the outset of the essay, two groups of men, the large herd and the few men of superior genius. The men of better parts must serve their country, as they did among the Romans and Greeks, opposing evil and promoting good government. In England, such men must come to the service of the ailing commonwealth. Like his Roman predecessor, the English gentleman had an obligation to serve the public, especially in the hour of peril when venality and private interest pervaded all ranks and orders. Those who were superior in rank and talent had the greater obligation of duty to their country. They had to rescue the state from the low and the mean who meddled in state affairs as if they were lotteries. Men of honor had to replace men of profit who, though inferior in every respect, lorded it over their superiors and all mankind. Bolingbroke was also critical in his *Spirit of Patriotism* of the Opposition he had left behind in England. The nobility were not meeting their obligations to the Commonwealth, the Opposition had become too concerned with their own interests, too much concerned with what would happen to them if Walpole fell, too little concerned with the need for fundamental changes. The Opposition should, Bolingbroke thought, be as disciplined, as prepared, and as hard working as the Government.

It is not difficult, after reading *A Letter on the Spirit of Patriotism*, to understand Bolingbroke's great appeal for Disraeli.[78] Both express an antibourgeois mood, a longing to restore an ideal past, and a call to the privileged to exercise the responsibilities and obligations incumbent upon their positions. Bolingbroke's concern with the young aristocrats, with young England, in these later years of his life, may also have impressed Disraeli. Bolingbroke wrote his *Letter* to the young Lord Cornbury, the great-grandson of Lord Clarendon:

> I expect little from the principal actors that tread the stage at present . . . these men have been clogged or misled, or overborne by others . . . I turn my eyes from the generation that is going off to the generation that is coming on the stage. I expect good from them, and from none of them more than from you, my Lord.[79]

In the late 1730's and early 1740's, a group of "boy patriots" that included Cornbury, Bathurst, Marchmont, Lyttelton, and William Pitt the Elder assembled around Bolingbroke and Frederick, the Prince of Wales. As with Disraeli's Young England, much of the energy of these boy patriots went into romantic nostalgia and poetry. Only Pitt among them would master the art of politics.

Bolingbroke's return to England in July 1738 coincided with the explosion of the political tension that had accumulated over the previous four years. Pitt had raised the hopes of the Opposition from the gloom of 1735 by becoming the spokesman of the traders and denouncing Walpole's foreign policy. Spain, in these years, put heavy pressure on the English with renewed demands for Gibraltar and the end of the Assiento, England's monopoly of the slave trade with the West Indies obtained at Utrecht. At the same time Spain pushed her commandeering of British seamen in West Indian waters. The Opposition complained of Captain Jenkin's humiliation and demanded war, while Walpole sought a convention with Spain that would bring peace.

In March 1739, the Opposition members of Parliament, led by Windham, seceded from the Commons when it voted to approve the convention with Spain. Bolingbroke approved of this dramatic gesture, but he made it clear that, at least for him, the protest was not simply against Walpole. It is clear that the "hatred of Walpole" theory is an inadequate explanation of Bolingbroke's actions and thought. He wrote to Marchmont on the subject of the secession.

Our patriots, for such they desire to be thought, and such I wish they were, made a declaration to the people of Britain when they made their secession, that they could do no real service to their country till the independency of Parliament was restored . . . Walpole is your target today, and any man his majesty pleases to name may be so tomorrow . . . I would contribute at any risk to save the British constitution and to establish the administration upon national principles . . . Restoring the independency of Parliament is the only secure way of correcting this and every other abuse of power.[80]

After Bolingbroke's departure in 1735, the Opposition had found a new focus around Frederick, Prince of Wales. The Leicester Square residence of Frederick, who, in keeping with the family tradition, hated his father, was the center for the circle of Opposition politicians that included Pitt, Windham, Cobham, and Marchmont. He also drew to him the writers of the Opposition: Pope, Johnson, Henry Fielding, David Mallet, and James Thomson, who sought the patronage they had failed to receive from George II or Walpole, "Bob the poets' foe."[81]

The central figure in the Prince's circle was George Lyttelton, his personal secretary. Lyttelton, a close friend of both Pope and Bolingbroke, effected the liaison between the literary and political branches of the Opposition in the late 1730's. On his return, Bolingbroke, the grand old man of the Opposition, was received back into this circle. He renewed his activity as a leader of the Opposition, and his work culminated in the creation of the book by which the entire movement has since been remembered—the *Idea of a Patriot King*.[82] The Commons and the nobility had failed to rescue the country and return it to original principles; the only remaining hope was the next monarch, Prince Frederick.

The *Idea of a Patriot King* opens with a description of corruption that pervaded all ranks in England from the vulgar to the highest in the land. All of Walpole's crimes were catalogued and the general rapaciousness after wealth described. The dying spirit of liberty in England could be revived only by a return to original principles, the principles of the constitution. According to Machiavelli, all governments degenerate and need to be drawn back to their original principles. The best way to achieve this return was through the emergence of a great man. A Patriot King was England's only hope. Bolingbroke, neither royalist nor absolutist, held no mystical fancies about kingship. A good disciple of Lord Halifax, he had earlier written of the king as "nothing more than a supreme magistrate, instituted for the service of the country." His lofty trappings, crown, and scepter, were merely "for getting the attention and reverence from the vulgar." But in this crisis, Bolingbroke writes, only a great man, a Patriot King, "a sort of standing miracle, so rarely seen," could rescue a country like England, so corrupt, so close to ruin.[83] The Patriot King would revive the traditional free constitution, would end the king's bondage to the minister and the legislature's to the executive. He would restore the mixed constitution, not be an absolute monarch. By setting his own lofty personal example of virtue, the Patriot King would lead his people away from the pursuit of private interest and gain. Public virtue and honor would once again be recognized as virtuous. He would purge his court of all men of self-interest and appoint only those who had remained true in recent years to the interest of the Commonwealth. He would be a monarch above party, the common father of all the people. His model would be the greatest of all monarchs—Elizabeth. He would be as beloved and as popular as she, and in his reign there would be a prosperous and expanding trade, the lifeblood of England's greatness. There would be few taxes and the specter of a national debt would be forever banished from her shores. The final rhapsodic lines of the essay describe a revived England under the Patriot King.

Concord will appear, breeding peace and prosperity on the happy land; joy sitting in every face, content in every heart; a people unoppressed, undisturbed, unalarmed; busy to improve their private property and the public stock; fleets covering the ocean, bringing home wealth by the returns of industry, carrying assistance or terror abroad by the direction of wisdom, and asserting triumphantly the right and honor of Great Britain, as far as waters roll and winds can waft them.[84]

If the strains of "Rule Britannia" seem to rise from these lines, it should be remembered that the anthem was itself a product of this circle around the Prince of Wales, the future Patriot King.[85] H. R. Trevor-Roper has made much of the longing for Elizabethan times characteristic of the disgruntled, declining gentry in the seventeenth century who longed to reenact memories of profitable sea victory over the Spanish, bountiful trade, and the content and joy that permeated the land in the days of Good Queen Bess. Few greater apotheoses of Elizabeth and her age, however, can be found than in the *Patriot King* of 1739 and "Rule Britannia" of 1740, a unique marriage of the gentry and the trader. Outside this bond stood what they sensed as their common enemy—Walpole, and the organized power of money.

After leaving the manuscript of the *Patriot King* with Pope, Bolingbroke returned once again to France where he resumed his philosophical writings. He had become thoroughly disillusioned with the chances of saving the English. Writing to Windham, he referred to the gentlemen of England as grown indifferent about the preservation of the British constitution. "A people cannot be saved against their will and Walpole may use them like the slaves they are and deserve to be."[86] The apathy of the English portended the doom of the great Commonwealth. Bolingbroke was convinced that the English had outlived their greatness and like the Romans would be conquered by the internal diseases of decline and degeneration. This sense of decline, so central a theme in Augustan thought, was rarely more clearly stated than in a letter of Bolingbroke's written to Marchmont from France in 1739. Even as these forebodings were being expressed, England stood, of course, on the threshold of its empire and its economic explosion. But greatness of this kind was far from Bolingbroke's ideal.

Are we not in the dotage of our Commonwealth, my Lord? are we not in the second infancy, when rattles and hobby-horses take up all our attention, and we truck for playthings our most essential interests? In a first infancy there is hope of amendment, the puerile habits wear off, and those of manhood succeed; reason grows stronger and admits of daily improvement. We observe, we reflect, we hear, we persuade ourselves, or we are persuaded by others. But in a second infancy, what hope remains? Reason grows weaker; the passions, the baser passions, the inferior sentiments of the heart, avarice, envy, self-conceit, and obstinacy grow stronger, and the habits we have then accompany us to the grave.[87]

In the midst of Bolingbroke's renewed interest in intellectual matters the Great Man stepped down, defeated on a minor issue. He resigned after twenty-two years in office as first minister and was immediately elevated to the Lords as Lord Orford, where to all intents and purposes his influence ended. Bolingbroke, who had settled in England once again, persisted in his opposition while others of the Opposition took positions in the new Pelham government. For a considerable time already Bolingbroke had warned that some persons had used the Opposition as a scaffolding for their own ambitions. "Newcastle," he wrote to Marchmont, "has often said that the late, which are, I suppose, the present measures of domestic government, are the sole expedient by which any administration can be carried on." A national party, thought Boling-broke, representing all segments of opinion, and repudiating the entire framework of the modern Whig innovations was the only solution, but one which "this vile generation has neither the virtue nor the ability to force."[88]

It was clear to Bolingbroke that Pelham and his brother, the Duke of Newcastle, had no intention of changing the foundations upon which Walpole had built his power, nor of governing for long with a coalition of all the parties. Bolingbroke was convinced that the situation had not been ameliorated, that the Pelhams were no better than Walpole, and that venality, corruption, and faction were as prevalent then as in 1710 or 1734. His personal chagrin at his treatment by Pitt and the old boy patriots compounded his disappointment. "Some who leaned upon me as their crutch in their days of lameness, have laid me by as a useless implement." If this was to be his reward for service, then once again he resolved "to retire for good and all from the world." This time he held to his resolve. His letters in the late 1740's reveal no interest in the passing events, only the sickly decline of the old man of mercury, now known to his friends as "the Hermit of Battersea."[89]

But the appearance in print of Pope's version of *The Idea of a Patriot King* in 1749 forced Bolingbroke back into the public spot-light. He brought out his own edition with the text as he preferred it to be remembered and, in that same year, wrote his final essay. Pulteney and Lyttelton had dropped their opposition, opportunisti-cally ending their careers with office and respectability. Not so with Bolingbroke, so often accused of opportunism. He ended his public career seven years after Walpole's fall, with the same slash-ing attack on the post-Revolutionary world that he had made twelve years before Walpole's rise to power. In *Some Reflections on the State of the Nation*, his last written work, Bolingbroke spoke of the new financial world with a bitterness not heard since the closing of Swift's *Examiner*.[90] The public debt had soared, he wrote, from £300,000 in 1688 to the dizzying sum of £80,000,000 in 1749, all resulting from the decision made in William's day, to forego financing wars by the existing revenue in order to secure the new government on the private fortunes of those who would lend it money.

Thus the method of funding and the trade of stock jobbing began. Thus were great companies created, the pretended servants, but in many respects the real masters of every administration, thus . . . the growth and spreading of that cancerous humor, which had begun to gnaw our vitals.[91]

The only possible solution Bolingbroke saw to England's problems was retrenchment and the reform of her government, a reduction of the power of money and a campaign for public frugality. The debt had to be eliminated and to this end the interest paid the fundholders had to be reduced. The merchants must be allowed to trade and landed men to plough and sow for their own and the community's good, "not for the userer and the stock jobbers, for those leeches who fill themselves continually with the blood of the nation and never cease to suck it." He acknowledged that the money men would complain at the campaign waged against them, but they must be reminded of the fundamental axiom of the English political tradition that had been lost sight of these past sixty years: "THE LANDED MEN ARE THE TRUE OWNERS OF OUR POLITICAL VESSEL; THE MONEYED MEN, AS SUCH, ARE NO MORE THAN PASSENGERS IN IT." At seventy-one, Bolingbroke summarized in this essay the essential message behind all that he had done and all that he had written since he entered public life a half-century earlier. Basic to his political career and what one can make of his political philosophy were social assumptions from which he never wavered. What is so striking is that Bolingbroke, so often charged with opportunism, with a lack of principles, was in fact committed to an overriding set of principles that have tended to elude even his most sympathetic students. In 1731, Bolingbroke had written to Swift that "as far as I am able to recollect, my way of thinking has been uniform enough for more than twenty years."[92] It remained so for the next twenty.

Bolingbroke died on December 12, 1751. His collected works were published three years later by his poet friend, David Mallet. Horace Walpole and Samuel Johnson have recorded the scandal and anger which met their publication,[93] but despite this immediate reaction, Bolingbroke's works, individual and collected, went through numerous editions in the eighteenth and nineteenth centuries, in all the languages of Europe. But how often was he read? George III and Disraeli notwithstanding, Burke's question of 1790 more than likely reflects the judgment of posterity, "Who now reads Bolingbroke, who ever read him through?"[94]

# II

## Walpole and the New Economic Order

Twenty years of war spawned new and powerful economic institutions in post-Revolutionary England. The Bank of England and other large moneyed companies either emerged or developed fully in these years, and the stock market grew into a thriving institution. A huge national debt, the widespread use of paper currency and credit, payments of interest to receivers of state annuities: all were part of the mystery of the new economic order. For many Englishmen this new economic order was symbolized by the trauma of the great South Sea Bubble. Like the Bubble, the new economic order seemed inscrutable, and dangerous. It portended radical change from traditional social and political ways.[1]

Economic innovations in Augustan England were both qualitative and quantitative. The financial developments reflected in banking, moneyed and joint stock companies, and stockjobbing were not completely new, but their size, scope, and impact certainly were. Banking, merchant, and commercial enterprises had previously been predominantly small, local affairs, usually of a family nature, or, at most, its commercial analogy, a merchant apprentice relationship. The novelty of the Augustan economy consisted in the size of its economic units. The growth of great banks, of huge moneyed and trading companies, and of a permanent London stock and money market paralleled the dramatic increase in the size of the debt.

It may have been the case that, as Defoe claimed, "not one in forty understands it," but the new world of public credit ultimately concerned all. It impinged on everyone's lives; yet few knew what it was, or even how to describe or define it. Defoe, who, perhaps more than any other Augustan, did understand the workings of public credit, has best described the sense of mystery which it evoked in his contemporaries.

Like the soul in the body it acts as all substance, yet it is itself immaterial; it gives motion, yet it cannot be said to exist; it creates forms, yet has it self no form; it is neither quantity nor quality, it has not whereness, or whenness, site or habit. If I should say it is the essential shadow of something that is not, should I not puzzle the thing rather than explain it, and leave you and myself more in the dark than we were before?[2]

The most important of these institutions and the center of the new economic and financial order was the Bank of England, a new economic institution with no roots in the British past. Banking itself had developed out of the extracurricular functions of the goldsmith. Makers and sellers of gold, silverware, and precious stones were by vocation naturally involved in finance.[3] In the Commonwealth period the government, which had previously relied mainly on the mercantile classes as a source of loans, turned to the goldsmiths to be its bankers.[4] After the Restoration the king still relied on the goldsmiths for advances in anticipation of the revenue. Goldsmiths might have continued indefinitely as a banking institution had not the long wars with France, begun under William III, forced a financial crisis for the government that was solved by the creation of a funded debt—a debt owned by lenders to the government; the Bank of England was erected on the basis of this debt. The goldsmith bankers first objected to the creation of the Bank and then opposed its monopoly, but they were unsuccessful in both cases.[5] Public finance ceased to be the profitable preserve of individual craftsmen because the liberal state needed a more powerful and centralized institution to underwrite its expansion.[6]

The Bank of England, wrote Bagehot, was originally "not only a finance company but a Whig finance company."[7] A child of politics, it was conceived in the Glorious Revolution, which by making England a participant in the continental struggle against France created the national debt. Its sponsors were not unaware of the political significance of the Bank and the funded debt. These new institutions involved the vested interests of the affluent in the success and perpetuity of the new monarchy and in the Revolutionary settlement. A fundholder would hardly consider recalling a

Pretender who would repudiate the debt raised by those who had dethroned him. That the Bank of England symbolized London's commitment to liberalism was seen clearly by the Tory Jonathan Swift. "Whoever were lenders to the government, would by the surest principle be obliged to support it."[8]

If the war were to be financed in the 1690's, something dramatic had to be done to provide for the striking increase in public expenditures incurred since the Revolution.[9] The solution was a bank modeled on the Bank of Amsterdam. The idea originated with William Paterson, a Scotsman, and was sponsored by Charles Montagu (later the Earl of Halifax in the Whig Junto), friend of Locke and Chancellor of the Exchequer in 1694. In the Italian city states public banks had existed for centuries, and in northern Europe they sprang up in the early seventeenth century in Amsterdam and Hamburg. The association of national banks with free cities or republics prompted talk of establishing one in England during Cromwell's Republic.[10] But after the Restoration a common argument against such an official bank was, in fact, this very association with nonmonarchical politics.[11] An important step in the acceptance of the Bank was the popularization in England of the Dutch and their institutions that came with the new monarch, and with the writings of Sir William Temple, a onetime envoy to Holland. Temple's *Observation on the United Province of Netherlands*, published in 1672, described Holland as the "greatest treasure, either real or imaginary, that is known anywhere in the world."[12] In 1694, under William and Mary, England copied the core financial institution of the Dutch, beginning what Disraeli would later call the long period of Dutch captivity. Temple's protégé, Swift, dissented from this haphazard cultural borrowing.

The pernicious counsels of borrowing money upon public funds of interest, as well as some other state-lessons, were taken indigested from the like practices among the Dutch, without allowing in the least for any differences in government, religion, law, custom, extent of country, or manners and dispositions of the people.[13]

Swift had learned well at the feet of his master. Temple's own cultural relativism cautioned against such transplantations. Temple had written of the Dutch, "Their greatness is a result of the vastness of their trade, in which their religion, their manners and dispositions, their situation and the form of their government were the chief ingredients."[14]

Paterson's idea was that an association of public creditors would raise a loan to the government that instead of being fixed for a limited period would return perpetual interest. The association would also be entitled to purchase from the government any outstanding government debts and would receive perpetual interest for them too. In addition to receiving interest in perpetuity, the association would be authorized by government charter to become a corporation empowered to issue circulating notes, to buy and sell bullion, and to deal in bills of exchange. Locke's friend Halifax, who was Chancellor of the Exchequer, threw the weight of the Government behind the bill and in 1694 the new company was chartered. The Company was authorized to raise £1,200,000 by subscription and to lend it to the government. Loyal subjects were invited to underwrite His Majesty's government and armies; private individuals could enter into contractual relationship with the state. In twelve days 1,272 individuals subscribed the necessary £1,200,000, and in less than a month the money was transferred to the Exchequer. If Locke's political ideas are sometimes caricatured for picturing the state as a joint-stock company, this caricature seems nowhere more appropriate than in the birth of the Bank. The scheme of Locke's friend Halifax had made 1,272 individuals actual owners of the state. Interestingly enough, Locke was among them.[15]

The initial subscribers included Godolphin and Marlborough, who put up £10,000 and matched the subscription of the King and Queen; and Halifax, who subscribed £2,000. If for no other reason than that the loan was taken up in twelve days, the vast majority of the initial subscribers were Londoners; 450 out of the first 500. The largest single holding, £166,855, was that of Sarah, the Duchess of Marlborough; the second, £104,625, was held by a Sephardic Jew, Francis Pereira.[16] Indeed, one important factor contributing to the unpopularity of the Bank, the debt, the moneyed companies, and the new financial order in general, was the popular prejudice against Jews and foreigners, who seemed to be connected with these institutions.[17] It was argued that tribute that would slowly drain England's treasure was being paid the Jews and the Dutch. The belief that England's debt was owned by foreigners was eventually not that far from the truth: by 1757 of the 3,294 voting proprietors of the Bank stock about 1,000 were Dutch or Flemish; of the 495 owners of the £4,000 which qualified one for governor of the Bank at least 105 had obviously Dutch names. One third to one fourth of the owners of shares in the joint-stock company, England, were nonnationals!

After the establishment of the Bank, the most dramatic event associated with the new financial order and the most frequently cited source of resentment among the gentry and lesser merchants was the sudden growth of the national debt. Before 1692, the debt had consisted only of a small number of short-term loans to the government made in anticipation of the revenue of the Crown, but the war and the new permanent funding innovations set the debt moving upward. Taken at five-year intervals from 1691, the debt grew at the following rate: 1691—£3.1 million; 1695—£8.4 million; 1700—£14.2 million; 1705—£13 million; 1710—£21.4 million; 1715—£37.4 million; and 1720—£54.0 million.[18] The bulk of this national debt was owed to three great moneyed companies: the Bank of England, the South Sea Company, and the East India Company. In 1714, of £36,000,000 in the debt a little less than half, £15,752,966, consisted of debts to these three companies. In 1727, of the £53,000,000 in the debt, nearly £47,500,000 was owed the three moneyed companies, and of this the largest part was owed the South Sea Company.[19]

In the eighteenth century many Englishmen were convinced that the national debt portended imminent doom for the nation. To the gentry, who regarded England as one large landed estate, and to the tradesman a national debt was an obvious burden and encumbrance like private debts. The independence of the private owner was obviously threatened until the debt was paid off. If not bankruptcy, then conquest by the French would be England's fate. A line of distinguished writers on public affairs that runs from Davenant through Bolingbroke, Hume, Blackstone, Price, and Paine attacked the debt and attributed most of England's ills to it. A typical grievance hurled at the debt is that of the anonymous pamphleteer who attacked those who supposedly benefited from it.

Who does not see that upon the first bustle in Europe which demands our interposition, the same taxes must be renewed, nay additional ones must be imposed, and all of them to be mortgaged at an exorbitant interest to Jews and stockjobbers. So that we might then see a debt of an 100 millions without a sinking fund to discharge it, after which, the merchant would trade, and the landed men would plow, not for themselves but for their usurious creditors.[20]

The Jews and stockjobbers were not the only ones who, according to the pamphleteer, benefited from the debt. A "sole minister," a single powerful minister, could put a large national debt to his own use:

for by our constitution, the Crown being the steward of all the public money, the minister by that means acquired a greater influence by the disposal of offices, which necessarily arose from the discharge and receipt of that immense sum. Thus the higher the debts of the nation are the more must the power of the sole minister increase.[21]

As soon as criticism of the debt came from the Opposition defense came from the Government. "Consider how much the public is the richer or poorer for the national debt. It is to the national debt we owe our public credit, and to this public credit may principally be ascribed those superior blessings, which are self-evident to every honest enquirer, which our ancestors never did enjoy."[22] Those who opposed the national debt were labeled by the Government's pamphleteer as opponents of the establishment which it underwrote.

The Sinking Fund set up in 1716 was intended to liquidate the debt in a few years but it had little effect on the size of the debt, for in 1733 Walpole raided the Fund, despite the purpose of its establishment, and used part of it for the year's expenses. Parliament concurred, and the Sinking Fund was, after 1733, damaged beyond repair as its misappropriation became a regular feature of the government's financial policy. Later in the century, the radical Price and William Pitt the Younger were to revive the Sinking Fund in another assault on the debt.

In addition to the birth of the Bank and the growth of the national debt, there also occurred in this Augustan era the striking growth of joint-stock companies, especially the South Sea Company and the East India Company. The stock market also developed and with it the practice of stockjobbing. The first English joint-stock companies had appeared much earlier, but their growth in size and importance is definitely associated with Augustan England.[23] At the end of Elizabeth's reign, for example, the total amount of capital invested in joint-stock companies was £10,000.

In 1695 it surpassed £4,000,000; in 1717, £20,000,000; and by 1720, the joint-stock companies represented a capital investment of about £50,000,000.[24]

The last decade of the seventeenth century was a period of great economic expansion in England characterized by a sense of buoyancy and confidence in the commercial world. This sense of optimism and of material promise produced the first generation of great English writers on economics: Sir William Petty, Gregory King, Charles Davenant, John Locke, Josiah Child, and the Tory free traders, Dudley North and Nicholas Barbon.[25] In spite of the war, the 1690's were a feverish period of private speculation. A surge of patents and inventions resulted in a burgeoning of joint-stock companies, the number increasing in the year 1693 alone from eleven to one hundred.[26] An important factor behind this boom in company promotion was the gradual abandonment of the Elizabethan practice of Crown and Parliamentary incorporation through charter, to be resurrected only after the Bubble in 1721. Until then, joint-stock ventures sprang up in large numbers, simply upon articles of association or a patent.[27] England had entered what Defoe called its "age of projects"; the projecting spirit passed over the land, and men tinkered and invested, their minds filled with plans.

This mood reached its climax in the fateful year of 1720, but it gave its stamp to the entire Augustan Age. The Puritans had resurrected Francis Bacon when they ruled England; now, when they were out of power, their academies sent forth Baconians learned in useful and practical subjects. The projector and the inventor were playing their part in subduing nature and bringing it under man's control, thus furthering Bacon's objective of contributing to the utility and happiness of man.[28]

The English spirit of technology, of projects, of conquering nature, would impress the French *philosophes* and their *Encyclopédie*.[29] They looked to their English patron saints, Bacon, Locke, and Newton, for their science, their psychology, and their ethics. Moreover, their English Trinity were all projectors. Locke and Newton, revising and modernizing the coinage, were also their inspirations.

Swift, Pope, and Bolingbroke rejected this projecting spirit and linked it to the new commercial order. The experience of the 1690's and the years leading to the Bubble indelibly joined, in their minds, the spirit of projects and innovation to the joint-stock company and what they considered the foul and pernicious practice of stockjobbing. The trauma of the Bubble reinforced for these Tory intellectuals the intimate association of projecting, commercialism, and social disorder.

Two companies emerged alongside the Bank as giants of the financial and economic world in the early eighteenth century. The East India Company was of seventeenth-century origin, but its great power and size came after it had settled its internal schism and emerged as one united company in 1709.[30] Like the East India Company the South Sea Company was founded in 1711 as a commercial and financial organization, but after 1720 it became only a financial one. The power of these two companies and the Bank was a direct result of their ownership of much of the national debt. Every government had to deal with these pillars of public finance, and depended on them to raise short- and long-term loans. The Bank was the main source of short-term credit and the other two of long-term funded loans. Treasury loans would be pledged at closed subscriptions, and individuals representing the Companies and special interests, like those of the Jews and the Dutch, would be notified by the Treasury. The Treasury would then settle the terms with the more prominent applicants. The largest creditors were invariably the three moneyed companies.[31]

Their indispensable connection with the government served these giant monopolies well in a period when sentiment was running against monopolies in trade. The pleas first heard from seventeenth-century Puritans for unrestricted commercial enterprise were revived by Bolingbroke's *Craftsman* and then the Hume-Smith school. It was primarily as political institutions, however, that the companies were attacked by both the Molesworth Commonwealthman and Bolingbroke's opposition, who argued that statesmen and Senators of the body politic assembled in Parliament were becoming mere lackeys of men from the City. The ideal commonwealth, fashioned in antiquity and the Tudor Age, envisioned no such dependency.

The practice of stockjobbing as a specialized transaction that accompanied the rise of the stock market was another post-Revolutionary innovation on the English scene because it required the impetus of the rapid expansion of joint-stock activity and the negotiable bills of the moneyed companies. No professional market for stocks existed in England until the 1690's and the reign of William III.[32] There had been brokers and assorted other financial intermediaries in the past, but it was not until the end of the seventeenth century and the beginning of the eighteenth that the stockjobber became the main agent of capital mobility. It was inevitable, then, that, like the Jew, the jobber became an object of scorn and ridicule. To its critics there was no greater symbol of this new era, no greater target for resentment than the stockjobber.

The resurrection of honesty and industry can never be hoped for, while this sort of vermin is suffered to crawl about, tainting our air, and putting everything out of course, subsisting by lies, and practicing vile tricks . . . They are rogues of prey, they are stockjobbers. They are a conspiracy of stockjobbers! A name which carries along with it such a detestable image, that it exceeds all human invention to aggravate it; nor can nature, with all her variety and stories furnish out everything to illustrate its deformities; nay, it gains visible advantages by the worst comparisons you can make. Your terror lessons, when you liken them to crocodiles and cannibals, who feed for hunger on human bodies. Well, but monstrous as they are, what would you do with them? The answer is short and at hand, hang them.[33]

In establishing a market in which stocks and shares had a quotable day-to-day price, London once again followed the Dutch example; a stock market along these lines had existed for some time in Amsterdam.[34] Another link was forged in the shackles of England's "Dutch captivity." The spark which fired the first real development of the market was the speculative mania of 1692-1694. In these years there appeared the first English financial journal that gave a weekly résumé of commercial and financial speculation with advice on such topics as "time bargains" and "selling short."[35] The new profession of stockbrokers shared the Royal Exchange with the merchants in the early 1690's. The merchants had had the Exchange as a bargaining area since Elizabeth's time.

By 1697 the jobbers had grown sufficiently in numbers to provoke a statute limiting the profession. The preamble accused brokers and stockjobbers of engaging in unjust practices of selling and discounting tallies, bank stock, bank bills, shares, and interest on joint-stocks. It also accused brokers of unlawfully combining to

47

raise or lower the value of securities for their own private advantage. On the grounds "that their number had very much increased during the few preceding years and were daily multiplying," restrictions were placed on their right to practice. Their number was limited to one hundred and they were required to identify themselves with silver tokens imprinted with Royal and City arms. The merchants shared this dislike of the stockjobbers; their Royal Exchange was made too noisy and bustling with these frantic dealers in stocks who were perpetually running and shouting. Stockjobbers, the merchants reasoned, tempted the public to ruin and polluted the Royal Exchange. In 1698 the merchants managed to force the stockbrokers to withdraw to nearby Exchange Alley and its coffee houses.[36] Wits and satirists would thenceforth talk of Exchange Alley (or Change Alley) in directing their barbs at the vermin, brokers.[37] Nonetheless, despite the constant criticism and ridicule of the jobber throughout the Augustan era, their historian points out that "as he bowed his head beneath the torrent of obloquy, he flourished."

Sir John Barnard, the Opposition's City spokesman, did lead a successful attack on stockjobbing in 1733, and if Barnard's legislation (7 George II, c.8) "to prevent the infamous practice of stock-jobbing" had been strictly enforced it would have put an end to speculation. It was not. The statute outlawed time bargains and dealings in futures: bargains in which the seller did not actually have the stock he was selling at the time of the sale could not be struck because debts contracted in such transactions would not be recoverable at common law. But by 1733 the speculative habit had taken too firm a root in England; it could not be uprooted by act of Parliament. The gamble went merrily on, however uncertain the position of the broker, and, as Defoe reported in his *Tour Thro' the Whole Island of Great Britain*, thousands of families flocked to London to buy and sell stocks. The statute, never effective, was repealed in 1860.[38]

## WALPOLE'S ROBINOCRACY AND THE NEW ECONOMIC ORDER

Walpole accepted the new financial order which had developed in post-Revolutionary England. This is to make no claim that Walpole was himself a capitalist or bourgeois figure. On the contrary, there is about his actions the traditional posture of the landed

and aristocratic man who controls and manages the merchant and the money man. Of gentry stock himself, he occasionally showed sympathy for the plight of the gentry, as when he proposed an excise scheme that would have reduced the land tax. Nevertheless, Walpole understood and welcomed the financial innovations so opposed by Bolingbroke and others in the Opposition. Walpole had few or no qualms about the values inherent in the financial revolution, and even fewer over any possible effect they might have on the constitution or the traditional ordering of society. The new institutions of the financial bourgeoisie were important to him primarily because they served his major interest—power, a pre-occupation that made him inevitably less a traditionalist than his reactionary opponents. One may argue, then, that it is merely by default and not by temperament that Walpole emerged as the political patron of financial capitalism; but whether by default or by conscious choice, Walpole's response to the new England was a very different one from that of Bolingbroke. His public performance and private dealings served to enhance the prestige and power of the men of money and to give official sanction to their path to social and political power. That his attitude had this effect was quite evident to his contemporaries. Lord Egmont wrote in his diary that Walpole "had no so great regard for any as for these little pickthanks and scrubs . . . in opposition to the old gentry of the kingdom."[39]

The support of the large financial interests in the City was one of the important sources of Walpole's strength. Lord John Hervey, the omniscient observer of his age, wrote that Walpole was "hated by the City of London because he never did anything for the trading part of it, nor aimed at any interest of theirs but a corrupt influence over the directors and governors of the great monied companies."[40] The large merchants, the men of the moneyed companies, and the brokers formed one small but powerful segment of the City, favorable to Walpole and the new order. The bulk of the City's small traders and merchants opposed both and were an important part of the Opposition. This division was reflected in London's government. The oligarchic Court of Aldermen contained twenty-five citizens who were generally rich and representative of the financial interests of the great companies. While Walpole was in power this body nearly always supported his policies. The Court

of Common Council contained 234 members and was more democratic; it remained in opposition. Walpole ratified the alliance of
his government and the "moneyed interest" of the Aldermen with
his London Election Act of 1725, which recognized the claim of
the Aldermen that they had veto power over the Common Council
as legitimate. The stability of Walpole's regime rested in part on
this relationship. He was assured that in return for his support the
moneyed companies would meet the short- and long-term borrowing
needs of his government.[41]

Walpole was particularly close to Sampson Gideon, the leading
financier of the age. Gideon could be found daily at Garroway's or
Jonathan's Coffee House in Exchange Alley, where he dealt in
government securities and stocks of the three moneyed companies.
After 1740, Gideon left the Alley for the more prestigious job of
banker to the government. As a jobber he was a close personal
friend of Walpole's, and as banker and financial advisor he was indispensable to Pelham, Walpole's successor. In an age when a fortune of £50,000 was considered a substantial achievement for a
"rich" London merchant, Gideon's career stands out as phenomenal. In 1719, he began with a capital of £1,500; under Walpole, his
jobbing brought it to £44,650. After twenty more years as banker
to England's war effort, he had a fortune of £350,000. Gideon is a
perfect example of the new gentleman, a theme which so preoccupied Defoe and the age. Because he was a Jew he was unable
to sit in Parliament, but by 1745 he had received a grant of arms
and set himself up as a country gentleman. He abandoned the
Jewish community in 1753 in hopes of a baronetcy or a peerage,
which he never received, but in 1759 he withheld a loan to the
Duke of Newcastle until his thirteen-year-old son, who had been
baptized, was created a baron.[42]

Walpole's Robinocracy was more than an ordinary friend of the
financial interest. Walpole's successful parliamentary whitewash in
1721 of the South Sea fiasco may have earned from his enemies the
epithet of "screen" but it also brought the lifelong gratitude of the
implicated financial community. In return for such favors, for contracts and continued support of the debt, funding, and stockjobbing,
Walpole was assured of votes in the Commons. The moneyed interest, recipient of so many favors from the government, was a

supporter of the government in power, which, for much of the early eighteenth century, was Walpole's.

Walpole did have his enemies in the City, the smaller merchants. Their spokesman, Sir John Barnard, repeatedly attacked the moneyed interest: men like Sampson Gideon in general, and Walpole's close affiliation with them in particular. Barnard, one of the four City members of Parliament, remained in opposition throughout Walpole's administration. Like Bolingbroke he was convinced that Walpole's ordering of the public funds had created two nations in England; it "divided the nation into two ranks of men, of which one are creditors and the other debtors. The creditors are the three great corporations and others, made up of natives and foreigners; the debtors are the landholders, the merchants, the shopkeepers, and all ranks and degrees of men throughout the Kingdom."[43]

In addition to their institutional interdependence, there were other strictly personal factors at work strengthening Walpole's ties to the moneyed interest. The civil servant, William Lowndes, Secretary of the Treasury and close friend of Walpole, sat in the Commons and was a convenient intermediary between the Bank (whose interests he also served), Parliament, and the Treasury. From Walpole's contemporaries and biographers it is clear that he was himself peculiarly adept in financial matters as Chancellor of the Exchequer in 1715-1717 and 1721-1742. After 1720, when he played an important role in bringing the Bank to the rescue of the South Sea Company, Walpole was in constant touch with the Bank directorate and the South Sea Company. His brother-in-law and then partner at the head of the government, Townshend, became a member of the General Court of the Bank in 1722, and remained on it until 1733, when he was elected Governor of the Bank of England. The Bank's dealings with the state were also "eased and sweetened" throughout Walpole's period by the Bank's custom of making a yearly New Year's gift of some 340 guineas to the officers of the Exchequer.[44]

However, Walpole's patronage of the new financial order involved more fundamental political motives. The new financial institutions were identified with the political settlement of 1688, and Walpole and the establishment Whigs pictured any opponent of these institutions as an opponent of the Revolution and of the Hanoverian succession. Walpole's pamphleteers answered Opposition attacks on the national debt, on stockjobbing, and demands for lower interests to fundholders, with just such an identification of the new financial order with the freedom acquired in 1688.

The national debt was contracted in defense of our liberties and properties and for the preservation of our most excellent constitution from popery and slavery. This encouraged the best subjects at the Revolution to venture their lives and fortunes in maintaining a long and expensive war in a firm dependence on Parliamentary faith and that public credit which arose from the force and unconfined liberty, so wisely given to every subject to dispose of his property or interest in the public funds. This created a new Commerce amongst mankind . . . without this commerce which gave birth to a new kind of species, it seems impossible that war could have been maintained . . . This commerce, this freedom for every subject to attach his property in the Funds, as occasion or convenience required, may undoubtedly be affirmed to be the support of public credit. It is in a great measure to this liberty that we owe the happy effects of the revolution, the blessings of peace, and the succession of the present royal family.[45]

This government pamphleteer then proceeded to attack Barnard's Opposition bill to curb stockjobbing, arguing that such restraints on the free liberty of the subject would not only impair credit, but would also have a deleterious political effect on the nation. The clamor against companies and stockjobbing endangered the settlement, "this darling child of liberty," so wisely and carefully nursed and cherished by the legislature. "Oh that the Lords Halifax and Godolphin were living to see an attempt made to destroy this uncontrolled circulation, this noble structure which they laboured so much to raise and establish!"[46] The reasoning of Walpole's pamphleteer is clear: to criticize the financial world of modern Whiggery is to challenge the political settlement of 1688.

Walpole's *London Journal* frequently gives evidence that it accepted the new economic order. Stockjobbing in and of itself is not in the least harmful, the *Journal* contends, when it is practiced honestly by brokers. When people pay for the stock, and buy and deliver what they sell, and no unfair methods are used to raise or lower the prices, then "to buy or sell stocks is as reputable as to buy or sell land."[47] Walpole was himself a great speculator. Contrary to the opinions of historians who have for decades seen him as sceptical of the South Sea Scheme, it is now known that Walpole had great holdings in the Company and that through judicious and careful speculation he amassed a great deal of money that he managed to save by pulling out in time.[48]

*The London Journal* used the same logic to defend the moneyed companies as it had used to defend jobbing. "It shews as great corruption of heart as any corruption these authors (*The Craftsman*) complain of, to insinuate, that all companies are villains." In 1735, *The Daily Gazetteer,* another Walpole sheet, defended the fundholders who, it insisted, deserved their interest. It was absurd, the paper argued, to see the population as mere hewers of wood and drawers of water who maintained the proprietors of the funds at a life of luxury. Those in *The Craftsman* who talked of ending the national debt and interest payment "would justly deserve to be hanged." It is no small coincidence that soon after Bolingbroke's second flight to France in 1735, *The Daily Gazetteer* said of *The Craftsman's* author "the proprietors of the Funds if not the people of England, have just reason to say, away with such a fellow from the earth, it is not fit that he should live."[49]

In 1730 one issue of Walpole's *London Journal* offered a lengthy defense and praise of the new and mysterious world of financial capitalism that so confused and angered the gentry and smaller merchants and their spokesmen in political and intellectual circles. The article, a hymn to money and credit, described the invention of paper money and credit institutions as contributing to the general public welfare, not only the enrichment of a few. "Bank notes, South Sea bonds, and any others answer our occasions the same as money. As money they are given also in circulation; they amount to near the value of so much coined gold." *The London Journal* went on to praise other new financial institutions. "The getting in of debts is business itself, and has been for some time a great part of the employment of our kingdom." Banks had also been of great use in the nation, "enabling dead money to be gathered into stocks and made to circulate in the form of Bonds or notes."[50]

Walpole illustrated his patronage of the new economic order by legislative action. He defended, for example, the renewal of monopoly charters to the trading and moneyed companies. When the East India Company's charter was up for renewal in 1730 and was under bitter attack by the Opposition, Walpole came to its defense. Petitions from hundreds of merchants demanding a freer and more open trade to the East Indies were presented to the House. On the floor, Barnard and William Pulteney spoke for the merchants, and Windham, Bolingbroke's spokesman, spoke against the Company. The storm was weathered by the Company; Walpole had an easy majority of 231 votes to 131. The Company, which had contributed £200,000 to Walpole's government, had its charter renewed until 1766.[51] Walpole persistently resisted parliamentary efforts to reduce the interest paid to fundholders. In 1737 the Opposition, led by Barnard, sought to lower the interest rate to three percent; this would include the interest paid to the government's creditors. The Opposition measure was intended to "ease the trader, manufacturer, farmer, and labourer of those taxes which bear the hardest on them and are discouragement to improvement of the land and enlargement of the trade of this kingdom."[52] Trade and land, it was contended, were being held at ransom by the moneyed interest, which contributed not one shilling toward the expense of the public. William Coxe, Walpole's first biographer, indicates that "Barnard's motion was principally defended by the landed and resisted by the moneyed interest."[53] Walpole pleaded the case of the public creditors. "The preference given to the funds arises from various causes, from the facility of receiving interest, cheapness of transfer and from none more than the faith placed in the national honour, which is bound to suffer no loss to fall on the public creditors."[54] Barnard's proposal was defeated.

Walpole seemed at times genuinely concerned with the plight of the landed classes. By his excise scheme he attempted to raise the excise on salt, tobacco, and wine, and to allow a reduction in land tax. But, one could argue, Walpole's acceptance of the new economic world was revealed even in this activity. In the Commons, Walpole justified the excise and its obvious imposition on the poor with the claim that everyone, including the poor, should be taxed. The landed had borne too much of the burden. The poor should pay too, since they also received benefits of the state's protection that were purchased by taxation. A government pamphlet used the same argument: "If he [the labourer] has no estate, yet he owes the protection of his life and liberty to the government, and should consequently contribute his mite to its support."[55] Implicit in Walpole's and the pamphleteer's position is an acceptance of the view of Hobbes and Locke that the state is the protector of rights and liberty, and should be subsidized by all those sheltered by the public sword. With respect to taxation, at least, Walpole's Lockean views extended to the lower orders. They were protected in life and liberty and should, therefore, pay taxes to the policeman state.[56] When the Opposition attacked Walpole's measure, it rejected the thoroughgoing Lockean attitude which lay behind it. The most important Opposition statement came from Lord Bathurst, the young friend and disciple of Bolingbroke. It is not surprising that the "possessive individualism" so characteristic of Locke's thought was rejected by Bolingbroke's spokesman, nostalgic for a world that knew no bourgeois values, and no Locke. In Bathurst's statement there is a lingering afterglow of the status model of society.[57]

In all cases it is hard, it is cruel to tax the poor journey men and day labourer, because it is not to be presumed that they can get anything more than bare subsistence by their daily labour. The profits that may be made go all to the benefit of the master who employs them. He it is that has the whole benefit of their labour and therefore ought to pay the taxes.[58]

There is, to be sure, a heavy dose of expediency in the gentry-based Opposition's rejection of Walpole's effort to alleviate the hardship of taxes on land. But one can also detect an element of principle here. It was the responsibility of the gentry to operate the government and to pay its costs, while laborers and tenants were to serve and obey. The gentry paid the revenue and looked after the poor; they could cede neither their privileges nor their duties. They reacted to Walpole's excise in terms which reflected their fear that such legislation might weaken their political influence; he who threatened their duties threatened their privileges.

# III

## Bolingbroke and the New England

Bolingbroke as J. H. Plumb tells us, had an uncanny ability to understand and exploit public opinion.[1] What he sensed was the discontent of a group of his contemporaries who felt that their lot had worsened, and that the traditional political and social order in which they played an important role was being undermined. Great changes were, in fact, taking place in the countryside during the Augustan years. The leading economic historian of the period, H. J. Habbakuk, has suggested that these developments contributed to the serious plight of the gentry in the early eighteenth century.[2] Professor Habbakuk's thesis assumes that it was Tawney who had accurately described the gentry's course in the seventeenth century, when the rise of the squirearchy provided the background to social change; but, he goes on, other important changes also took place in rural society after the Glorious Revolution. "There was a general drift of property in the sixty years after 1690 in favor of the large estate and great lord. While the movement probably was not so decisive as that which in the hundred years before 1640 consolidated the squirearchy it clearly marks one of the great changes in the disposition of English landed property."[3]

Habbakuk's research discloses that if one divides English landed society of the period into three groups: peers, substantial squires, and smaller squires, then the amount of land possessed by the upper two classes of large proprietors increased considerably from 1640 to 1740. The years 1680-1740 saw a particularly appreciable decline in the area of land owned by small squires and landed gentry.[4] The increased vitality of large landed estates was not primarily the result of economic advantages they possessed, but, in part, caused by certain legal developments such as increased entailing of estates,

56

which enabled a father to keep the family estates intact in the hands of a succession of older sons, and to prevent the estates from being reduced by bequests to younger sons.[5] The most important factor contributing to the difficulties of the small gentry, however, was the nearly twenty years of war with France under William and Anne.

The high land tax levied to finance the war fell most heavily on the landed gentry. Before the war the land tax varied from year to year, but only twice reached four shillings in the pound of the landowner's income between 1667 and 1690. In the war years, 1692-1715, a steady tax of four shillings in the pound was levied. The tax levied on rents fell with particular hardship on those smaller landowners who depended entirely on rents as a source of income. In addition, the low price of agricultural produce from 1702 to 1706, during the most desperate years of the war, made it more difficult for landed men to pay their taxes.[6] Only those landowners who had a source of income other than their land were able to pay their taxes and survive this difficult period. Those able to do this tended to be the owners of the larger estates and older families who had benefited from the war's effect of increasing the machinery of the central government by acquiring offices, commissions, and ambassadorships. The smaller gentry, the class most free from debt in the seventeenth century, was forced in this later period to mortgage heavily. Thus one can find an act in the reign of Anne, to reduce the rate of interest, prefaced:

> Whereas the heavy burden of the late long and expensive war hath been chiefly borne by the owners of the land of this kingdom, by reason whereof they have been necessitated to contract very large debts, and thereby, and by the abatement in the value of their lands, are become greatly impoverished . . .[7]

The statute proceeds to single out for particularly heavy fines, "all and every scrivener and scriveners, broker and brokers, solicitor and solicitors, driver and drivers of bargains for contracts." The scriveners' function in the estate market was the symbol to the debt-ridden gentry of their plight.

An historian of eighteenth-century life in Northumberland reports the virtual liquidation of scores of lesser Catholic gentry in the early years of the century. Scarcely a Roman Catholic gentleman in the north country escaped inclusion on registers of mortgaged estates. This led, in the years between the Restoration and 1750, to the near disappearance of the smaller gentry in the area, and the rise of vast agglomerations of landed estates; it was also, not surprisingly, accompanied by a noticeable political impact. "One begins to suspect that the last civil war in England, the Jacobite, was due in no small degree to the desperate poverty of the northern Catholic gentry. Not that bankruptcy was a monopoly of adherents to the old faith, many others had little to lose."[8] Bolingbroke the gentry apologist and Bolingbroke the temporary Jacobite seem not that incompatible.

Statements of contemporaries substantiate the research of historians.

I believe it can be easily demonstrated, that the freeholders have contributed more towards the expense of the two last wars, than was ever known in any country in the world; for I am thoroughly persuaded that after deducting four shillings in the pound for the land tax, losses by insolvent tenants, reparations, the assessments for the militia and the payment of parochial duties, their clear income in most counties would not excel seven shillings and sixpence in the pound, which indeed exterminated nine parts in ten, of all the gentlemen of middling estates.[9]

Daniel Defoe's observations on the plight of the rural gentry while on his travels through England and Wales corroborate these economic data. Another observer, an anonymous pamphleteer, summed up the fate of the gentry in anguished terms.

Other countries have had, and possibly still have, a gentry and nobility equal to ours; and out of this stock warriors, statesmen, and patriots have at different times sprung up, almost in every soil. But in this country alone, for many ages that middle class of men, higher than the peasant, and lower than the gentleman, hath subsisted independent, who like an isthmus, hath divided and withstood the fury of popular insurrection and the arrogant incroachments of greatness, saving alike this bounded monarchy from confusion and tyranny. Pity it is that such a bulwark should now be undermined and moulder into ruin. With the yeoman, the middle gentry of small landed estates, seen hastening to annihilation, the few remaining (for they every day decrease) are possibly the most miserable beings amongst us, with nothing left undiminished that belonged to their fathers, but pride and appetite beyond their fortunes. And those taxes, which have near devoured their little substance, have, in no inconsiderable degree, impaired the possessions of the greatest.[10]

The smaller gentry, beset by debt, dreaded the end of their independent existence. Their land was being absorbed by larger estates whose owners could meet the tax burden, and by purchasers new to the land. The development at the turn of the century of the national debt and of funding operations opened a large new field of investment, so that land, which had once appeared as the only secure investment, now had a rival as merchants invested heavily in the government. Those who chose to buy land were now more likely influenced by considerations of social prestige and political power than by the prospect of profitable investment. The local gentry were being replaced by lawyers, doctors, goldsmiths, and tradesmen. Most conspicuous among the newcomers, however, were those who had drawn their fortunes from government during the years of the war. Typical of this group was Daniel Finch, the Earl of Nottingham, who, but for his huge gains in office "it is certain . . . would not have bought so large an estate as Burley." War, by enlarging the ranks of government servants, made fortunes and positions for new men in much the same way as, in the Tudor Age, the new bureaucracy of the centralizing monarchy had. The declining small gentry felt themselves victims of a conspiratorial pincer movement. The war which necessitated the high land tax, the initial cause of their woes, seemed to benefit only those who had connections with the government and who were able to survive using their non-landed income to pay their taxes. The managers of the war, government officers in London or in the field, who were financed by the land tax, were using the fruits of place to buy into the land and squeeze out the small gentry. The palaces at Burley and Blenheim were monuments to this process.[11]

Another group of men seemed to profit from this war paid for by the gentry's land taxes—the money men, the owners of the state debt. These men collected yearly interest from the government and paid no taxes. The great war and its debt filled their pockets, and they, too, came to the land seeking position and prestige with their new-found wealth. This encircling movement was responsible for the plight of the small gentry. They were compelled, in effect, to exhaust their financial energies in helping to create the class that would dispossess them. In addition to their feeling that they were being victimized by a conspiracy of commerce and government, the gentry felt resentment for another reason—the intangible and impersonal quality of the new financial order which seemed responsible for their plight. In Bolingbroke's day the reaction of the gentry and small traders to the new phenomena of mysterious public credit, paper transactions, and large new financial institutions can be construed as an early form of populist reaction to the modern economic and social world, a phenomenon which would emerge in other nations when they entered this stage of development.

We have heard such an analysis before. Trevor-Roper describes the seventeenth century in terms of the plight of the gentry.[12] Confronted by a conspiracy of office holders and new moneyed men from London, the declining gentry, he contends, indulged their despair in radical political activity and in talk about the ideal order for which they longed, which had been described by Harrington. Could it be, then, as J. G. A. Pocock suggests, that Trevor-Roper's political analysis of the decline of the gentry applies better to the later period, 1640 to 1740?[13] Gentry politics of discontent seem to explain the nihilism and negativism of the Jacobite 1715 and 1745 better than the Great Rebellion. Bolingbroke would then be the appropriate political philosopher of the declining gentry. He embodies the attitudes, aspirations, and frustrations of a declining class in a much more direct and self-conscious manner than does Harrington, whom Trevor-Roper ties to the plight of the gentry. Bolingbroke is the conservative and "populist" spokesman for the declining gentry. Being an aristocrat, he was concerned with the threat posed by the new order to the traditional role of his own class as well as to the gentry who had constituted the wide and solid base of the ruling class.

Reactionary populist leaders need not be small farmers, threatened artisans, or shopkeepers. In the united front of a populist reaction to early capitalism it is appropriate—most especially in one of its first manifestations—that the generals were well bred and the troops were yeomen farmers and small traders. They could make common cause so easily because they both perceived the extent of the threat. Bolingbroke's career and writings bear an amazing consistency when they are seen in this light. From 1701 to 1715 he championed the antiwar, antimoneyed interest in Parliament. His populist tendency may account for the seeming aberration of his Jacobite years, and explain the perpetual attack in all his political writings on the new role of finance in society. He emerged as the full-blown spokesman of discontent in his opposition to Walpole. He had discovered the source of the conspiracy which depressed aristocracy, gentry, intellectuals, and small traders alike. But it was really the new composition of English finance, not Walpole, which was the nemesis that brought an end to the traditional constitution in which, since the days of the Tudors, the aristocracy and gentry had stood paramount.

Interestingly enough, another and rather unexpected source of gentry resentment in this period was the use made of the writings of Locke by the financial community. The defenders of the new economy used Locke to answer the arguments of the gentry, who, in their search for an explanation of their plight, saw only factors external to themselves. One contemporary gentry spokesman included even the government in a long list of those responsible for gentry hardship. "You certainly ruin those that have only land to depend on to enrich Dutch, Jews, French and other foreigners, scoundrel stock jobbers and tally jobbers who have been sucking out our vitals for many years."[14] The financial community responded by citing Locke's comments in an essay of 1691 in which he had described the plight of the landed as caused by no one but themselves. It was an argument later used by Defoe.

. . . ill husbandry, neglect of government and religion, depraved education, introduce debauchery and living beyond means and debts increase. This is generally the cause why men part with their land . . . the usual struggle and contest, as I said before, in the decays of wealth and riches is between the landed men and the merchant, with whom I may here join the moneyed man. The landed man finds himself aggrieved by the falling of his rents, and the straitening of his fortune, whilst the moneyed man keeps up his gain, and the merchant thrives and grows rich by trade. These he thinks steal his income into their pockets, build their fortunes upon his ruin and engross more of the riches of the nation than comes to their share. He therefore endeavors by laws to keep up the value of lands (and reduce the rate of profit) which he suspects lessened by the others' excess of profit: But all in vain. The cause is mistaken and the remedy too. It is not the merchant's nor the moneyed man's gain that makes land fall, but the want of money and lessening of our treasure wasted by extravagant expenses. If the landed gentleman will have and by his example make it fashionable to have more claret, spice and silk and other foreign consumable wares than our exportation of commodities does exchange for, money must unavoidably follow to balance the account and pay the debt . . . We must not therefore impute the falling of the rents, or of the price of land, to high interest, nor if ill husbandry has wasted our riches, hope by such kinds of laws to raise them to their former value. I humbly conceive we shall in vain endeavor it, by the fall of interest.[15]

The gentry felt, on the contrary, that they would be saved and the moneyed interests punished if only the land tax were reduced and the interest rate paid to receivers of state annuities lowered. "The monsters who were enriched by exorbitant premiums, annuities, and dividends should be compelled to bear some share." This same disgruntled commentator would have instituted a confiscatory tax on the holders of stock in the Bank, and the South Sea Company, for they had "amassed their fortunes upon the wants of the public."[16] To counter these demands for low interest, the money men once again cited Locke. A pamphleteer who attacked the proposed lowering of interest in 1751 wrote, "I may I think declare my opinion the more boldly because I find the famous Mr. Locke was of the same opinion . . . that great man was against it."[17] Locke's reasoning in 1691 was equally appropriate in 1751, added the pamphleteer. Borrowers and lenders should make their own bargains, and civil laws should not interfere with the automatic workings of the laws of nature. Moreover, according to Locke's essay, the receivers of interest need have no shame. Lockean sentiments such as the following were not inclined to impress the hard-pressed gentry.

It follows that borrowing money upon use is not only by the necessity of affairs and the constitution of human society unavoidable to some men, but that also to receive profits from the loan of money is as equitable and lawful as receiving rent for land, and more tolerable to the borrower, notwithstanding the opinion of some over-scrupulous men.[18]

What Locke had written in 1691 was also cited in opposition to those advocating a lower land tax, for had he not written that land must inevitably bear the brunt of taxes? The declining gentry could hardly be pleased with this pessimism of their Mr. Locke.

Lay the taxes how you will, land everywhere in proportion bears the greater share of the burden . . . struggle and continue as you will, lay your taxes as you please, the traders will shift it off from their own gain, the merchants will bear the least part of it, and grow poor last. In Holland itself where trade is so loaded, who I pray, grows richest, the landholder, or the trader? Which of them is pinched and wants money most? . . . I challenge any one to show me a country wherein there is any considerable public charge raised, where the land does not most sensibly feel it, and in proportion, bear much the greater part of it.[19]

The gentry had yet another reason to be wary of Mr. Locke. He and his political friends, Montagu and John Somers, and the great Isaac Newton had played an important role in the recoinage of 1696-1699 in which new coins were minted and old light (clipped) coins were removed from circulation.[20] This made circulating medium in general more scarce, which had a particularly stringent effect on the gentry because much of the clipped currency was in the countryside, and had often been used to pay the land tax. Government receivers now refused to take the debased currency, and so further fanned the fires of gentry discontent.[21] So much, then, for the early eighteenth-century gentry and the onetime "gentry spokesman," John Locke.

### THE BANK CRISIS OF 1710 AND THE BUBBLE OF 1720

Bolingbroke built his career upon the discontent of the gentry. An assault upon its alleged source, the new financial order, is involved in all his writings. The economic and social developments of the period were inextricably bound to the political attitudes found in Bolingbroke's circle. These developments could not go unnoticed because two jarring historical events brought them to the immediate perception of Tory intellectuals. The Bank crisis of 1710 warned of the potential danger in the new order and the South Sea Bubble of 1720 seemed to verify its horrifying actuality.

Bolingbroke and his circle were obsessed with the political power of money; it was one of their constant charges that this power had been institutionalized and enabled to command the commonwealth. Behind many of these fears lay the memory of events in June and August 1710, when the leaders of the Bank of England had tried to dictate policy to the Queen of England. The Sacheverell trial in 1710 had inflamed the London mob to turn upon all traces of popery and dissent. Not satisfied with burning chapels alone, the mob had threatened to storm the Bank itself, full of gold and Whiggery. The Bank was protected, and perhaps even saved, by squadrons of Horse Guards who rode from St. James to scatter the rioters.[22] The Bank directors, who feared that the encouragement of this passion had come from rumored changes in Anne's ministry, sent the Governor and Deputy Governor and two other gentlemen of the Bank to "attend Her Majesty to desire that she would make no further alterations in the ministry which must affect so much all the public credit."[23] Their plea was ineffective, and Sunderland was dismissed two days later. In August, the Bank responded by refusing a loan to support continued army, navy, and transport services. It told Godolphin, still in office, that it had refused the loan because many were fearful for the security of the Hanoverian Protestant succession: credit was falling and the Bank feared that it might fall even lower because of talk that the Queen would dissolve Parliament and make further changes. The Bank directors asked Godolphin to speak to the Queen. He did as they asked and was dismissed by the Queen. Contemporary opinion had it that his dismissal was precipitated specifically by Anne's anger at this moneyed impertinence.

The dismissal was occasioned upon a representation he carried to the Queen from the Bank in which they expressed an unwillingness to lend money till Her Majesty had made a further declaration that she intended no further changes, nor a dissolution; upon which though she expressed no great dislike at that time, the next morning she wrote to him to break his staff himself to save her the trouble of taking it away.[24]

The potential political power of the new economic order presented itself clearly to Bolingbroke in these developments of the summer of 1710 that brought Harley and himself back to power. It was to these events that he referred in his dramatic pleas to Parliament when he presented his Landed Qualification Bill in 1711. He referred again to the incidents of the summer of 1710 in his letter to Windham. "The Bank had been extravagant enough to pull off the mask and when the Queen seemed to intend a change in her ministry, they had deputied some of their members to represent against it."[25] Incidents like the Bank crisis represented a departure from the past. Swift's *Examiner* of April 19, 1711, attests to its considerable impact on the Tory intellectuals.

What people then are these in a corner, to whom the constitution must truckle? . . . What new maxims are these, which neither we nor our forefathers ever heard of before, and which no wise Institution would ever allow. Must our laws from henceforward pass the Bank and East India Company or have their Royal Assent before they are in force?[26]

Another and even more important shock associated with the new economic order was the South Sea Bubble of 1720. In this catastrophe the entire system seemed involved and indicted—the moneyed companies, the projecting spirit, the funds, the debts, and the stock-jobbers. After 1720, the Tory intellectuals would have a lasting memory of social chaos, of what they considered the imminent collapse of the established ranks and orders, and of the discord and confusion that come with the end of rank and order.

The Bank crisis of 1710 was the first step in the complex set of events that culminated in the Bubble.[27] The South Sea Company was conceived at the time of the Bank's pressure on the government in 1710. Harley, Anne's new minister, backed it in the hope that it would be a Tory rival to the Whig Bank. The new company offered to buy up the debts of almost ten million pounds that the government owed its creditors; in turn the Company demanded a monopoly of trade to the South Seas from the new Tory government. It was felt by the Company that the potential profit of the trade would prompt former government debtors to invest in their new venture. Had it not been for John Law and his speculative activity in France, little more might have been heard of the South Sea Company. It could have gone on peacefully collecting the annual interest of six percent that the government paid it for having taken over ten million pounds of debt. It might have been remembered only as a respectable commercial failure. But the South Sea Company attained historical notoriety because Mr. John Blunt, son of a Rochester shoemaker, former petty scrivener and leading director of the Company was fascinated by the events in France, and conceived a plan for England similar to Law's audacious scheme for the French economy. In a daring takeover bid, the South Sea Company would assume the whole of the national debt, which in 1719 amounted to fifty million pounds: thirty million pounds borrowed from the public at large, and twenty million from the East India Company and the Bank of England.

During the spring and summer months of 1719, the South Sea Company burgeoned, and although Law's scheme in France collapsed, little attention was paid to this in England. Mr. Blunt's assumption had paid off. Amid vague rumors that the Assiento

Trade would be enlarged, and that the South Sea Company was negotiating for trading rights in Africa, the price of Mr. Blunt's stock soared. It continued to climb as the general mania for speculation spread throughout the country. Blunt assisted this by sending Company money to holders of South Sea stock and encouraging them to purchase even more Company stock. In January 1720 the price of the Company's stock stood at £128; in March it sold for £300; by May it had reached £500; and by the end of May the price was £710. In early August South Sea Company stocks climbed to their greatest heights, first £1,000 then £1,100. Some voices of gloom were heard in those early spring months. Lord North wrote that the scheme "was calculated for the enriching of a few and the impoverishing of a great many; and not only made for but countenanced and authorized the fraudulent and pernicious practice of stockjobbing, which diverted the genius of the people from trade and industry."[28] An anonymous pamphleteer scorned the speculative hysteria of his countrymen.

> The South Sea stock is risen to so monstrous an excess, that it puts an affront upon all sense and reason; a set of crafty men having undertaken to delude the world with an opinion that they can by a little hocus-pocus management, make a single unit become a good ten.[29]

But few listened. That summer most Englishmen were intoxicated by the first heady draughts of financial capitalism. The mystery of credit, the projecting spirit, the speculative impulse, and the proliferation of joint-stock companies combined to produce the great Bubble. In April and May alone, fifty new companies were launched, few bothering even with the formality of a charter. As the restless dynamic spirit of the innovating bourgeoisie made its historical debut, conversation in the coffee houses along Exchange Alley was filled with tales and descriptions of new ventures. The summer of 1720 saw the formation of the London insurance market with the establishment of the London Assurance Company and the Royal Exchange Assurance. The year 1720 also saw the formation of the Welsh Copper Company, a company to build houses in London and Westminster, the York Building Company, and numerous others which dealt in woolen and cloth manufactures.

The ingenious projecting spirit so ably described by Defoe manifested itself in numerous less reliable capital undertakings. A list of the new companies founded in 1720 must also include the Bleaching of Hair Company, Insurance on Horses Company, a company for the Transmutation of Quicksilver, a company to Insure Marriages from Divorce, and another to design an air pump for the brain. Subscriptions were opened and filled immediately for a company to plant mulberry trees and breed silkworms in Chelsea Park. Another company would produce a cannon with the capability to discharge round and square cannon balls and bullets. The mania possessing the English that summer is best illustrated by the subscription of three thousand pounds in one day for "a company to carry on an undertaking of great advantage but nobody to know what it is."[30]

Fortunes were being made by everyone, or so it seemed. Credit was the new alchemy. The King had bought and then sold at a clear profit of £86,000 and made John Blunt a baronet. Walpole, himself a heavy speculator, recommended the South Sea stock to his friends, although he managed to sell his own stock in time. New fortunes were made, and others were lost. A contemporary journalist wrote, "we are informed that since the hurly-burly of stock jobbing there has appeared in London 200 new coaches and chariots besides as many more now on the stocks in the coach-makers' yards; above 4,000 embroidered coats; about 3,000 gold watches at the sides of whores and wives; and some few private acts of charity." An anonymous playwright has a well-dressed woman ask of a man of substance, "How long have you been a gentleman?" "About a week, Madame," answers the speculator.[31]

On August 18th the Bubble burst. In his zeal to close out some of the many upstart ventures that were rivals for investment Blunt had writs served on those companies that had no charters. By doing this he inadvertently precipitated the collapse. The stocks of the illegal companies fell, and with them the public confidence. Speculators rushed to sell their South Sea stock because many had shares in more than one company and needed cash to meet their obligations when the other stocks fell. The collapse came quickly. South Sea stock fell from £900 on August 17 to £190 on September 28.

There were many ruined fortunes. The Duke of Chandos lost the £300,000 he had made as Marlborough's Paymaster of the Forces. Two newspaper accounts give the sense of despair and helplessness felt by contemporaries before this mysterious turn of fate.

67

You may see second-hand coaches; second-hand gold watches, cast off diamond watches and earrings to be sold; servants already want places who were, but a little while ago, so saucy and insolent, no wages and no kind of usage could oblige them. The streets are full of rich liveries to be sold, nay, and full of rich embroidered petticoats, rich, embroidered coats and waistcoats; in a word every place is full of the ruin of Exchange Alley.

The far greater number who are involved in this public calamity appear with such dejected looks, that a man of little skill in the art of physiognomy may easily distinguish them. Exchange Alley sounds no longer of thousands got in an instant, but on the contrary all corners of the town are filled with the groans of the afflicted, and they who lately rode in great state to that famous mart of money, now humbly condescend to walk the streets on foot, and instead of adding to their equipages, have at once lost their estates.[32]

The Tory intellectuals would never forget this chaotic and confused nightmare. The ease with which the social order had been threatened and gentlemen made and unmade, would forever be identified with the Bubble and the new commercial order which produced it. Pope, Prior, and Gay actually lost small amounts of money. In France, Bolingbroke heard of the Bubble and its effects from one of its victims when the Duke of Chandos wrote him on October 5.

I have seen great variety of fortunes, but in all my life I never saw so universal a sense of misery as I did last week; the distress mankind was in was inconceivable and a general Bankruptcy was apprehended. God be thanked the ruine that threatened the Publick is pretty well blown over, but the destruction the fall of stocks and the loss of credit, hath brought upon private families is never to be retrieved and the number of families of all degrees have suffered accordingly. Lord Harcourt from being worth a profit of 100,000 pounds, I fear hath hardly saved 10,000 and in my fortune, I assure you I have lost within this month 500,000 pounds.[33]

In 1721 Bolingbroke read an anonymous volume of *Persian Letters* that concluded with an attack on the new economics in France in general, and on John Law and his schemes in particular. Much of what Montesquieu wrote in those *Persian Letters* on the French commercial order would be repeated in Bolingbroke's writings on England.

The great Bubble epitomized for Bolingbroke's circle an England

diseased in its political and social order. The money men with their
financial innovations had threatened degree, and it was inevitable
that confusion and chaos would follow any tampering with the assigned ranks and places of the traditional order. The attitude of the
Tory intellectual to his age was shaped by the experience of the
Bubble. The Bubble could never be forgotten, because, in the words
of Pope, it marked the moment when:

> At length corruption, like a general flood
> (So long by watchful Ministers withstood)
> Shall deluge all; and Avarice, creeping on.
> Spread like a lowborn mist, and blot the Sun;
> Statesman and Patriot ply alike the stocks,
> Peer and butler share alike the Box,
> And Judges job and Bishops bite the Town,
> And mighty Dukes pack cards for half-a-crown
> See Britain sunk in lucre's sordid charms;[34]

An anonymous pamphlet of 1721 sounded the lesson to be learned
from the experience of the previous year. God, it revealed, had
visited England to make it feel the fatal effects of its corruption and
folly. Now England must set upon the course of reformation which
consisted of restoring its religion, industry, frugality, and public
spirit. Men should first cease decrying religion. Having done this,
the nation had to turn to hard work. The only way England could
be wealthy was through the natural productive methods of land
and trade, not through the public gaming table where "money is
shifted from hand to hand in such a blind fortuitous manner, that
some men shall from nothing in an instant acquire vast estates
without the least desert; while others are as suddenly stript of
plentiful fortunes." Frugality of manner, the pamphlet continued,
is the nourishment and strength of the body politic, while luxury
is the natural cause of decay and ruin in the community. The English were becoming as helpless as the ancient Romans, and would
soon be a corrupt and ruined people, drowning in luxury. There
had to be a revival of public spirit. Men must be turned from cen-
tering all their efforts upon their private interests. Corruption had
become a national disease which infected all His Majesty's subjects.

The south sea affair is not the original evil or the greatest source of
our misfortune; it is but the natural effect of these principles which for

many years have been propagated with great industry. And as a sharp distemper by reclaiming a man from intemperance may prolong his life, so it is not improbable but this public calamity that lieth so heavy on the nation may prevent its ruin . . . if it should turn our thought from cousenage and stock-jobbing to industry and frugal methods of life; In fine if it should revive and inflame that native spark of British worth and honor which hath too long lain smothered and oppressed.[35]

This response to the Bubble, in its despair, resentment, and call for reformation, suggests the attitude of the Tory intellectuals and especially of Bolingbroke during the following twenty years.

### THE NEW ECONOMY, CORRUPTION, AND THE MODEL OF ROME

In Bolingbroke's *Craftsman*, the central organ of the Opposition, weekly articles no less severe than Bolingbroke's other published works battled the new order. The focus of the attacks was the belief—in *The Craftsman's* words—that a different kind of property of a most precarious and uncertain nature had arisen since 1688. This new form of property was quickly translated into the "new sort of power sprung up, since the Revolution," which tended to the destruction of the constitution.[36] *The Craftsman* listed the offensive elements of the new order as the national debt, stockjobbing, and the moneyed companies.

The national debt was the fountain from which flowed all the evils of the new order. In *The Craftsman's* opinion, the debt stood behind the Bank and the tremendous power of the East India and South Sea Companies. It endorsed the easy pursuit of wealth by the steady interest it paid its fundholders, an interest that caused heavy taxes to be levied on the oppressed gentry. The debt gave rise to the new and mysterious world of public finance with its "kind of false wealth, called paper credit." A large debt and high taxes also provided multitudes of new offices and employments, and, *The Craftsman* considered, crippled trade because no nation would deal with a country so vulnerable.[37] *The Craftsman's* attitude was dominated by the widespread fear that the colossal and ever-increasing debt would bring about the bankruptcy and ruin of England. It was argued that a nation was, after all, but one extended estate. Should an estate go deeply into debt it would be ruined, and such was the fate predicted for England. *The Craftsman* deplored Walpole's defense of the debt as economically useful and politically essential. It satirized a fictional Walpole supporter explaining to some simple and honest men why a man should let his estate fall into debt.

I will undertake to demonstrate the justness of it to the meanest capacity whereupon he called for a pen and ink and scrawled over a sheet of paper with figures, schemes and calculations, by which means he puzzled the understandings of the company in so masterly a manner that his opponents were obliged to give up the point and drop the dispute . . . It was undeniably a great advantage to any gentleman to be in debt, and mortgage his estate, because said he, it keeps those persons, who lend the money, in a constant dependence on him who borrows it and strengthens the title to his estate, by lodging his securities in other hands.[38]

Stockjobbers were another frequent target of *The Craftsman*. Number 47, a "Persian Letter" from Usbeck, an imaginary traveller in England, to his homeland describes the existence among the Christians of "a peculiar sort called stock-jobbers," men whom the Christians call Jews. They live and grow rich, "not by Traffick, nor by arts, or science, or industry, or labour, or mechanicks, or navigation, or warfare, or any other business of use or advantage to mankind." This peculiar breed of men, he goes on, utter strange sounds in an inarticulate manner and walk about wildly. Usbeck concluded the letter by questioning how long it must be before this false and imaginary commerce would end all solid trade. The broker and stockjobber could never be forgiven the insecurity they brought to the ownership of property. *The Craftsman* argued that English government, unlike French, had never before allowed property to be precarious and subject to the will of the prince. This security, the distinguishing character of English government, was now weakened, because brokers rendered estates uncertain and dependent on the will of men in power. A few men could "with a breath blow away my estate, make me worth nothing today, who yesterday had a handsome income." Since stockjobbing had flourished, trade and useful work in general had declined; the easy way to acquire riches drained the time and attention of too many. The stockjobber was the lowest of creatures; of them and of their ever-present partners, the schemers and projectors, *The Craftsman* wrote, "like cankers they preyed on the vitals of their country till they had reduced it to the most declining condition."[39]

The third most offensive elements in the new order were the three great companies. *The Craftsman,* representing the sentiments of the city small trader rather than any commitment to free trade, repeatedly assaulted the monopoly privileges of the three companies. Such exclusive corporations were prejudicial to commerce and therefore pernicious in a trading kingdom. "Freedom of trade is the spring of riches."[40] Not only were the companies enemies to freedom of trade, but also to political liberty, since their vast political powers extended from electing members of Parliament to intimate connections with Walpole and the Robinocracy. The traditional constitution was at their mercy.

Companies, like upstart men, had existed before, but Augustan man had to reckon with institutions whose scope was larger than any previously known. *The Craftsman* described these institutions as "monstrous members and societies in the Body politic, grown too big for the whole kingdom." The size of the elements in the economic revolution staggered the imagination. The debt was a sum incomprehensible in its greatness, the trading companies were organizations with national and world-wide involvements, and the Bank loomed as large as the state itself. The war of the Spanish succession was of a dimension that Englishmen had never before experienced; it uprooted thousands of men and sent them thousands of miles away.

A decisive break with the past was taking place in English social history during the Augustan period. A traditional order was giving way to institutions of a centralized and commercial society, and to an increasingly urban and middle class world. Small and personal units were being replaced by larger and more remote ones. *The Craftsman* said of the monstrous companies, "they have bodies, but no souls, nor consequently consciences."[41] The new depersonalized world seemed to render the individual helpless before forces much larger than himself. These impersonal forces operated the credit mechanism and determined the value or lack of value in the individual's tallies and estates. The individual landowner or small trader seemed no longer capable of controlling his own destiny, but felt himself to be at the mercy of outside and impersonal forces manipulated by men he did not know or trust. The Opposition's attack on the standing army must be understood partly as a rejection of an impersonal professional and rootless organization in the place of a more personal and locally based militia in which each man and his neighbor could perceive his own contributions. It is no accident that the Augustan satirists were so fascinated with the relativity of size; their daily experience made this an ever-present concern.

Another characteristic of the new order seemed to be the centrality of money. *The Craftsman* wrote in March 1727 that preoccupation with money was a sickness which had descended on Great Britain since the Revolution. It had changed the nature of the people, the institutions of society, and the constitution. It was truly "the root of all evil." It seemed to *The Craftsman* to be the major force contributing to the depersonalization of society and the destruction of the traditional bonds which naturally held men together, and led to the imposition of an artificial basis of social relations. It had become the strongest cement in the world, "a more lasting tie than honour, friendship, relation, consanguinity, or unity of affections." Money and the new financial order, it was argued, were destroying the familiar society of gentry England. Under the patronage of Walpole, money had become the very "rule and sinew of government."[42]

In *A Dissertation upon Parties*, Bolingbroke described how money had become the only real power, and how it, and not the prerogative claims of the seventeenth century, would be the ruin of the constitution.[43] We know now that Bolingbroke's prediction was inaccurate; the gentry and their power would not pass as quickly as some feared in this first flush of anguish at the new power of money. Genteel England would survive and preserve its power for some time, but England's values would never again be the same. Bolingbroke and his following recognized the change, and their feeling that it was immense was more than justified. In his terms the new England represented a corrupt society far different from the England of his nobler ancestors. Shortly before his death, Bolingbroke wrote in a letter to Chesterfield "the very genius of our people is changed both in public and private life . . . the spirit of private interest prevails among us."[44] Englishmen of olden times, Bolingbroke thought, were men of economy, probity, and simple manners, and showed more of honor and industry than of pride or vanity. Since the Revolution, however, Englishmen had ceased to be plain, rough, and good-natured; corruption and luxury having been spread and avowed, decay appeared everywhere, and wit, good sense, and public spirit all declined together. Like the poets of his youth who protested against luxury, Bolingbroke could see only the "venality of all orders and all ranks of men." Politicians, lawyers, doctors, and clergymen headed his corrupt procession of Augustan men, who, seeking only lucre, had substituted avarice for honor. Their concern was only the "rapacious eagerness after wealth" which mired all England in the profusion of their luxury. The English mind, he wrote, so enervated by luxury, was now incapable of great and generous sentiments inspired by virtue; it could only produce soft ideas and wanton delicacies. For this reason, Bolingbroke, like Pope, saw in his age a dearth of wit and learning and all about him "modern dullness and stupidity." Men of merit and ability could justly complain, but it was futile to expect that in such a rapacious and selfish age arts, wit, or learning could thrive. The only ability in this age, wrote Bolingbroke, was a sordid genius for tricks and cunning which revealed itself in jobbing and other iniquitous arts.[45]

This corrupt age was epitomized for Bolingbroke by the venality that pervaded politics for which he held money and its new role in society to be responsible. A corrupt Parliament and first minister had resulted from a corrupt and mercenary society, and had reciprocated by encouraging the society by example and by the sanction of public authority. Had not wise men, Bolingbroke asked, from Aristotle and Cicero in antiquity to Machiavelli in modern times written that people were only as virtuous as their leaders?[46] Bolingbroke and his *Craftsman* assaulted corruption and luxury, and even advocated sumptuary laws. They attacked Walpole for presiding over the corrupt order and unashamedly defending it.[47] To the Tories Walpole seemed to proclaim moral anarchy when he insisted that corruption, far from threatening the constitution, saved it, and that luxury and self-interest were useful and necessary, as Bernard Mandeville, the philosopher of the new order, had written.

In a letter to Chesterfield, Bolingbroke objected to the way Walpole accepted the central thesis of Mandeville's *Fable of the Bees*.

Not content to neglect he ridiculed every public virtue. Not content to ridicule them, he established every opposite vice, and took off that remnant of shame which might have been improved to check, and under a better administration, to reform them.[48]

But Bolingbroke was no perfectionist; he did admit that corruption was inevitable, "for no human institution can arrive at perfection." There will always be some evil, he wrote in *The Spirit of Patriotism*; some corruption is necessary "to maintain subordination and to carry on even good government." Electoral and aristocratic dependence is useful and necessary, as is some of the Crown's patronage. What was lamentable, however, was the increase in the financial means of corruption, which was being employed for the benefit of the new financial oligarchy and not for the monarchy.[49]

It was natural that Bolingbroke, the humanist scholar, viewed corruption in Augustan England in the light of the Roman model. He conceived history's function as teaching present and future ages to be wiser and happier by giving them the examples of former times. It was not by accident, then, that Bolingbroke was concerned with the fall of states, especially Rome. Roman experience taught Bolingbroke that the forerunners and causes of the loss of liberty were the decay of virtue and public spirit, luxury and extravagance in expense, and venality and corruption in private and public affairs. Unlike Commonwealthmen like Walter Moyle or Harrington, Bolingbroke did not offer any explanation of Rome's decline in terms of property holdings and subsequent changes in power. He reserved his Harringtonian analysis for England, and did not read it back into antiquity. His analysis of Roman decline is almost pure Machiavelli. Frugality and temperance had accounted for the original greatness of Sparta and Rome, only to be displaced later by luxury and prodigality.[50] In both *A Dissertation upon Parties* and *Remarks on the History of England*, Bolingbroke devoted an entire letter to holding out for England the fate of Rome. Like England's, Rome's grandeur had developed over centuries, and continued as long as she had preserved her virtue, and her citizens' primary concern was the common weal. When she grew corrupt and venal "her power and her glory could not long survive." Public spirit declined when citizens thought only of themselves, factions sprang up, and the commonwealth was left to madmen and wretches "whose talents would scarce have recommended them to the meanest offices in the virtuous and prosperous ages of the commonwealth." He warned that a similar fate awaited England if there were no return to the original principles of the glorious and incorruptible past.

She who had been the envy, as well as the mistress of nations, fell to be an object of their scorn, or of their pity . . . Into such a state, the difference of times, and of other circumstances considered, at least, into a state as miserable as this, will the people of Britain fall, and deserve to fall.[51]

POLITICS AND THE NEW ECONOMY: LEADERSHIP,<br>BALANCE, AND THE "GENUINE" POLITY

An important reason for England's decline, according to Bolingbroke, was that the traditional order, which had placed supreme value on a natural leadership of virtuous and learned men, had been superseded by a new ideal that proclaimed that "he with the most money was the best man." In *A Dissertation upon Parties*, Bolingbroke wrote that no phenomenon of recent years was more striking and astonishing than the elevation of people to the highest posts of power and authority "who had not, either from their obscure birth, or their low talents, or their still lower habits, the least occasion ever to dream of such elevation." The new leadership came from men out to make their families, who rose through fraud and corruption, not through their own virtue. This could only happen, Bolingbroke thought, in a society where money had dissolved the natural political order, where the new power of liquid assets dissolved the traditional structure of authority and submission. Inferior men were thus enabled to lord it over men who were in every natural way their superiors, and men "born to serve and obey"—stockjobbers, money men, and all of Walpole's clique—had come to command even government itself. In the *Dissertation*, Bolingbroke wrote that even the power of the medieval petty tyrants, the great lords and great prelates, was preferable to the modern men in power.

How preferable will subjection to those powerful landlords (whom the Commonality were accustomed to serve, and by whom, if they suffered on the one hand, they had considerable advantages on the other) how preferable, indeed, will this subjection appear to them, when they shall see the whole nation oppressed by a few upstarts in power: often by the meanest, always by the worst of their fellow-subjects, by men who owe their elevation and riches neither to merit, nor birth, but to the favor of weak princes, and to the spoils of their country, beggared by their rapine.[52]

76

In the guise of a discussion of the excessive power of freed imperial Roman slaves *The Craftsman* satirized upstart leaders. The Romans, lords of the world, "had to put their necks under the feet of the dregs of the human race." Those vile Roman upstarts could not love the Senate or any men great in blood, fortune, or virtue. "Observe the strange inversion of all order and sense! Dignity debased; how vilely is the function of a consul prostituted!" In another essay, "Novi Homines," *The Craftsman* again ridiculed men born to mean circumstances and raised to great power. Men of superior rank think it a diminution of their character to oppress and insult those beneath them. Upstarts, on the contrary, use their inferiors ill, the better to distinguish themselves from their former associates.[53] The message was clear enough. Even the lower elements of every community were best governed by men of superior merit and virtue who were discovered among those of greater rank in the social hierarchy. Unfortunately for the aristocracy and gentry, and, as Bolingbroke felt, for the British Constitution, the moneyed men with their quickly acquired and artificial power paid no heed to the requirement of a proper political order.

The new economic order had, moreover, in Bolingbroke's opinion, a much more serious effect on the political world than simply bringing upstarts to ruling positions. It threatened the basic constitutional balance perfected in the Tudor Age. It is here that one finds the core of Bolingbroke's argument; it brings together his Harringtonian views, his reactions to his age, his concern for balance, and his nostalgia for the reign of Elizabeth. In both his *Remarks* and his *Dissertation*, Bolingbroke described property changes during the reigns of Henry VII and Henry VIII as "opening a way to the Commons to increase their property, and consequently their power in the state." This new power came, not from any new functions, but "purely by the manner in which their independency, the effect of their property, enabled them to exercise the same powers which they enjoyed before." Elizabeth had had the wisdom to discern the growing alteration of property, and had at once accommodated the whole system of her government to this great change. In her reign, as a result of the alteration in the state of property and power, "England was brought to the true poise of a mixed government." It achieved the greatest perfection attainable by any free government. The excellency of the British

Constitution having been "settled about the time of Queen Elizabeth," there was no other era of English history that deserved to be studied more.[54]

This Tudor balance came under fire in the seventeenth century when the Stuarts attempted to assert the power of one part, and, in Bolingbroke's opinion, caused the Civil War. The virtuous gentry, at the center of the new and powerful Commons of Elizabeth's reign, fought a defensive war, not in an aggressive effort to seize all power, but to retain the power already rightfully theirs. The balance was restored in 1688 when the British Constitution was once again set right. But, Bolingbroke believed, a new and more powerful threat to the balance arose after 1688—money, more dangerous than even the pretensions of Stuart prerogative.[55]

In Bolingbroke's opinion, the new financial innovations increased the power of the executive, the Crown and its ministers, to such an extent that the Tudor balance was placed in jeopardy. The debt, the funds, and high taxes increased the officers of government and created a "vast number of new dependents on the crown." The minister's manipulation of the new financial world, his use of money to influence and corrupt, made the legislature virtually dependent on the Crown. The new composition of the revenue became a great source of corruption, and as a result "this change in the state and property of the public revenue hath made a change in the constitution, since it gives a power unknown in former times, to one of the three estates." Schemers, jobbers, and projectors controlling the new economic world worked relentlessly and successfully to draw real property, formerly diffused among thousands, into the pockets of a few moneyed men who surrounded the minister. The rise of moneyed property since 1688 translated itself into an alteration of power relations. Landed property was no longer equated with power. Power was now held by men with no stake in England's soil. Harrington's law of balance, reasoned Bolingbroke, apparently held for property other than land as it had once held for land. "The power of money, as the world is now constituted, is real power," wrote Bolingbroke.[56] A frightened Harringtonian, he realized that the principle of balance now worked against the gentry. The principle meant an end to the ideal of a "gentry paradise" described by Harrington and desired by like-minded apologists for the gentry of the post-Revolutionary era such as Bolingbroke.[57] The Tudor balance, which for Bolingbroke had centered on a powerful Commons led by the gentry, had been destroyed when the Commons became weak and dependent on the minister and his moneyed men. The new economic order had destroyed the basic element in the traditional constitution, balance, and with it the constitution itself. In the *Dissertation*, Bolingbroke summarized his reading of English history from Henry VII to Walpole: "that very change in the state of property and power, which improved our constitution so much, contribute[s] to the destruction of it."[58]

Bolingbroke saw the ideal political world as a "genuine" polity, a commonwealth where politics was part of a functional order carried on by the natural leaders of society.[59] In such an order government sprang from the patriarchal roots of the landed family, and public service was as much the duty and responsibility of heads of families and localities as was their care and control of the core family. In the "genuine" polity, "the image of a free people" writes Bolingbroke, "is that of a patriarchal family, where the head and all the members are united by one common interest."[60] Government was not yet an artificial function whereby men came together and rationally conceived laws. A "genuine" order needed few laws, because the dealings of men were prescribed by time-honored codes of duty and honor. In such a system, a much less clear-cut distinction between public and private relations existed because men in society were held together by the natural bonds of family, geography, and interest rather than by an artificial act which had brought together isolated individuals. The order and links in God's social structure had existed long before man, and thus, in Bolingbroke's "genuine" polity, man's entrance into society placed him among natural affiliations and natural relations to others, whether as governor or as governed, as relative or as neighbor. The passing of this "genuine" order was described in a poem by one of the later nostalgic Tory poets, Oliver Goldsmith, author of the first full-length biography of Lord Bolingbroke and of *The Deserted Village*, the classic eighteenth-century literary rejection of the new order. In *The Traveller* (1764), Goldsmith described the demise of a "genuine" political system.

As nature's ties decay,
As duty, love, and honour fail to sway,
Fictitious bonds, the bonds of wealth and law,
Still gather strength, and force unwilling awe.[61]

Bolingbroke's idealized notion of political society has in it a strong dose of Aristotelian political and economic wisdom. At the center of Bolingbroke's imagery, as in Aristotle's notions of politics, is the household or family unit with the independent master at its head, and in a fixed subordinate position beneath him, dependent servants. For both Aristotle and Bolingbroke independence was equated with the possession of real property and dependence with its absence. For this reason money men were the natural servants of the landed political masters. Both envisioned an aristocracy of the learned and well born at the apex of the polity, above the independent men who made up the broad base of the ruling class.[62] Bolingbroke's ideal of a "genuine" Aristotelian political and economic order presumes a world without capitalism and without liberalism, where the prevailing values are independence and dependence, and concern master and servant, rather than equality and inequality, which concern capitalists and proletariat.[63]

The assumption that some men were intended to be natural leaders of society was basic to Bolingbroke's ideal polity. In his *Letters on the Study and Use of History*, Bolingbroke wrote that one of the distinguishing features of England's free government was that in it a man was designed for public service by his birth. In other countries the question of who was to occupy the different posts in the administration was often settled by the whim of the prince, but in England men were "called in a particular manner by their rank." The obligation to serve one's country increased in proportion to the rank one held. In his *Letter on the Spirit of Patriotism*, Bolingbroke urged the nobility and gentry, the true leaders of society, to rescue the English Constitution.

In that essay, he invoked another feature of his ideal polity, the image of the classical orator. The true statesman was wholly a public man, eloquent and learned, and dedicated selflessly to the community. Such men were noble and of virtuous character, and were capable of resisting their passions and self-interest so that they spoke and pleaded for the common weal. Bolingbroke's description of a good minister reads like a description of the perfect classical orator.

He is wise, generous, and full of the virtues of his ancestors. He is educated in his country's constitution, laws and interests. He is just in his dealings, and moderate in his pleasures. When speaking, he addresses himself to the good sense of others, not to their passions or interests. He is not solicitous for position because he wants it, but because position wants him.[64]

A most important aspect of the "genuine" ideal is a concern for the public good. Every man, *The Craftsman* writes, must be persuaded that he is but a member of society, "that he can no more subsist alone than a limb, when it is torn from the rest of the body." When individuals consider themselves distinct from the community and strive only for their own interests, their minds are contracted to narrow and selfish views. A preoccupation with self-interest distinguishes the modern great man from the past ideal, for today's great man acquired his position by understanding the paltry business of scriveners and jobbers and by acquiring the tricks of Exchange Alley, not by learning and concern for the common weal. There was a time, however, when public spirit characterized public men.

The good of his country ought to be the principal view of every good man; which, as romantick as it may seem, was not altogether an unfashionable topick in the good old days of Queen Elizabeth; which our author presumes to lay down as a pattern to all succeeding reigns.[65]

Political man in Bolingbroke's "genuine" political society was an independent man, an owner of property who was therefore capable of exercising his own judgment on matters of state, calling upon his own wisdom, virtue, and good sense. He was not dependent on other politicians, ministers, or financial institutions for his course of action; nor were political men, as a body, dependent on dependent men for whom tallies, stocks, or other interests determined political interests. The function of government was not to pursue any special policy; it was to protect the propertied base for the continued independence of the individual. Under Walpole, however, money and the new financial institutions threatened to end this sacred independence.

In a series of "advice to Freeholders" on parliamentary elections, *The Craftsman* drove home the necessity of returning to Parliament local men with gentry estates, men whose independence was indicated by their roots in landed property. Bolingbroke and *The Craftsman* consistently worked for a Place Bill that would take away seats from the stockjobbers and moneyed upstarts and exclude dependent members of Parliament whose seats would then return to "the old country interest of the best families in the Kingdom." Such a law would be just because it would return to the landed what was, by nature, rightfully theirs. If a Place Bill were passed, every country gentleman would regain his seat and thus "again enjoy the natural Rights to which he was born."[66] Political control in a "genuine" society belonged with the landed families in each locality, argued Bolingbroke's Opposition.

As long as the private interest of the generality of the voters depends upon the great and rich families in the several counties, cities, and boroughs, to which they belong, our liberty will be safe; for then the Crown, in order to secure a majority in the House of Commons, must always first secure a majority of the great and rich families of the Kingdom. And this they can never do but by a just, prudent, and wise administration. The only way of establishing an arbitrary government . . . is to procure that influence to centre in the Crown only, which was formerly divided among the great families.[67]

The new financial order was the great threat to Bolingbroke's "genuine" polity. Money knew no traditional ties of family, honor, and friendship. It dissolved with indifference the hierarchical relationships of the past and ushered in an unnatural social and political mobility. The face-to-face political and social life of a natural political order had known no vast and impersonal institutions like the Bank and the moneyed companies. Huge debts, funds, and mysterious credit arrangements were "bastards" and unnatural intrusions into the simple and "genuine" politics of Arcadia. The entire set of "bastard" and unnatural innovations signalled the decline of the cultural and political leadership of the gentry, the nobility, and the humanist intellectual. The new man was not a gentleman, but an unnatural urban man who owned liquid assets but had no stake in the soil, the natural source of virtue. The sense of the passing of the "genuine" political order is well illustrated by Hume in his late pessimistic Tory period.[68] His essay, *Of Public Credit*, epitomizes the despair that he shared with such earlier Augustan writers like Bolingbroke. It describes an England oppressed with a huge debt, high taxes, avaricious jobbers and schemers, and speculates on the total effect of the new order.

In this unnatural state of society, the only persons who possess any revenue beyond the immediate effects of their industry are the stock-holders . . . these are men who have no connexions with the state, who can enjoy their revenue in any part of the globe in which they chuse to reside, who will naturally bury themselves in the capital or great cities . . . Adieu to all ideas of nobility, gentry and family! The stocks can be transferred in an instant, and being in such a fluctuating state, will seldom be transmitted during three generations from father to son. Or were they to remain even so long in one family, they convey no heredi-tary authority or credit to the possessor, and by this means, the severed ranks of men which form a kind of independent magistracy in a state, instituted by the hand of nature, are entirely lost, and every man in authority derives his influence from the commission alone of the sovereign.[69]

Bolingbroke had written that in Britain's free government the inter-mediate magistrates were independent and emerged naturally; only in despotic systems were they chosen by the prince. England, he felt, had now become such a despotic system. "Adieu," then, "to all ideas of nobility, gentry and family!"

# IV

## Bolingbroke on Natural Law, Society, and the Origins of Government

The "genuine" political society had been undermined, according to Bolingbroke, by the destructive work of the economic and social developments in England after 1688, and, equally, by the destructive impact of the liberal and individualistic ideas of John Locke. Thus, one finds in Bolingbroke's discussion of natural law and the origin of government a critique of Locke. It emerges from the depths of Bolingbroke's discussion, which begins with the contention that he is merely offering a reading of natural law in order to mediate between the metaphysical whimsies of the Platonists Cudworth and Clark and the gross absurdities of Hobbes. The Cambridge school of Platonists had erred in seeing morality as an eternal essence antecedent even to the deliberate determination of God, and Hobbes had erred in assuming the contrary—that no moral duty existed until man deliberately made such distinctions in his positive laws. Both of these extremes should be avoided; one should neither "soar so high as Plato and Cudworth," nor "sink so low . . . as Hobbes."[1] Natural law, properly understood, does not antecede the deliberate will of God, but does antecede civil society. Bolingbroke ostensibly set himself the task of answering both the Platonists and Hobbes by reaffirming the tradition of Stoic and Christian natural law. In the course of this endeavor, however, he turned this tradition against Locke, its most recent and distinguished exponent.

### NATURAL LAW, PLATONISTS, AND HOBBES

Plato and his modern Cambridge disciples were particularly disliked by Bolingbroke. He despised them for being presumptuous and arrogant metaphysicians who wove labyrinthine systems out of their wild imaginations. At best they were "pneumatic philosophers" dealing with spirits; at worst they were poets whose minds had fled observable phenomena to embrace dreams and fancies.

Cudworth and Clark wrote that the natural law was derived from eternal and necessary essences of justice, equity, goodness, and truth. The obligation to act in harmony with these essences was the core of the duty imposed upon man by natural law. These great principles of morality were independent of the will of God and antecedent to it; they were the sole criterion of moral good and evil, since will could not be the source of natural law in a truly rational universe.[2]

To destroy these arguments of the Cambridge Platonists, Bolingbroke called upon the great enemy of all such metaphysicians, Locke, whose *Essay on Human Understanding* is described by Bolingbroke as "the most complete work of this kind that any language can boast." Locke, the empiricist, humbled the pride of the metaphysicians by pointing out that their talk of eternal essences and necessary fitness of things was not based on observable phenomena of nature. Bolingbroke repeated Locke's contention that all knowledge came from outside the mind in the form of received sensations. The sensationalist psychology of the master taught that men could have no idea of real essences and no innate perceptions of eternal moral principles. The simple ideas received by experience and the more complex ones generated in the mind by reflection were all that men could know. The essences referred to by the Platonists did not exist because the mind could not perceive them. According to Locke's premises Clark and Cudworth exaggerated the power of the mind beyond the narrow limits of its competence. To base natural law on an assumed power of man's mind to perceive eternal and abstract essences of morality is to "entertain a high opinion, and to make extravagant encomiums of our intellect."[3] Moreover, it is demeaning to God to suggest that morality is not a product of His will, but is antecedent to Him.

When he discussed the question of natural law and will Bolingbroke turned to Hobbes. Hobbes' insistence that will is the source of moral law was useful to Bolingbroke when he wanted to counter the Platonist rejection of will. To the extent that he agreed that natural law was positive and promulgated by the will of God, Hobbes' argument seemed acceptable. But more than this divine element of will, Bolingbroke would not accept. He rejected Hobbes'

85

contention that the will that makes moral distinctions effective derives from the Leviathan, the power created when the state of nature becomes civil society. To refute Hobbes, Bolingbroke called upon the traditional view of natural law which had developed in Rome and the Christian world. Distinctions between moral good and evil, between just and unjust, were not established by civil authority. Moral obligations derive from an anterior law of nature, not from the laws of society. Civil societies could not have been formed had there not been the prior laws of nature. The mere will of a human legislator is not a firm enough foundation on which to base morality. Will may constrain and force and even create an outward or physical base to obligation, Bolingbroke conceded, but it imposes no inward moral necessity. Such necessity arises only from the law of the divine legislator whose promulgation of this law coincided with His creation of moral agents. The law of their nature was the product of His will. Natural law is the origin of all positive laws. Civil law is merely a gloss on God's law made by men and altered by their will. Natural law is God's basic law and determines the morality of men's actions.

The relationship between this God and man, Bolingbroke suggests, is political and paternal: we stand as "subjects and servants to a gracious and beneficent lord and master, who gives us laws neither ambiguous nor captious, and who commands us nothing which it is not our interest to perform."[4]

Natural law, however, is not simply God's law; it is also reason's law, and is therefore available to all rational creatures. The principles of reason are plain and simple, and have universal application. Bolingbroke contends that the principles of rational natural law are so simple that if they appear intricate and complex it is only because writers on the subject like Grotius and Pufendorf "puzzle and perplex the plainest thing in the world."[5] Bolingbroke suggests that the precepts of natural law that guide and govern human conduct are in fact collected by man's reason *a posteriori* from experience and observation. In this way, men discover God's will. At some point in dealing with one another it becomes evident to rational men in all societies that certain actions contribute to the happiness of individuals and society. These acts men label virtuous. The principles of morality discovered by such experience "are properly called laws of nature." Bolingbroke is so intent on destroying the *a priori* position of the Platonists that he applies Locke's empiricism to an end never intended by him—an empirical natural law:

> Let us consider then how it [the mind] is constituted . . . to what ends we are directed. Let us trust to pure intellect a little less than we are advised to do, and to our senses a little more. When we have examined and compared the informations we receive from these, and have reasoned *a posteriori* from the works to the will of God, from the constitution of the system wherein we are placed by Him to our interest and duty in it, we shall have laid the foundations of morality on a rock, instead of laying them on the moving sands, or the hollow ground, that metaphysicians point out to us.[6]

Here is a prefiguring of the empirical doctrine of natural law that would emerge full blown in the French Enlightenment.[7] But it is more likely that Bolingbroke, rather than proposing a new theory, was simply carried away by his Lockean zeal in his attack on Cudworth and Clark. His natural law, like Locke's, was really that of the older tradition—the discovery of God's rational moral code for man. His major concern was not to enlarge upon the notions of natural law advanced by Cicero, Grotius, or even Locke, but to assert that natural law and morality existed before any legislative act of human will.

Bolingbroke contends that the obligations imposed by natural law are few. One of its most basic principles is universal benevolence, for "God has made benevolence to all rational beings the fundamental law of our nature." Other natural moral obligations derived from reason include the duty to administer justice and to keep compacts. It is evident, however, that civil laws do not perfectly reflect these imperatives of natural law. Bolingbroke suggests this should not lead one to conclude, as had Montaigne, that since there are vast numbers of human laws which have no universal approval and which violate alleged moral principles, there can be no natural law. The existence of imperfect civil laws does not prove that natural law does not exist, but only "that civil laws have been made without a sufficient and constant regard to it." Legislators and priests have misread the law of nature, and have, therefore, perpetuated unnatural institutions, customs, and prejudices through fraud and ignorance. If reason were universally adhered to, these irrational customs and illegal institutions would pass away and "mankind would reach the perfection of their nature." If reason had not been superseded, then all men would live under the same rules "and civil government would have been uniform in the whole world, as well as conformable to nature, and to reason, and the state of mankind would have arrived at human perfection."[8]

It is a mistake, however, to read Bolingbroke's notions of natural law as if they culminate in optimistic rationalism with some implicit revolutionary call. Burke was the first to misrepresent Bolingbroke in this way, when he suggested that Bolingbroke called upon reason to end the empire of prejudice and prescription.[9] This was not Bolingbroke's intention. He did write that men's reason had been seduced by false appearances and that these seductions, confirmed by law and religion, had barred mankind from perfection. But his recognition of imperfection did not lead him to assault the institutions and prejudices that barred the perfect realization of rational and natural law. His reasons are clearly stated. "It was not in the councils of the most high, which it becomes us to adore and not to examine, that this should be so." God has made men such that passions, appetites, and ignorance often have greater force than reason, and thus irrational will often prevails over rational nature. To the extent it does, it is determined by God that the state of mankind will be less than perfect; and that it will not attain the perfection of rational natural law. In the *Patriot King* Bolingbroke cautions "that perfect schemes are not adapted to our imperfect state." He who would read Bolingbroke as an optimistic rationalist must remember Bolingbroke's theodicy, and its central tenet, resignation before God's incomprehensible order. To complain of the weakness and fallibility of man's reason and of his incomplete adherence to natural law would be to overlook man's assigned place in the chain of being. It is no revolutionary rationalist who could say: "if our reasoning faculties were more perfect than they are, the order of intellectual beings would be broken unnecessarily, and man would be raised above his proper form . . . The reason he has is sufficient for him in the state allotted to him."[10]

### THE ORIGINS OF POLITICAL SOCIETY

The final obligation imposed by natural law is one with which man's inferior and inadequate reason cannot interfere because it is impelled by the additional force of instinct. When God created man

He made a rational creature "by nature fit for society."[11] Boling-broke's discussion of natural law leads logically to an analysis of the origins of political society. His description of the natural social inclinations of man is part of his general assault on Hobbes. Boling-broke attacks the asocial individualism of Hobbes' state of nature and its image of man's ceaseless pursuit of self-interest. Men, wrote Bolingbroke, were never in a state of absolute individuality before the institution of civil society; they are instinctively social and, like animals, herd with those of their own species. Because men are human, an intellectual sympathy also prompts them to unite with their fellows. In holding this view Bolingbroke borrowed arguments from theorists of natural law, Cicero, Grotius, and Pufendorf, who wrote before Locke, and stressed the inherent sociability of men. He also borrowed arguments from the Aristotelian tradition which depicted man as a social animal by nature.

He probably also called upon the writings of the third Earl of Shaftesbury, who, in his *Characteristicks*, had criticized the individualism of the contractualist argument. Although he did not mention the name of Hobbes or of his former tutor, Locke, Shaftesbury had them in mind when he wrote that the contractualist erred in not seeing man as innately sociable. Shaftesbury argued that a herding instinct is basic to all men's psychology. Writers on society, he wrote, were too preoccupied with this plaything—the state of nature. "The learned have such a fancy for this notion, and love to talk of this imaginary state of nature." Morality is based on innate ideas, and political society is also instinctual and natural, and not a product of artifice or contrivance.

How the wit of men should so puzzle this cause as to make civil government and society appear a kind of invention and creature of art, I know not. For my own part, methinks, this herding principle and associating inclination, is seen so natural and strong in most men, that one might readily affirm 'twas even from the violence of this passion that so much disorder arose in the general society of mankind.[12]

There never was, he contends, a state of nature where men were unassociated—"That it was their natural state to live thus separate can never without absurdity be allowed." Shaftesbury also criticized Hobbes for describing morality as a product merely of civil legislation. There are innate in men at all times, Shaftesbury asserts, moral obligations of faith, justice, honesty, and virtue which must operate even in a postulated state of nature. Civil union does not make right or wrong; it would be as wrong to break a promise in natural society as in civil government.[13]

Bolingbroke is at one with Shaftesbury in considering men's sociability to be the basis of the natural origins of society. He did not accept Shaftesbury's belief that men are sociable because of some innate benevolence that prompts them to seek communal well-being.[14] According to Bolingbroke, men "have a natural sociability; that is we are determined by self-love to seek our pleasure and our utility in society." But he departs from Shaftesbury's position when he bases sociability on the instinct of self-love and not on a moral sense. "Self-love, the original spring of human actions, directs us necessarily to sociability." Satisfaction of mutual wants demands sociability. But even if the motives of utility were lacking, men would fly from absolute solitude and seek simple human conversation.

The most powerful determinant of man's sociability, however, is God, who, desiring that men live in communities, has insured this sociability by the psychological composition with which he has endowed his creatures. Instinct leads men to seek pleasures that lead inexorably to the sociability of man and woman. The rudimentary instinctual basis of sociability that leads men and women to sexual pleasure is part of a law of nature that utilizes its energy so that men will live in community. There is further pleasure involved in the bringing forth of offspring and family life. It is true that as the circle of involvement widens to family, community, country, and mankind, reason displaces instinct and men may seek long-term happiness rather than fleeting pleasures. Men are moved from the instinctive to the rational law of nature and accept its moral virtues of justice, benevolence, and concern for the public good because their reason informs them that private good depends upon the happiness of society. But man never effectively transcends self-love. Men love themselves in their love for their families, friends, and neighbors, love themselves in the political body to which they belong, and finally love themselves when extending benevolence to the whole race of mankind.[15] In his total unwillingness to dismiss self-love, Bolingbroke unites it with social concern by finding the true fulfillment of the former in the latter. Pope understood Bolingbroke's reasoning and wrote:

> Thus God and Nature linked the general frame,
> And bade Self-love and Social be the same.[16]

In his *Characteristicks*, Shaftesbury had specifically criticized just such a doctrinal merger of selfishness and benevolence. He singled out in particular those who see "the love of kindred, children, and posterity" as "purely love of self." He also criticized those who suggested that "the love of one's country and love of mankind must also be self-love." Bolingbroke was, in his turn, no less critical of those who talked of the irrelevance of self-love, or of the instinctually benevolent nature of man and his innate moral sense. Bolingbroke must certainly have had Shaftesbury in mind when he turned on those who believed in a "moral sense; for to assume any such natural instinct is as absurd as to assume innate ideas, or any other of the Platonic whimsies."[17] As he tried to walk the middle path between the Cambridge Platonists and Hobbes, so here, too, Bolingbroke sought the middle ground between the benevolence of Shaftesbury and the egoism of Hobbes.

But on the question of the sociability of man and the natural basis of society and civil government Bolingbroke stood solidly beside Shaftesbury in criticizing Hobbes and Locke. The contrast of natural society and political society was a false one, wrote Bolingbroke, if it implied that a nonpolitical existence preceded man's deliberate creation of civil authority. Some form of government had existed ever since man's and woman's instinctual pursuit of pleasure led them to live together and then to love themselves in their children. In such acts of generation paternal government was established. Government and political authority were not creations of voluntary will; their foundations lay in nature. Man was led to political society by the hand of God, not by his own conscious or deliberate choice. Bolingbroke calls this earliest form of political existence "natural political society" or "natural government" in contrast to the later stage of political society created by the art of man which he calls "political societies of human invention" or "civil government."[18] Natural society is not anarchic because it has no isolated individuals. In the state of nature individuality pertained only to individual families.

By this logic, Bolingbroke criticizes Hobbes' image of the ruthless war of all against all in individualistic natural society, when each individual "supposes him [self] to have a right to everything, and to be a rival and enemy on that account to every other man." Such individual anarchy and ruthless competition, Bolingbroke contends, never did, in fact, exist. Men, whose basic reflexes are cooperative, never stood so utterly alone. "We are born to assist, and to be assisted by one another." Bolingbroke has no attachment to the social outlook that underlies liberal ideology. Natural society was a political society, he suggests, and had no unbridled freedom to be lost in some later establishment of government. Men, dispersed in families, formed numerous distinct political societies under paternal government. Fathers were the chief magistrates and kept peace and order in the relatively small and homogeneous society by their natural authority. Bolingbroke went so far as to explain taboos against incest as the recognition that in "natural political society" whatever tended to diminish the reverence for parents diminished their authority and thus threatened to "dissolve the order of those little commonwealths." Inherent in natural society is "authority, subordination, order and union necessary to well being." The liberal notion that consent is the only legitimate basis for political obligation is rejected completely.[19]

But Bolingbroke is no Filmer. He writes of a paternal authority destined to give way to the political society of human invention, "not the royal fatherhood of that ridiculous writer Filmer." Divine right and absolute power of kings, ideas that Filmer had advanced, were "a silly and slavish notion," "one of the greatest absurdities that was ever committed to paper."[20] Bolingbroke had made his peace with 1688; he had no desire to perpetuate royal fatherhood.

Nevertheless, Bolingbroke's account of the rise of artificial government is different from the liberal views which had emerged in the 1680's. The act of association which established civil society was a product of reason as natural society had been of instinct, but, Bolingbroke insists, "civil governments were formed not by the concurrence of individuals, but by the association of families." He suggests two motives which might have moved families to enter into such compacts—utility and fear. Quarrelsome families might break apart and in the next generation would become separate societies no longer regarding a common political authority, "whose eye was over the whole community," and who could intervene when mutual injuries occurred. Or the case might arise of two different families living in close neighborhood who experienced conflict and tension.

In such a case too, paternal authority would be inadequate. The motive behind union in these cases would be the convenience and utility of a common judge; but, unlike Locke, Bolingbroke sees this motive leading families, not individuals, to "coalite amicably by covenants."

Families, however, may not always be so rational and cooperative. Strong families often threatened weak ones who, in response, unite into larger artificial bodies. Fear is also a principal inducement to the erection of civil authority, as Hobbes had contended; but, once again, it is families Bolingbroke describes, not Hobbesian individuals. This search into the motivation behind the creation of civil government may be completely unnecessary, however, for compact and covenant need not be the only foundations of political society. In a significant anticipation of Hume's critique of contractual thinking, Bolingbroke throws out the suggestion that, more often than not, families were brought together by war and conquest and not by consent.[21]

The communities produced by the union of different families contained heterogeneous populations drawn together by accidental ties. Paternal magistrates were unable to exercise authority in these altered circumstances; yet the covenant demanded a supreme power to enforce its observance. Artificial political authority filled the gap, replacing natural political authority by a power superior to that of fathers of families. This new civil authority established "rather by art or by force, than by nature," was monarchical. Writers who think that men originally in a state of natural freedom and equality established government and chose democracy are wrong, Bolingbroke contends. Let such writers simply consult ancient wisdom. Lycurgus, for one, understood the easy transition from paternal to monarchical government. When advised to establish a popular government in Sparta, he told his advisor to "try in the first place to establish democracy in his own family." Even more important than the authority of Lycurgus was that of Aristotle, whose influence was so strong in Bolingbroke's discussion of the origin of political society (as indeed it would be in so many of his social and political views). Had not the wise Aristotle begun his *Politics* with just such an account of the transition from paternal to regal government?[22]

It is classical political wisdom that Bolingbroke has in mind again when he describes the character of these first kings. They were great and wise legislators who assembled families and clans into larger and more civilized communities. The first kings were "philosophical legislators, who succeeded to the authority of fathers of families." These men, wiser and more just than the rest, invented useful arts of life and established order and good government. They taught men to promote the happiness of individuals by promoting the happiness of the public. They also taught the lesson "of preserving liberty by subjection to law." The plain and simple rules which had been the appropriate basis of natural law under paternal government needed extension in the more complex society formed by the union of families. Philosophers and legislators arose capable of collecting the precepts of the law of nature from God's work and the invariable course of events. Their superior reason enabled them to make the proper and necessary deductions from these precepts and to apply them in all those cases which concerned man's duty to God or his fellow man. They instructed their fellow men and gave them laws. Legislators like Moses and Solon used law to reform the manners of the people they civilized and to improve their social life. These laws, written and unwritten, occasional and permanent, were not given by virtue of any royal prerogative. No constituted legislative power stood behind their deeds; on the contrary, they "were chosen kings, because they were chosen legislators." It was the goodness, wisdom, and justice of their laws which recommended these great men to civil authority and which kept them there. The sovereignty of the first kings and legislators was earned simply by their great and good deeds. They received power from the people and were ultimately accountable to them for its exercise. This first form of civil government "is of human institution, established by the people and for the people," made by men and submitted to by their consent.[23] Filmer is wrong, then, in his claim that Adam was an absolute monarch by right of creation whose prerogative descends to all kings, and leaves all others slaves by birth who have no right to choose forms of government or governors.

Bolingbroke's emphasis on the monarch's need for the consent of the governed, and of government's duty to pursue the good of the governed, coupled with his general assault on Filmer, might seem to place Bolingbroke among those whose ideas grew out of

1688. But in his opposition to Filmer and divine right, Bolingbroke has in mind an older image of consent and political obligation rather than the new ideology of rights. The good of the governed is not achieved when the civil authority meets the demands and terms of contract set by those who consent to it; it is found in the paternalism of older views in which authority comes from above and knowing what is best for the governed earns public consent. In Bolingbroke's opinion the function of artificial government is still paternal. In natural society sovereignty had been in the hands of fathers who exercised it not for their own sakes, "but for the sake of their offspring." So it is in civil government. Nature instituted natural government and directed human reason to artificial government. "She meant the same in both cases, the good of the governed." In describing the "good of the governed" in civil government, Bolingbroke is not concerned with rights or liberty. He merely repeats the formula for paternal authority: "She [nature] intended, no doubt, that they who had been treated like children, under the influence of instinct, should be treated so likewise, under the influence of reason."[24]

### BOLINGBROKE AND LOCKE

Something is missing from Bolingbroke's discussion of the origin and nature of political society; he has ignored Locke, an omission all the more striking because Bolingbroke was clearly a disciple of the empiricist Locke. Bolingbroke accepted 1688, but he rejected the ideology of liberalism found in Locke's *Treatises of Civil Government*. He agreed with Locke in emphasizing consent, the artificial origins of civil government, and the significance of covenants. But Bolingbroke still disagreed with fundamental ideas in Locke's thought.

Nowhere in Bolingbroke's discussion is it ever suggested that men enter society to protect rights and property. The individualist bias that Locke's assumptions about natural rights give to his more traditional notions about natural law is totally absent from Bolingbroke's analysis. It does not signify much that they shared some concepts. Consent and compact were notions long-established in medieval political thought, and particularly in writings about natural law, before Locke. Bolingbroke's agreement with Locke that the origins of civil authority were artificial is vitiated by

Bolingbroke's contention that natural society was little different from civil society because both were characterized by subordination and government. Bolingbroke's theory of natural law and political society is a mixture of Aristotelian and Stoic ideas and of medieval and sixteenth-century views on natural law.[25] It sees the origin of political society in families and paternal authority, and the function of government in civil society as not protection of individual rights, but as what it had been in natural society: the maintenance of peace and order, the rendering of justice according to natural law, and paternal concern for the good of the people.

Bolingbroke does more than simply ignore Locke's liberal positions. His discussion of the origin of political society culminates in a direct attack on Locke. Fragment XIII of *The Philosophical Essays* is devoted entirely to criticism of the eminent Whig's philosophy and of the view of the world that Bolingbroke sensed lay behind it. Bolingbroke suggests that Locke reasoned inconsistently and "on a false foundation." It is inconsistent to acknowledge that paternal government preceded civil, as Locke sometimes did, and then to describe the rise of civil government as if it were the first authority that brought men into subordination. How, Bolingbroke inquires, could Locke's "solitary vagabonds," his "strolling savages" suddenly accept the laws of civil government if they had previously "known no subordination"? Locke had reasoned falsely because "mankind was never in such a state of nature." The origins of civil government cannot, Bolingbroke contends, be discovered by digging into a country's history or tradition. All one can do is "guess with great probability" by making analogies from what one knows. Locke's theory, a "speculative whimsy," contradicts such analogous thinking as well as the clearly perceivable constitution of human nature, both of which tell us that civil government probably grew out of natural government. Men were never solitary individuals "out of all society in their natural state." Locke's doctrine is false because proper reasoning confirms what Bolingbroke had been saying: "Civil governments were formed not by the concurrence of individuals, but by the associations of families."[26]

Bolingbroke was aware of the revolutionary potential of Locke's ideas. Locke's stress on the natural independence of solitary individuals is related logically to his view of men "as equal one amongst another." Bolingbroke thought that Locke's arguments based on the natural equality and freedom of mankind "carry his notions on the subject a little further than nature, and the reason of things will allow." Much more damning, however, is Bolingbroke's conviction that such notions subvert the established order. The principle of the hierarchical ordering of society is threatened when the principle of natural equality is adhered to. Distinctions vanish, the social order can be overturned, and havoc ensues. "He who sits on a throne would inhabit a cottage, and he who holds a plough would wield a sceptre."[27] The conviction that a state of perfect freedom such as Locke described would result in total chaos and anarchy prompted Bolingbroke to suggest, as Shaftesbury had done earlier, that Locke was little different from Hobbes.[28] Mankind possessed of such freedom would have come into "a state of war and violence, of mutual and alternate oppression, as really as that which Hobbes imagined to have been the state of nature." This anarchy would be compounded by each man's right to execute the law of nature. To talk of each individual executing justice for himself is not only "language unworthy of Mr. Locke," but implies the same absurdities as did the ideas of Hobbes. Each man's pretending to be judge and executioner of the law of nature would lead to a tyranny and oppression as brutish as ever conceived of by the philosopher of Malmesbury. Thus it is, writes Bolingbroke, "that the state of mankind under the law of nature, according to Locke, would have been very little, if at all, better than the state of nature before there was any such thing as law, according to Hobbes." The part of Locke's thought that looked backward, the traditional doctrine of natural law, Bolingbroke could accept, but he rejects the bourgeois individualism imparted by the new reading of natural right. Bolingbroke turns his back on the liberal ideology of Locke as he asks "to what purpose it was to make any abstract system of rights, that never did nor could exist . . . a method of establishing civil government that never could be taken." Locke, he concludes, presents "a notion of natural liberty very different from the real constitution of nature." Our real nature demands that there always be authority; if it were ever lacking men would live in the nightmare world of the Hobbesian state of war.[29]

Lest his readers be shocked by this attack on the great Locke, Bolingbroke tempers his critique by suggesting that it was only Locke's excessive zeal to destroy Filmer's false notions of government which set him off on the other extreme of assuming a state of nature that never could have existed and a freedom and equality with such subversive implications. Locke's failure is common "to men of the greatest genius, when they grow to be over fond of an hypothesis," who pursue their abstract thought beyond common sense and in the end "maintain propositions so little conformable to the real constitution of things."[30] Nothing, however, can soften the challenge to Locke that Bollingbroke poses. Locke's ideas on the origin of political society were directly relevant to the emergence of bourgeois, liberal, and individualist notions of politics in his day; Bolingbroke's rejection of these Lockean ideas was part of his overall rejection of the liberal world, which increasingly justified its existence with these very ideas: Bolingbroke's political ideals are aristocratic and paternal. Men are not naturally free and equal, nor is government instituted to protect natural rights. His opposition to Locke is inevitable; the social forces he represented are very different from those whose champion Locke had become. Locke's political thought became the ideology of a middle class individualism that stressed individual freedom, self-interest, and competition as positive social values. Bolingbroke's political thought is the ideology of a family-centered aristocracy and gentry. Fathers, paternal authority, subordination, rank, cooperation, and public service are the dimensions of this ideology's superstructure.

Seen in this light, Bolingbroke's attacks on Locke's individualism, natural freedom, natural equality, and natural right take on added significance. So, too, does Bolingbroke's equation of Locke with Hobbes. In Bolingbroke's *Philosophical Fragments* he had criticized Hobbes for claiming that men were mere individuals and not members of commonwealths, that men had the right to all things and were rivals and enemies to one another. In his polemical writings, Bolingbroke also decries as the great evils of his age the individualism, self interest, freedom, and equality depicted by these theorists as the state of nature. These very ideals were those he found in the new economic and social order that was destroying the traditional structure of society. It is more than coincidental that in his last work, *Some Reflections on the Present State of the Nation*, his most scathing attack on the corruption and degeneracy of his age, Bolingbroke compares the English to those very men in the Hobbesian state of nature to which Locke's writings seemed to lead.

What expectation can be entertained of raising a disinterested public spirit among men who have no other principle than that of private interest, who are individuals rather than fellow citizens, who prey on one another, and are in a state of civil society, much like to Hobbes' men in his supposed state of nature.[31]

It must be granted that repeated references to original contracts are scattered throughout Bolingbroke's writings and might lead one to think him a follower of Locke. In *A Dissertation upon Parties,* for example, Bolingbroke wrote about the king governing since 1688 in terms that imply an original contract that made his office conditional and subject to forfeiture. *The Idea of a Patriot King* also describes the relationship between the people and the government as if it is formed when the people consent, by an act of contract, to the appointment of civil authority over them. It bears repeating, however, that Bolingbroke did not think of the covenant that is the basis for artificial civil government as a product of universal participation, and did not think it a covenant to protect rights. There is no initial coming together of all to form a political community; political community already exists as a natural and God-given phenomenon. The covenant is solely between the people (a small number of them at that—family heads) and a prince. There is no mention of natural rights or their protection as the foundation of civil governments in the terms of the covenant. All that is intended is "to maintain the same degree of peace and good order in communities more numerous." Men establish civil government through a contract "because popular liberty without government will degenerate into license." The ultimate end of government is to achieve the good of the people, and through contract "governors are therefore appointed for this end." Bolingbroke's contract does not mention personal or property rights; it merely describes a "bargain" struck between the prince and the people.[32] His theory of contract differs from Locke's; its terms do not belong exclusively to Restoration liberalism. They go back to late medieval descriptions of a contract between prince and people, and to notions of consent found in the political thought of such writers as Marsilio, William of Occam, and the authors of the *Vindicae Contra Tyrannos.*

In Bolingbroke's notion of contract is also found the late medieval flavor of Hooker, propagandist for Elizabeth, that prince who most nobly embodied the values of peace, good order, and great and good actions. Bolingbroke calls upon a more traditional and less revolutionary notion of contract than Locke. Reformation and late medieval theorists like Hooker prepared notions of contract that articulated the limitations that should operate on a prince in a good Christian state. Such a contract also seemed implicit in feudal oaths of allegiance that detailed the reciprocal duties of king and vassal. Monarchy was limited by the public good and to this extent implied accountability to the people.

In a passage from his *Remarks on the History of England* Bolingbroke's notion of contract and consent is clearly indicated.

> The union we speak of between prince and people, neither can nor ought to subsist on any other terms, than those of good government on one part, and of gratitude and expectation on the other. This union may be, and hath been maintained by absolute princes with their people; because it is not impossible that an absolute prince should be a wise and good man.[33]

The English, however, are fortunate that their constitution limits the king while it demands that he give "good government." This union had been violated most dramatically in the seventeenth century by James I, Charles I, the usurping Cromwell, and James II. Only in the reign of Elizabeth were great deeds accomplished by a monarch in contract with a grateful and expectant people. Bolingbroke could easily assimilate 1688 to these late medieval views by arguing that the Revolution merely deposed a prince who had broken the fundamental covenant with his people. The people consisted of the great men in the community, the natural political leadership of gentry and nobility who, being bearers of ancient paternal authority, still exercised authority and justice over retainers and dependents in the countryside. In return for his maintenance of the *salus populi*, they pledged their obedience to the king. When he broke the contract by threatening the church, by ceasing to maintain peace and good order, and by abdicating the throne in his flight, they replaced him.[34]

Intrinsically related to Bolingbroke's rejection of the liberal and voluntarist view of the world propounded by Locke, is his acceptance of the older idea of the Great Chain of Being. An old concept with roots in neo-Platonic and Christian cosmology, the doctrine received its great statements in English thought from Renaissance humanists like Sir Thomas Elyot, Shakespeare, and Raleigh.[35] After its almost total disappearance in seventeenth-century English thought, it reappeared in an extraordinary revival among Bolingbroke's circle of Augustan humanists. The concept juxtaposes order, duty, function, and hierarchy on the one hand and anarchy, rights, mobility, and individualism on the other. In Bolingbroke's hands the concept was used to defend an ideal socio-political order that he alleged was passing and to brand the agent of that change as sinful.

His description of the chain of being emerges in those philosophical essays in which he outlines his notion of theodicy. God's justice, as Bolingbroke sees it, is vindicated in spite of man's suffering because man is not the center of God's universe, and the universe does not exist solely for man's happiness.[36] God's universe contains an infinite number of creatures who form a ladder above man to God, and below him to animal and vegetable life and inanimate creation. To imagine oneself the object of God's special concern is prideful, since it places one above one's place in the great chain, all the links of which must be God's equal concern. This hierarchical world view, found in Bolingbroke's religious writings, is the source of his "Tory Cosmology" as it was for the cosmology of the Renaissance humanists and would be for that of Swift and Pope. God's Great Chain of Being has its secular analogy in men's social and political ranks which are as fixed and determined as the hierarchy of creation. In the social world each man has an assigned station with attendant duties and functions, and the social order is characterized by authority and subordination. The appropriate response of the individual is resignation to the will of God who has placed him in his particular rank.

The wisdom and the goodness of God are therefore manifest. I thank thee, O my Creator! that I am placed in a rank . . . to which I belong: a rank wherein I am made capable of knowing thee, and of discovering thy will, the perfection of my own nature and the means of my happiness.[37]

The immense design of God's order is contrived so that "the whole order and system . . . would be disordered and spoiled if any alteration was made in either."[38] Each man must accept his station, "the place he is to inhabit . . . the part he is to act." Bolingbroke's words are directed at the prideful men of Walpole's age who were destroying this divine structure in their disregard for rank, duty, and authority.

In the conclusion to his description of the chain of being and its violators in his *Philosophical Fragments*, Bolingbroke illustrates the fundamental unity of the Augustan critics by invoking his dear Dean Swift. If men, Bolingbroke writes, seek to be inferior or superior to what they are intended to be, and do not keep to the rank God intended for them, they will appear as preposterous creatures in God's system. "Gulliver's horses made a very absurd figure in the place of men, and men would make one as absurd in the place of horses."[39] Locke's ideas, Bolingbroke believed, encouraged such acts of pride and their absurd and sometimes monstrous results. Belief in natural freedom and equality would destroy a static and hierarchical order that had fixed social and political distinctions. Locke's system failed to take into consideration the fixed distinctions between the ploughman, the cottager, and the magistrate. A world with social relations determined by contract had no place for assigned rank; a view of the world that valued individualism and social mobility achieved by acquisition did not accord with Bolingbroke's emphasis on the static and functional ordering of men and offices.

One specific application of Bolingbroke's social and political reading of the chain of being was his insistence that there were those whose specific function was to govern, and others whose function was to be governed. Yet another dimension of Bolingbroke's repudiation of the liberal view of the world can be found in this notion of an inevitable division between those destined to lead and those to be led. His defense of the special merits and claims of great men and great families contrasts with what he considered the liberal's disregard for such distinctions in their indiscriminate description of "the people." It is an important aspect of Bolingbroke's aristocratic response to Locke's liberal challenge.[40] Bolingbroke suggests that a basic and recurring division runs through the history of mankind between "the multitudes designed to obey, and . . . the few designed to govern." In paternal government this division is quite obvious, but even at the critical stage of political evolution when natural governments pass into artificial governments the few emerge, the philosophical legislators, "men of more genius than the common herd." As it was the case at the birth of political society that a few men were better able to understand the laws of nature, so it is always the case, Bolingbroke contends, that a few are set apart to govern.

All men are directed to submit to government but "some men are designed to take care of that government."[41] That this is so is a result of man's basic nature, which is so constituted that constant battle is waged within each individual between his reason and his passions. The passions, writes Bolingbroke, lead men to immediate and less important pleasures, whereas reason, slower and more deliberate, leads men to more lasting but more remote pleasures. There is a striking similarity to Hume's contrast between calm and violent passions in Bolingbroke's judgment that "the influence of reason is slow and calm, that of the passions sudden and violent."[42] From this psychological distinction, Bolingbroke drew the same aristocratic conclusions as Hume would. People in whom slow and calm reason predominates should constitute the political leadership. These more rational people are born to be guides in formulating laws to the many, in whom sudden and violent passions rule. The vulgar masses "know little and believe much"; they are ill-informed and "incapable of judging for themselves," but the rational few are the educated and wellborn. Education helps reason control the passions, and the leisure and affluence provided by high social standing allow one to continue the cultivation of reason.[43]

That Bolingbroke envisioned the nobility and the greater gentry as the source of natural leadership by rational men was made clear in his essay *On the Spirit of Patriotism*. Written in 1736 as a letter to Lord Cornbury, it is a plea to the younger generation of the landed and noble classes to recapture the leadership of English political society from the new men around Walpole. Men of good breeding, like Cornbury, are set apart by the Author of nature. "These are they who engross almost the whole reason of the species; who are born to instruct, to guide, and to preserve; who are designed to be the tutors and the guardians of human kind." Such men are superior spirits, men who even from infancy "were born for something more, and better." Their rank and situation in society denote for them one vocation—government, "which it is not lawful for them to resist, nor even to neglect." Such men are set out in the social chain of being as governors whose function is to preserve the strength and splendor of the commonwealth. Lord Cornbury and other sons of great landed families were those few men of reason "designed to take care of that government on which the common happiness depends." With aristocratic views such as these, no wonder Bolingbroke's essays and *The Craftsman* returned time and again to the theme of an England where a new social and political order had arisen. In this new social order moneyed men of no social rank, and men who generally lacked quality were seen moving to the center of the political stage. These men, the paper suggested, made of politics a far different thing than when it was the preserve of noble and landed gentlemen. The ability to govern is a product of long experience, not a skill acquired overnight, and such experience comes only with the generations of leadership that rightfully accompany rank.[44]

A final area in which Bolingbroke is critical of Locke concerns the relationship of the religious realm to the political. This disagreement points to their fundamental differences over the nature and purposes of the state. Bolingbroke, a great critic of organized religion from a religious and philosophical point of view, was at the same time, like Machiavelli, convinced of its social and political utility. Doctrinally, he could not tolerate the notion of eternal punishment in another life, yet he recognized that this sanction was a powerful force upholding the laws of men and strengthening government. Like Machiavelli with his praise of Numa, the classicist Bolingbroke could not find enough praise for the antique lawgiver's manipulation of religion as an expedient to encourage obedience and public spirit. There are some, however, Bolingbroke writes, who would question this secular application of religion. (He does not mention Locke, but it could easily be Locke's *Letters on Toleration* that he has in mind.) These men argue that religious and civil societies are widely different in the purposes of their institutions, and are therefore independent of each other. Because religious society deals with the salvation of souls and civil society with the security of temporal interests, this position, Bolingbroke writes, asserts that the state can punish only overt acts and must take no notice of what passes in the mind and does not assert itself in criminal action. Bolingbroke rejects this attitude; his position is that of an intrenched Erastian; he also rejects Locke's limitation of the magistrate's concerns to only negative protection of temporal natural rights.[45]

Now in answer to all this we may deny, with Truth and reason on our side, that the avowed ends of religious and the real ends of civil societies, are so distinct as to require distinct powers, and a mutual independence. The salvation of souls is not the immediate end of civil government . . . But if to abstain from evil, and to do good works, be means of salvation, the means of salvation are objects of civil government. It is the duty of princes and magistrates to promote a strict observation of the law of nature, of private and public morality, and to make those who live in subjection to them good men, in order to make them good citizens.[46]

It was not only Locke whom Bolingbroke was attacking, but also Walpole, who accepted the novel liberal idea of a limited magistrate. *The Daily Gazetteer,* one of Walpole's papers, had articulated this liberal idea in an attack on the Opposition in 1735. It rejected the Opposition demand for governmental action to end luxury and corruption by asserting that such action was outside the legitimate sphere of the magistrate's power. "There is no remedy for this but what is in ourselves," it wrote. People may do what they please with their property and persons so long as they do not injure others: "'tis out of the power of all the laws to hinder Them." Government cannot interfere with their freedom and fortunes "under a pretence of preventing luxury." Walpole's *Daily Gazetteer* concluded its attack on the Opposition with the declaration that "the end and design of government is not to keep us from hurting ourselves, but to keep others from hurting us; if governments would do that, 'tis enough; 'tis all that men desire of them."[47] But government, for Bolingbroke, one of whose models was the classical world, could never be relegated to a mere policeman protecting rights. Part of the function of government was positive education in virtue and the shaping of better and more moral men. Here was the culmination of Bolingbroke's charges against the England that had developed since 1688. In this new order, as he saw it depicted by its great theorist, Locke, and practiced by Walpole, government only acted as an umpire over the ceaseless acquisition of wealth which endangered the traditional social structure. Limiting itself to "the security of temporal interests" it overlooked its more traditional role of leading men to the good life.

### THE PRECURSORS: LESLIE, SHAFTESBURY, AND TEMPLE

The ideological motivation for Bolingbroke's rejection of Locke's liberalism is clear enough, but what is not so apparent are the intellectual sources of this theme of Bolingbroke's thought. Much of his political thought could, of course, be derived from classical sources and the tradition of natural law. Both traditions are full of potential arguments against the novel aspects of Locke's thought. Particularly striking in this respect is the similarity between much of Bolingbroke's description of the combined patriarchal and contractual origins of government and the views of Pufendorf.[48] More immediate, however, in time and place are possible English influences on his thought. There is Shaftesbury, who, as was noted above, was critical of the theories of contract prepared by both Hobbes and Locke. Shaftesbury's preoccupation with the naturalness of civil government prompted him to suggest that, deprived of it, men are lost and helpless like children without a father. Shaftesbury's opposition to the contractualists contains hints of patriarchal ideas. In these, he might be said to approach the insights of twentieth-century psychological studies of political leadership and the cult of the father.

If men really have no public parent, no magistrate in common to cherish and protect them, they will still imagine they have such a one; and, like new-born creatures who have never seen their dam will fancy one for themselves, and apply (as by nature prompted) to some like form, for favour and protection. In the room of a true foster-father and chief, they will take after a false one; and in the room of a legal government and just prince, obey even a tyrant, and endure a whole lineage and succession of such.[49]

The writings of Leslie, as native to England as Shaftesbury's, are even more probably a source of Bolingbroke's ideas on natural society and civil government. Charles Leslie, a nonjuring Anglican, had been the first outspoken critic of Locke. He had taken a patriarchal position in numerous sermons and publications in the early years of the eighteenth century.[50] Leslie's most significant public utterances were expressed in debate with Benjamin Hoadly, a Whig churchman and popularizer of Locke, who would soon be a favorite of Robert Walpole's. Leslie's critique of Locke, like Shaftesbury's, centered on the notion of the contractual origin of government. The idea that men chose themselves to be members of a political society by a voluntary act was contrary to both sacred and profane history. He contended that such an act was sociologically impossible, because such a view posits man born a free adult who experiences no childhood dependence on parents, and no womanly dependence on a husband. Locke's fundamental error, in Leslie's opinion, was his irreligion. Government was a creation of God for man, not man's own creation; it was described in Scripture; to deny this is blasphemy. Kingdoms are like families and families do not choose their fathers. In language much like that Bolingbroke would use, Leslie claimed that Locke's account violated the fundamental religious foundation of government by

supposing (against the plain matter of fact in the scriptures) that God did ordain no government at all among mankind, but left them, like the Brute Beasts, to range about in the wide world, every man and his children (like a fox and his cubs) to ravage and prey where they cou'd. Till at last, by their own sagacity, they found out that contrivance of government; and erected it by the plurality of Voices; and upon their own authority; to which God being oblig'd to concur, it is become Divine; And the Voice of the people, from that time forth, was the Voice of God.[51]

Leslie's alternative was a patriarchal theory of government that described the king as the father of society. Like Filmer, he thought that the patriarchal genesis of government was binding throughout the millenia. Society is not made up of free floating, rootless individuals able to contrive their own roles and destinies. "It is most natural that authority should descend, that is, be derived from a superior to an inferior, from God to fathers and Kings, and from Kings and fathers to sons and servants." Men's duties are determined by their places in the hierarchical order which ascends to the king. Man's proper role is to accept this natural and necessary provision of God, established for man's own protection, just as the helpless bee submitted to the "master-bee." Leslie argued that Locke's theory, by its rejection of this stable and structured order, would lead only to the chaos and discord feared by Tudor and Augustan humanists. The nonjuror Leslie's cry against the contractualist involves ideas similar to the cosmology of a stable and hierarchical world implied by Shakespeare, Elyot, Bolingbroke, Swift, and Pope.

These men leave no principle, no constitution, no thing in the world certain, but uncertainty! They are the antipodes to all government, method or settlement! They are perfect Babel and Confusion! Fitted to pull down everything; but to build up Nothing. There can be no peace or quietness where they live, and have any power.[52]

Bolingbroke knew Leslie and his writings. In *A Dissertation upon Parties* he specifically rejects them and equates Leslie's ideals with those of the Stuarts. "Let neither the polemical skill of Leslie nor the antique erudition of Bedford persuade us to put on again those old shackles of false law, false reason, and false gospel, which were forged before the Revolution and broken to pieces by it."[53] Bolingbroke apparently had little taste for Leslie's warmed-over Filmer, but Leslie's influence on Bolingbroke's attitudes on contract and the hierarchical nature of society cannot be dismissed as lightly as Bolingbroke might have wished.

There is yet another possible English source for Bolingbroke's assault on the contractualists, one who, unlike Filmer and Leslie, was eminently respectable, highly regarded, and widely read and quoted by Augustan writers. In much of Bolingbroke's critique of Hobbes and Locke the arguments are nearly identical with those penned by Sir William Temple in his *Essay upon the Origin and Nature of Government,* a Restoration attack on the theory of social contract. To the great Macaulay, this essay of the 1670's seemed "exceedingly childish," but Bolingbroke thought highly enough of Temple's work to incorporate its arguments into his own theory.[54]

In his *Essay* Temple contended that natural sources of authority were "truer originals of all government among men, than any contracts." He attacked the rationalist theory of social contract and the state of nature, put forth by the "great writers concerning politics and law," Pufendorf, Grotius, and Hooker on the one hand, and by Thomas Hobbes on the other. The first group described men as sociable creatures, "naturally disposed to live in numbers and troop together." Hobbes, on the contrary, saw natural men as instinctively "creatures of prey, and in a state of war one with another." The two schools can still be spoken of as one, wrote Temple: whichever disposition, social or antisocial, is assigned mankind by the contract writer, mankind must be assumed to have, at some point, realized the necessity of leaving the state of nature and rationally agreed on rules by which each individual willfully consents to a government he has himself created. Temple rejects this notion that mutual consent is responsible for the "rise of all civil governments."

I do not know if men are like sheep, why they need government; or if they are like wolves, how they can suffer it. Nor have I read where the orders of any state have been agreed on by mutual contract among great numbers of men, meeting together in that natural state of war, where every man takes himself to have equal right to everything.[55]

Government, Temple contends, is not a product of a voluntary contract; it is a natural patriarchal phenomenon. The natural authority of the patriarch existed long before any contract established civil government. A state of nature with isolated and free individuals never existed; the natural government of family heads existed in the first natural society. This paternal authority was derived not from prerogative but from the father's deeds and the children's high opinion of his wisdom, goodness, valor, and piety. His children had seen him feed them, protect them, dispense to them his goods with discretion according to their needs. In turn, they willingly accepted his authority.[56] Contract, then, had nothing to do with the origin of political authority, although nonpatriarchal institutions did finally evolve from these patriarchal origins.

In describing this transition, Temple's argument is virtually identical with the later explanation offered by Bolingbroke. Governments founded on contracts, Temple suggests, ultimately do succeed governments first founded on natural authority, but it is not isolated individuals who so come together. "We must imagine the first numbers of them, who in any place agree upon any civil constitutions, to assemble not as so many single heads, but as so many heads of families." Temple offers as the motive behind the creation of civil authority by natural governments the security achieved by the unification of numerous families who come together for protection against the invasions of other aggressive, perhaps barbaric, families. Behind their bond is the convenient mutual safety afforded them by their unity.[57]

The basis of the contract, then, is mere utility, not obligations imposed by natural law to protect natural rights. This theory of Temple's was accepted by Bolingbroke and anticipates Hume. Temple and Bolingbroke anticipate another of Hume's charges against the theory of a social contract; although he thought that the contract is drawn up by family heads as the basis for civil authority, Temple concedes that most often the source of political obligation is derived from forceful conquest whereby the vanquished families became subjects to their conquerors.[58]

Locke's contractual theory based on an individualist state of nature and the protection of natural rights was penned after Temple's critique. It remained for Bolingbroke to revive Temple's theory of the origin of government and to use it in an attack on Locke, as Temple had used it in an attack on Grotius and Hobbes. Temple's patriarchal argument was a safe one for Bolingbroke to use since it applied only to the origins of government. Unlike Leslie's and Filmer's, Temple's argument had no partisan ties to issues of the day, to contemporary royalism or Jacobite agitation. But Bolingbroke's use of Temple's ideas would inevitably be bound to the contemporary Augustan scene. Bolingbroke's theoretical attack on Locke's contractual theory and individualism was, after all, but a part of Bolingbroke's general attack on the new Whig world of England after 1688.

# V

## Walpole on Politics and the English Constitution

Walpole, seldom thought of as a political thinker, is noted rather for the institutional innovations that contributed so greatly to the stability of government that his twenty-one years as first minister brought to Great Britain. The political community over which he presided was in virtual agreement on the Whig principles of 1688.[1] The ideological fervor of the seventeenth century characterized by political and religious divisions had subsided. The Tories, although not discredited as Jacobites, sulked in their country houses or sat independently in the back benches of the Commons, aloof from the game of politics. Walpole's great achievement was the creation of parliamentary majorities in this age of consensus. His solution was a rigorously articulated system of corruption. At the heart of this system was Walpole's power as First Lord of the Treasury and his possession of the full favor and confidence of the Court.

Walpole solidified his power by using the Crown's tremendous power of patronage; both Georges usually followed his advice in their appointments. From recipients of places and their relatives Walpole exacted allegiance to his leadership in the Commons. Placemen were allowed to sit in the Commons, and Walpole's legions steadfastly resisted the perennial Opposition bill to bar pensioners and placemen from future sessions of the Commons. Walpole also used the patronage of the Crown to help secure election victories. In elections such as that of 1727, Walpole and the Duke of Newcastle used patronage, bribery, and any form of influence to insure the victory of men loyal to the Treasury party. Bolingbroke's *Craftsman,* no impartial observer, to be sure, described the workings of the electoral process in the countryside in words that might suitably serve as commentary for Hogarth's depiction of an eighteenth-century election.

He hath done everything usual on such occasions to reconcile himself to the electors; the streets have constantly swum in ale, and the good women have been almost cloy'd with kissing. In short there hath been such a continual scene of drunkenness, rioting and insolence on one side and of abject flattery, cringing and preposterous adulation on the other, that I am ready heartily sick of the place.[2]

After an election, offices, large or small, would be hawked to relatives, friends, and dependents of relatives and friends of the successful candidates on the understanding that the beneficiary's political influence would be at Walpole's disposal. Nearly all the jobs and offices in the king's household and civil service, and nearly all the appointments in the armed forces and the church were made by Walpole. In this way he created the Treasury party, reliable support for his ministry, and the basis for the political stability of England until the turbulent years of George III.[3]

The nature of Walpole's system was well understood by his opposition. The analysis offered in *The Craftsman,* less its partisan anger, anticipates Sir Lewis Namier's extensive research into eighteenth-century corruption.

There is a practice still more illegal and dangerous, which was complained of in former reigns; I mean, that of issuing great sums of money out of the Treasury, for electing such persons into Parliament, as would act agreeably to the views and inclinations of men in power and amply reimburse what had been profusely expended on their account . . . These practices are now wisely provided against by divers wholesome laws: and it will not, I hope, ever be in the power of any overgrown Minister, for the future, to sit magisterially in his arm chair, and choose a Parliament by his fire side; threatening some, who have displeased him, with opening the floodgates of the Treasury upon them; and obliging others to make their applications to him, instead of those, whom they are to represent; disposing of Boroughs, cities and counties, according to how his vanity, interest or ambition shall direct him.[4]

The ironic pose is dropped in a later issue of *The Craftsman.* Court boroughs, Treasury boroughs, Admiralty boroughs, and Post office boroughs, it suggests, are dependent on the government departments located in their areas and obliged to choose representatives nominated by them. This "cantoning out the boroughs of England among court favorites, gives us a very strong idea of the power of the minister."[5] Those who were returned to the Commons on their own were seduced by places or pensions given to them directly or to their friends and dependents. Whatever the cash price, loyalty to Walpole was an essential part of the bargain. *The Craftsman* self-righteously described the Treasury party as the great sovereign of all England.

Let us suppose that a Parliament should at any time be called, in which one fifth part of the Boroughs should, according to the modern phrase, take a recommendation from the Treasury, and chuse persons who are utterly strangers to them merely under that influence, obtained by a distribution of places, or money, or perhaps both amongst the electors. Now, in this case, I should be glad to know, whether persons so elected can be properly called representatives of the people, or whether they are not rather commissioners from the Treasury; whether laws made by the force of their votes can be justly called laws made by the consent of the people.[6]

Walpole's long rule prompted general debate over another institutional innovation: the phenomenon of the "prime" minister. Henry Pelham was the first man to be called "prime" minister without pejorative connotations; but it was during Walpole's rule that the modern meaning of the term first emerged, for Walpole determined all domestic policy from his post as First Lord of the Treasury, and, after he ousted his brother-in-law, Lord Townshend, he seems to have determined all foreign policy as well. He exacted a form of cabinet supremacy and collective responsibility, if only by overcoming and turning out rival ministers. He also remained leader of the Commons, rejecting the traditional custom of his predecessors of moving to the Upper House. But Walpole's emergence as the first minister was based on more than his consummate skill as a politician. He had become indispensable to the new dynasty. His knowledge of the Commons and his ability to exact his will from his dependent herd made his services essential to the Hanoverians, newcomers to parliamentary politics. That George I could speak no English is not true but what is true is that both George I and George II were more preoccupied with their beloved Hanover than with England. Because of this lack of concern they seldom attended the Cabinet Council. George II, reluctant to return from Hanover in 1755, articulated this early Hanoverian attitude. "There are kings enough in England. I am nothing there. I am old and want rest and should only go to be plagued and teased there about that D----d House of Commons."[7] It is not surprising that the minister who controlled the Commons could emerge as "prime" minister in such a situation.

There had been talk earlier of Godolphin having been prime minister or Premier in the reign of Anne, but Anne made it quite clear by ousting him in 1710 that he was but a servant, entirely responsible to her. In her letter of dismissal she wrote to Godolphin, "The many unkind returns which I have received from you, and especially what you said to me personally before the Lords, make it impossible for me to continue you any longer in my service."[8] What alarmed opponents of Walpole was that, far from being the servant of the Crown, he seemed to be the essential energy of the government, engrossing all functions and holding the Crown captive. The *Grub Street Journal* in 1732 described this new phenomenon, a "prime" minister.

A Prime Minister is a person who in the name and by the authority of the supreme power, manages all affairs of states, disposes of all preferments, presides over the receipt and disbursement of public money; and has all the essential power of a monarch, without the pomp and the name.[9]

As might be expected, Bolingbroke's *Craftsman* also attacked Walpole for this constitutional innovation. In 1727 it stated:

In absolute monarchies, we generally find a person invested by the Prince with the sole management and direction of all his affairs, under the title of Prime Minister, who is, by virtue of his office, as he commonly proves himself to be by his actions, an arbitrary Viceroy or deputy tyrant. But the power of such a minister seems to be inconsistent with the nature of a free state, whether a Commonwealth or a limited monarchy, because the absolute uncontrolable will of one man has been generally found to end in the destruction of liberty in general.[10]

*The Craftsman* attacked Walpole's direction of all the offices of government: army, commerce, foreign alliances, and revenues. This overreaching by one ambitious minister was, it protested, a notion foreign to the English Constitution.

In former times every great officer of the Crown used to act independently of other ministers in his department; but some ambitious designing men of modern times, not being contented with one of these great trusts, have found out a method of engrossing them all to themselves, under the notion of a Prime Minister, which is likewise a title of foreign extraction, and only another word for a vice-roy, or Deputy sovereign, to whom all the minor ministers are required to yield implicit obedience, under pain of his highest displeasure. This sovereign minister nearly *primum mobile* sets all the wheels of government going.[11]

These charges of *The Craftsman* were echoed by the peers who in 1740 unsuccessfully sought to remove Walpole on a charge that he was a "prime minister." The protest stated in part: "A sole or even a first minister is an office unknown to the law of Britain, inconsistent with the Constitution of this country and destructive of liberty in any government whatever."[12] Walpole denied the charge and his obedient Commons exonerated him. He was thus officially not a prime minister.

### WALPOLE AND POLITICAL IDEAS

Concurrently with his important institutional innovations, Walpole sponsored a set of political principles and ideas. It may seem unusual to claim this for one so traditionally recognized only as a consummate practitioner of political skills; indeed, the consensus among students of Walpole is that his mind was commonplace, dull, lacking in brilliance and insight, and that he cared little for the world of learning and ideas. Politics was power and the art of management. His lack of learning and brilliance had little effect, however, on his capacity for leadership; he had a remarkable ability of "evoking in other men a sense of security, of competence, of dependability."[13] This most successful of politicians can, however, be identified with something approaching a set of political principles, often in sharp contrast to those of Bolingbroke.

Reconstructing such a distinct position is difficult since Walpole wrote little of consequence and since his speeches in Parliament have little theoretical value. One must, therefore, look to the large body of writing which he sponsored and subsidized to express his views; in these pamphlets and newspapers published by his government one finds a view of politics and society that may be labeled Walpole's.

During his administration, a steady stream of pamphlets poured forth from J. Roberts, the government printer, in which the position of Walpole's government was often ably put by such distinguished men as Bishop Hoadly, Daniel Defoe, Lord Hervey, Thomas Gordon, and Horatio Walpole. It was in the weekly newspaper war, however, that Walpole's views were most consistently and succinctly articulated; contemporaries had no doubt that the voice that answered and attacked *The Craftsman* belonged to Walpole's government. Swift wrote in 1727 to Sheridan:

It is certain that Walpole is peevish and disconnected, and stoops to the vilest offices of hireling scoundrels to write Billingsgate of the lowest and most prostitute kind and has none but beasts and blockheads for his penmen, whom he pays in ready guineas very liberally.[14]

Secret parliamentary investigation in 1742 into Walpole's conduct in office revealed the extent of Walpole's liberal purchase of penmen.[15] The sum of £50,000 was paid in the years 1732-1742 to authors and printers of newspapers, the most popular of these being *The London Journal*. Until 1722, the *Journal* had been the vehicle for John Trenchard's and Thomas Gordon's biting attacks on Walpole in their *Cato's Letters*. In September 1722, the *Journal* entered the Government service, becoming Walpole's chief theoretical spokesman over the many years of conflict with Bolingbroke's *Craftsman*.[16] Walpole subsidized its new writers and printers, and ordered its free and speedy delivery through the post office—benefits denied the Opposition press. Two other Walpole newspapers, the *Daily Courant* and the *Free Briton,* were also distributed through the post office. *The Craftsman* complained of this in 1731, claiming that hundreds of copies of these three government papers plus scores of less well-known newspapers were being distributed at a cost of £20,000 per annum.

The mercenaries of the post house are the wholesale dealers, who convey them to the excise and customs house officers, and these hawk them out to the coffee houses and inns, unregulated and duty free.[17]

In sharp contrast with the luminaries in the service of the Opposition, and even with his pamphleteers, the men who wrote for Walpole's newspapers were relative nonentities whose names mean nothing today. The weekly political essay in his chief paper, *The London Journal,* was written by James Pitt under the pseudonym, Francis Osborne. Pitt, a schoolmaster from Norwich in Walpole's native East Anglia, was well-versed in his Locke, and his weekly debate with Bolingbroke's *Craftsman* is an important example of political writing in this era. Walpole must have been pleased with Pitt's performance, for after the writer took over the *Journal* in the late 1720's, Walpole had the number distributed by the post office increased from 650 to 2700.[18]

The essays in the *Free Briton* signed "Francis Walsingham" were written by a young lawyer, Francis Arnall, perhaps the wittiest of Walpole's writers. The secret committee of 1742 reveals that Arnall received nearly £11,000 from Walpole in the space of the four years 1731-1735. Arnall would be consigned to obscurity along with his co-worker Pitt, but that Pope chose to immortalize him in *The Dunciad:* "No crab more active in the dirty dance Downward to climb and backward to advance."[19] In 1735, the *Daily Courant,* the *Free Briton* and *The London Journal* ended their separate existences and merged into *The Daily Gazetteer. The Craftsman* was answered on Thursdays by Walsingham, and on Saturdays by Osborne. By early 1736, the *Gazetteer* also faded out of existence and, with *The Craftsman* subdued by Bolingbroke's absence, the tenyear newspaper warfare came to an end. Lord Hervey, an important figure himself in articulating the Walpole position, was convinced that *The Craftsman* had gotten the better of this duel. All the best writers had written for it, he contended, whereas the government papers were written only for hire, giving "the readers as little pleasure, as they did service to their paymasters."[20]

The basic positions of Walpole's political thought, as articulated by his publicists, were derived from the writings of John Locke. An important position was thus achieved for Locke's ideas when they were given the official stamp of the government and the Whig Establishment. Cited in Walpole's press, Locke's ideas became part of the general political debate for large numbers at the level of the coffee house. Men were born into a state of nature in which they were naturally equal, wrote *The London Journal.* They lived in this state and had rights to their persons and property and all the means necessary to preserve these. (The American Indian was for *The London Journal* as for Locke a good example of men in such a natural state.) In this state of nature all men had a right not only to their persons but to all that they could honestly acquire by their own labor; no man had a right to the person or property of another. These rights were derived from the law of nature; "men would have them were there no civil government upon earth." A civil government was necessary, nevertheless, because "in a state of nature every man must be necessarily judge of the breach of the law of nature (even in his own case) and executioner too."[21] The people came together, therefore, in a contract and set up a common judge for the better security of their lives and possessions.

Thomas Gordon, who was late in his career one of Walpole's chief writers, made Locke's argument the core of his *Essay on Government*. Men left the state of nature and set up governments because "confusion arose from men being judges in their own cause, and their own avengers."[22] This common power, or civil government, to be justly instituted, must have the consent of the people. "The fountain and original of all just power must be from the people."

Conquest, the *Journal* wrote, gave no right to govern, for government is instituted solely for the sake of the people, and for the security of their persons and property. There could be no other explanation of the origins of government. Pitt wrote in the *Journal*: "If men could be as secure in their possessions without civil government, as with it, then all civil government would be thoroughly ridiculous and absolutely useless." Locke's message had been well learned; the theorist of *The London Journal* wrote: "civil liberty consists in the security of property."[23] Arguments from natural rights, indeed, the entire body of Locke's thought, were not the exclusive property of a small group of clandestine "real Whigs" in the early eighteenth century.[24] Spokesmen for that most establishment of Whigs, Walpole, repeatedly invoked Locke.

The views on church and state found in *The London Journal* were also Locke's and represented the liberal position in opposition to the Erastian position of Bolingbroke. The civil magistrate, wrote Walpole's paper, deals only with civil interests, execution of the laws, and securing to all the subjects the possession of things belonging to this life. He can do nothing that does not involve the use of power. Power can in turn relate only to property, life, liberty and money and is out of place in the domain of religion. "Government cannot subsist without the exercise of power, but Religion is totally subverted by the exercise of power; 'tis indeed the life of Governments, but the death of Religion."[25] Religious obedience, unlike civil obedience, comes from understanding and reason alone.

Employing force or the civil power in religion, the *Journal* concludes, undermines its very essence.

This use and acceptance of Locke's political principles by Walpole's writers was predictable; these principles lay behind the developing economic institutions which they also accepted. Bolingbroke's doubts about the new order led him to question its Lockean foundation. In other areas of his political thought, as well, Walpole's positions were the opposite of Bolingbroke's. If Bolingbroke attacked corruption, Walpole defended it; if Bolingbroke denied party differences, Walpole stressed their importance.

### WALPOLE ON POLITICAL PARTIES

Walpole's writers argued that party differences did exist in their era. The claims of Bolingbroke and *The Craftsman* were wrong; parties were not dead in the kingdom, "they only pretend to be asleep."[26] Party differences were significant and real. The Tories were still the divine righters of the seventeenth century, and the agents of the Pretender, while the government Whigs alone remained true to Whig principles. A rare government venture into satire illustrates this insistence on the persistence of party differences. *A Full and True Account of the Strange and Miraculous Conversion of the Tories in Great Britain by the Preaching of Caleb d'Anvers, Prophet and Apostle to these Nations* ridicules *The Craftsman's* fictional editor for his claims about the alleged transformation of Toryism. St. Caleb, clearly Bolingbroke, has purged the Tories of their old principles, the pamphleteer writes, and they no longer adhere to the principles of Sir Robert Filmer, where "Kings are to look upon their Subjects as the ground they tread on, formed for their sole use and advantage, and men were to be fed and guided by priests." How wonderful, the pamphleteer concludes, that St. Caleb has made good little Whigs of all these former madmen![27]

In his insistence on the existence of real party differences, Walpole was the first of a long line of Whigs to see eighteenth-century politics as a struggle between two parties, each possessing a clear and well-defined ideology: the Whigs representing progress, the Tories, reaction. To later Whig writers, it seemed inevitable that these two parties should have existed in the eighteenth century, because they saw political history as determined by an iron law of human nature which Macaulay proclaimed: "Through the whole of the great movement (from Magna Carta to the Reform Act of 1832) there have been under some name or other two sets of men, those who were before their age, and those who were behind it."[28] The law is immortalized more colloquially in the Gilbertian lyric

> That every boy and every gal that's born into the world
>    alive,
> Is either a little Liberal or else a little Conservative!

As Bolingbroke's denial of party differences and his description of the antagonism between the Court and independent gentlemen anticipated Namier's interpretations of the eighteenth century, so Walpole's partisan zeal to discredit Bolingbroke by pinning the Tory label on him led Walpole to anticipate later Whig attitudes. His press insisted that parties had maintained their differences, and that they could not lose them. There was an immutable law of politics which invariably produces two parties. Parties could not change their nature any more than could particular men. Human nature, wrote the *Journal,* inexorably produced two kinds of Englishmen.

> It is equally impossible for a true Whig to come into this chimerical coalition, as it would be to reconcile the two sides of an express contradiction; or to perform any other of the greatest absurdities in Nature. Experience is the best guide in political as well as in natural knowledge; and in this case, all the Experiments that have ever been tried, demonstrate one invariable phenomenon of Whig and Tory.[29]

Even more surprising is the *Journal's* suggestion that parties are a healthy phenomenon. In an age characterized by violent opposition to faction and party Walpole's writers stand out as exceptions in their favorable reaction. All free countries, *The London Journal* asserts, will have parties. To those who claim that no country in the world was ever as infested with parties as England, the reply is "'tis so far from being a reproach, that 'tis an honor to us; and shews, that we have a sense of liberty and public virtue."[30] No wonder, then, that Burke looked back on Walpole as a practitioner of party government with such pleasure. Burke, the zealous missionary of party, had only praise for Walpole.

> Sir Robert was an honorable man and a sound Whig. He was not as the Jacobites and discontented Whigs of his time have represented him,

and as ill-informed people still represent him, a prodigal and corrupt minister. They charged him in their libels and seditious conversations as having first reduced corruption into a system. Such was their cant. But he was far from governing by corruption. He governed by party attachments. The charge of systematic corruption is less applicable to him, perhaps than to any minister who ever served the Crown for so great a length of time.[31]

### WALPOLE ON CORRUPTION

Walpole's defense of this corruption, whose existence as a deliberate system Burke denied, is the heart of his political thought. In the famous speech of 1734 defending the Septennial Act, in which he attacked Bolingbroke as an "anti-Minister," Walpole brushed off the charges of bribery and corruption with an insight commonplace to students of corruption, from Namier to students of American urban politics. Walpole told the members of the Commons that corruption marked a healthy political system; was it not easier to bribe when a political community was ideologically unified and when little partisanship divided it? In such a case, he added, where corruption, and not ideology, solidified attachments corruption was less dangerous.[32] *The London Journal* defended corruption on one occasion as a fact of modern life, like the standing army and the riot act; "it was a result of the present circumstances of the world, the natural condition of human affairs." It was foolhardy for the Opposition to expect all members of Parliament to be independent. Men could not be shaken from their natural dependencies. It was unjust and immoral to expect electors to vote against the man to whom they and their families were obliged. The Place Bill, perenially sought by the Opposition, operated on a false premise which assumed that place corrupted men and that serving the government was itself corruption, while, on the contrary, the *Journal* argued, serving a government was not itself corruption, nor did holding a place under the King incapacitate a man from serving the people as well.[33]

That the fruits of power—places, honors, and preferments—were distributed only to the Whigs was as it should be. They were less bribes to sway men from their own judgment than they were rewards for their service. "His Majesty knows who were the persons that brought his Family to the throne, and for what reasons they brought him." It is only justice to reward friends, as it would indeed be bribery and corruption to give places to enemies.[34] The gentry-based Opposition recoiled at Walpole's corrupt system precisely because of the effect of its monopoly of offices on the traditional relationship of property and power. Not only did Walpole accept the charge, but his writers emphasized it and proudly flaunted this consequence before the discontented gentry. The Government pamphlet of 1731, *The Case of the Opposition Stated Between the Craftsman and the People* makes this quite clear.

The Tory interest grows weak and the Whigs powerful by the disposition of favours and employments. For if the profit of serving the publick in places be computed at any sum, and this be raised equally upon the people, that party which is admitted into trust will have more than a retribution, whilst the other party is like a scale, continually losing weight, without any new accession to maintain the balance; so that in a certain process of time the losing party must quite dwindle to nothing, and that the prevailing party, by continuing in employments of profit, must become able to purchase all the lands in the Kingdom.[35]

The *Free Briton,* another of Walpole's papers, repeated this argument in 1732, in answer to a *Craftsman* attack on the attempts being made by new men in the countryside to upset longstanding landholding arrangements by using the ill-gotten gains of office and the money market. The power and property of the state, the paper argued, could not be divided among Whigs and Tories, parties for and against the establishment. All property and influence should be on the side of the present settlement. The scale of the Pretender's backers, all Tories of course, should be empty. Only when the Whigs held all the land would the king be secure; the offices dispensed by the executive enabled the Whigs to purchase this land.[36]

The most important defense of corruption offered by the Walpole forces was, however, neither the first argument from the nature of the times and human nature, nor the second one which weakly cloaked economic interest. The major defense insisted that without corruption the constitution would not function properly. The excellence and perfection of the constitution consisted in the balance of power being divided among the three parts of the legislature. But since—as Harrington had clearly shown—power follows property, the balance of power had come to rest too strongly on the side of the Commons, which now possessed some seventeen-twentieths of the land. Added to this natural power of the Commons was its sole ability to give public money. The king no longer possessed great Crown lands and had to receive whatever money he had from the lower house. Only one safeguard preserved the traditional mixed constitution from the great danger of imbalance. Though the people had the natural foundation of power, property, the king "especially since the Revolution has got a large artificial power, by having so many places of profit at his disposal." Walpole's press argued that only through the disposal of these places of honor, profit, and trust in the civil, military, and ecclesiastical establishment could the monarch hold his place in the constitutional balance. The existence of the noble and glorious mixed constitution depended on the existence of corruption. If the dependencies created by place were taken away, the monarchy could not stand, and mixed government would fall.[37]

The enemies of corruption who attacked the places in the king's gift were enemies of the monarch, seeking to deprive him of everything that gave him real power. If the Commons had the power to dispose of places and jobs all power would rest in the popular branch, and England would be governed by a democracy. Walpole's writers had more damning labels to hang upon the Opposition than "Jacobite" or "Tory"; they could also brand them radical democrats. *The Craftsman's* attack on corruption, Walpole's publicists contended, was an attempt to overthrow the traditional constitution.

Liberty, then, is only the pretense of the Opposition. Their real design rather than not get into power, is to overturn the constitution: they did, indeed, at first preserve some decency in their conversation and writings, and seemed to level their pieces at the ministry only. But now finding the court firm and steady, they appear in earnest for subverting the ancient government of England, and setting up a Democracy. This is the burden of their late writings; and for this end, they are always lessening the power of the King, and increasing the power of the people.[38]

Although Bolingbroke argued that corruption endangered the independence of the Commons and encouraged the supremacy of the executive, Walpole answered that corruption in fact counteracted the increased power of the popular branch and therefore preserved the balance. David Hume was less than original, then, in his often quoted defense of corruption in his essay "Of the Independence of Parliament." He, too, wrote that English mixed government was threatened by the great power of the House of Commons. How could this part of the constitution be confined within its proper limits, Hume asked. His answer came straight from the justification of corruption found in Walpole's press. The many offices at the Crown's disposal would preserve the ancient constitution from danger. Call this whatever invidious name you please, Hume wrote, dependence or even corruption, "but some degree and kind of it are inseparable from the very nature of the Constitution and necessary to the preservation of our mixed government."[39]

### WALPOLE ON MIXED GOVERNMENT AND REPRESENTATION

However much, in practice, Walpole may have contributed to the breakdown of the balance of power through executive manipulation and management of the legislature, he was, in theory, firmly committed to the ideal of the mixed constitution and the balance of the three branches of the legislature. Speaking to the Commons on the debate over the Septennial Act in 1734, Walpole could well have been using Polybius as his text.

Ours is a mixed government, and the perfection of our Constitution consists in this, that the monarchical, aristocratic, and democratical forms of government are mixt and interwoven in ours, so as to give all the advantages of each, without subjecting us to the danger and inconveniences of either.[40]

Bolingbroke's demands for the independence of Parliament, its freedom from ministerial control, was the particular target of Walpole's theorists. Such an independence would be too great for the constitution to bear. Bolingbroke's formulation of this principle in his *Remarks on the History of England*, which appeared in *The Craftsman* in 1730, triggered Walpole's reaction. Bolingbroke had said, "In a constitution like ours the safety of the whole depends on the balance of the parts, and the balance of the parts on their mutual independency on one another."[41] Walpole's *London Journal* answered that it was impossible, given the nature of things, for the legislative power to be independent of the executive. The constitution consisted, to be sure, of three distinct powers, but they were not absolutely independent. If they were absolutely independent there would result only contention and dispute till one power got the better of the other. Not only were Bolingbroke and his *Craftsman* radical democrats, they were also speculative Utopian schemers.

'Tis necessary, therefore, in order to the due exercise of government, that these powers which are distinct, and have a negative on each other, should also have a mutual dependency and mutual expectations; 'Tis in vain to carry virtue up to a Romance and fly to Harrington's *Oceana* and schemes of government which never existed but in Men's heads.[42]

In defending their version of the mixed constitution Walpole's writers invoked arguments from human nature that traditionally underscored the liberal commitment to the balance of powers. The nature of man is such that he is not to be trusted with uncontrolled power. "He is not to be trusted with power which is not checked by other power." It has thus been the wisdom of some states since the ancient governments of Greece and Rome, "to limit and divide sovereign power, so as to make it conducive to the sole end of it, the good of mankind." The English constitution allows each power to be distinct enough to be a check upon any increase of power attempted by the others. But, contrary to Bolingbroke's views—as construed by Walpole's press—there can be no absolute independence of the parts for, "human affairs are not to be reduced to mathematical calculations, nor can the balance of power, so often talk'd on, but never well explained, be so settled that the several parts which constitute the government shall be equally powerful, and so equally independent." The total independence allegedly sought by Bolingbroke would lead only to inaction. The imprecise balance which allows for executive intervention in the legislature by the tool of corruption is a much greater safeguard of the true balance of power, which is characterized by mutual dependency of the parts.[43]

Walpole's political thought is rounded out by his views on the nature of representation which arose from his partisan involvements in 1732 and 1733. His views on representation add another dimension to Walpole's political ideas that must have impressed Burke, for in these years Walpole's ministry attacked the radical idea that the Member of Parliament is a delegate of the people.

The immediate context for this reaction was the excise crisis in 1732, which saw the petitioning, instructing, and even threatening of Members of Parliament by the many who sought to defeat Walpole's scheme. The legislature of England, wrote *The London Journal*, is the only power and the sole authority in England; the people have no voice over this supreme authority. To claim that they do is to speak of rebellion and of taking the government into their own hands. The power of the people extends only to the constituent act of establishing the government. When the government is settled and the power of legislation given to a body chosen to represent the community, "then the original power of the people in their collective body ceases, for the sole power and the sole authority is invested in the persons chosen, who are to judge and act for us in all matter relating to legislation."[44]

Walpole's *Journal* was careful to anticipate the radical retort implicit in Locke's discussion of the "Dissolution of Government" in the *Second Treatise*.[45] It claimed that when Locke talked of a supreme power of the community to save itself from the legislature's invasion of property and liberty, he surely meant a residual power to be called upon for something much more fundamental than a tax on tobacco. Only when the constitution itself was threatened by the legislature could the government be dissolved, it suggested, and only after it had been dissolved, did the people regain their power and authority. As long as the constitution was preserved, the *Journal* reasoned, the people had no right to instruct their members on what laws they should make, or how taxes should be raised. The members of the legislature might ask advice and the subjects might even petition them, but that was all.

We have no authority over them, we cannot command them; we gave them power to make laws for us, and chose them, because we judged they had abilities and integrity enough to do their duty: But they must judge what laws are best for us; what taxes are most proper. If we don't like what they have done, we are at liberty, when the time is expired, to chuse others; this, and this only is our power. But we have no right to send threatening letters, and insolent instructions, authorisation orders and commands to those persons in whom we have lodged the supreme power of legislation.[46]

*The Craftsman* led the attack on the Excise Bill and took the radical position on the representative's function, so providing one more reason for Walpole's press to label Bolingbroke a dangerous radical. Walpole's writers argued that if the people were allowed the power that Bolingbroke claimed for them, the mixed constitution would fall before an omnipotent popular branch, which would be overwhelmingly dependent on the fancies of the mob.

The terms of Walpole's attack on Bolingbroke's "radicalism" would be echoed in the theory of representation Burke enshrined in his famous letter to the Bristol constituents. But Burke was not the only eighteenth-century theorist who could have used this aspect of Walpole's political thought. Hume's understanding of the nature of representation corresponds to Walpole's and forms a convenient link between Walpole and Burke.[47]

### WALPOLE ON ENGLISH HISTORY

A final area of interest in this survey of Walpole's political and constitutional ideas is his reading of English history which emerged in the vigorous debate on the nature of the English past that was waged between his forces and Bolingbroke's in the 1730's. Buried in the newspapers and journals of those years is a fascinating episode in the history of English historiography noted in 1734 by Lyttelton's observant Persian.

My long stay in the country gave me leisure to read a good deal; I applied myself to history, particularly that of England; for rightly to understand what a nation is, one should previously learn what it has been. If I complained of the different accounts which are given by the English of themselves in their present circumstances, I have no less reason to complain of their historians: Past transactions are so variously related and with such a mixture of prejudice on both sides, that it is as hard to know truth from their relations, as religion from the comments of the divines.[48]

As in the seventeenth century, English political writers in the age of Walpole and Bolingbroke projected their partisanship onto different readings of the past.[49] The interpretation of the past became another weapon in the arsenal each amassed against the other. In this sense the historical debate in the 1730's was a mirror of the political tension that characterized the Augustan period. But what is unique about their differences here is that, more than in any other area of their disagreement, Bolingbroke, the champion of the Tory Opposition, wrapped himself in the noble flag of Whiggery and covered the Whig Walpole with the ignominious standard of Toryism. And he was justified in so doing; in their attitudes to English history, Bolingbroke was the disciple of Edward Coke and Algernon Sidney, while Walpole was the follower of the royalist Tory, Dr. Robert Brady.

Behind the Walpole-Bolingbroke debate in the 1730's lay the late seventeenth century controversy on the nature of English history described in J. G. A. Pocock's masterful study, in which Dr. Brady answered the Whig notions of an immemorial constitution found in William Petyt, William Atwood, and the *Argumentum Anti-Normanicum*. Brady wrote that William I was a conqueror who had completely altered English law and government by importing feudal tenures. Brady was ruthlessly single-minded and, facilitated by his royalist partisanship, he abandoned the ingrained image of the ancient constitution and embraced the new, more accurate feudal history of Sir Henry Spelman and Sir William Dugdale.[50] He denied Petyt's claim that a class of freeholders maintaining continuity with Anglo-Saxon society had survived the Conquest. In Brady's writings the entire medieval population was depicted as tenants in military service to some higher lord with the chain of tenure leading ultimately to the grand suzerain, the king. In such a totally feudal society there were no freeholders. Before Edward I's reign in the late thirteenth century, wrote Brady, no commoner sat on the king's feudal council. The council had been comprised only of the king's tenants in chief—the bishops, earls, and barons. Like Spelman, he asserted that the Commons emerged gradually as lesser tenants evolved into freeholding knights through the commutation of their feudal obligations. Magna Carta, for Brady, was merely a demand for relaxation of feudal service and a call to the more powerful barons to implement feudal privileges of council and advice; it represented no appeal to any older pre-feudal ancient law.

Such was Brady's history, offered "to teach the people loyalty and obedience and frustrate the designs of the seditious."[51] No omnipotent Parliament and elective Crown could threaten the Stuarts if the claim that the ancient constitution had accorded power to Parliament was erroneous. During the years of the Exclusion crisis, Brady's scholarship was at the service of Filmer's position; it maintained the omnipotence of the Crown and the subjugation to it of the law, liberties, and Commons of England.

The Royalist cause of Filmer and Brady was rejected in 1688. It has been assumed that with this defeat the influence of Brady's history declined. Herbert Butterfield and D. C. Douglas have written that with the Whig victory in 1688 Whig historiography also triumphed, and that Brady and his feudal history were forgotten until its revival and final acceptance in the nineteenth century.[52] Pocock writes that after the expulsion of his patrons, the Stuarts, Brady was ignored; with the Revolution came "the rejection of his historical ideas." The Revolution legitimized the historical doctrine of the victors and their notion of an ancient constitution became the ideology of the successful Whigs in the eighteenth century.[53] Brady had to wait, it has been assumed, for the romantic historians of the nineteenth century to justify his early and perceptive insights into the real nature of the English middle ages.

A study of the political press in the Augustan period indicates, however, that Brady's scholarship did not have to wait so long for its revival. Dr. Brady found important disciples only a half-century after his eclipse and, what is more startling, his champions were the spokesmen for the most successful of the Whig bene-ficiaries of 1688, Robert Walpole. But, though the Brady position was adopted as the historical attitude of the Whigs, its partisan use was a very different one. The dynamics of Augustan politics led Walpole to embrace the theories of the Tory Brady, because Boling-broke made partisan use of the Whig common law myth of an ancient and immemorial constitution. Brady's scholarship was thus made respectable long before the nineteenth century, and it was a Whig government that took this step so crucial for future students of English history.

Bolingbroke's use of Whig history served obvious partisan pur-poses. How better to attack Walpole than with traditional Whig conceptions of the past! The present corrupt age, Bolingbroke maintained, was one of slavery compared to the great freedoms of the past. In both the *Remarks on the History of England* and *A Dissertation upon Parties*, Bolingbroke concluded that the ancient English were freemen: "in all their ages, Britain hath been the Temple, as it were, of liberty."[54] But this glorious and continuous tradition of freedom was once again threatened, as it had been in the seventeenth century by the Stuarts. In 1730, the English were not free. The Revolution, which had sought to restore the ancient constitution and its freedoms, was betrayed by the new political and economic world of Robert Walpole. Despotism was reducing the English to slavery and the longing for the freedoms of old England could be met only by a Machiavellian *ricorso*, a return to the first principles of the ancient constitution. Annual parliaments, a militia, and the exclusion of placemen were steps toward a freer past, and were associated with an old England, which was everywhere being replaced by new and disturbing innovations. Bolingbroke had learned well the lesson of the seventeenth-century common lawyers and the Whigs of the Exclusion crisis. To the English political mind a most effective way to combat a contemporary evil was the use of an historical argument that contrasted present slavery and lack of freedom with an idyllic image of a free past. Bolingbroke was a Whig historian because his opposition to Walpole and to the new England over which Walpole presided made him one.

If opposing Walpole made Bolingbroke a Whig historian, then Bolingbroke's charges, cloaked in the theory of the ancient constitution, made Walpole's press Tory historians.[55] In the desire to prove that Walpole's administration and post-Revolutionary Whiggery in general had enlarged the degree of English freedom it was necessary for ministerial writers to destroy Bolingbroke's picture of a free past and to replace it with Dr. Brady's description of English history.

The birth of real freedom in England was the Glorious Revolution, proclaimed Walpole's press. Bolingbroke's belief that the Revolution did not alter, but merely renewed the constitution was rejected as the *Gazetteer* asked, "a renewal of what? a renewal of a non-entity. We never before had a constitution as was settled at the Revolution. That sure can't be renewed which never existed."[56] There were no freedoms to renew, because old England had been steeped in slavery. To praise old England, as Bolingbroke did, was to condone misery, for, in the words of *The London Journal*, "new England, or the present state of things caused by the Revolution, as far exceeds the old, as light does darkness, as liberty does slavery; or as happiness does misery." Four years later, *The London Journal* repeated this claim: "The modern constitution is infinitely better than the ancient constitution in any point of time, from the Saxons down to that glorious period of the Revolution."[57] Bolingbroke's history, in the view of Walpole's press, inaccurately praised English ancestors for possessing a spirit of liberty that was "unknown to all the world." Even more absurd was the foolish description of the Normans' sudden seizure and conversion by this spirit after their arrival. An anonymous writer in *The Daily Gazetteer* exclaims scornfully: "what heroic tales are here! more idle and romantic than those of Gargantua," and regrets that he is "ashamed of my ancestors for deserving these encomiums so little; and of my contemporaries for bestowing them so ignorantly."[58] In 1733 *The London Journal* wrote that Machiavelli would surely blush at the ignorance and impudence of the Opposition, which enlisted his principles in a false belief that the ancient constitution had declined.

The very reverse is true of our government, which was bad in the beginning, made better by degrees and is brought to perfection at last . . . To bring the government of England back to its first principles is to bring the people back to absolute slavery. The primitive purity of our constitution was that the people had no share in the government, but were the villains, vassals, or bondsmen of the Lords: a sort of cattle bought and sold with the land.[59]

In its zeal to demolish the argument for a free ancient constitution, Walpole's press found in Brady's scholarship an answer to Bolingbroke's idyllic portrayal of the past. Brady's feudal history now found an official champion. *The London Journal* wrote, "to wish a return of the ancient constitution is wishing for but one freeholder, and that was the King, he was the only freeman, the only unconditional independent, and absolute freeholder."[60]

To prove that the people of England were not free in the middle ages, ministerial writers depicted those centuries in the stark feudal terms first articulated by Spelman and Brady. They even superimposed this feudal image on the Saxon period to show how illusory it was to talk of power in the hands of the people, even in that supposedly golden age. The Witenagemot, related *The London Journal*, was composed of the king, abbots, princes, barons, and the tenants who held of the king *in capite*. No freeholders were to be found there; the common people were then only a crowd of "rude, scarce humanized fighting beggars." After the

Conquest, "the King became grand landlord of the Kingdom." The barons who held their lands of him by military service were little absolute sovereigns over their own tenants and slaves. "The King, Church, and Barons had then all the lands in the Kingdom; the people had no property." Since the commoners had no property they had no freedom; they were simply the tools of their masters. Occasionally they might be assembled into the armies of the king, church, and barons, but they never fought for liberty; they fought because "their sovereign lords commanded them, and would starve or hang them, if they did not." What wretched stuff, then, is this of Bolingbroke, "our great master of history" when he writes of the spirit of liberty diffused through the whole mass of people. Nothing could be further from the truth, wrote *The London Journal*, for "we were then a nation of little independent sovereigns, with each his slaves about him."[61] As another writer put it

Authorities are endless; I could produce a thousand to prove the truth of the proposition, that the old English were slaves by virtue of the constitution, or slaves by law established. I know no infamy in speaking truth; and the truth is, that in those days there was one continual chain of vassalage from the King down to the meanest slave; and the chain of vassalage was according to the law of England.[62]

Walpole's Whig camp denied any immemorial representation of commoners. Parliament was itself a development of feudal obligations, a council to which the chief tenants of the suzerain were summoned and in which the tenants expected to give advice. The king, according to Walpole's publicists, sent for his greater tenants himself and ordered his sheriffs to send some of the lesser tenants; this is all demonstrable from the wording of the Magna Carta. "The people chose nobody; for these greater and lesser tenants were hereditary members, sent for by the king, to sit in council by virtue of their tenures, but not chosen by the people." For two centuries after the Conquest the king's council was regal and aristocratic, and the people had no role in making the laws. It was inconceivable that persons could participate in government, when, as lowly vassals, they were looked upon as mere livestock. The king, church, and nobility would have treated the people as cattle, "knocked them o' the head and eaten them, had not these vassals been of more service to them when alive and the cattle more pleasant to their taste when dead."[63] It was equally absurd for Bolingbroke to talk of annual parliaments as part of the ancient constitution because the calling of the feudal curia depended ultimately on the whim of the great landlords of England. To talk of annual parliaments even in Saxon times was a distortion of historical fact, wrote *The London Journal.*[64]

Like Brady and Dugdale, Walpole's writers located the first appearance of the Commons in the reign of Henry III. *The Daily Gazetteer's* account followed closely that of the Royalist Dugdale in explaining the emergence of the Commons as merely a byproduct of Simon de Montfort's political ambitions. "To such low beginnings," it wrote, "and such private views, do we owe the origins and foundations of all our liberties." But Walpole's apologists were willing to attribute the origins of the Commons and its emergence out of the feudal structure to causes beyond the competition of nobility and monarch for political allies. They addressed themselves to the problem of the decline of feudalism, which, as Pocock points out, is a question that the Tory feudal historians of the seventeenth century had never successfully handled. The Walpole press cited Harrington and his description of the new distribution of power created by the changed balance of property brought on by Tudor legislation. It even anticipated the "hardship of the nobility" thesis of more modern scholarship with a description of a hard-pressed nobility caught in the price revolution, overextending itself in fashionable luxury, and leaving its estates to be broken up, "which the Commons, grown wise and industrious by the enchanting novelty of property, got into their hands."[65] But, in their description of the decline of feudalism, Walpole's writers went beyond Harrington's analysis to arguments that neither he, Brady, nor Spelman had advanced.

*The London Journal* described certain economic developments "about two centuries after the Conquest," important for changing the distribution of power under feudalism and contributing to the emergence of the Commons. These developments "began to vary the model and draw it nearer the present form of government." Commoners in Cornwall exported tin, and in other areas of England earned money by exporting wool. By the fruits of this commercial activity, wrote the *Journal*, feudal duties could often be commuted and privileges and charters obtained. Some localities even received the privilege of sending up representatives to Parliament. *The Daily Gazetteer* pointed to the development one hundred years later, in the fourteenth-century reign of Edward III (1327-1377), of the wool trade, which also gave new weight and power to the commoners.[66] This was the explanation Walpole's press gave for what Spelman and Brady had earlier described as the emergence of the commoner from the lesser tenants—a phenomenon which these seventeenth-century historians had not sought to explore further.

Another aspect of Bolingbroke's Whig history contested by Walpole's defenders was Bolingbroke's division of the English past into alternating periods of good monarchs who served the cause of freedom, and bad monarchs who opposed it. Walpole's writers could not accept the notion that the people had had more or less freedom in different reigns, depending on their own watchful defense of the ancient constitution and its spirit. Lord Hervey questioned this particular aspect of Bolingbroke's historical doctrine, and surveying the long line of monarchs since the Conquest, found none worthy of any of the praise bestowed by Bolingbroke. Hervey's argument that all monarchs before the Revolution had been tyrants brought the Walpole position to its logical conclusion. The past was totally unfree. Even Elizabeth was criticized. Under her, the people did not "enjoy the least shadow of liberty." "Never were the reins of prerogative held with a stricter hand or the yoke of slavery faster bound upon the people's neck than at this period of time." Star chambers were no sign of freedom. When people fought, in the past, it was not for liberty, but for a master; it "never aimed at striking off one chain, but in order to put on another." His conclusion was simple and straightforward: until the Revolution there was no such thing as liberty. *The London Journal* joined Hervey in debunking Elizabeth, the favorite of Bolingbroke and the Opposition, to illustrate the lack of freedom under all monarchs before 1688. "The Government of this Kingdom, since the Revolution, and under the present royal family, excels hers, almost as much as a government by laws does a government by arbitrary power."[67] All the historical conflicts that Bolingbroke had described as battles won or lost for freedom and the ancient constitution left the sorry lot of the people much what it had been.

Walpole's journalists were well aware that their history followed

Brady's and therefore opposed that written by seventeenth-century Whig heroes like Sidney, James Tyrrel, and William Petyt, who were advocates of the ancient constitution. *The Daily Gazetteer* admitted in July 1735: "I agree with Brady in many of his facts, and think them undoubted records and true testimonies."[68] The writer was equally quick, however, to dissociate himself from everything but Brady's scholarship, denying that he shared any of the learned doctor's political principles and the use he made of his studies. It is nonetheless remarkable that, forty-six years after the Revolution, a Whig ministry officially endorsed the historical findings of the Tory Dr. Brady.

Walpole's publicists exonerated their seventeenth-century Whig predecessors from their historiographical errors. When they defended the antiquity of Parliament their intentions had been honorable, which was more than could be said of Bolingbroke. The seventeenth-century Whigs had feared the use that could be made of the novelty of Parliament by an arbitrary court; so they had insisted, incorrectly, on the freedom of the ancient constitution and the antiquity of Parliament. There is perhaps no greater indication of the Whig acceptance of Brady's scholarship than the comment of Walpole's press on Sidney—"of immortal memory; who, had he lived in these days, would never have wrote his book."[69]

But Walpole's writers also clearly indicated that though they accepted Tory history they did not accept Tory politics. This self-conscious effort to differentiate themselves from Brady's political principles can be seen in their response to *The Craftsman's* charge that to insist on a lack of freedom in the past implied the ministry's acknowledgment and approval of a present deficiency. *The Daily Gazetteer* replied: "What have facts to do with principles? Or how does it appear that because our ancestors were slaves, we ought not to be free?" Why can it not be the case, it went on, that even if Englishmen in the past were not free, that "liberty was our original right, our right from nature or reason."[70] Brady's history can be rescued from Brady's politics only by Locke's principles.

The most important aspect of the debate is that Walpole's Whig publicists endorsed the historical views of the Tory Brady. By doing this, they helped remove some of the partisan fog that made it difficult to interpret the English feudal past. In the long run, Brady's views on English history would become the accepted interpretation.

Trevelyan, the most widely read of twentieth-century English Whig historians, writes almost as an aside: "The Witan was not the origin of the later English Parliament, which grew up out of Anglo-Norman institutions; nor was the Witan a popular or representative body."[71] When Englishmen commemorated the seven hundredth anniversary of their Parliament in 1965 there were no dissents from Brady's scholarship. Sir Robert Walpole had endorsed it long before Englishmen were so unanimous. The partisan motivation for his use of Brady is self-evident. How better to disprove Bolingbroke's claim of a present extinction of ancient freedoms than to show that freedom was non-existent in a past when people were virtually slaves? Reduced to their simplest terms, the historical positions of Bolingbroke and Walpole amount to little more than the simple device of brightening the present by dimming the past, or vice versa. If the past were so unpleasant and devoid of freedom as Walpole's press implied, could the subject of George II doubt that he was better off under the ministry of Robert Walpole?[72]

# VI

## Bolingbroke on Politics and the English Constitution

> The full, the perfect plan
> Of Britain's matchless constitution, mixt
> Of mutual checking and supporting powers,
> Kings, Lords, and Commons.
>
> —JAMES THOMSON, *Liberty,* LONDON, 1736

### BALANCE AND MIXED GOVERNMENT

Praise of the virtuous British government and her matchless mixed government and balanced constitution is found in virtually all Augustan writings on politics.[1] Behind much of this Augustan praise of mixed government lay reference to the classical writings of Aristotle, Polybius, and Cicero, which had apparently set forth, for all time and for all political systems, the principle that a combination of monarchy, aristocracy, and democracy checked the characteristic vice of each while combining their characteristic virtues. Tyranny, faction, and violence would be mutually curbed, while power, wisdom, and virtue would be combined.

This classical wisdom had been systematically applied to English government for the first time in the sixteenth century, when Puritans, Jesuits, and Marian Exiles alleged that the Tudor monarchy violated the principles of mixed government found in the classical texts.[2] Although John Aylmer, Robert Parsons, John Ponet, and Thomas Cartwright contended that the classical praise of mixed government was meaningful and relevant to contemporary political debate, they also made clear the fundamentally contentious nature of invoking the principle. The ideal of mixed government would thenceforth usually be articulated for the purpose of drawing attention to alleged departure from the ideal. This expediential dimension of invoking the principle would be evident in the seventeenth-century confrontation of Charles I and Parliament and again in the eighteenth-century dispute between Bolingbroke and Walpole.

Augustan writers on politics often referred to the classical sources of the doctrine of mixed government. Swift, Bolingbroke, and Commonwealthmen like Walter Moyle were familiar with and constantly cited the key texts. Their firm belief in the relevance of the classical version of mixed government to the eighteenth-century political scene is illustrated in Augustan works such as that of Edward Spelman, whose *A Fragment out of the Sixth Book of Polybius* had "prefixed a preface, wherein the system of Polybius is applied to the government of England."[3] But this was by no means the only indication. A great deal of the vogue for both Machiavelli and Harrington in this period is attributable to their praise of classical mixed government. Bolingbroke's circle was, in particular, fascinated by this aspect of classical thought, not only because they were humanists, but also because of the hope the principle held that a truly mixed government could postpone degeneration and decline. Obsessed with a sense of the corruption of English government and society, it was inevitable that Bolingbroke's followers found the framework for their preoccupation in a body of thought similarly concerned with the problems of corruption, decline, and regeneration.

Newton's thought was another powerful intellectual force shaping Augustan concern with balance. The mechanistic spirit that had so pervaded seventeenth-century thought (as seen, for example, in Harrington's preoccupation with equilibrium) was powerfully reinforced in the eighteenth century by the Newtonian picture of the world. The play of balance and checks in the political world corresponded, it was believed, to the fundamental harmony and balance in the universe. If the universe were a clock set going by a great and wise clockmaker, then government was also a delicately calibrated machine set in motion by some original great legislator, a Lycurgus or Solon. God did not have to return to rewind His balanced universe, as great men and Patriot Kings had to rewind the political machine and reset their springs and balance wheels; but this was only as it should be, for man was certainly an inferior workman compared with his God.

J. T. Desaguliers' opposition poem, *The Newtonian System of the World, the Best Model of Government,* written in 1728, is an interesting manifestation of this Newtonian influence in the political thought of the period. In the preface, the poet writes that he has "considered Government as a phenomenon, and looks upon that form of it to be the most perfect, which does most nearly resemble the natural government of our system, according to the laws settled by the all-wise and almighty architect of the universe." The poem describes the decline of true balance in the political world, and pleads, "But boldly let thy perfect model be/ NEWTON's (the only true) Philosophy."[4]

A passage in *A Dissertation upon Parties* bears further witness to the imprint of Newton's ideas on political thought in this period. Bolingbroke's description of the power of the King of England after 1688 is given in Newtonian terms.

> He can move no longer in another orbit from his people, and, like some superior planet, attract, repel, influence, and direct their motions by his own. He and they are parts of the same system, intimately joined and co-operating together, acting and acted upon, limiting and limited, controlling and controlled by one another.[5]

Another intellectual source of the Augustan preoccupation with balance was the gothic model. Tacitus' *Germania* was continually referred to in this period and descriptions of the mixed institutions of Saxon government could often be found in Augustan writing, although the gothic model never had as powerful a hold on eighteenth-century thought in England as it had on seventeenth-century political writing, or on eighteenth-century thought in France. For many eighteenth-century Englishmen the gothic model never survived the blow administered by Harrington. When they did not look to the classics, Bolingbroke and Swift, however, would often speak of the mixed constitution as a noble gothic invention.[6]

Intellectual sources for the model of mixed government—classical wisdom, the Newtonian world view, and the gothic model—do not, however, completely account for the Augustan infatuation with a mixed and balanced constitution. A much more important influence was the legacy of English political and constitutional experience. In the seventeenth century participants in the constitutional struggles identified their positions with the defense of mixed government and attacked their opponents' as departures from it.[7] The Levellers were exceptions who argued that the tripartite government of kings, lords, and Commons was a mark of Norman bondage;[8] but most defenders of the Commons against the Stuarts held to the theory that mixed government was a product of the nation's gothic past. Parliament's supporters were not the only ones, however, to argue the principle of mixed government. In his famous "Answer to the Nineteen Propositions," Charles I publicly identified the Crown with the notion that English government was a mixture of monarchy, aristocracy, and democracy. Charles' pronouncement, "the cardinal document in the theory of mixed government," gave the theory a respectability and widespread fame it could have acquired in no other way.[9] His use of it was typically expediential and opportunistic; it enabled him to answer the demands of the Long Parliament by wrapping himself in Parliament's own cloak of mixed government. To grant their demands, he answered, would upset the balance between king, lords, and Commons, and destroy the balanced constitution which "the experience and wisdom of your ancestors hath so moulded."[10]

The principle received its permanent sanctification when Englishmen rejected the Republic in 1660 and the unlimited monarchy in 1688, marking mixed government as a firmly entrenched product of the nation's experience. Mixed government was "the fundamental assumption" of the eighteenth-century constitution.[11] Francis Atterbury, the voice of high Toryism, reflected the consensus when, in a sermon before the House of Commons in 1701, on the anniversary of the restoration of Charles II, he called the mixed government of the English "a model and standard for all others." The English constitution was "wisely moulded, out of all the different Forms and Kinds of Civil Government." It was a "Constitution, nicely poiz'd between the extremes of too much liberty, and too much power; the several parts of it having a Proper Check upon each other."[12]

Atterbury's sentiments are much like those of Halifax, who had earlier described the English constitution as a noble *via media*. This great exponent of mixed government had written that the British constitution itself was an embodiment of the trimmer's instincts. It rejected the extremes of monarchy and commonwealth, reconciled dominion and liberty, vassalage and obedience, "devouring prerogative and licentious freedom." The composite was the best position. "Ours is a happy mixture and a wise choice of what is best in others." Halifax's blending of Aristotelian ideals with English experience strikingly anticipated the mood of later Augustan thought. He suggested that not only its constitution, but all the dimensions of its national existence matched England to the classical model of moderation and balance. Mixed government was only a part of a much more fundamental approximation of English life to Aristotelian moderation where not only political but all wisdom and virtue lay in the mean.

Our climate is a trimmer, between that part of the world where men are roasted, and the other where they are frozen; our church is a Trimmer between the phrenzy of Platonick visions and the lethargic innocence of popish dreams; our laws are trimmers, between the excess of unbounded power, and the extravagance of liberty not enough restrained; true virtue hath ever been thought a trimmer, dwelling in the middle between the two extremes.[13]

However much eighteenth-century Englishmen might talk of its continuity or its age-old character, fundamental changes in the strictly political dimension of England's *via media* had taken place in the seventeenth century. The constitutional settlement resulted in a different understanding of mixed government with Commons and Lords now sharing governing power with the king. The older notion vested sovereignty solely in the king. He alone governed the realm; this meant that his powers included those of declaring and promulgating statutes. His power was balanced, according to the older notion, by the Commons, which was entrusted to raise revenue and impeach officials. The Lords maintained the balance, and by its judicial power kept the law of the land. After the Revolution, however, mixed government meant sharing the sovereign legislative power. At least legislative power over the realm was shared among what Charles I had described as the three "estates" of the king, Lords, and Commons.[14]

This fundamental change hidden within the similarity of expression did not deter the Augustans from writing of a continuous tradition of mixed government. It was considered part of their constitutional heritage with firm roots in the political history and experience of the country. On any issue that involved the interrelationship of the various branches of government the principle would be invoked.

Two such occasions arose in the early years of Bolingbroke's career. They brought home to him and to all Augustans the principles of balance. Like most Englishmen of his age Bolingbroke learned about the balance of powers and about mixed constitutions during the impeachment of the Whig lords in 1701, and in the controversy over the Peerage Bill in 1719. On both occasions specific policy issues were raised that filled the air with talk of balance. Writers defended the principle and accused their opponents of upsetting the balance of mixed government by misguided Parliamentary action. With the exception of Swift few who participated in these two incidents stressed classical ideas.[15] Their principal source of authority was English history and the wonderfully balanced constitution evolved by their glorious ancestors. An important political work exemplifying this tendency emerged from the impeachment crisis. In August of 1701, the youthful Bolingbroke wrote to Sir John Trumbull, his intellectual mentor.

> I have lately read a book which you doubtless have had sent you. It is Sir Humphrey Mackworth's *Vindication of the Rights of the Commons* and am very pleased with it. It contains a great deal of plain truth and exposes to the eyes of the people a just draught of our admirable constitution.[16]

Mackworth described England's mixed constitution as derived from English practices, not from any intellectual model. The three powers in government, he argued, represented the interests of the kingdom: the king, who is common father of the country; the Lords, men of great honor, quality, and estate; and the Commons, representing the people. One also finds in Mackworth's essay the beginnings of a functional differentiation for each branch; he describes the king expediting, the Commons deciding, and the Lords adjudicating.[17] Functional differentiation had always been implicit in the notions of mixed government; it could be found in Harrington and as far back as the Aristotelian division of political authority into deliberative, executive, and judicial activity.[18] What Mackworth begins, however, is the conscious identification of the three powers with the three functions, an identification that could be meaningful in England only after the Revolutionary settlement. This interpretation of the constitution in terms of a functional separation of governing powers stands very much alone, however.

The prevailing interpretation of mixed government was not Mackworth's but the one to which Bolingbroke and Walpole adhered, in which government was seen as consisting of the three different interests of the realm sharing the legislative power. The remaining part of Mackworth's analysis, however, is at one with the prevailing notion—he depicts the lesson of English history to be that the three interests of king, Commons, and Lords are "mutual securities for the common safety, and as checks one upon the other."[19]

The Peerage Bill of 1719, which would have set a fixed limit to the number of Lords and removed the Crown's power to appoint new peers, gave rise to a controversy in which nearly the entire English political community debated the principles of a mixed and balanced constitution. The pamphlet literature produced by this controversy provides some interesting insights into Augustan views on mixed government.[20] Once again the principle of mixed government was paraded in a contentious setting. The opponents of the bill saw it ruining the balance by giving too much power to Lords; the proponents saw it restoring the balance by making Lords equal to the other branches. Stanhope, the sponsor of the bill, did refer to the Roman Senate in debate, but most members of Parliament and pamphleteers were more concerned about traditional English practices and their relevance for this bill.[21] The debate over the Peerage Bill reveals, in addition, that the three branches of government were still seen in traditional terms as three parts of the legislature and not as three separate functional powers. The pamphleteers wrote of the mutual checks and balances as Mackworth had, and many commented on the corrupting influence of power.[22] These were stock aspects of the principle of mixed government.

These events of 1701 and 1719 illustrate dramatically that although some Englishmen might cite classical wisdom or even the model of natural science as the rationale for their mixed government, most understood mixed government in terms of English experience. Mixed and balanced government had been perfected in English constitutional practice, and any tampering with this balance had to be accommodated to the English genius, which in the past had made their constitution the most perfect of any to be found in free governments. This was the burden of the political debate in 1701 and 1719, as also in 1730 and 1734.

Bolingbroke's thoughts on balance and the mixed constitution were derived less from Polybius or Tacitus than from his knowledge and concern with English experience. It was this concern that shaped his attack on Walpole, whom he considered to be destroying the perfect balance of the mixed constitution. Bolingbroke's theory of mixed government made no pretensions to abstract or theoretical speculation on politics; it was firmly rooted in the experience of his age. No wonder, then, that Bolingbroke saw so much "plain truth" in Mackworth's admirable book of 1701, for there Mackworth had written:

But the excellence of the government of England is not only proved by reason, but by long experience; this nation having for many ages, flourished under the same constitution of government by Kings, Lords, and Commons, and from generation to generation preserved their liberties, whilst many of our neighbors have lost their ancient forms of government, and their liberties together.[23]

Bolingbroke's views on mixed government have little novelty about them. His enlistment of the principle in the attack on Walpole merely repeats what is common to his age, and, indeed, to Walpole.

An interesting interpretation of Bolingbroke's political writings, however, denies that his views were altogether traditional and makes him out to be the author of a new theory of the separation of powers, which, it is also claimed, is the source of Montesquieu's notions.

The claim that Bolingbroke is the teacher of Montesquieu goes back at least as far as Henri See's history of eighteenth-century French political thought, in which Bolingbroke's influence on Montesquieu is paired with Locke's.[24] But the extended thesis of Bolingbroke's novelty and influence on the great French writer has been developed more recently by Robert Shackleton of Oxford.[25] His argument is twofold. He considers Bolingbroke the author of views on the separation of powers that were a novel departure from traditional ideas on the mixed state. He also claims that Montesquieu, who learned of Bolingbroke's ideas in *The Craftsman*, constructed from them his unique notion of liberty as consisting in a rigid separation of governmental powers.

The evidence that Montesquieu had read Bolingbroke in *The Craftsman* is incontestable, but one may question the initial premise

of the argument, the alleged novelty and importance of Bolingbroke's theoretical views. Shackleton contends that three features
distinguish the idea of separation of powers from the notion of
mixed government. The latter, he holds, merely denotes the situation in which a state is composed of all three of the simple forms
of government—legislative power is divided and held jointly by
monarch, nobles, and people. From Polybius until the eighteenth
century, this had been the prevailing notion, he argues. But he sees
separation of powers as a completely different idea that supported
the division of political authority into three separate functions and
that would be assigned to distinct and independent bodies. A second distinguishing feature, Shackleton contends, is that the separation of powers also stresses the checking and balancing of one
power against another, whereas the mixed state combines all interests solely to prevent or stall the inevitable degeneration of
government, not to check power. Checking and balancing is an
outgrowth of the third and most distinctive feature of the separation of powers, a distrust of power itself, which, Shackleton suggests, is not present in the idea of the mixed state. He argues that
these three features of the "separation of powers" are found in the
theories of Bolingbroke, who put forward this novel doctrine with
persistence and vigor in *The Craftsman*. "It was thence Montesquieu
derived the notion, which when he refined it and systematised it,
was to become his most distinctive and influential contribution to
constitutional theory."[26] But one may ask whether Bolingbroke's
ideas were really that novel and whether these distinctions are really
tenable.

The key passage which ostensibly shows that Bolingbroke held
new ideas on the separation of powers, is found in *The Craftsman*
of June 27, 1730 (later published as Letter II of Bolingbroke's *Remarks on the History of England*). It allegedly advocates the independence of the executive and the legislature in the following
language. "In a Constitution like ours the safety of the whole depends on the Balance of the parts and the Balance of the parts on
their mutual independency on one another."[27] That this statement
goes beyond the traditional notion of the mixed state is apparently
proven by citing the reaction to this *Craftsman* comment by the
Government's *London Journal*. The *Journal* claimed this independency to be not only a constitutional innovation but also sheer

imagination; absolutely distinct powers were mere Utopian fancy. The king, the *Journal* claimed, was an essential part of the legislature.[28]

Shackleton reasons from this debate that since Bolingbroke's opponents discerned in his comments principles at variance with the traditional notion of mixed state, the novelty must have really existed. Since the *Journal* accused Bolingbroke of wanting to grant the king only executive power and the Commons the entire legislative power, that is what Bolingbroke must have wanted. But a partisan reading of what was itself a partisan charge cannot be taken for truth itself. Bolingbroke had no intention of excluding the king from the legislature and giving the lawmaking function solely to Parliament. *The Craftsman's* answers to *The London Journal's* charges indicate that Bolingbroke sought to end only "corrupt" interference by the throne in the legislature, not its rightful participation as one of the three branches sharing legislative authority. What Bolingbroke desired was a return to the purity of the mixed state, not any novel and rigid partitioning of executive and legislative power. There is, he wrote, both a necessary "constitutional dependency" by which each participant in the legislative power controls the other, and a "constitutional independency" that prevents one branch from totally subverting the others' share in the legislative power. His call for independence was merely a plea for an end to the corrupt and unconstitutional dependence of Parliament on the executive that Walpole's regime had brought about.[29]

Bolingbroke's notion of a simultaneous "dependency" and "independency" of the three constitutional branches was not a novel distinction; it can be found, for example, in Mackworth's book of 1701. Mackworth had written "The King, Lords, and Commons must agree together, and assist each other in the exercise of their several and respective powers [mutual dependency] without the least encroachment upon one another, or else they will not answer the end for which they were established [mutual independency]."[30]

Both Walpole and Bolingbroke were engaging in the, by then, familiar process of accusing the other of advocating departures from the traditional mixed constitution. Walpole's press accused the Opposition of seeking to take away the Crown's power of place and jobs, which would then force the Crown to become dependent on the Commons. The Government opposed this potential dependence by using the very partisan language, calling for distinct and independent powers of legislature and executive, that Shackleton finds so novel and important in Bolingbroke! In what might be taken as an even stronger statement of separation of powers than the passage cited from *The Craftsman,* Walpole's *Free Britain* declared in 1732:

> In all free countries, the legislative and executive powers are distinct authorities vested in different bodies of persons. To the legislature belong the original of laws; to the magistrate the execution of these laws. Hence it is that as by keeping those two great powers distinct, a state is free and happy; so in all despotick governments, the legislative and executive powers are blended together.[31]

*The Craftsman's* response to *The London Journal's* charge that it sought a novel division of power that excluded the throne from the legislature indicated that Bolingbroke had no new notion of a separation of powers in mind, but only a partisan charge within the traditional structure of a mixed constitution.

> An independent House of Commons, or an independent House of Lords is as inconsistent with our Constitution as an independent, that is absolute King . . . The House of Commons considered as one part of the Legislature, ought not to be Independent of the other parts, which are the House of Lords and the King . . . In this sense then the several estates of the Legislature are dependent on each other . . . whereas if the exercise of any corrupt influence should be allow'd, the branch of the Legislature would gain such an ascendent over the others; that the Balance of our constitution would be broken.[32]

The second essential of the separation of powers that Shackleton discovered in Bolingbroke's writings, the checking and balancing of power, is neither unique to his writings not to a theory of separation of powers. It is an implicit assumption of the theory of mixed government that may be found in political writing from Plato's *Laws* to the theories offered by Walpole's press. Polybius, whom Shackleton acknowledges the great theorist of the mixed state, thought that checks and balances were the secret of Lycurgus' policy and of the Roman constitution. Machiavelli had written that "these three powers will keep each other reciprocally in check."[33] The notion was a common ingredient of Augustan writing on mixed government. Atterbury spoke of such checking in his sermon cited above, Thomson in his poem, *Liberty,* Mackworth in his book, and the pamphleteers of 1719 in their discussions of the Peerage Bill.

The third feature of the separation of powers, distrust of power itself, merits closer attention. Shackleton claims that Montesquieu found this attitude in Bolingbroke, and that for Bolingbroke it was the essential element of a novel notion of separation of powers. Because Bolingbroke felt that power corrupts he hit upon the novel notion of dividing its exercise among distinct hands independent of one another. Montesquieu's *Spicilege* does contain a direct quotation from *The Craftsman* of June 13, 1730: "The love of power is natural. It is insatiable, almost constantly whetted, never cloyed by possession." Elsewhere in *The Craftsman,* Bolingbroke wrote, "power is a thing of the most intoxicating nature, it ought always to have some checks on it."[34]

No doubt such sentiments were basic to Montesquieu's and all liberal notions of separating, checking, and balancing power. But they were not unique to Bolingbroke. Montesquieu could have derived them from numerous other more respectable and impressive sources. The notion was not unique to a theory of separation of powers and was held by all those whom Shackleton would relegate to mere theorists of the mixed state. Kurt von Fritz has shown that Plato was preoccupied with the inevitable corruption that results when men possess unchecked power; so were Polybius and all theorists of the mixed constitution in antiquity.[35] The seventeenth-century Commonwealthmen Harrington and Sidney, were equally convinced of the classical notion that mixed government overcame the evil that emerged when men possessed power. Among Bolingbroke's own contemporaries, the Augustan Commonwealthmen, especially John Trenchard and Thomas Gordon, one finds as a recurring theme this notion of checking power because of its intrinsic corrupting effect. Shaftesbury who rejected Hobbes' idea of "power insatiably coveted by all," proposed "a right division and balance of power." The idea was so widespread in Augustan England that even Walpole's *London Journal,* which Shackleton depicts as the upholder of the mixed state against Bolingbroke's novel ideas wrote: "For such is the nature of man, that he is not to be trusted with power which is not checked by other powers, as our fore-fathers well judged."[36]

Bolingbroke's notions of balance and checking power were firmly set in conventional English wisdom and constitutional experience. The only unique aspect of his thought on this issue was his application of the suspicion of power not to the functional differentiation of branches of government, but to the novel theory of opposition. His constitutional ideas on balance were traditional ones; only in his articulation of a theory of opposition based on the distrust of power would he break new ground.

This should not suggest that Montesquieu learned nothing from Bolingbroke during his visit to England. Although Bolingbroke was not the source of a new theoretical concept of the separation of powers, he was to a great extent, as Shackleton's research makes clear, the source of Montesquieu's general impressions of English government.[37] He need not have been the only source, however, because Walpole's administration and his press were as eager to describe English government as a mixed constitution as were Bolingbroke and *The Craftsman*. Montesquieu found the image of a balanced government being championed by both camps, each accusing the other of endangering the balance with corrupt practices or utopian legislative reforms. Montesquieu could have found *The Craftsman* so carried away by its partisan zeal that it appeared to advocate a novel separation and independence of function, but he could have found the same argumentative leap in Walpole's *Free Briton*. But these were rhetorical exceptions to the theory held by both camps, exceptions that zealous to attack alleged dependence, overemphasized independence. But independence is not the same thing as separation. Partisan cries defended the independent share of legislative power possessed by either the Crown or Parliament, as the case applied. They did not defend separate functions of legislating and executing.

The theoretical notion of a functional separation of powers could not be found in Bolingbroke's writings. But Bolingbroke's traditional ideas on mixed government were still, themselves, important for Montesquieu, apologist for the French noble reaction—he could use the model of mixed government in England as an argument against *la thèse royale* that rejected the balancing power of the Parlements.[38] What mattered most about the ideal government of *les Anglais,* which Montesquieu pictured for the French, was the mixture of power between the central royal administration and the intermediary powers of the political community, the Commons and

Lords sitting in Parliament. In the perspective of Montesquieu's restatement of *la thèse nobilaire* in the middle decades of eighteenth-century France, what is important in his understanding of England is not his discovery there of the new theory of the separation of powers, but the hard social and political fact he discovers there—the sharing of power as opposed to its centralization.

It now becomes clear why Bolingbroke rather than Walpole impressed Montesquieu. Bolingbroke and Montesquieu shared similar social perspectives; they were both spokesmen for aristocratic reaction. They are their respective countries' paradigms of reactive conservatism during the Enlightenment. Bolingbroke's lament at the way corruption at the royal and administrative center was ruining the independent power of substantial men in Parliament was more likely to impress Montesquieu than Walpole's argument that place bills left the monarch powerless. Because their partisan purposes were so similar Montesquieu took Bolingbroke's stand and made it, and not Walpole's, the basis for his description of the British constitution. Walpole talked of mixed government and balance, but Montesquieu may have sensed that behind Walpole's ministerial cry lay a reality reminiscent of *la thèse royale*.[39]

Through Book XI of *L'Esprit Des Lois* Bolingbroke's writings on mixed government and the British constitution entered the constitutional conflicts of eighteenth-century France. But Montesquieu was not the only Frenchman to use Bolingbroke's comments on the mixed British constitution in the battles of eighteenth-century French politics. His writings were utilized by the Marquis d'Argenson for the very opposite purpose, the defense of *la thèse royale*.

D'Argenson, a member of the Club de l'Entresol and its historian, knew Bolingbroke in his years of exile and renewed this earlier acquaintance when Bolingbroke returned to France in 1735, and d'Argenson visited him often at Chanteloup. Unlike most of the members of the Club de l'Entresol, d'Argenson was a critic of Boulainvilliers and a stauch exponent of *la thèse royale*.[40] His important work, *Considerations sur le gouvernement Ancien et Present de la France*, was written and circulated in manuscript in the late 1730's, but not published until after his service as foreign minister and his death.[41] The work rejects the Germanic theory of French history and its eighteenth-century application, the theory of intermediate powers, mixed government, and power of the Parlements.

D'Argenson offers instead a model of strong royal power held by an enlightened and reforming monarch.[42]

In his attack on mixed government in general, and on *la thèse nobilaire* in particular, d'Argenson set out to destroy what he considered the myth of its perfect embodiment in the English government, so effectively utilized by the French *nobilaire*. His *Considerations* contains an important digression on English government which contends that, far from being a model of perfection, it was corrupt, imperfect, and despotic.[43] D'Argenson had never been to England, but he used the arguments of his friend Bolingbroke. He had read *The Craftsman* and often met with Bolingbroke in 1735-1736, the years in which he wrote his treatise. Bolingbroke's critique of Walpole emerges from the pages of *The Considerations!*

The scourge of England, d'Argenson wrote, was its national debt, an obstacle to all great achievements. The state was poor, and the few private individuals who were rich were not concerned with the common interest. "Tout s'occupe de l'argent, tout va a l'argent chez eux, et tout cela ressemble mal aux Romains." England was governed despotically, "par ce qu'on appelle le ministre, invention qui étoit encore inconnue aux Anciens." A new element had entered into political life. Tyranny was no longer the province of an Emperor, a Senate, victorious generals, or favorites, but instead was incorporated in the office of a modern minister, "un ministre stipule pour le Roi, mais il travaille . . . pour lui-même." Financial corruption and the institution of the minister had turned the much praised English government into a despotism. "L'habitude d'aimer l'argent corrompt égalisment les moeurs et la politique d'Angleterre; la corruption des suffrages dans le Parlement y est devenu un moyen aise d'introduire le Despotisme." The gifts of office and pension wielded by a skillful minister result in an overbearing executive whose great power is acquired by his skill in creating a deferential assembly. This, he concludes, is the much lauded ideal of *la thèse nobilaire*.

Voilà pourtant quel est le chef d'oeuvre de l'esprit humain dans le juste melange de trois espèces de gouvernement; ces trois rivals ne cessent jamais de se combattre jusqu'a l'entièr anéantissement de deux; elles peuvent bien être admises pour etre consultées, ou pour rester en subordination l'une de l'autre, mais tant qu'elles se trouveront en concurrence de droit et de force, elles se choquent et se détruisent à la fin.[44]

Bolingbroke's partisan vision of the English constitution was put to use by both sides in the French dispute. Montesquieu, who knew of corruption in England,[45] preferred to see its government in the ideal prescriptive terms of Bolingbroke's theory of mixed government, which corresponded to his own objectives as a theorist of *la thèse nobilaire;* but Bolingbroke's description of what the English constitution really was like was utilized by d'Argenson to attack the model of *les Anglais* and serve his interests as theorist of *la thèse royale.*

One may question the accuracy of Bolingbroke's claims that the practices of Walpole's administration spelled an end to the fundamental balance of the English mixed constitution. Bolingbroke was wrong. Walpole and David Hume were more perceptive and accurate analysts of mixed government. Were it not for the extensive parliamentary influence exercised by the Crown that allowed many Members of Parliament to be tied to the executive, the settlements of 1688 and 1715 would have given preponderant power to Parliament. Corruption preserved the mixed constitution in the eighteenth century to such an extent that one analyst claims that this period was indeed the only time when England enjoyed a truly balanced constitution. "The relationship between King and Commons in the eighteenth century was for the first and last time a balanced relationship between two more or less equal partners."[46] Bolingbroke's place bills would have undermined the mixed constitution. (The balance was ultimately shattered in the half-century between 1780 and 1832, when the Crown's influence over the Commons was drastically reduced by the elimination of places. The House of Commons emerged as the supreme power when its counterbalance, the monarch, was thrust from politics. Its victory was short-lived, however, because the supreme power would soon be the extra-Parliamentary forces of party and electorate.) Walpole must be credited with holding the line. Had Bolingbroke governed, mixed government might have died much earlier. He did not govern, however, and one cannot really know whether he would have done other than Walpole. Bolingbroke the conservative wrote and thought in reactive terms. He seized upon the notion of mixed government because it suited his broader purpose of rejecting Walpole and the new order by attacking the supposed political effects of this new order in language meaningful to the political mind of Augustan England.

PARTY AND OPPOSITION

Bolingbroke's distaste for parties and factions, like his concern with mixed government, was a characteristic feature of Augustan political thought.[47] This disdain was not derived from an individualist philosophy or democratic notions that the Member of Parliament was a delegate of the people, views which prompted later liberal and radical antipathy to party.[48] It was simply that parties, the Augustans felt, pretended to promote the public good, but their real objective was power and prizes. The party man ceased to be a free agent, and, having conceded his own freedom, he was unfit to be trusted with the liberty of the people. Parties confined men's thought in a narrow mold, denying them the liberty of private opinion. The exclusiveness of party was particularly intolerable to men like Halifax, in many ways the archetypal Augustan, who wrote that even "the best party is a kind of conspiracy against the rest of the nation. Like the Jews and the Gentiles, all those are off-scowrings of the world."[49] The most general criticism offered by Augustan writers was that party and faction violated independence. Their image of an ideal Member of Parliament was a holdover from that of Shaftesbury's country party of the preceding century. He should be an independent landed gentleman, free to criticize the executive. This independence was damaged and even ruined when he became a mere puppet whose strings were pulled by the Court, Bank, moneyed companies, or factions and parties. John Toland, the Commonwealthman, described party men as "no longer voluntary agents, but so many Engines merely turned about by a mechanic motion."[50]

The recurring condemnation of faction and party found in Augustan political writings should not blind one, however, to the several instances in the period when party was accepted as inevitable, and indeed useful. In Temple's writings, for example, faction was not seen as an unnatural creation of evil men that could easily be overcome by moral suasion and invocations of national interest. It was, on the contrary, a natural manifestation of discontent among men who disliked their "unequal condition"; it was also a reflection of the "restless humour" inherent in men's temperaments. A half century later the Earl of Egmont similarly wrote of faction as an inevitable development when a difference in income and social level caused some to be discontented.[51] The Aristotelian wisdom of

153

these comments is seen again in Shaftesbury's realistic analysis of faction. He regarded factions and parties as inevitable, albeit unhealthy, developments of the "associating spirit," which, always seeking new social combinations, forms "wheels within wheels" and in political constitutions "one empire within another." A paradoxical situation arose in which sociability led to separateness and selfishness because separate societies within the political society were spawned.

And the associating genius of man is never better proved than in those very societies, which are formed in opposition to the general core of mankind, and to the real interest of the state. In short, the very spirit of faction, for the greatest part, seems to be no other than the abuse or irregularity of that social love and common affection which is natural to mankind.[52]

In Augustan political writing one can even find a defense of the positive value of parties. Walpole's acceptance and justification of party has already been noted. There were also other less biased defenders of party in this period. In the tolerant thought of Toland, who, on most occasions, had only scorn for party, there is found the germ of the defense of party offered by liberals to this day. In 1705 Toland wrote, "a great variety of opinion is a certain sign of a free government," and in 1717 he suggested that all divisions in the state were not in themselves pernicious. Parties in the state were often comparable to heresy in the church, he wrote. "Sometimes they make it better and sometimes they make it worse, but held in their bounds, they always keep it from stagnation." Toland could have found the same notion in Temple, who had written: "a weak or unequal faction, in any state, may serve perhaps to enliven or animate the vigor of a government." Even so staunch an opposition writer as Lyttelton saw the possibility of good in parties. "Parties in society," he wrote, "are like tempests in the natural world; they cause indeed, a very great disturbance, and when violent, tear up everything that opposes them, but then they purge away noxious qualities, and prevent a stagnation which would be fatal."[53]

Augustan praise of faction and party received its most definitive statement by Edward Spelman in 1743. It is found in the preface to his translation of Polybius in which he seeks to apply the wisdom of antiquity to England. "In all free governments there ever were and ever will be parties," he wrote. The free governments in Sparta, Rome, and Athens all had their conflicts between aristocratic and democratic parties, whereas in the despotism of Persia, the only contest was "who should be the greatest slaves."[54] Different understandings, education, and attachments will necessarily produce different ways of thinking, Spelman concludes, that will and should be reflected in different parties in the political world. Should party be extinguished from England, the English, he contends, would become slaves. "Parties, therefore are not only the effect, but the support of liberty." Spelman suggests that the great utility of party is the opposition of one out of power to another in power, which prevents the latter "from pursuing bold measures, which an uncontrolled power might otherwise tempt them to engage in." His image is a fully developed theory of alternative governing parties.

A thirst of power, irritated by disappointments, animates the application of the opposers to public affairs, infinitely more than the languid impulse of national considerations: By this means, they grow able statesmen, and, when they come to be ministers, are not only capable of defending bad schemes, but when they please, of learning good ones . . . Another great advantage that accrues to the people from this opposition is that each party by appealing to them upon all occasions, constitutes them judges of every contest.[55]

In his emphasis on opposition, Spelman's views are quite close to those of Bolingbroke, who allegedly deplored party.

It is, however, as a figure in the more prevalent mood of Augustan political thought that rejected party that Bolingbroke is traditionally read, and with good reason. Both his writings and political program called for an abandonment of irrelevant party distinctions and for the creation of a national government above parties. His position was, of course, a partisan one, determined by the configuration of party politics in his day; still, in his condemnation of parties, Bolingbroke had much to say of a lasting significance.

His description of the decline of seventeenth-century ideological differences between Whig and Tory, which left only conflict over persons and power, anticipates findings of modern British historians.[56] He showed insight in his analysis of both the material and ideal motivations which caused men to unite in party, as his *Letter to Sir William Windham* indicates.[57] And although a recent critic of Bolingbroke has charged that he did not "examine with any penetration the irrational elements in factional strife,"[58] it could be argued that the irrational tendency of parties was actually the basis of Bolingbroke's most interesting and consistent condemnation of party. In the *Remarks on the History of England* he wrote that in parties "prejudices concerning men and things" grew up and were strengthened until they "obtained an uncontrollable influence" over men's conduct. *A Dissertation upon Parties* four years later finds him commenting that the heady atmosphere of parties "can hurry even reasonable men to act on the most absurd, and honest men on the most unjustifiable principles." He suggested in *The Idea of a Patriot King* that one who had not been inside of parties could have no idea that "reason has small effect on members. A turn of imagination, often as violent and as sudden as a gust of wind, determines their conduct."[59] Few men were better qualified to write of the irrational excesses of party than Bolingbroke, minister of the Queen from 1710-1714.

That Bolingbroke was the enemy of party after his fall from power, indeed, that he was the best example of disdain for party among eighteenth-century political writers, is the conventional interpretation of Bolingbroke's writings on party.[60] This interpretation has recently been amended to suggest that Bolingbroke's great disdain for party enunciated in the *Patriot King* was the real inspiration behind Burke's praise of party in his *Considerations Upon Present Discontents*.[61] A challenge has been offered to this traditional view by Professor Kurt Kluxen's study of Bolingbroke.[62] In what can only be described as an intellectual tour de force, Kluxen devotes the largest part of his book to describing Bolingbroke as the great theorist of party. In Kluxen's judgment, Bolingbroke's political thought is rooted in ethical, psychological, and philosophical conceptions, the core of which is the Stoic and Christian image of man's bifurcated personality. This assumption regards reason and passion, social love and private interest, as waging eternal combat within all men. Kluxen suggests that Bolingbroke projects this internal personal conflict onto the body politic where the ethical and psychological battle is waged by political parties. Government parties represent the lower self of the passions, and opposition parties embody the higher self of reason. Kluxen claims that because Bolingbroke saw this internal conflict as the only means by which the personality developed, he considered the conflict of party in the political world necessary, inevitable, and a prerequisite for a moral and harmoniously integrated political community. Bolingbroke's oft repeated disparagement of parties arose, then, from a belief that the Patriot King could internalize the conflict of passions and reason again, and eliminate the necessity for overt party conflict. In his reign, the traditional conflict would be waged within the person of the Patriot King, who would reconcile the two warring psychological factions. Parties could be laid to rest, then, only if a Patriot King were miraculously to arise. But the idea of a Patriot King is doomed to failure, adds Kluxen. Not only has he never risen, but he never can arise. The political community must therefore always externalize the conflict between higher and lower self in political parties—government and opposition. This, Kluxen contends, was really Bolingbroke's message for the eighteenth century, a message, Kluxen holds, relevant for a free world in 1955.[63]

This reading of Bolingbroke's thought in idealist categories, would be quite unrecognizable to Bolingbroke. He did praise reason and disparage the empire of passion in his philosophical writings, but nowhere did he imply this to be relevant to his discussion of parties. Professor Kluxen over-intellectualizes Bolingbroke's political writings, which were much more historically and socially oriented. In the face of all that Bolingbroke has said on social and economic matters in his political works, in *The Craftsman,* in his correspondence, Kluxen asserts that such questions were totally irrelevant in Bolingbroke's political thought, which consists only of philosophical, ethical, and psychological categories.[64] Kluxen's description of Bolingbroke does, however, serve the very useful function of directing attention to a Bolingbroke who is not simply a stereotype of Augustan enmity toward party.

A more modest claim for Bolingbroke's theory of parties could have equally interesting contemporary applications. Bolingbroke's defense of an opposition party whose avowed principle was the transcendence of party is the model for what has come to be the traditional "Tory theory of party." This may help to explain the appeal of his notions to such twentieth-century Tories as George Young, who applied the *Patriot King* to England in the 1930's, and even to R. A. Butler in 1963.[65] In *The Conservative Case,* a detailed exposition of Tory party beliefs, Quintin Hogg describes the Tory party as a national party dedicated to principles, "which stand over and above party affiliations" and thereby opposed to the socialist party, whose class consciousness commits it to one interest within the community.[66] The Tory party claims to be a party embracing all the people and all their interests rather than the self-interest of narrow groups. In Harold Macmillan's words, "The Labour Party is a class party . . . They build on division. We are a national party. We build on unity."[67] This claim is strikingly similar to Bolingbroke's for his opposition party, a party whose ideal motivation was the public transcendence of narrow party affiliations. It can be argued that Bolingbroke found party acceptable if, as his own claimed, it represented the interest and concerns of the nation; whereas the Walpole Whigs, representing the interest of but one class in the community (the financiers and money men) were an unacceptable faction. No doubt the limitation of Hogg's claim is that the transcendence of his party actually represents the interest of the privileged; this limitation can also be charged to Bolingbroke, but it does not destroy his subjective conception of a national party above interest.

Central to the interpretation of Bolingbroke as a Tory theorist of party is the distinction he makes between party and faction. A party, he writes, is a national body "authorized by the voice of the country," whereas a faction is initiated and maintained on the particular prejudices or interests of an exclusive set of men. Bolingbroke described the party transcending party when he described the true country party. "A party thus constituted, is improperly called party. It is the nation, speaking and acting in the discourse and conduct of particular men." Quintin Hogg could not improve upon this as a statement of the Tory conception of party. Bolingbroke had only words of praise for the country party that effected the Revolution, for its interests were the nation's. "But this national party degenerated soon into factions; that is, the national interest became soon a secondary and subservient motive." Government, he wrote, is carried on by two sets of men. Those who combine to seek their own narrow interests or the interests of segments of the community are properly labelled factions; those who seek a national interest beyond their own are properly called parties. But, writes Bolingbroke, if one insists on calling them all parties, one must find some other way to distinguish them, "and nothing can be more reasonable than to admit the nominal division of constitutionalists and anti-constitutionalists."[68] Such are, he writes, the parties of Walpole's day, although it would be preferable to call the former a party and the latter a faction.

That the Patriot King should espouse no party and his government should be above parties is in fact a statement of the Tory view, found in the writings of Disraeli, Randolph Churchill, and Hogg, that Tory government is not party government, but service to the entire nation "over and above party affiliations." Interesting in this light is Sir Hugh Cecil's observation that George III, far from being an opponent of party government, "was as no other King of this country has ever been; he was a party leader." He, not Bolingbroke, Cecil suggests, revived the Tory party.[69] When a Patriot King rules, Bolingbroke contends, and the opposition is in power, "he will distinguish the voice of his people from the clamor of a faction, and will hearken to it;"[70] there will be national government above party. When Tories of today are out of power, they contend that faction governs in the guise of particular class interests; the national party is the opposition. The same held true in the eighteenth century; Walpole's government was considered factious by Bolingbroke, and his own Opposition the true national party.

After both the Glorious Revolution and Bolingbroke had cleared the air of seventeenth-century Tory notions, Bolingbroke set forth the Tory theory of party that still holds today. Essential to this continuity has been the perpetual confrontation of the status quo by demands for change. Bolingbroke and his Opposition represented groups in the community resisting change and assaults on their power. In their reaction they wrapped themselves in the cloak of the nation to distinguish themselves from those who sought change and whom they described as seeking only narrow interests. The truly national party was the status quo party above narrow interests; its opponents were labelled factious. This is still the characteristic Tory reflex to which Mr. Hogg bears witness; contemporary Tories merely call class what Bolingbroke called narrow interest. The national party, wrote Bolingbroke, concerned with the entire community, was the constitutional party, and the factious and self-interested were the anti-constitutionalists. This distinction helps to explain the hold of Bolingbroke's theory of party on Tory thought. Bolingbroke's rule for determining which was a national party and which a factious one survives in Quintin Hogg's Tory ethos.

The sole question will therefore be, which was the factious side? Now to determine this, we need only inquire, which side was for usurping on the other; which was for preserving and which for altering the established constitution of government.[71]

When one turns from his general thoughts on party to Bolingbroke's specific defense of opposition, one sees clearly that he did make an important contribution to the development of constitutional thought. He based his justification of opposition on the assumption that power and authority are "bewitching and enchanting things" which make those who possess them "giddy and wanton." Individuals in power as well as ministries must be checked by an opposition ever eager to call notice to the misuse of power. "Liberty cannot be long secure, in any country, unless a personal jealousy watches over it."[72]

The theory of opposition is developed in Bolingbroke's *A Letter on the Spirit of Patriotism,* written when he sensed that the more ambitious members of his coalition were ready to bolt the cause. Opposition, he writes, is a duty, not an adventure, and must be undertaken seriously and steadily. The opposition is the supporter of good, and controller of bad government, the guardian of public liberty. Bolingbroke refers specifically to "an opposing party," whose task it is to "oppose systematically a wise to a silly, an honest to an iniquitous, scheme of government."[73] Nearly eighty years before John Cam Hobhouse coined the phrase "His Majesty's Opposition," Bolingbroke described Parliament as divided into two parties: a government party and an opposition party.[74] Every member of Parliament, he wrote, is appointed to promote good and oppose bad government, "and if not vested with the power of a minister of state, yet vested with the superior power of controlling those who are appointed such by the crown . . ."[75] Even more striking is Bolingbroke's description of this opposition party as one capable of being a possible alternative to the one in power.

They who engage in opposition, are under as great obligations to prepare themselves to control, as they who serve the crown are under to prepare themselves to carry on, the administration: . . . a party, formed for this purpose, do not act like good citizens, nor honest men, unless they propose true, as well as oppose false measures of government.[76]

The opposition party must systematically contrast on every occasion the policy that the public interest dictates with that presented by the prince and his ministers. But it must also propose alternative programs, for "opposition, should be a system of conduct likewise, an opposite, but not a dependent system."[77]

Before any theory of opposition could be assimilated into the British constitution, a clear distinction had to be made between opposing the king and opposing his ministers. This Bolingbroke did by suggesting that the king is an essential aspect of the constitution but his ministers are merely parts of the government. To criticize the king would be an unconstitutional act, but to criticize the government is justified. This required that Bolingbroke further distinguish between the government and the constitution, which he did in *A Dissertation upon Parties*. A constitution is the totality of laws, institutions, and customs that "compose the general system, according to which the community hath agreed to be governed"; whereas a government is merely the "particular tenor of conduct" by which magistrates administer public affairs. The task of the opposition, then, is to guarantee that the governors actually do govern at any particular time "as they ought to govern at all times." The opposition is to judge the actions of the government by the criterion of the constitution.[78] These views anticipate the nineteenth-century theory that the opposition is the watchdog and safeguard of the constitution against rash actions of the government.

Archibald Foord, historian of His Majesty's Opposition, insists correctly that Bolingbroke's partisan vision would not have allowed for an opposition as an enduring and beneficent institution.[79] But Bolingbroke's theoretical justification for his own Opposition and his labored distinction between government and constitution laid much of the foundation for what would later become the theory of His Majesty's Opposition. In the realm of practice Bolingbroke's party also made significant contributions to the institutionalization of the opposition. As Walpole's long tenure helped institutionalize the notion of "the" minister, so Bolingbroke's activity over so long a period led to the frequent appearance of the phrase, "the" opposition.

Other features of what would become the traditional practice of the opposition first appeared in these years. Bolingbroke's parliamentary forces, for example, consistently sat on the left of the speaker, the leading orators on the lower benches across from the government bench. This practice may have arisen simply because the leaders wanted good seats and therefore came early, or because these seats provided a good vantage point from which to face and challenge Walpole. In any case, after 1734 the Opposition spokesmen in different areas sat across from the relevant minister and directed their comments to "the gentleman across the way."[80]

Walpole's writers, as one might expect, criticized Bolingbroke's theory of opposition. In April 1734, *The London Journal* attacked his distinction between government and constitution and repeated its familiar charge that the Opposition was really a treasonous attack on George II. What annoyed the *Journal* most was Bolingbroke's call for a continued, persistent, and systematic opposition. The belief that opposition was permanently justified simply because "it keeps them in awe and upon their guard is as immoral a proposition as ever was advanced." The *Journal,* however, could not completely forget its own Whig principles, so on occasion its anger was tempered: "I affirmed in my last that opposition was necessary in a free government, and was the child of liberty; and so it is, but methinks the child should not always be crying."[81]

Even after Walpole's defeat, Bolingbroke urged the Opposition to continue its work, writing that, "to reform the state, therefore is and ought to be, the object of your opposition, as well as to reform the administration."[82] It was more than Walpole that he opposed. Others might join the new government, but in his opinion opposition was still needed. Bolingbroke's position appeared in a series of pamphlets written in 1743 to answer Egmont's claim that opposition was no longer justified.[83] These pamphlets demanded that opposition to the political and social order of the money men continue. One by one grievances were reviewed—debt, gentry hardship, stockjobbers, the large number of government officers, moneyed companies, social and political upstarts, bought and bribed commoners. One anonymous writer, after surveying the long list of socioeconomic grievances that still persisted, concluded:

The principles of the opposition itself are perfectly just and everlastingly the same. An opposition aims at a change of measures, and not of men, and therefore is never in a greater probability of succeeding when such as compose it are bound to each other than by no other tie than that of sameness of sentiment . . . We have examined the grounds and reasons of the Opposition. We have considered the nature of those things of which we complain independent of their relation to ourselves, and we have seen that they are real and not imaginary evils; that they are productive of ruinous consequences.[84]

### THE PATRIOT KING: MACHIAVELLI AND THE HUMANIST PRINCE

Bolingbroke's remedy for these "real and not imaginary evils" so "productive of ruinous consequences" is found in *The Idea of a Patriot King,* the summation of his political writings and career. A corrupt people could be reformed only by a great man who ruled alone, above all factions and parties. Only in this way could a degenerate constitution be returned to its lost virtue. Bolingbroke had read his Machiavelli carefully.[85]

Felix Rabb's recent study, though concerned with an earlier period, speculates quite accurately that Machiavelli's influence on Bolingbroke and other Augustan political writers was considerable. However, a new feature was visible in Machiavelli's Augustan face. In the sixteenth century, Englishmen could be found who were impressed because Machiavelli avoided questions of ultimate justification and limited theology to one sphere and politics to another. Some seventeenth-century Englishmen were impressed by Machiavelli's discussion of the autonomy of politics, his realism, his description of politics as a rational pursuit of power; others in that century were impressed by Machiavelli's republicanism and his attachment to the classical mixed constitution.[86] Bolingbroke and Augustan writers, however, read Machiavelli in a new light, as a theorist of corruption and regeneration.

The vogue of Machiavelli in Augustan England extended beyond Bolingbroke and Hume. He was favorably cited by countless pamphleteers, journalists, and minor writers. The anonymous author of *An Essay Towards the Ruin of Great Britain* invoked Machiavelli in his diatribe against the South Sea Bubble, which he thought was an external calamity that might return English government to its true principles.[87] Another writer used Machiavelli in a tract on the Peerage Bill in 1719 to describe mixed government's superior stability and resistance to the inevitable degenerative cycle.[88] Bolingbroke's newspaper waxed warm and cold about Machiavelli. It could on one occasion write, "some have learned well from their mischievous master Machiavelli how to suppress while leaving the appearance of Freedom"; or on another write that the *Prince,* was written by "one of the best writers upon Politicks."[89] On one occasion *The Craftsman* suggested that Machiavelli's vivid picture of political cynicism and naked power was intended to frighten men into the proper pursuit of liberty and morality. The issue of October 5, 1734, contains a letter from one Nicolo Machiavelli, who describes the European scene from his vantage point in the nether world. Contained in the defense of his writings is an allusion to Walpole.

For though I have been represented as a Patron of arbitrary power, my writings are witnesses to the contrary, when thoroughly understood, and prove me a much better friend to the cause of liberty than some noisy Pretenders amongst you, who have actually reduced into practice most of these rules, which I designed only as scarecrows, and to paint tyranny in the blackest colors; but the world seems to be now pretty well satisfied as to that point, and hath already begun to do me Justice.[90]

Even Walpole's *London Journal* wrote favorably of Machiavelli as the theorist of regeneration. He had taught, the paper contended, that "we must bring things back to their original standard for all things gather rust by time . . . it is necessary once in an age or two, to make a noble stand and bring governments back to their first principles."[91] This, Walpole's paper proudly proclaimed, had been accomplished in 1688; thus it rejected the Opposition thesis that such a rejuvenation was still needed.

Dr. Charles Davenant, one of the era's keenest Machiavellians, introduced the basic theme of Machiavelli's thought as the Augustans applied it, the *ritorno ai principii*. If the body politic is to be long-lived, perhaps even immortal, Davenant wrote, its youth must be renewed. It must be returned to the principles upon which it was first founded. The Machiavellian image of the great man reformer found in Bolingbroke's *Patriot King* was clearly envisioned by Davenant.

This deep statesman, Machiavelli, has a saying in another place well worthy of eternal remembrance; that the Prince who aims at glory and reputation in the world, should desire a government where the manners of his subjects are corrupted and depraved not to subvert and destroy it like Caesar, but to rectify and restore it like Romulus; than which the heavens cannot confer, nor man propose to himself a greater honour.[92]

Davenant believed, as did Machiavelli, that his contemporaries needed to recapture the spirit of public service illustrated by the Romans. The English economist even repeated Machiavelli's praise of Numa, who perceived the importance of religion as an agent to inculcate this virtue of public service.[93] Walter Moyle, an Augustan Commonwealthman, similarly cited Machiavelli in his *An Essay upon the Constitution of the Roman Government*, which was written as an attack on constitutional developments in the England of his day. Machiavelli used Roman experience to awaken his Italian contemporaries. Part of his popularity with Augustan writers lay in their efforts to do the same for their corrupt society.

Machiavel, and other modern writers of politics, lay down for a certain maxim, that commonwealths cannot subsist, unless they are frequently renewed by their magistrates either by reviving the reverence and terror of their laws, or by restoring the ancient virtue and disciplines or by a thorough reformation of those corruptions and disorders which the depravity of human nature will introduce.[94]

John Trenchard of *Cato's Letters* was another Augustan impressed with the wise Florentine. "The great authority Machiavel tells us that no government can long subsist but by recurring often to its first principles."[95] In a pamphlet of 1720, Trenchard described George I as a great man at the head of a corrupted people, who would have the honor of restoring their virtue and reforming their constitution.[96] Machiavelli's Italian prince was thus transformed into an English king nineteen years before Bolingbroke transformed him into Prince Fred.

The degree to which Bolingbroke was influenced by Machiavelli reflects, therefore, a tendency typical of his age. Machiavelli's appeal to Bolingbroke lay partly in his championship of mixed government, but primarily in his classical preoccupation with corruption and decline. He was the major theorist of decline, preoccupied, as was Bolingbroke, with Roman and contemporary models of corrupt and declining society. Against threatening corruption, it is Machiavelli's *ritorno ai principii* that Bolingbroke urges. He could recognize in his England the familiar features of decay that Machiavelli had described in the sixteenth-century Italian Republics. Like Rome in its declining days, Italy was overcome with corruption, a disease embodied both in a spirit of luxury and the failure of public spirit. Religion had failed to offer a positive inducement to public spirit, and the individual cared little for the general welfare. Machiavelli's writings were rooted in the deadening of political consciousness and declining participation in politics of the old civic ruling class of his day. The degeneration of public spirit was symbolized by the demise of the militia and its replacement by mercenaries who fought for gain, not for love of city.[97] Much of the Opposition's criticism of the standing army in eighteenth-century England came from just such an idealization of the militiaman as a public-spirited citizen. For one writer of this era, the creation of a national militia seemed the only way a corrupt England could be saved from the fate of Rome. Selfish Englishmen beset by a lust for gain could recapture their public spirit only through an extensive militia which would effect a national rebirth.[98]

Machiavelli saw but one effective remedy for such a corrupt people, and even that was destined to failure if the people were totally corrupt. They must renew and renovate, bring back their constitution to its original precepts. It is conceivable, Machiavelli wrote, that such a return could be brought about by calamitous external blows, and the essayist on the South Sea Bubble thought so too. In general, however, Machiavelli, and Bolingbroke after him, thought that reform could come only from an internal development like the emergence of a great man, a creative political architect who builds and repairs states. Such a prince, guided only by the intention to promote the public good, could rescue a corrupt people.[99]

Bolingbroke did not accept all of Machiavelli's teachings. He could see no value in factions as Machiavelli had, nor did he share the Florentine's negative views on landed gentlemen. But the most significant area in which Bolingbroke's thought differs from Machiavelli's is in the explanation of the political decline and corruption that preoccupied them both. Machiavelli saw the roots of decline inherent in human nature and its inevitable tendency, shared with all things, to degenerate unless periodically rejuvenated.[100] Bolingbroke, however, like Harrington, thought corruption a product, not of some invariable human nature, but of the social and economic structure of society.[101] He diagnosed the corruption of Walpole's England not in terms of man's spirit, but in the structural terms of his condition. He differed from Machiavelli in this respect; that is, he differed in all his writings except the *Patriot King*.

In this, his most famous work, he abandoned Harrington and accepted the humanism of Machiavelli. To this extent, the *Patriot King* constitutes his great failure: its humanist solution remains futile before the inexorable economic and political developments that he himself had so ably described. Nothing can really be done to rescue England, if its salvation demands a *"deus ex fortuna."*

The freedom of a constitution, writes Bolingbroke in the *Patriot King,* rests on two foundations; the "orders" of the community— the "different classes and assemblies of men, with different powers and privileges"—and the "spirit and character of the people."[102] The Patriot King who seeks to reform a corrupt people in order to reestablish a free constitution will not alter the powers and privileges of the orders and classes, for this would cause too great a shock to the body politic, and, moreover, it would be impossible in a corrupt commonwealth. His methods must be moral, not political. The reforming Patriot King must be a humanist prince who influences by his moral example, and not a political reformer who deals with classes, powers, and privileges.

> To preserve liberty by new laws and new schemes of government, whilst the corruption of a people continues and grows, is absolutely impossible: but to restore and preserve it under old laws, and an old constitution, by reinfusing into the minds of men the spirit of this constitution, is not only possible, but is, in a particular manner, easy to a King.[103]

The Patriot King, whose own moral example and virtue alone will return the body politic to its lost liberty and true principles, is "the most powerful of all reformers" who can renew the spirit of liberty in people's minds. "Under him they [his people] will not only cease to do evil, but learn to do well." Overnight, "a new people will seem to arise with a new King." The Patriot King will perform several positive deeds; he will dismiss corrupt advisers, rule without party, and choose virtuous patriots to govern with him. No more than this is outlined, however, no new policy, no specific reforms.[104] The moral example of this humanist Prince is all that is required to restore the political and social balance of class and privilege which had been corrupted and destroyed over the past half-century.

As soon as a Patriot King is raised to the throne, the panacea is applied; the spirit of the constitution revives of course; and, as fast as it revives, the orders and form of the constitution are restored to their primitive integrity.

In this, his penultimate argument, Bolingbroke abandoned his Harringtonian insight into the structural changes in English society—that change in the balance of property was the root of hateful corruption. Like Machiavelli, Bolingbroke, in the *Patriot King*, regards political degeneration as inevitable in all systems, regardless of their structural uniqueness.

Absolute stability is not to be expected in anything human . . . The best instituted governments, like the best constituted animal bodies, carry in them the seeds of their destruction: and, though they grow and improve for a time, they will soon tend visibly to their dissolution.[105]

Bolingbroke's prescription for regeneration in the *Patriot King* assumed that degeneration is caused by a decline in virtue; he assumed a moral change rather than the institutional change he had himself diagnosed. Convinced of the prospects for moral reform through an exemplary Patriot King, Bolingbroke devoted the last pages of his essay to a minute description of the desirable private and public character of this King. He outlined his proper education, upbringing, and social dealings, all of which were designed to make him a "great and good man." Bolingbroke's retreat into humanism is completed when he offers a "mirror for princes," an "education for a Christian Prince," a "book for governors."[106] With this minute description of princely deportment, the *Patriot King* also becomes the most ludicrous example of Bolingbroke's insistence on the theatrical image of politics over the administrative image. How appropriate, then, that the essay ends by invoking that greatest and most dazzling of all political actors—Elizabeth.

The *Patriot King*, the great testament of Bolingbroke's Opposition, explains and bears witness to the movement's failure. In all his writings he attributed the rise of corruption and the passing of the ideal order to the social and economic changes in England since the Revolution, yet here he suggests that the only way to reestablish the ideal order is the moral example and theatrical deportment of a humanist prince. Bolingbroke, because of his humanist obsession with morality, example, and the just ruler, befuddled his institutional insights. His cause was doomed to failure by more than the death of Frederick. By the middle of the eighteenth century it is even doubtful whether political action could have restored the past; but there is no doubt that the old order could not have been recaptured by humanist methods and aesthetic performances. Bolingbroke's humanist Prince was a hopeless anachronism in the England of 1749. The month *The Patriot King* was published, Horace Walpole peremptorily dismissed "the absurdity and impracticality of this kind of system."[107]

### BOLINGBROKE AND THE RADICAL THEORY OF REPRESENTATION

Horace Walpole's father had often labelled Bolingbroke a radical in the course of their many disagreements. By the end of the century English radicals did, in fact, look upon Bolingbroke with great favor and continually cited his texts. His history, emphasizing lost Saxon freedoms, fitted well into radical historical notions. Like the radicals, he, too, was a critic of the government of eighteenth-century England; much of his nostalgia for the simple, more virtuous past could appeal to the republicanism of Georgian radicals. Much of what Bolingbroke had said of Walpole could be said of George III, Lords Bute and North—and it was.[108] Moreover, Bolingbroke had the unmistakable attraction to the radicals at the end of the century of having been the century's most famous critic of parliamentary corruption.

One interesting radical use of Bolingbroke was that made by the London Society for Constitutional Information. The Society, whose members included John Cartwright, Thomas Hollis, John Jebb, Capell Lofft, Richard Price, and Horne Tooke, circulated "minutes" which consisted of extracts from "lovers of freedom" chosen on approval by two thirds of the membership. In June 1782, Lofft included in these radical papers of correspondence a lengthy quotation from Bolingbroke's *Dissertation upon Parties*. The radicals saw Bolingbroke as the democrat attacked in Walpole's press. The extract from this "lover of liberty" dealt with the failure of government after the Revolution to accomplish the great design of 1688.

The benefit was not secured to us. The just expectation of the nation could not be answered unless the freedom of elections, and the frequency, integrity and independency of Parliaments were sufficiently provided for. These are the essentials of British liberty . . . Nor does the security of our liberty consist only in frequent sessions of Parliament; but it consists

likewise in frequent new Parliaments. The plain intent and scheme of
our constitution provides that the representatives of the people should
have frequent opportunity to communicate together about national
grievances and to obtain the redress of them; and that people should
have frequent opportunities of calling their representatives to account,
as it were, for the discharge of the trust committed to them, and of
approving or disapproving of their conduct by electing or not electing
them anew.[109]

There was more of Bolingbroke in the Society's minutes. One of
its weekly letters predicted the fate of Rome for England because
of the contagion that accompanied excessive prosperity. "That contagion has long been circulating in secret through this devoted land
corroding the vitals of the constitution." Luxury and avarice have
led "to a contempt for the virtuous simplicity of ancient manners."
This new commercial age has "a multiplicity of laws, contrary to
the principles of a free government." Accompanying this radical
evocation of Bolingbroke's nostalgia for a simpler society and
government there is an echo of the *Patriot King.* "The executive
power has been clogged and encumbered and deprived of that
energy which is necessary to maintain the honor and safety of the
nation." Party government, wrote the anonymous radical correspondent, has forced the King to have recourse to corruption.
Ministerial influence has only bad effects on the constitutional structure, but Royal prerogative, wrote the Society spokesman, "is part
of the law and the constitution and is necessary to give energy
and vigor to the state." A monarch should be above parties and
above ministers, both of which "impede every national effort."[110]
For a time, at least, this radical Society saw some hope for reform
in the Crown, if only the Crown were not hampered by the two
modern innovations of party and prime minister.

Bolingbroke's appeal to the radicals is illustrated again in Richard
Price's essay on the national debt written in 1771, in which there is,
woven into his lengthy prophecy of England's ruin from this
monstrous burden, an attack on Walpole and praise for his "Patriot"
Opposition.[111] Not only had Walpole raided the Sinking Fund, but
he had also instituted the practice of using the fund and its offices
to corrupt Parliament and the entire nation. Against these abuses
Bolingbroke's patriots had appealed, Price wrote, but to no avail,
and these evils still beset the nation. Bolingbroke, the great antago-

nist of the evil Walpole, emerges the hero, albeit an unsuccessful one. Bolingbroke's fate was a unique one. At the end of the century he was consulted by both of Burke's enemies, the King and the radicals. No wonder Burke had so little love for the enemy of Walpole.[112]

That Bolingbroke and his Opposition appeared to later radicals with a radical face is neither surprising nor difficult to reconcile with his basic conservatism. Part of the ideological dynamic of his politics was "populist," even though an early and most aristocratic populist manifestation, and inherent in populism is a force at once intensely radical and reactionary. It is always "the people," be they yeoman farmers, urban small traders, or failing gentry who are being victimized by the small conspiratorial financial interests. In Bolingbroke's view, these conspirators had captured the government; the King, ministers, and legislature spoke at their bidding. Bolingbroke's Opposition inevitably took on a popular tone in its perpetual plaint that the government and its ministers and legislature were alienated from the people, the true source of power. There was, of course, much more to Bolingbroke's Opposition than this. What concerned him particularly was that the conspiracy of government and vested interest had removed "the people's" natural leadership from power. In defending the one, however, he often had to defend the other; for "the people" and the aristocratic leadership faced the same enemy.

In opposing the middle class and its liberal and capitalist order, there was a natural alliance between the interests of the aristocracy and those of "the people." John Gay of Bolingbroke's circle could write *The Beggar's Opera* from the right, but it could be used with few changes by Berthold Brecht two centuries later, for the left.

In accounting for Bolingbroke's radical aspect one must also add the English spirit of his "Tory radicalism" that would so impress Disraeli. Bolingbroke recognized in the 1730's that a tactical alliance with the people could further conservative objectives. The Tories could exploit the substantial sympathy with their outlook found among the deferential masses. The city mob in the early eighteenth century was, although not overtly Jacobite, certainly easy prey to Tory manipulation. The London workers and tradesmen who flocked to Atterbury's Jacobite fold in 1722 have been immortalized by Hogarth, who showed them displaying their reactionary and xenophobic politics.[113] Understandably, then, both Lyttelton and Bolingbroke's *Craftsman* spoke out against and demanded the repeal of the Riot Act, which, although it throttled the political activity of the mob, had been continually defended by the Whigs since the crisis of 1715.[114] A political program that had at its center a sentimental longing for a golden past and good Queen Bess could easily appeal to the popular elements in the community. So for reasons both of ideological dynamics and strategic considerations Bolingbroke would often appear the radical.

But Bolingbroke was no true radical, no more than Disraeli, who in 1831, as a young man of twenty-seven was turning to Bolingbroke's writings. On the surface they both wore radical masks, but in their innermost thoughts they cherished sweet memories of a nobler and simpler age that had been forever lost. Only to the extent that some figures of the English radical tradition also sought that golden age before capitalism can Bolingbroke seem a bedfellow of the radicals. Otherwise it is clear that his radical positions were merely partisan whips with which to lash the political practice of the Robinocracy, as befitted a noble defender of the people against ministerial oppression.

It was just such a situation which prompted the principal manifestation of what might be called Bolingbroke's radical views. He took the position of champion of the people in the debate with Walpole on the nature of representation that emerged from the excise crisis of the early 1730's.

The radical theory that the representative was a delegate of his constituents, which Bolingbroke espoused, has roots deep in the medieval constitution. As far back as the fourteenth century the notion that the representative acted as an attorney for his constituents' interest can be found. This view of the Member of Parliament was revived in the constitutional crisis of the seventeenth century, when freeholders sent many instructions to those whom they considered their delegates in the Commons. Another example of this practice is found in Andrew Marvell's correspondence with his constituents in the corporation of Hull. Marvell wrote the corporation in 1670: "What is your opinion at Hull of the Bill from the Lords for general naturalization of all foreigners that shall take the oaths of allegiance and supremacy?"[115] In 1681, Shaftesbury actually circulated a form of instructions suitable for use by county constituencies in instructing their representatives on exclusion. This conception of the representative's role would be central to later eighteenth-century radical thought, but in the interim its principal champions were Bolingbroke and his Opposition.

Burke's theory of representation had an equally long tradition behind it. Coke, in his *Institutes of the Laws of England*, wrote, "though one be chosen for one particular county or borough, yet when he is returned, and sits in Parliament, he serveth for the whole realm."[116] In the century and a half that separated Coke and Burke, Walpole's theorists were the most consistent supporters of this view. When they objected to instructions and "commands" ordering Members of Parliament to oppose the Excise Bill, Walpole's writers were objecting to the theory of representation implied by such "commands," a theory they thought radical, democratic, and because it would increase the power of the people a threat to the mixed constitution. Walpole's theorists rejected the Opposition's juxtaposition of the people and Parliament and the radical inference that the people had the supreme authority. In 1734, *The London Journal* wrote: "What enormous nonsense is this. The King is to know no voice of the people, but by their representatives; the Parliament is the only voice of the Nation he is to hearken to."[117] To refute such radical and democratic nonsense, *The London Journal* called upon the authority of the great Whig and republican hero, Algernon Sidney whose *Discourse concerning Government* contained views similar to Coke's and Walpole's theories. The *Journal* quoted Sidney's comments:

> Every county does not make a distinct body, having in itself a sovereign power, but is a member of that Great Body which comprehends the whole NATION. 'Tis not therefore for Kent or Suffix, Lewes or Maidstone, but for the whole nation, that the members chosen for those places, are sent to serve in Parliament . . . they are not strictly and properly obliged to give an account of their actions to any, unless the whole Body of the Nation for which they serve could be assembled.[118]

Bolingbroke, whose partisan interests were well served by the people's claim to instruct their representatives against the excise scheme, adhered to the delegate theory. Thus, *The Craftsman*, objecting to *The London Journal's* attacks on the application of the constituencies to their representatives answered

There may be cases put, where the very best things be turned to an ill use, but instructions from corporations have been, and may be, of singular use to the cause of liberty, on some important occasions.[119]

Bolingbroke's newspaper asked the *Journal* "whether the members of the House of Commons are the people's representatives or not; and whether, unlike all other deputies and trustees, they are absolutely independent of their principals and constituents." *The Craftsman's* position was founded more firmly on medieval precedent than on any democratic instincts such as would prompt the London Society for Constitutional Information, but later radicals also accepted the medieval argument. Parliaments, *The Craftsman* wrote, were formerly called on particular emergencies of state, at which time the people were informed of the problem for which the Parliament was called, "and therefore were enabled to acquaint the elected with their sense of the matter, before they came to town." Should anything unexpected occur during the sitting, the Commoners usually "desired leave to consult their constituents, before they came to any resolutions." *The Craftsman* was not above drawing upon the radical strain in Locke to prove its point. Like the later radicals, it did not hesitate to confront Parliament with the extraparliamentary political community.

The community says he [Locke] perpetually retains a supreme power of saving themselves from the attempts and designs of any body, even of their legislators, whenever they shall be so foolish, or so wicked as to lay and carry on designs against the liberties and properties of the subject.[120]

*The Craftsman* proclaimed itself the champion of such a community, whose members had sense and virtue; whereas Walpole, it wrote, considered the common people "stupid, dregs and vulgar."[121] The marriage of mob and gentleman was sanctified by their common opposition to Walpole, his excise, and his world.

The debate on the nature of representation was revived in an even more bitter exchange during the last years of Walpole's rule and immediately after his fall. The positions were the same: Bolingbroke's Opposition upheld the right of constituents to instruct their delegates; Walpole and the Government Whigs denounced this as a radical innovation destructive of the balance of government. The historical props for this second stage of the debate were the many petitions and instructions sent to Members of Parliament demanding a declaration of war against Spain, and, once war had been declared, the continuation of war grants. There were also instructions calling for place bills, triennial parliaments, and an investigation into Walpole's financial manipulations. As in the later Wilkes affair, the center of popular agitation from 1739 to 1743 was the corporations of Westminster and London, although instructions on the war often came from merchants in interested cities such as Bristol.

Lord Egmont's Government tract, *Faction Detected by the Evidence of the Facts*, criticized the Opposition's radical tactics. A small misguided group in Westminster, he wrote, had drawn up instructions to their Members of Parliament. "This notion of it being the duty of every M.P. to vote in every instance as his constituents should direct him is a thing in the highest degree absurd." It is a fundamental change from the constitution which presumes "that no man, after he is chosen, is to consider himself as a member for any particular place, but as a representative for the whole nation."[122] The Opposition's principle, he wrote, would alter the constitution, making it into a democracy. The people were erroneously setting themselves up as superior to the whole legislature and attempting to resume that vague and loose authority that all peoples who enter into political society "divest themselves of and delegate for ever from themselves."[123] The Opposition's attitude made the representative a mere creature of the people, as among the Dutch. (At last the Government was able to accuse the Opposition of importing evil Dutch practices!) The Government newspaper, *The Daily Gazetteer*, added in 1742 that instructions to Members left representative government totally uncertain and chaotic. The Government's views were thoroughly compatible with those of Burke, who would later react to similar radical demands.

But surely a representative is one who stands in the place of another, with power to act for that other as if he, or if he represents more, as if they were present, and acting for themselves. Yet instructions quite alter the case, and from a representative make such a member a mere deputy, governed by other folks' sentiments which nothing in our constitution warrants, and which the whole frame of it tacitly condemns.[124]

In the renewed debate of 1739 to 1743, the Opposition once again sponsored the delegate theory of representation. In *The Craftsman* and in the same set of pamphlets that had answered Egmont's attack on the continuation of the Opposition, the people's case was defended from the criticism of the establishment Whig government. One might have expected that Bolingbroke's view that his Opposition was a national party above sectional interests would conflict with this endorsement of local constituency pressure, but a reconciliation was not difficult. It could be argued simply that the views of the people when they instructed their local M.P.'s reflected the consensus of the nation, and opposed the narrower views of the Government, which was now in the hands of the moneyed interest. Bolingbroke's endorsement of this radical concept of the representative can further be explained by the concept's affinity to traditional Tory notions of a state that was functional and corporate, where all interests received their representation; an idea which, like Bolingbroke's image of a national party, is no stranger to twentieth-century Tory thought.[125]

One Opposition pamphlet answered Egmont by denying that the people, in originally divesting themselves of power to their representatives, ever intended "to delegate it forever from themselves." It proceeded to attack the Government's view that the people had obtained too much power by quoting Bolingbroke's *Remarks on the History of England* to the effect that the people had had more freedom in Saxon England.[126] *The Craftsman*, still the leading spokesman for the Opposition, commented in 1739 that "the collective body of the people have a right to petition or instruct their representatives in answer to the ministerial writers who have laboured the contrary." Has not any man, it asked, "a just right to instruct his attorney, trustee, delegate, representative, or by what ever other name he may be called, in all points relating to his interests"? Surely, no man in his right senses "would continue such a person in his trust, if he refused to follow his directions, or acted contrary to them." *The Craftsman* was adamant in its insistence that such practices had had a hallowed place in the medieval constitution. Three years later it wrote: "The claim of the people to instruct their representatives is no novelty, and their right to do it was never called in question before."[127]

Several decades before the debate between Burke and the radicals on the people's role in instructing their representatives, the same battle was waged between Walpole's Whigs and Bolingbroke's

Opposition. From Burke's later comments on these events at the end of Walpole's reign it is evident how disturbed he was by the precedent they seemed to establish for popular control of political decisions. He was convinced that the Opposition, the poets, and the mob had forced Walpole and his party government into a war they did not desire.[128] One more item had been added to the list of Burke's objections to Bolingbroke. Not only was he the great enemy of organized religion and parties, but he was also a radical. That Burke saw only this radical dimension of Bolingbroke's thought helps explain his *Vindication of Natural Society*, the earliest of Burke's political works, which rails against Bolingbroke's thought as a radical and utopian scheme to do away with government and authority. Burke, who should have known better, saw Bolingbroke simply as a radical.[129] Burke may have been prompted by wishful thinking to ask "Who now reads Bolingbroke?"

### BOLINGBROKE ON ENGLISH HISTORY

The Bolingbroke and Walpole forces were engaged in another significant debate in the 1730's that helped endear Bolingbroke to radicals later in the century.[130] Herbert Butterfield has written that "one man in the eighteenth century wrote essays so full of the song of liberty that he has been called the founder of the Whig interpretation; yet he was none other than the politician Bolingbroke, notorious in his day and ever since as the wildest and wickedest of Tories."[131]

Bolingbroke, in his *Remarks on the History of England* and *A Dissertation upon Parties*, revived seventeenth-century common law and Whig notions of an ancient constitution with immemorial free institutions. The *History*, written in 1730, provided the opening statement in the five-year debate that raged between the Walpole and Bolingbroke camps. It was followed in 1734 by the *Dissertation*, which renewed opposition to Walpole's "Tory" historians. Though the bulk of the debate was carried on in newspaper articles in 1734 and 1735, the initial spark was struck by these two works of Bolingbroke's, which, it must be remembered, first appeared weekly, in the pages of *The Craftsman*.

In his *Remarks on the History of England*, Bolingbroke's prose on the continuity of English freedom was no less exalted than that of any seventeenth-century Whig. He found the roots of English freedom in the original British and Saxon constitutions. In the Saxon constitution, he wrote, the "supreme power centered in the Witenagemot, composed of the king, the lords, and the Saxon freemen, that original sketch of a British Parliament." The people had had great power in the democratic Saxon commonwealth, "and these principles prevailed through all subsequent changes." As for William the Conqueror, "neither he nor they [his two sons] could destroy the old Constitution."[132] Not only could they not extinguish the old spirit of liberty, they were in fact inspired and seized by it themselves. For Bolingbroke, the Magna Carta represented a milestone in the people's watchful protection of the spirit of liberty, a victory for the continuity of Saxon freedoms. The middle ages, in Bolingbroke's history, was a stage upon which the people continually defended the spirit of freedom against kings, barons, and clergy. Some kings were good and furthered these free institutions while others opposed them; the total freedom varied according to the political developments of each reign.

Bolingbroke's Harringtonian perception of the rise of the Commons under the Tudors and his general preference for the Elizabethan Age and its balance—which Harrington did not share—did not interfere with his belief in immemorial popular freedom residing in a representative body of commoners. To be sure, Henry VIII's actions had given the Commons great power, but only such as it had enjoyed formerly. Tudor constitutional arrangements returned the English "to the principles of government which had prevailed amongst our Saxon ancestors."[133] Although the power of the Commons had declined under the Norman and subsequent dynasties, it was never extinct; under the Tudors it was merely revitalized in full Saxon measure.

Week after week during this five-year period, Bolingbroke's *Craftsman* defended the theory of the ancient constitution from the history proposed by Walpole's publicists, a "novel and pernicious doctrine, first advanced by the Tories, and since adopted by our modern Whigs, that liberty is not our ancient inheritance but only an acquisition since the Revolution."[134] The Revolution, *The Craftsman* contended, was merely a renewal of the ancient spirit of liberty; it did not mark the end of centuries of tyranny and slavery. In July 1735, *The Craftsman* stated the theory of the ancient constitution again, in all its pristine seventeenth-century phraseology.

From the earliest accounts of time, our ancestors in Germany were a free people, and had a right to assent or dissent to all laws; that right was exercised and preserved under the Saxon and Norman Kings, even to our days; and may an uninterrupted exercise thereof continue till time shall be no more.[135]

*The Craftsman* constantly reiterated Bolingbroke's central contention that the Commons had sat continuously in Parliament from the Saxon era through the Norman invasion and into the present day. "The Commons of England were an essential and constituent part of the Saxon general councils."[136] Even in the two centuries between the Conquest and Simon de Montfort, the Commons had been represented. *The Craftsman* also insisted that William I had in fact made no conquest of England. As proof, it cited the Whig *Argumentum Anti-Normanicum*, the appearance of which in 1680 had moved Brady to his assault on all such Whig theories of the ancient constitution.[137] Bolingbroke's journal answered Walpole's feudal history with a complete denial that William I had effected any discontinuity. He had not abolished Saxon law, nor had he become supreme landlord over all the land which he then parceled to his retainers. The common councils of Parliament, which met in his reign, included English barons, churchmen, and commoners, as well as William's French nobility. Invoking the support of a famous seventeenth-century lawyer and believer in the ancient constitution to make this point, *The Craftsman* continued: "The truth of this account is confirmed by the authority of the Lord Chief Justice Hales in his *History of the Common Law*, where he says that William I made the laws of Edward the Confessor the rules of his government, and added very few new ones to them." Furthermore, Magna Carta and the coronation oath of Edward II had the Norman kings swear allegiance to the native Saxon laws. Walpole's press spoke the seventeenth-century Tory language of feudalism and slavery; Bolingbroke's press answered with traditional Whig pieties.

Our government by King and estates of Parliament is as ancient as anything can be remembered of the nation . . . the attempt of altering it, in all ages, accounted Treason. This is our government; and thus it is established, and for ages and immemorial Time has thus continued . . . The grand court of Parliament was in substance the same as it was before the coming in of this conqueror . . . 'tis not to be deny'd but that the same courts which were in the Saxon time . . . continued after William I was made King; and the footsteps of them remain to this day.[138]

In using these arguments *The Craftsman* saw itself firmly in the tradition of such great Whig patriots as Petyt, Sidney, and Tyrrel, in contrast to a "set of men who call themselves the advocates of a Whig ministry, defend those prerogative principles, and lick up the spittle of such slavish writers as Brady and his followers."[139]

*The Craftsman* also denied the Walpole writers' claim that the people had never profited from changes in government before the Revolution, but had merely transferred subjection from one tyrant to another. On the contrary, it insisted, the people and the spirit of liberty had, in fact, flourished in certain reigns, particularly those of Edward III, Henry V, and Elizabeth. Nor could Walpole's press simply concede that people had been "happier" in those reigns; it was clear that they had also been freer. *The London Journal* and *The Daily Gazetteer* were accused of making no distinction between the best princes and the worst. "Normans, Plantagenets, Tudors, and Stuarts are lumped together as an uninterrupted succession of tyrants or idiots, who seem to have mounted the throne for no other purpose than to furnish them with an opportunity of complimenting the present times."[140]

The Government's effort to indicate its acceptance of Brady's history only and not his Tory politics had led it to claim that, at bottom, the rights of reason and nature were sufficient grounds upon which to base English freedoms and that these rights were compatible with a long history of slavery. This position was also questioned by *The Craftsman*. People cherished and held on only to those public rights that had acquired strength through long prescription and long possession. Walpole's press "has led us into a strange wild goose chase, about the natural rights of mankind." Do they really think that "old constitutions, solemnly established and frequently confirmed" are not a more powerful foundation for freedom than timeless and abstract rights of nature? Those who argue that if liberty were but a year old in England it would stand as good a chance to survive, and be regarded as an Englishman's natural right, as would a liberty handed down through the ages—such men are blind to the "natural temper of mankind, more tenacious of ancient birthrights than of any modern acquisitions."[141]

The eager search for authorities with which to support the two positions in the debate on history between Bolingbroke and the Whigs led to a final interesting about-face in the attitudes the two camps took to the leading Augustan historian of England, the Huguenot Rapin de Thoyras. H. R. Trevor-Roper writes that he was "the official historian of his triumphant patrons, the English Whigs."[142] Trevor-Roper goes on to suggest that David Hume directed his Tory history specifically against the Whig history written by Rapin. What has not been known before is that the ministerial writers under Walpole had already criticized Rapin and chosen Tory history, and that Bolingbroke had emerged as the champion of the official Whig historian. Bolingbroke cited Rapin's Whig history so often in his *Remarks* and *Dissertation*, and *The Craftsman* used it so extensively, that Hervey was prompted to refer to him as "the *Craftsman's* own political evangelist, Rapin."[143] The ministerial *Daily Gazetteer* wrote of the official Whig historian, "The *Craftsman* knows very little of the English history, except what it has gleaned from the dullest of dull writers, Rapin, who hath writ without genius or perfect knowledge of his subject." *The Craftsman* jumped to Rapin's defense claiming that "no historian was ever so universally read." It added that the true cause of the resentment against him was that he, a model Whig, had spoken glowingly of the ancient constitution, so that the general drift of his history did not serve the purposes of Walpole.[144] Twenty years before Hume discredited Rapin and embraced Brady's views on feudalism and the ancient constitution, Walpole's publicists had broken the same ground.[145] Bolingbroke was, paradoxically, the champion of the "official" Whig historian.

### BOLINGBROKE: THEORIST OF INTERNATIONAL RELATIONS

Bolingbroke is not only remembered as a writer on English history or as the perpetual opponent of Walpole. History also remembers him as the architect of the Treaty of Utrecht. It is only natural, then, that in the course of his long career he had a great deal to say on the principles by which states did and should deal with one another. In negotiations for a commercial treaty with France, for example, Bolingbroke assumed a position virtually identical with that of nineteenth-century liberals like Cobden who felt that peace and cooperation would result from lowering trade barriers. Nations, he assumed, whose mutual interests were served by trade, could not desire war with one another.

But by far the most important principle of international politics found in Bolingbroke's writings was the balance of power. This principle had been discussed earlier in the writings of Bacon and Halifax, but in Bolingbroke it received its most early reasoned statement among English writers. In his diplomatic correspondence, his history of England, his articles in *The Craftsman*, concern with the balance of power emerges as the cardinal prescription for England's dealings with the outside world.

'Tis not the Emperor, nor France, nor Spain, nor this nor t'other Potentate, to whom we must keep up a perpetual opposition, or grant a constant assistance; power will always be fluctuating amongst the princes of Europe and wherever the present flow of it appears, there is our enemy, there the proper object of our fears.[146]

England's proper role was that of the "balancer" seeking to maintain the equilibrium upon which its safety depended, "to hinder it from being destroyed, by preventing too much power from falling into one scale." Her primary interest was to guarantee that no single power emerged on the continent, for "if a superior power gives the law to the continent, I apprehend that it will give it to us, too, in some great degree." One of the criteria by which Bolingbroke judged the English monarchs was their faithful adherence to the balance of power. Elizabeth stood highest; Cromwell and the Stuarts stood near the bottom because of their alliances with the superior powers of Spain and France.[147]

In adhering to the principle of the balance of power, Bolingbroke projected onto the international sphere the preoccupation with balance and limitations on power which characterized his image of the English constitution. The very terminology of the domestic equilibrium could be transferred to the international. Like the three branches of government, the ruling houses of Europe had fairly well-defined limits of influence and control. If one power transcended its limits, the others banded together to defeat it or discourage its effort. Bolingbroke saw both constitutional and international politics in terms that postulated rival independent powers who were still interdependent enough to check a single power's claims to hegemony. Polybius' famous sixth book used language that could describe both balances of power.

For when any branch of it, swelling beyond its bounds, becomes ambitious, and aims at unwarrantable power, it is manifest that no one of them being, as I have said, absolute, but the designs of each subject to the contradiction and control of the other two, no one can run into any excess of power or arrogance; but all three must remain in the terms prescribed by the constitution, either by being defeated in their attempts to exceed them, or, by being prevented, through the fear of the other two, from attempting it.[148]

It only remained for Bolingbroke to transfer to the international order the peculiarly English constitutional preoccupation with equilibrium, checks, and balance. In making this transferral, he would often be imitated in the next two hundred and fifty years of English political writing.

Two twentieth-century commentators, Hans Kohn and Carleton Hayes, have attributed to Bolingbroke an important role in another area where political thought meets international relations, namely in formulating early ideas of English nationalism.[149] There is in *The Craftsman's* campaigns against Spain and France and in the *Patriot King* and its association with the war propaganda of 1739, a chauvinism and strident nationalism that borders on the xenophobic, but it is inaccurate to blame this on Bolingbroke's Toryism, as the late Professor Carleton Hayes did. In these passages, Bolingbroke is no more self-righteous about England, no more imperialistic, than the great Commonwealthmen of the seventeenth century—Milton, Harrington, and Sidney.

A better case, however, can be made to prove that Bolingbroke was a nationalist from his elucidation of what would become the traditional Tory emphasis on patriotism: service and concern for the nation and its interests as the overriding value in politics. The *Patriot King*, which presents an image of a national party and national interests that transcend narrow and sectional private interest, is the most important text for this interpretation, but the idea is writ large in other Bolingbroke writings and in his career as Opposition philosopher. National unity and harmony meant as much to Bolingbroke as to Tory writers to this day; to this extent, he was a nationalist. But to leap from Bolingbroke's Tory emphasis on patriotic concern for the nation to the claim that "in the garden of Fascist Italy, Bolingbroke might perhaps discover the perfect specimen of the species of shrub which he had tried to cultivate in a hothouse long ago," is clearly untenable. It is an unwarranted attribution of modern evils to men of the past.[150] Nor can one justifiably argue, like Hayes, that Bolingbroke represents a great turning point from the religion of Christianity to the romantic and explosive religion of nationalism. Bolingbroke was too much of a stoic and cosmopolitan thinker of the Enlightenment to be guilty of this post-Enlightenment heresy. The internationalism of the Enlightenment is uppermost in his *Reflections upon Exile* while his Tory "patriotism" lies in abeyance.

Among numberless extravagances which have passed through the minds of men, we may justly reckon for one that notion of a secret affection, independent of our reason, and superior to our reason, which we are supposed to have for our country; as if there were some physical virtue in every spot of ground which necessarily produced this effect in every one born upon it . . . There is nothing, surely, more groundless than the notion here advanced, nothing more absurd . . . A wise man looks on himself as a citizen of the world: and, when you ask him where his country lies, points, like Anaxagoras, with his fingers to the heavens.[151]

Even if it be granted that Bolingbroke was a "patriotic" nationalist when not in exile, it should be noted that he was not an expansionist, like the seventeenth-century Commonwealth nationalists. As often with nationalists, a heavy streak of isolationism runs through his writings on England's dealings with the outside world. This isolationism is an outgrowth of Bolingbroke's emphasis on the supremacy of national interest in determining foreign policy. In his discussion of national interest Bolingbroke emerges an early proponent of what has come to be called the realist theory of international politics, which in England is most closely identified with Tory writers and statesmen.[152] In the nineteenth century this view could be found in Canning, and in the twentieth most strikingly in Sir Winston Churchill, a descendant of Marlborough. Tory realism holds that the determining factor in a state's attitude to other states is its national interest, not sentiment, morality, or ideology. The opposing liberal view on international politics has, from the seventeenth century to the present day, worked for the state to achieve certain ideological goals in the international sphere such as freedom, free trade, national self-determination, opposition to despotism, or nuclear disarmament.

Bolingbroke's writings on foreign policy read like a realist primer. His constant complaint about the War of the Spanish Succession was that after 1706 England was no longer fighting for her own national interest, but for the sake of her allies and particular interests within the national community. "The reasons of ambition, avarice, and private interests which engaged the princes and states of the confederacy to depart from the principles of the grand alliance, were no reasons for Great Britain." England's national interest had been achieved in checking Louis; there was no need for a moral crusade to secure the Spanish throne for the Emperor. The English should not be friends or enemies to Austria or the Bourbons by virtue of mere passion and sentiment. "A wise Prince, and a wise people, bear no regard to other states, except that which arises from the coincidence or repugnancy of their several interests; and this regard must therefore vary as these interests do, in the perpetual fluctuation of human affairs." So Elizabeth and her people opposed Austria and supported the House of Bourbon in the sixteenth century, but Anne and her people supported Austria and opposed the House of Bourbon in the eighteenth century. It is laid down in *The Craftsman* as a "never failing maxim, that no treaty will be kept long which is not for the interest of both the parties." On another occasion the paper called upon the English "even to break our word, for once with our neighbors" on Gibraltar, since to do so would better serve the English national interest.[153]

When Bolingbroke's Tory realism defined the English national interest, there emerged a strikingly isolationist streak. The major determinant of England's interest is that she is an island. It is essential, therefore, that she have a strong navy to protect her moat, as it were, and that she not meddle in European politics unless the balance is seriously threatened, and then only with her navy. Elizabeth's glorious reign had illustrated that peace could be enjoyed on an island while the neighboring continent was laid waste by war. "But our own [eighteenth-century] histories will show us likewise, how an island may approach, as it were, too near the continent, and be fatally drawn into that great vortex." The continental powers must, for their own safety, always be busy outside their borders negotiating treaties and alliances. An island, however, "need not take up the policy of the continent, to enter into the system of alliances we have been speaking of," or "enter deep into the quarrel, or involve themselves intricately."[154] One historian has recently suggested that the strain of isolationist thought in Bolingbroke's writings was an important European source for Washington's Farewell Address and its warning against foreign entanglements.[155] Particularly meaningful to Washington was the statement of English aloofness contained in the *Patriot King*.

Other Nations must watch over every motion of their neighbors; penetrate, if they can, every design; foresee every minute event; and take part by some engagement or other in almost every conjuncture that arises. But as we cannot be easily, nor suddenly attacked, and as we ought not to aim at any acquisition of territory on the continent, it may be our interest to watch the secret workings of the several councils abroad; to advise and warn; to abet and oppose, but it never can be our true interest easily and officiously to enter into action, much less into engagements that imply action and expense.[156]

Whatever Bolingbroke wrote served a definite partisan purpose. The Opposition, throughout the 1730's, attacked Walpole's preoccupation with endless European treaties, especially conventions with Spain that settled nothing, and left Spain free to violate English interests. The only appropriate response to Spain was, in the opinion of the Opposition, a war at sea in the grand Elizabethan manner. Bolingbroke's criticism was also directed to the Crown's concern with European politics because of its interest in Hanover. Bolingbroke was less than eager that George should involve the English in his continental aspirations.

Bolingbroke may have been a nationalist preoccupied with patriotic service, but his nation was not expansionist or interventionist. His Tory realism might encourage wars at sea to protect England's interests, but it did not seek to spread any moral attitude or political ideology, as seventeenth-century Commonwealthmen had sought to do; it did not seek to intervene on the continent in the name of liberalism and freedom as nineteenth-century liberals sought to do.

A final realist insight into the nature of the international order brings us full circle in this discussion of Bolingbroke's political writings. In his critique of Hobbes and Locke Bolingbroke suggested that their competitive and individualist model was much more appropriate for describing nations in the international community. Sovereign states, with no law above them or common judge to settle their differences, existed in that individualist world that Hobbes and Locke had described for man. Bolingbroke rejected their ideas ultimately by banishing them from domestic politics and relegating them to, what he considered, the more appropriate realm of interactions between and among states.

However unlike nations may be to nations in their dispositions and manners, all of them, even the weakest, seek their own advantage real or imaginary, at the expense of others. Thus have the civil societies of men acted towards one another from their primitive institutions . . . whilst every particular state has gone through various forms of government and revolutions of fortune, the universal state of mankind has been little less than a state of perpetual anarchy. Families kept men out of that state of individuality which Hobbes, and even Locke supposes. But political societies have been always individuals.[157]

# VII

## Defoe and the Literature of the New Age

Christopher Hill has described 1688 as the turning point between two radically different civilizations in England.[1] Setting upon the Dutch course, England became an economic power; national greatness would thenceforth be measured in commercial terms. Late in the seventeenth century and early in the eighteenth century the foundations were laid in England for an economic system, dominated by exchange, that would finally put to rest the medieval synthesis of ethics and economics. Augustan England, with its development of a rudimentary capitalist system and middle class, marks the decisive break with the spirit of the Middle Ages.[2]

Walpole presided over some of the early years of this new civilization, perfectly willing to harness its new institutions and new spirit to his own ends; in his pay, however, was someone more openly disposed to sing the praises of the new civilization. Daniel Defoe was the lyric poet of this new world; his writings captured and immortalized the spirit of the age. Walpole may not have been completely at one with Defoe, "the first great apologist of the English middle class,"[3] but Defoe's attitudes perfectly embodied all that Bolingbroke and his circle found distasteful in the age of Walpole. Walpole himself does not serve posterity as a symbol of the new commercial age; he had in his employ, however, the man who best embodied its political, social, and cultural values.

Defoe's party affiliations were less than consistent. He always managed to write for the party in power, a characteristic unusual among the writers in this period. Despite the obvious opportunism his huge literary output is unmistakably consistent in its wholehearted acceptance of the new world of bourgeois liberalism. Even during Defoe's early association with the Tories he was closest to the most "commercial" of them, Robert Harley. In 1715 he began working for Walpole and never stopped.[4]

One of Defoe's most ingenious assignments for Walpole was his collaboration with Opposition journals. Capitalizing on Defoe's previous position of trust with the Tories, Walpole had him join the Tory weekly, *Mists*, and suppress from within articles offensive to the Government. For ten years Defoe maintained this ruse of working with Tory journals (*Mercurius Politicus*, *Mists*, and *Applebee*) while taking the sting out of their criticism of the Government. He also emerged during the same ten years as one of Walpole's chief propagandists, writing scores of tracts which defended English prosperity and the new order, and dispelling with optimism the gloom purveyed by the Opposition.[5]

His most enduring piece of propaganda for Walpole is the *Journal of the Plague Year*. The possibility that an epidemic in Marseilles might be spread to London by the merchant fleet prompted Walpole in 1720-1721 to demand from the Commons a quarantine act that would, if necessary, restrict shipping and give the government power to meet the epidemic. Throughout the agitation Walpole employed Defoe to impress Londoners with the horrors of the plague in France and the need for government action. The campaign culminated in March 1722 with the appearance of Defoe's famous *Journal*, depicting conditions in 1665, when the streets of London rang with the cry to bring out the dead. Such grizzly horrors of pestilence and death argued well that a grave need existed for the strong action sought by Walpole's government.

But it was not only in such obvious political propaganda that Defoe served Walpole. All that Defoe wrote paid tribute to the ideas, institutions, and society that had developed since the Revolution and over which Walpole presided. Walpole understood his man well: Defoe, not Colley Cibber, was the true laureate of the age.[6]

Fundamental to Defoe's political writings were the ideas of Locke. During his early years when he edited *The Review*, he used Locke to answer the arguments for divine right and patriarchal government that had appeared in *The Rehearsal*, journal of the nonjuror Charles Leslie. His popularizations of Locke's ideas on the state of nature, property, contract, and consent have led one observer to describe Defoe as "the most thoroughgoing exponent of Whig principles during the early years of the eighteenth century."[7]

Defoe wrote that the institution of property is necessary to the formation of society. The private possession of property is lawful and just for anyone who will "seize upon, and possess as his own, any part of the creation of God, not inhabited or possess'd before— and Priority of Possession is a just Right of Property." Men enter civil society to protect their property; the origin of government is a self-conscious and deliberate act of rational men. It is interesting in the light of his later writings that Defoe suggested that if twenty men who "had never known men" were set on an island, "the first thing they would apply to by the light of nature after food, would be to settle government among them."[8]

These Lockean themes occur again in his poem, *Juro Divino*. When government is established "*Safety* with *Right* and *Property* combines." Government is created by people and consented to for the safety and security it gives their persons and property. There is also a large dose of Hobbes in this early theoretical poem.

> Nature has left this *Tincture in the Blood*,
> That all Men *would be tyrants* if they cou'd:
> If they forbear their Neighbours to devour,
> 'Tis not for want of *Will*, but want of *Pow'r*;[9]

Behind the formation of government are both the protection of property and the defense of oneself against neighbors who would devour.[10] Locke and Hobbes are common authorities for the self-same truth. The identification of the contractual origins of government with that of self-love that prompted Shaftesbury and Bolingbroke to criticize Hobbes and Locke appealed to Defoe, who was much more sympathetic to its individualist liberal implications. He could easily accept its fundamental assumption that self-interested individuals were at the bottom of all political and economic activity. "Self, in a word, governs the whole world; The present race of Men all come into it. 'Tis the foundation of every prospect in Life, The beginning and end of our actions." His poetry expresses the same sentiment:

> Self-love's the Ground of all the things we do,
> Which they that talk on't least do most pursue.[11]

Men never transcend this self-love in Defoe's view, as they do in Bolingbroke's and Pope's.

Although *Robinson Crusoe* may not be "the great allegory of the Capitalist system,"[12] it is certainly an articulate and lyrical rendering of Locke's ideas. The isolated individual is depicted free of society, history, and tradition. Crusoe, who laments that he "was reduced to a mere state of nature," must set about rationally constructing his own life. He worked his island, so by natural right "the whole country was my own mere property." When the Spanish and Portuguese shipwrecks intrude, Crusoe insists that a written contract be drawn up and creates a political society in which he is to be recognized as the legitimate governing authority. By this compact all consent to be "entirely under and subjected to his commands." Hobbes' influence is also detected in Robinson Crusoe. After discovering the savages, Defoe's isolated individual is obsessed by fear of sudden destruction. He hides in his cave, refusing to leave, "in the constant snare of the fear of man." Like Hobbes, who had described in a memorable passage how fear, in the state of nature, led to the neglect of industry, building, navigation, and all forms of enterprise, so Defoe shows Crusoe's obsessive fear interfering with his efforts to improve the island. "The frights I had been in about these savage wretches, and the concern I had been in for my own preservation, had taken off the edge of my invention for my own conveniences." He is forced to give up making his bread and perfecting his grindstone; he has only time for preserving himself. Crusoe's fear disappears, however, with his subjection of Friday and the establishment of civil society on the island when reason leads Crusoe and the newcomers to enter into contract. The anarchy of the state of nature is ended and the freedom of all is limited by establishing the rule of law. The persons, homes, and farms of all inhabitants are made secure and the island community is made peaceful.

Defoe's explicit use of Hobbes' and Locke's ideas, so basic to the emerging individualist and liberal ideology, was by no means his most important contribution to the new social order in Augustan England. His entire literary and political output glories in the new age. Swift, the frustrated and gloomy aristocrat, and Defoe, the restless and optimistic bourgeois created the complementary representatives of this age. Defoe accepted and rejoiced in the age of Walpole; Swift rejected it with satire, horror, and bitterness. Crusoe traveled the globe because there were never enough worlds for the bourgeois hero to conquer showing an optimism that seems hollow and pathetic when reflected in the hapless voyages of Gulliver.

In no book is the spirit of this age better captured than in Defoe's *Essay on Projects*. Defoe writes that in 1688 England entered what he calls the "Projecting Age." No previous age had produced such a degree of scheming and inventing "in matters of negotiation and methods of civil polity" as this age. Written in the midst of the inventive and speculative boom of the late '90's, Defoe's description of projecting England applies equally well, if not better, to the following decades. The source of the energy which "every day produces new contrivances, engines and projects to get money," was the war with France, whose losses and depredation forced men to turn their wits to new inventions. This projecting spirit lay behind the new economic ventures and innovations of the period: the banks, stocks, stockjobbing, and assurance societies. Such economic projects benefited the public by improving trade, employing the poor, and helping the circulation and increase of the kingdom's public stock. New discoveries in trade and new credit facilities "are without question of as great benefit, as any discoveries made in the works of nature by all the academies and royal societies in the world." The Bank and stockjobbing had nursed the spirit of projecting; in turn, projecting "has very diligently pimped for its foster parent."[13]

Defoe, the unabashed modern, conceded that the ancients had had their inventions and undertakings, their Noah's Ark and Tower of Babel, but, he argued, no previous age had produced such technology, such engines, and instruments as England since 1688. Defoe was careful to describe the entrepreneurial aspect of this "projecting humour" which pervaded the land. The projector could rightfully expect an allowance of one-half the profits for himself; there was no reason why the author of contrivances and schemes "should not reap the harvest of his own ingenuity."[14] It was, after all, his due reward for an earnest and industrious use of his wits. The *Essay* concludes with a long list of Defoe's own proposals for new projects: country banks, improved highways, body insurance, disability pensions, "fool-houses," an English academy to encourage learning and establish the purity of the language, another academy for military studies, and yet another for the teaching of women. For the rest of his life Defoe was himself a projector, seeking to prevent robberies, to lessen the number of streetwalkers, to make perfume from the glandular secretions of cats.[15] Like Robinson Crusoe, he could well say of himself, "my head . . . was filled with projects and designs."

It is more than likely that Defoe was closely involved in the most important economic projects of his day. One biographer thinks Defoe may well have advised Halifax on the two most daring financial measures of the 1690's, the founding of the Bank of England and the new coinage.[16] Much more significant and clear-cut, however, is his role with Harley in the founding of the South Sea Company in 1711. Defoe had little to do with the financial aspect of Harley's plan, the assumption of the debt, but he played a large part in its commercial and trading aspects. Here, in Defoe's plan for the South Seas, the projecting and bourgeois spirits of the age meet. Ever since the days of William III, Defoe had been preoccupied with a project for English trade and colonial expansion in South America and Mexico, where he saw new worlds and markets to conquer, and great wealth and profits to be taken. Defoe proposed, unsuccessfully, to William, that English colonies be set up in Chile and on the Atlantic coast. He proposed it once again to Godolphin, and in 1710 and 1711 he wrote of the project in his *Review* with glowing descriptions of the wealth to be had for the daring men willing to undertake the risk. He sent a draft of his proposal to Harley, his patron and employer at that point. It is not improbable that the South Sea project was the end result of Defoe's work and his crowning glory as a projector.[17] Only John Law's project in Mississippi would surpass this exploitative and acquisitive dream of Defoe's.

In both his career and his writings Defoe embodied the projecting spirit—the restless and optimistic desire to tinker with and change society and nature. Tradition, the inherited social order, and nature ceased to be sacred before the projector and tinkerer. His wholly progressive spirit gloried in inventions and newness, in solving traditional problems, in conquering new worlds. His practical and utilitarian spirit enshrined the useful, the handy, the profitable; his was the spirit of self-interest, avarice, and individualism. Projecting man, free of any functional duty to any organic social structure, stood alone, creating and shaping his own world and his own destiny. His was the spirit of Locke's man, of Robinson

Crusoe, a necessary ingredient of the capitalist creed. How apt, then, that Defoe's *Essay on Projects* should have profoundly impressed the man whom Max Weber saw embodying the spirit of capitalism "in almost classical purity." Benjamin Franklin, describing his father's library in his autobiography, wrote of a particular book "of Defoe's called an *Essay on Projects* . . . which perhaps gave me a turn of thinking that had an influence on some of the principal events of my life."[18]

This projecting spirit was particularly despised by Bolingbroke's circle. Its principal manifestation in financial innovations seemed to spell doom for the aristocratic and gentry society they favored.[19] Tinkering and scheming showed little reverence for the traditional order of society, and brought chaos and disorder to the established social structure. Restlessness and eagerness to transform appalled classicists whose eyes were firmly fixed on the past. The words "project" and "scheme" were anathema to Walpole's Tory critics, and could serve only in their satires, like the "project" to eliminate overpopulation from Ireland. But the projector and tinkerer were seen as more than socially and politically dangerous. For Swift, as well as for Bolingbroke, he was a blasphemer, committing the sin of Pride, in much the same way as Marlowe saw his Doctor Faustus assuming too great a role in manipulating his own world, interfering too much in a divinely ordained hierarchy and nature.

Defoe spoke for the new age in terms even more basic than those of the projecting spirit. Like Walpole's opponents, he sensed that the new age of projects would have a fundamental impact on the social and political structure of England. It would produce social mobility dramatic enough to supplant the distinctions of rank by an utter confusion of rank. Defoe agreed with the gloomy Tory satirists that Augustan England marked the passing of nobility and gentry supremacy. But his every poem, novel, and pamphlet wholeheartedly endorsed this change. The theme of the work that first brought him literary fame was, for example, an attack on the arrogant presumptuousness of the English upper classes. *The True-Born Englishman*, written in 1701, was as an answer to pamphlets attacking William III as a foreigner lacking English ancestry and birth.[20] The preface announces Defoe's intention of destroying the "vanity of those who talk of their antiquity, and value themselves upon their pedigree, their ancient families, and being true-born."

These claims to gentility are ridiculed by Defoe's argument *ab origine*.

> And here begins our ancient pedigree
> That so exalts our poor nobility:
> 'Tis that from some French trooper they derive,
> Who with the Norman Bastard did arrive (Part I, lines 22-25).

The poem is more than a defense of William. Sweeping aside claims to gentility based on birth and blood, Defoe launches a spirited defense of the social claims of the rising middle class.

> For fame of families is all a cheat
> 'Tis personal virtue only makes us great (Conclusion, lines 25-26).

This is a theme to which Defoe would often return; wealth now determines the rank of men in England. This is as it should be! A new nobility, a modern nobility, had arisen in Augustan England.

> Wealth, howsoever got, in England makes
> Lords of merchants, gentlemen of rakes.
> Antiquities and birth are needless here;
> 'Tis impudence and money makes a peer (Part I, lines 8-11).

A new kind of gentleman was responsible for the greatness of England. In his *Review,* Defoe seldom failed to point out that a vigorous middle class, not the idle squirearchy and their agrarian economy, provided the national energy. The gentry, he charged, played a minor role in the war with France; instead, they hunted, raced, gamed, and drank. They were "bred boors, empty and swinish sots and fops."

A great deal of the blame belonged to their impractical education with its useless classical bias. *The Review* cut to the very heart of the Opposition's political ideal when it attacked the alleged superiority of humanist training for the governing elite. The true-bred merchant, Defoe contended, is a universal scholar whose "learning excells the meer scholar in Greek and Latin, as much as that does the illiterate Person that cannot read or write." The merchant understands languages without books, geography without maps; "his foreign exchanges speak all tongues." He is most qualified for employment in the state "by a general knowledge of things and men."[21] These are the men who should govern the state not the effeminate and improperly educated specimens produced by the gentry and nobility. In this rejection of humanist education, Defoe mirrored values of the new age that so frightened men whose sights were set on the past.

He spoke for, and was read by a class totally alien to Bolingbroke, Swift, Pope, and Gay. These brothers of the Scriblerus Club thought Defoe's work socially and intellectually inferior, a fact indicated by its success with the new and bourgeois reading public.[22] They regarded his work as another illustration of the progress of "dullness" that rejected their humanist political, social, and cultural ideals. Defoe's *Tour Thro' the Whole Island of Great Britain* proudly proclaims that he would not write of the River Thames as a setting for water nymphs or river muses. This would do for "ancient poets," but for Defoe the Thames was something else, and so he described it as an avenue of trade, the booming artery upon which England's commercial greatness lay.[23]

Middle class readers in Augustan England could find their values and aspirations accurately rendered in Defoe's long string of successful novels where birth and ancestry mattered little. Crusoe's father pleads with his son to accept his God-given place in the "upper station of low life" and leave off his fanciful aspirations—advice that Crusoe refuses. The traditional hierarchy would not impede the adventurous seeker of gain in post-Revolutionary England. Walpole's men and Defoe's heroes cheerfully cast off obsolete social encumbrances of class, place, and station, when a world was to be won for the asking.[24] Crusoe does move up—a message that could not have been lost on middle-class readers who shared Defoe's aspirations to gentility. After his years of hard work, Crusoe looks upon his island home and contemplates himself with pleasure as "king and lord of all this country." His home he calls his "estate," his plantation on the other side of the island he calls his "country seat." If only he could convey it all back to England, he thinks, he "might have it in inheritance as complete as any lord of a manor."

Preoccupation with upward social mobility is reflected in Defoe's constant theme of colonization. Settling in a new world became an easy way for individuals of the lower and middle stations to better their fortunes. All that mattered was hard work; one could succeed there regardless of ancestry or birth. Moll Flanders is told by her mother that in the colonies, "many a Newgate-bird becomes a great man." Moll's own experience bears out the truth of her mother's words. Moll and one of her husbands, Colonel Jack, both convicted felons, make their mark in America, return to England, buy an estate, and live forever after as gentleman and gentlewoman. Unlike Moll, Colonel Jack was of gentle blood, but to no avail; his life brought only poverty, poor education, and crime. He, too, earned gentility only after a sojourn in the colonies with its attendant hard work.

These tales not only catered to his readers' aspirations but also reflect Defoe's own preoccupation with moving up in the social hierarchy. In 1706 he had been legally declared a gentleman although he was totally lacking in the claims of birth and ancestry.[25] Why should successful men of the lower and middle stations not aspire to gentility? Are they not superior to the older gentle classes? It is Defoe who speaks in the persona of the great money man Sir Robert Clayton, when the latter advises Roxanna to marry her Dutch lover.

Sir Robert said, and I found it to be true, that a true-bred merchant is the best gentleman in the nation; that in knowledge, in manners, in judgment of things, the merchant outdid many of the nobility; that having once mastered the world, and being above the demand of business, though no real estate, they were then superior to most gentlemen, even in estates.[26]

When Defoe returned to the essay and the political and economic pamphlet in his last years, the message was the same as in his novels. England faced a new social phenomenon, "difficult to describe and not less difficult to give a name to."[27] But, Defoe was up to the task. In his *Tour Thro' the Whole Island of Great Britain, Complete English Tradesman, Plan of English Commerce,* and *Complete English Gentleman,* he described the economic and social leadership of the nobility and gentry being replaced by the rising wealth and prominence of the middle class. These works, products of the Walpole years 1724-1731, were more effective than Walpole's press in answering the political and literary assaults of Bolingbroke's Opposition. Their exaltation of a growing and prosperous England exudes optimism. Defoe welcomed every change and improvement while Bolingbroke, Swift, and Pope wallowed in gloom and despair. Defoe wrote of growth, they of decay; he wrote of

England's greatness, they of her decline; he wrote of the virtuous English and they of the corrupt. He wrote of the wondrous rise of the middle class, they of the lamentable fall of the nobility and gentry.

On his tour, Defoe noted with pleasure how the increase in wealth of the city of London had spread into the country, "and plants families and fortunes, who in another age will equal the families of the ancient gentry." *The Complete English Tradesman* marvels at the new England where many noble seats are erected by trades-men or sons of tradesmen, "while the seats and castles of the an-cient gentry, like their families, look worn out and fallen into decay." All over England Defoe found ancient families "worn out by time and misfortunes, their estates possessed by a new race of tradesmen grown into families of gentry." Ideologists are wont to exaggerate, and Defoe was no exception. Self-proclaimed apologist for the rising middle class, he perceived social change in the same total and dramatic terms as did angry apologists for the declining gentry. In his *Plan for English Commerce* Defoe claims boldly that "the nobility and ancient gentry have almost everywhere sold their estates, and the commonality and tradesmen have bought them; so that now the gentry are richer than the nobility, and the tradesmen are richer than them all." Everywhere he saw self-made men like himself marching to the Herald's office searching for coats of arms to paint upon their coaches. But Defoe, the keen observer, went even further and suggested that the most significant explanation of the new facts of English life were the "abundance of . . . modern ad-vantages and private ways of getting money . . . the law, trade, war, navigation, improvement of stocks, and loans on public funds."[28]

Defoe drew the very political conclusions that Bolingbroke's cir-cle so dreaded. The new men, Defoe suggested, should take over the positions of political leadership in the nation. They, rather than those born of gentle and ancient family, were the rightful ruling class. The new men of business had an important national role to play. "The wise, sober, modest tradesman, when he is thriven and grown rich, is really a valuable man"; when he retires from busi-ness, he has more opportunity to do good than anyone else in the community, because his "special experience and knowledge of business" qualify him more than "men of ten times [his] learning and education." Retired men of business, Defoe suggests, are the "natural magistrates and general peacemakers of the country." In *The Review* he had argued that tradesmen had taken over the traditional place of the nobility and gentry as warriors; fifteen years later he went further.

After a generation or two, the tradesman's children, or at least his grandchildren come to be as good gentlemen, statesmen, Parliamentmen, Privy Councilors, Judges, Bishops, and Noblemen, as those of the highest birth and the most ancient families.[29]

In *The Craftsman* and most especially in the *Patriot King,* Bolingbroke did praise the value of trade, departing somewhat from past gentry and aristocratic attitudes enshrined in two centuries of literary and political writing. He was obliged, in part, to pay such respect because of the important role that the small traders, led by Barnard, played in the politics of the Opposition. But Bolingbroke's praise of trade could also find its legitimacy in the mercantilist views of the Elizabethans who saw trade solely as a contribution to the greatness and power of the state. In such a view the social hierarchy neither excludes nor is threatened by the merchant who contributes to the well-being and solidity of the entire structure, and who knows that his place as a merchant renders him unfit to rule. The gloom of Bolingbroke's circle is all the more understandable in the light of Defoe's message. Sad would be the fate of England, they held, if the ruling class came not from the country house, but from the counting house!

In the world of Augustan letters Defoe did not stand alone as defender of the social and political aspirations of the new class of men. The neoclassical principle of decorum in characterization still forced most writers to see society as a tightly organized and stable hierarchy with well-defined ranks and gradations. Characters had to mirror the harmonious scheme of the ideal order with the qualities appropriate for each rank.[30] Seventeenth-century dramatists had depicted merchants and financiers in terms appropriate to those who occupied a lower rank—they were covetous and usurious, stupid and immoral. Even early eighteenth-century Whig playwrights like Congreve, Vanbrugh, and Farquhar shared the neoclassical contempt for the men of the City and Exchange Alley.[31] Pope and Swift remained true to this principle of decorum, but a significant shift of opinion took place among later Whig writers.

After the settlement of the Crown and the rise of Walpole, the Whig alliance with the financial community came more and more to be reflected in sympathetic literary treatments of merchants and money men. Whig writers wrote both of the dignity of the moneyed class and of its arrival into the high places of the social and political world. As was abundantly clear to critics like Pope, Whig social doctrine was undermining traditional neoclassical conceptions of characterization and society.[32]

One of the Whigs who, along with Defoe, violated the decorum of character, was Sir Richard Steele, who emerged in the second and third decades of the eighteenth century as propagandist for men of business and men of money. As far back as 1710 in *The Spectator,* Steele had put beside Sir Roger de Coverley, a gentleman of ancient descent, Sir Andrew Freeport, a man of great eminence in the City, of whom one could say "a general trader of good sense is pleasanter company than a general scholar."[33]

The assimilation of the middle order of merchants and financiers into the gentry was not new to the English social scene. What was new in the propaganda of Defoe and Steele was the firm belief that successful moneyed men were in their own right entitled to a high place in social esteem and political power regardless of their ability to become gentlemen through marriage or purchase of land. This is the theme of Steele's *The Conscious Lovers,* staged in 1722. In terms that could well serve as the manifesto of the new order and its social outlook, Steele's hero proclaims:

We merchants are a species of gentry that have grown into this world the last century, and are as honourable, and almost as useful, as you landed folk, that have always thought yourselves so much above us.[34]

Even Colley Cibber, Walpole's titled laureate, echoed these sentiments. To the Opposition, he was therefore more than the symbol of the artistic degeneration of Walpole's England; he was also a propagandist for its new social values. In his play *The Refusal,* Cibber gives his merchant hero a claim that confirmed the worst fears of Bolingbroke and his group. The age of gentlemen has passed, the hero asserts; they will find "'tis not your court, but City-Politicians must do the Nation's business at last . . . We have made money, man: Money! Money! there's the health and lifeblood of a government."[35]

### BERNARD MANDEVILLE: PHILOSOPHER OF AVARICE

In Defoe and Steele, Walpole's England had poet and publicist. It acquired a philosopher in Bernard Mandeville. Mandeville (1670-1733) may be considered an opponent of Shaftesbury's benevolence or a forerunner of late eighteenth-century utilitarianism.[36] Historians of economic thought also sometimes claim him, although they cannot agree on whether his thought is mercantilist or laissez-faire.[37] But Mandeville may also be read in the intellectual context of his own age as an important formulator of new values for post-Revolutionary England. Confronted by the economic innovations of the years 1688-1725, England needed to reassess her values. Mandeville's achievement was the expression of values that supplanted humanism, appropriate for the emerging social structure.

Mandeville's famous poem, *The Grumbling Hive—or Knaves Turned Honest,* a poetic formulation of the later *Fable of the Bees,*[38] appeared in 1705. One student of Mandeville believes this poetic praise of corruption to have been a Whig tract intended to exonerate Marlborough and others in office from charges of bribery, fraud, and dishonesty.[39] Much more than a defense of Marlborough, the poem is a complex catalogue of all the corrupt individuals necessary for a flourishing society. In this general defense of corruption, Mandeville answers a group of poets of the preceding fifteen years who had attacked luxury, second-rate poets who bear an interesting, albeit seldom acknowledged relationship to the social and moral thought of Augustan England. These poets had produced a series of long moral poems between 1695 and 1710 arguing the corrupting power of money on all classes of society. Their appearance coincided with, and appears to have been the first reaction to, the birth of the Bank and the corporate and stock boom of the late '90's.[40] These fairly insignificant poets expressed the first intellectual reactions to the new financial institutions and the new prominence of money in society, themes that would be revived and given more skillful and enduring treatment by the giants of Augustan letters, Swift, Pope, and Gay. But their work had the one lasting distinction that these minor poets provoked Mandeville to his famous defense of money, luxury, and corruption.

Mandeville's beehive was a stage on which all manner of corrupt Englishmen were displayed; the sharpers, the parasites, the pimps, the players, the pickpockets, and all the others who fed on their industrious neighbors. Gay would assemble the same cast for *The Beggar's Opera,* but for very different purposes. In this portrayal of lawyers, physicians, priests, soldiers, and judges as totally corrupt, Mandeville followed the convention of the earlier poets.

> All Trades and Places knew Some cheat
> No Calling was without deceit.

But here the similarity ends, for Mandeville saw nothing wrong with such corruption; it was, in fact, an indispensable agent for good.

> Thus every Part was full of Vice,
> Yet the whole Mass a Paradise . . .
> Such were the Blessings of that State;
> Their Crimes conspir'd to make them great.

Luxury and pride employed the millions. Trade and commerce prospered as the vain bees dressed, ate, and outfitted themselves in luxury.

But soon, amidst this plenty, a cry went up: "damn the cheats," "the land must sink for all its fraud," a cry to be chorused by Bolingbroke and his circle for the next forty-five years. The cry was more successful in the poem however; fraud was dispelled from the hive and honesty filled the hearts of the bees; the professions became honest, and luxury was outlawed.

> Now mind the glorious Hive, and see
> How Honesty and Trade agree.

Merchants left the sea, companies closed down, industry was neglected, all were content "And neither seek nor covet more." The moral of the tale is clear, to all those meddling and virtuous politicians who busy themselves in decrying the prodigality and luxury of the times.

> Then leave complaints: fools only strive
> To make a great, an honest hive.[41]

Nine years later, in 1714, Mandeville published his poem with a lengthy introduction and set of "Remarks," in which form the *Fable* has come down to the present day. He had had enough of

*The Examiner*'s complaining of the moneyed interest, the Bank, and corruption in general. His *Fable of the Bees, or Private Vices, Public Benefits,* appeared when, at the height of their political ascendancy, the Tories' yearning for the simplicity of pre-Revolutionary days was reflected in agitation for sumptuary laws to curb the luxury that they alleged corrupted public manners and extinguished public spirit.[42] The *Fable* not only undermined the Tory position of 1714, but in its many revisions and republications in the years before Mandeville's death in 1733, it persisted as the most telling critique of the humanist values dear to the Opposition, and accepted the values implicit in the new socioeconomic order.[43]

Mandeville's method in his "Remarks" was to take traditional values, such as virtue and honor, and show either their less than admirable origins, or the futility of seeking their implementation. At the same time he sought to demonstrate that what appeared to be social evils, such as pride, prodigality, and corruption had beneficial results. The analysis resulted in the paradoxical conclusion that men steeped in vice made society flourish. The origin of virtue, he wrote, was simply the deception of savage man by skillful politicians who called virtue what men did to benefit others, so that virtue was contrary to man's real impulses. These standards of morality worked out by skillful politicians had a useful social function, but their total fulfillment would be economically disastrous since the wealth and grandeur of a society depended on the persistence of vice. Those who committed immoral deeds had to be reproved; but moral imperatives should only check vice, never vanquish it. A prosperous society would not talk of virtue and public service; it would instead harness the energy of self-interest. There was no quality so beneficial to society as pride. If pride were to disappear, so would economic prosperity; but, mercifully, such a virtuous age would never dawn. Mandeville also praised luxury and profuseness. He devoted a large part of his "Remarks" to lauding expenditure and denouncing frugality, which, "like honesty, is a mean starving virtue, which is only fit for small societies of good peaceable men."[44]

In the "Remarks" Mandeville ridicules the Tory critique of the Whig economy. Retrenchment and retreat to an era with no national debt, no banking and credit facilities, no speculative projects, no corporate moneyed giants, no hordes of corrupt government officials, is both impossible and undesirable. Mandeville was a philosopher of an age of self-interest and prodigality who had little appetite for the austere moderation of the Opposition's classical ideal. He dismissed with contempt their obsessive fear that luxury would enervate and emasculate. The Spaniard with his powdered wig and laced shirt was as brave beside his cannon, Mandeville writes, as the "most stinking slovens in their own Hair, tho' it had not been comb'd in a Month"; enough, then, with talk of sturdy, brave, and frugal ancestors uncorrupted by a moneyed and luxurious society. Mandeville, an eminently realistic man of the new age, could say, "all the Cardinal Virtues together won't so much as procure a tolerable Coat or a Porridge-Pot among them." The world of Mandeville, like that of Defoe, is far different from the nostalgic ideal of Bolingbroke and his followers. Mandeville belongs in the world of Walpole, where "great wealth and foreign treasure will ever scorn to come among men unless you admit their inseparable companions, avarice and luxury."[45] No wonder, then, that Bolingbroke's *Craftsman* singled out Mandeville in 1732 the apologist of the corrupt age.[46]

# VIII

## The Nostalgia of the Augustan Poets

From his entry into public life until his decline in old age, Boling-broke attracted about him most of the creative writers and wits of the period. Pope, Swift, Gay, and Lyttelton were important writers and thinkers in their own right, who, as a group, shared common values on social and political questions. Their bias was traditional and Tory, idealizing an aristocratic and gentry society. To the extent they sensed this society's decline, they responded with gloom, ridicule, satire, and misanthropy. Some found outlets in chauvin-ism, others in the political thought of reaction. Dominating their individual expressions was a common alienation from the age. Horace Walpole noted this with ridicule later in the century.

Last night at Strawberry Hill, I took up, to divert my thoughts, a volume of letters to Swift from Bolingbroke, Bathurst and Gay; and what was there but lamentations on the ruin of England, in that era of its peace and prosperity, from wretches who thought their own want of power as a proof that their country was undone.[1]

Walpole was quite right. Such lamentation on the decline and ruin of England was misplaced. The very years that heard these cries of woe were laying the foundations for England's Industrial Revolution and the acme of her greatness. In one sense, however, Bolingbroke, Swift, Gay, and Pope were accurate in speaking of decay and ruin, for their England was passing. Their want of power, in a sense more meaningful than suggested by Horace Walpole, was proof enough to them that their country was undone. In the extensive correspondence that passed among Bolingbroke, Pope, and Swift there is a consciousness of their bond as a peculiar triumvirate set apart from the world around them.[2] Their sense of alienation is revealed in a playful trifle found in a letter from Bolingbroke to Swift. There is no small bitterness in the humorous suggestion that they leave the world behind and establish their own perfect society. Only a Utopia would recapture their lost world:

> My spleen against Europe has more than once made me think of buying the dominion of Bermuda, and spending the remainder of my days as far as possible from those people with whom I have passed the first and greatest part of my life . . . what say you? Will you leave your Hibernian flock to some other shepherd and transplant yourself with me into the middle of the Atlantic Ocean? We will form a society more reasonable and more useful there.[3]

### THE SAVAGE INDIGNATION OF DEAN SWIFT[4]

During the years when Bolingbroke's London-based Opposition scored the contemporary scene, the most scathing denunciation of English folly came from a far-removed Irish Deanery where the aging Jonathan Swift inveighed against his former countrymen as the "most pernicious race of little odious vermin that nature ever suffered to crawl upon the face of the earth."[5] When his pessimism bordered on sheer misanthropy, Swift illustrated the Tory intellectual's most extreme alienation from the Augustan Age. Even Bolingbroke would recoil from this picture of utter depravity; he wrote to Swift that he "could never find in my heart to be so thoroughly angry with the simple, false capricious [world]."[6]

In reconstructing Swift's actual political beliefs, there is no better place to begin than with his "political testament" which he included in a letter to Pope.[7] It opens with a firm declaration against a popish successor and then moves to "revolution principles." Swift approves of violent change in government only when the evils attendant on it are less than the grievances under existing government, which he "take[s] to be the case in the Prince of Orange's expedition." He opposes standing armies in peacetime, for they inevitably enslave a country, and he approves of annual parliaments, adding somewhat rhapsodically, that he loves "the wisdom of that Gothic institution." Annual parliaments would remove the "commerce of corruption" between the ministry and the deputies, so dangerous to liberty and the balance of mixed government. The testament includes an attack on the moneyed power set up "about thirty years ago." Moneyed men should play no role in politics, Swift suggests, for "there could not be a truer maxim in our government than this, that the possessors of the soil are the best judges what is for the advantage of the kingdom." Swift's social and political views would be clear even had he not so explicitly catalogued them in this letter. The Augustan poet and writer, like his Roman archetype, was a public man who perceived his function in part as service to the commonwealth and its statesmen; thus much of Swift's energy and writing was directed to public questions. His responses reflected very closely the political and social views of his good friend, Harry St. John.

Swift's first important political position was, however, opposite to that taken by Bolingbroke. Bolingbroke favored the Tory Commons' impeachment of Whig lords in 1701; Swift, writing then for the Whigs, claimed that the action violated the balance of power essential to a mixed and, therefore, free government.[8] Their disagreement on the immediate issue was of little importance; Swift's theoretical defense of mixed and balanced government in his *Discourse on the Contests and Dissensions Between the Nobles and Commons in Athens and Rome* was based on principles with which Bolingbroke was in perfect accord. It is an eternal rule of politics, Swift suggested, that only mixed governments are free and that in any free government there must be an exact balance between the three powers. Tyranny results when any one force has all power in its scale. In the *Discourse*, Swift rejects the Goths as source of this wise system. It "was by no means a gothick invention"; nor did it come solely from antique wisdom. In an argument much like Harrington's, Swift finds the source of mixed government to lie in nature and reason. Any people that meet together as a civil society, by family government or compact, will inevitably divide themselves into three powers, Swift wrote. Firstly, nature and reason lead them to choose one eminent spirit as leader to defend the country. Secondly, the "natural division of power" leads men with large possessions to secure their property by some great council or senate of nobles. What remains, the body of the people, becomes the third power of this natural balance.[9]

The remainder of the essay treats the lessons to be learned from antiquity. Rome, Athens, and Sparta, we are told by Polybius, recognized the reason of mixed government and perfected the form. Eventually dissensions between the people and the nobility destroyed the balance, and one power claimed all. In every case, Swift contended in 1701, the over-reacher was the people. In Athens the tyranny of the people split apart Solon's balance, in Rome the plebians destroyed the mixed government by their assaults on the patricians. Once the balance was broken, decay and degeneration inevitably followed. As Polybius taught, all political forms tend to decline and die; they are immortal only if the balance of power is maintained.

The political implications of this argument for England in 1701 were self-evident. The impeachment proceedings of the Commons represented too great an assertion of power which would, as in antiquity, destroy the balance within the mixed government. Swift traced the rise of the Commons' power in terms derived from Harrington that described how the alterations of property under the early Tudors were reflected in changed relations of power. Like Bolingbroke, Swift wrote, "In the middle of Elizabeth's reign the power was at a more equal balance than ever before or since."[10] His views on balance and mixed government rested on the same assumptions as Bolingbroke's. In later years Swift, too, would see the Crown and ministry as the menace to the balance, and would agree with Bolingbroke that the Tudor balance and the English constitution faced ruin unless the equal power of the Commons was maintained. He argued this in *The Examiner*, and in *Gulliver's Travels* he implies that Lilliput had once had a balanced constitution that had degenerated through the corrupt system of the King and his advisors. By contrast, the Brobdingnagians had a well-functioning mixed government of nobility, people, and King.[11]

In his *Discourse* of 1701, Swift also attacked parties and factions. In parties, he wrote, man "had neither thoughts, nor actions, nor talk that he [could] call his own; but all conveyed to him by his leader, as wind is through an organ." If men were left unorganized and uninfluenced by other men or groups, prudence and the public good would emerge from their deliberations; otherwise folly and vice would predominate. In his *Examiner*, Swift often returned to the theme of parties. They were senseless distinctions that only divided a nation, particularly senseless now that the modern Whig had come so close to the position of the old Tory. Like Bolingbroke, Swift tended to equate party government and tyranny with Whig supremacy, and a national government above parties, and therefore free, with Tory hegemony. By 1726, and the publication of *Gulliver's Travels*, the Opposition, led by Bolingbroke, was convinced that all party differences had vanished, and that Walpole continued using these meaningless distinctions only to perpetuate Whig control. Swift immortalized this position in his description of the struggle between parties in Lilliput, "each recognised from the high and low heels on their shoes, by which they distinguish themselves." This "meaningful" distinction prompted the Lilliputian King to employ only low heels in the government and to bestow the gifts of the Crown only to such loyal subjects as so distinguished themselves. As one might expect, Brobdingnag is free of parties; indeed, its monarch is a veritable Patriot King; a statesman above parties, learned, of good parts, and solicitous for his people. In return, he is loved by his subjects and, far from becoming their absolute master, as he could, he confines his government to the narrow bounds of common sense and reason.[12]

Another political principle given prominence in the letter cited above from Swift to Pope was a preference for a gentry-based political structure. Like Bolingbroke, Swift thought the post-Revolutionary financial innovations a powerful threat to the old order. In *The Examiner*, Swift described the vast fortunes being made in funds and stock, "so that power which according to the old maxim, was used to follow land, is now gone over to money."[13] The Tudor balance was being seriously undermined, he feared, by a new and frightening alteration of property. Almost more than Bolingbroke, Swift was responsible for identifying the rise of the new Whig political order with the increasing significance of money. In his political writings of 1710-1715, written in active association with the Tory government, Swift dwelt upon the nexus of Whig, Bank, and moneyed men. After the Revolution, he explained, the government intentionally set about cultivating a moneyed interest because the gentry were no longer a reliable enough base upon which to build the new reign. It was decided, he suggests, that lenders to the government would be the surest support; hence the creation of the debt, the Bank of England, and the funds. Whigs argued, he wrote, that it was in the interest of the public to be in debt since men who held the debt would firmly support the government. So a moneyed interest developed soon after the Revolution, an army of clever and cunning men of business and credit, whose job it was to supervise and operate the new financial system. These moneyed men were firm in their support of the party that stood for debt and interest.[14] They took over the estates of the impoverished gentry and bought their way into Parliament by their vast reservoir of paper property. In 1710 these retailers of money dared even to threaten the legislature and monarch of the land with their demands.

The money man, the jobber, and the banker, he contended, had befuddled the simple gentry with an incomprehensible world, "such a mystery of iniquity, and such an unintelligible jargon of terms to involve it in, as were never known in any other age or country of the world." In *Gulliver's Travels* the Lilliputians try hard to safeguard their goods from thieves, "but honesty hath no fence against superior cunning," where the buying, selling, and dealing upon credit is itself theft. Fraud is practiced in Lilliput with impunity. The Patriot King of the Brobdingnagians could not understand this phenomenon of debt. How could Guilliver's native land, he asks, expend twice as much as its revenue? If "he was . . . at a loss how a Kingdom could run out of its estate like a private person," so, too, felt Swift, were many of the English gentry.[15]

The King of Brobdingnag queried Gulliver on whether the commoners chose as their representatives strangers with fat purses of money or landed men from the neighborhood. Gulliver replied that more and more men of money were chosen, despite the prescriptions of the Landed Qualification Act. No one had had greater praise for this Law of 1711 than Swift, who called it "the greatest security that ever was contrived for preserving the Constitution which otherwise might, in a little time, lie wholly at the mercy of the moneyed interest," whose property was "only what is transient or imaginary."[16] Men of imaginary and liquid property obviously cared little for the commonwealth, since no tangible part of it was their own. They could leave the inn or get off the ship whenever they wished.

The new order, Swift contended, not only debilitated the gentry and the gentry constitution, but it also ushered in an age of projects, which, although they moved Defoe to ecstasy, reduced Swift to despair. The Bank, the debt, corporations, imaginary credit, were, he held, all devilish schemes concocted out of the imaginations of upstart men who manipulated the given order.[17] In *Gulliver's Travels* Swift turned the full fury of his "savage indignation" on this projecting spirit. Part III describes the Grand Academy of Lagado, where researchers were busily engaged in such fruitless investigations as seeking to extract sunbeams out of cucumbers.[18] This portrayal of the Academy is the ultimate rejection by the tradition-bound Augustan of the visionary scheme of Bacon's House of Intellect in the *New Atlantis* and the effrontery of the Royal Society. It can also be read as a satire on political projectors, on men scheming to upset the traditional political order, as can Swift's *Irish Tracts*, written in 1721, that attacked the attempt to establish a Bank of Ireland in Dublin.[19] In these, Swift ridiculed the project in satirical essays that described the scheme in phraseology reminiscent of the projecting boom of 1720 in England. The projected Bank was the "wonderful wonder of Wonders, which was the wonder of all the wonders that ever the world wondered at." The Irish Bank, Swift wrote, would only benefit the moneyed men at the expense of the landed classes; it was worthy only of contempt. The projects carried on at the Academy of Lagado, as well as the scatological preoccupations of the academicians, were no more absurd to Swift than many of the schemes floated as corporate ventures in 1719 and 1720.[20]

Swift's satire on the projecting age of financial innovation reaches its peak when he leads Gulliver through Balnibarbi, where men, though busy in the streets and fields, produce nothing. Everyone walks fast there, works hard, and gestures wildly, but nothing grows; jobbers and moneyed men, despite their frenzied activity, contribute nothing to the productive stock of the nation. Gulliver is informed that all estates, houses, and agricultural undertakings in Balnibarbi have been remodeled according to a new system. Forty years earlier the Academy of Projects, it seems, had contrived new rules and methods for agriculture and building, new instruments and tools for all trades and manufactures, so that the fruit of the earth would come to maturity in whatever season one desired and "increase an hundred fold more than they do at present, with innumerable other happy proposals." Gulliver learns that, unhappily, none of the projects was yet perfected; meanwhile the country lay poor and wasted. This, however, did not prevent the enterprising spirits of the Academy from devising more schemes and projects that would ruin more houses and impoverish more honest yeomen. Gulliver's guide through this wasted land, Lord Munodi, had refused to remodel his house and destroy his plantations according to the new system specified by the Academy of

Projects. His reaction to the projecting age is much like Swift's, for he

> was content to go on in the old forms, to live in the houses his ancestors had built, and act as they did in every part of life without innovation . . . Some few other persons of quality and gentry had done the same, but were looked on with an eye of contempt and ill will.[21]

Jonathan Swift thought that the projecting spirit which tempted men to tinker with the status quo involved dangerous interference with God's cosmic order, both social and natural. Such experimentation and innovation could lead only to ruin.

Swift, as well as Bolingbroke, regarded his age as totally corrupt, and involved in a complete social, political, and moral decline. His correspondence from Ireland during the years of the Opposition's greatest activity reveals the extent to which he shared its major assumptions. In 1730 he wrote to Bolingbroke comparing his Lordship's wartime ministry with that of the last sixteen years of peace, and complained that the nation now had a huge debt and "corruption, like avarice, has no bounds." The devil could take those politics, "where a dunce might govern for a dozen years together." The following year he wrote to Gay, marvelling at the number of virtuous men who had banded together from various parties to oppose the corruption embracing England. "If this be disaffection, pray God send me always among the disaffected." Writing to William Pulteney in 1735, he lamented that no nation could experience liberty under one-tenth the luxury of the present age, nor one-millionth of the corruptions. "The Gothic system of limited monarchy is extinguished." This is inevitable, he adds, when a single upstart man, "without a superior advantage either of body or mind, can attack twenty millions, and drag them at his chariot wheels."[22]

In one of his Irish sermons, *Doing Good*, Swift singled out the decline of public spirit and the rise of private interest as the cause of "such a base, corrupted, wicked age as this we live in." Members of a commonwealth, he preached, must love the public more than themselves. This love "was in ancient times properly known by the name of virtue." Today, however, few people thought of their country, and in the pursuit of their own interest, would sacrifice a whole nation.[23] He developed this idea in *Gulliver's Travels*. In

Glubbdubdrib Gulliver called before him the noble Senate of Rome and compared that virtuous public-spirited body with the modern representatives. "The first seemed to be an assembly of heroes and demigods; the other a knot of peddlars, pickpockets, highwaymen, and bullies." The modern legislator was qualified only by his ignorance, idleness, and vice. The nobility, he contended, were as corrupt as the commoners. Gulliver corrects his Houyhnhnm master's misconception of English nobility by informing him that they are in fact bred from childhood in idleness and luxury and often contract odious diseases from lewd women. Far from being public-spirited and virtuous men, they are dull, ignorant, proud, and care little about the duties to the commonwealth incumbent upon their position. Swift rounds out his attack on the corrupt English political structure in his description of its third branch. Gulliver describes for the Houyhnhnms a "first or chief minister" who sought only wealth, power, and titles. Such a minister has all the jobs at his disposal and keeps himself in power by bribing the majority of the Senate. Such ministers, pickpocketing commoners, and scrofulous nobility make up the excellent English constitution, "deservedly the wonder and envy of the whole world."[24]

The financial innovations of modern Whiggery were responsible for such total corruption, but sharing the blame were the ideas of Mandeville and his defense of this new world of money and vice. Corruption, wrote Swift, had grown high and so quick "by the force of luxury so lately introduced."[25] In his discussions with the Houyhnhnms, Gulliver criticizes the very set of immoral men— forgers, gamers, robbers, pimps, liars, thieves—that Mandeville hailed as the mark of a flourishing society. Such men, explained Gulliver, are the inevitable and tragic result of the Yahoo preoccupation with money and their importation of luxuries that only debase and corrupt. Yahoos and mankind are prompted by the same principle of avarice.[26] The Spartan order of the Houyhnhnm's may be unattainable, but it was a model that haunted the Tory intellectual. Nor should one overlook in this vein Swift's satiric masterpiece. His *Modest Proposal*, in which he suggests that the private vice of eating children would lead to the public virtue of solving the dual problems of famine and overpopulation, is both a satire on businesslike projectors and Mandevillean ethics.

Gulliver's lament reflects the nostalgia Swift shared with his friends. The very nature of Englishmen had changed. The words are Gulliver's, but they could as easily be from the *Remarks on the History of England*, *A Dissertation upon Parties*, or *The Idea of a Patriot King*.

> I descended so low as to desire that some English yeoman of the old stamp might be summoned to appear, once so famous for the simplicity of their manners, diet and dress, for justice in their dealings, for the true spirit of liberty, for their valour and love of their country. Neither could I be wholly unmoved after comparing the living with the dead, when I considered how all these pure native virtues were prostituted for a piece of money by their grandchildren.[27]

The principal feature of Swift's ideal image of the world, on the other hand, is the hierarchical ordering of society and nature according to the divinely ordained chain of being.[28] Swift, like Bolingbroke, placed himself in opposition to Locke's theories of voluntary contract sponsored by the emerging middle class. Like angels in the cosmic order, individuals in society, Swift contended, were stationed as links in a hierarchical chain of being, each with an assigned place. Degree and order ruled both God's universe and man's world.

Swift came to this principle from both his humanist and Christian sympathies. Lovejoy has traced the notion of the chain of being back to its classical roots in Platonic, Neo-platonic, and Stoic thought, whence it became a basic part of the medieval Christian world view. Swift's notion of the chain of being also owed much to the social and political elaboration of the idea by English Renaissance humanists like Elyot.[29] Moreover, as an apologist for the aristocracy and gentry Swift could not conceive society without degree and place, without authority and submission. Beneath the humanist prince, at the apex of authority, stood the virtuous and public-spirited nobility and gentry, and below them farmers, merchants, traders, artisans, workers, and servants. Swift's clearest statement of these views is found in his Irish sermon *On Mutual Subjection*.

> As God hath contrived all the works of nature to be useful and in some manner a support to each other, by which the whole frame of the world under His Providence is preserved and kept up; so, among Mankind, our particular stations are appointed to each of us by God Al-

mighty, wherein we are obliged to act, as far as our power reacheth, toward the good of the whole community. And he who doth not perform that part assigned him toward advancing the Benefit of the Whole, in proportion to his opportunities and abilities, is not only a useless, but a very mischievous member of the Publick.[30]

God sees no station as more honorable than another. Submission and authority, Swift wrote, were not necessary to flatter the vanity of the governor, but to prevent sedition through disobedience. Servants obey masters, children their fathers, wives their husbands; otherwise, there would be only great confusion. We have not come very far from the English Renaissance and Shakespeare's "Take but degree away and hark what discord follows."

In another sermon, *On Brotherly Love*, Swift berates "that unhappy disposition towards politicks among the trading people." Politics have not been their concern in the past and should not be so now, because their station is to serve and not to govern. Their threat to the functional order is "some humiliation to the wise and mighty of this world." He returned to this theme in another sermon, *On False Witness*, urging the tradesmen and lower orders to have nothing to do with politics, "or the government of the world, in the nature of which it is certain you are utterly ignorant." In Lilliput, Swift's fictional England, the Lilliputians violated these notions by giving the leadership of public affairs to anyone, as if virtue were distributed equally throughout society, and as if they thought "truth, justice, temperance and the like to be in every man's power." Swift, like Gulliver, was shocked at such beliefs, which ran contrary "to that profound veneration which I am naturally apt to pay to persons of high rank."[31] On the contemporary controversy over charity schools, Swift agreed with criticisms that suggested that the schools were training pupils for jobs above their stations. They should not be taught too much, only enough to suit them "for the very meanest trade," the most important of which would produce a large body of well-behaved servants.[32]

It is natural, then, that Swift's criticism of the new financial order in England stressed its assault on the traditional prescriptions of place in the chain of being. He describes the money men, scriveners, attorneys, stockjobbers, and other retailers of fraud as "able to overreach others much wiser than themselves." They commit the same sin of pride as Lucifer, who had likewise rebelled against his divinely appointed status. These overreachers, Swift argued in *The Examiner*, were now in control of much of the nation's money and power, even though "by their birth, education, and merit, (they) could pretend to no higher than to wear our liveries."[33] In Lilliput, government preferment ignored those of good birth or liberal education and established as criteria for advancement excellence in knavish games such as rope walking and stick jumping. Agility at the Exchange or agility at games are scarcely talents necessary for governing, the Dean implies.[34] In his emphasis on good birth Swift makes even fewer concessions to virtue and merit than did the other Tory intellectuals or their spiritual ancestors, the Renaissance humanists.[35] His *Examiner* criticizes those who argue that virtue and merit are more important than birth, family, and ancient nobility. Recalling the argument of his *Discourse on the Contests and Dissensions* of 1701, he noted that the first cause of Roman ruin was the plebian encroachment upon the patricians. The difference in blood, he argued, was not wholly imaginary. A liberal education, travel, and example of ancestors were advantages that men of better family possessed over the vulgar. Those who rose from obscure birth to great station would inevitably retain some sordid vices of parentage or education, usually avarice and corruption. He does concede that virtue and merit in low birth could occasionally be compatible with statesmanship, "a pearl holds its value although it be found in a dunghill." He quickly adds, however, that "that is not the most probable place to search for it."[36] For Swift, no upstart money man could be a pearl. The pearls fit for governing were made by God and one could find them easily enough by their station, that of country gentry and nobility. The proud men of finance who paid no heed to God's order would accelerate the pace of decline and ruin inevitable in a society without hierarchy where discord and confusion reigned, and corruption went unchecked.

This concept of a chain of being, and the prospect of prideful man wrecking its order, gives structure to a Christian and humanist reading of *Gulliver's Travels*. The position man occupies in the chain of being is a middle state where, half-divine and half-bestial, half-reason and half-passion, he must struggle against an inherent duality in his nature. In the words of Pope man is

> Placed on this isthmus of a middle state,
> A Being darkly wise, and rudely great . . .

He hangs between; in doubt to act, or rest;
In doubt to deem himself a God, or Beast;
In doubt his Mind or Body to prefer . . .[37]

Properly restrained, and inspired by a good example, the humanist like Swift felt that man is capable of keeping his bestial element under control. Medieval beast fables served the humanist well when he wished to ridicule overreaching man who threatened the natural order. Should the basic structure of nature be violated, the traditional relationship between man and beast was likewise threatened, and man appeared more monster than man. Grotesqueness and monstrosity were used as devices for characterization throughout Elizabethan and Jacobean drama. The overreacher destroys the balance and order inherent in nature and will be affected either physically, or mentally. And so the Renaissance Marlowe dooms his Faustus. It is not surprising, then, that Walpole and his race of money men should have been so often satirized by Bolingbroke, Swift, and *The Craftsman* in monstrous and bestial terms. They had committed the sin of tampering with divinely ordained relationships.

### ALEXANDER POPE—OPPOSITION "LAUREATE"

The Augustan poet, like Gulliver, wrote "for the noblest end, to inform and instruct mankind."[38] If the tool of satire was occasionally frivolous, nevertheless it trained to virtue; this notion linked these eighteenth-century intellectuals to their Renaissance and classical ancestors. The new England of Robert Walpole seemed to turn a deaf ear, however, to the admonitions of the poets. In a letter to Pope, Swift complained that the poets of their age were ineffective compared with the golden age of Augustus, when they had "driven the world before them."[39] In Augustan England, the poet who most closely approximated the classical model of public moral teacher was Alexander Pope. Lyttelton exhorted him in 1738:

I wish . . . for nothing more than to exhort and animate you not to bury your excellent talents in a philosophical indolence, but to employ them as you have often done, in the service of virtue . . . some sparks of public virtue are yet alive, which such a spirit as you might blow into a flame . . . though you can't raise her up such ministers, or such senators as you desire yet your writings will . . . be an honour to your country, at a time when it has hardly anything else to be proud of.[40]

Pope was truly like the classicist conception of the poet, for he addressed himself in his poetry to the same grave public concerns as his friends Bolingbroke and Swift did in their prose. He, too, saw the traditional hierarchical ordering of English society and the humanistic values upon which it rested threatened by Walpole and his world. He deftly employed the sharp-edged tool of his satire against what he considered the vicious fools and dunces who displaced the men of wit and good sense.

In *The Dunciad* of 1728, Pope ridiculed Walpole's England in terms no less slashing than Swift's picture of the Lilliputians. Society, full of fools and knaves, bereft of virtue, wit, and good sense, was presided over by the "Great Dunce," Walpole, who had imported from France such noble arts as teaching "Kings to fiddle, and ... Senates to dance." This supreme tyrant enslaved his King, commanded all three estates, and made "ONE MIGHTY DUNCIAD OF THE LAND."[41] Pope returned to an overt attack on Walpole in 1738 and 1739, the years of his closest association with the patriot circle around Frederick. The poet answered Lyttelton's call to speak out publicly with an *Epilogue to the Satires* in 1738. Under Walpole, England had bid "adieu distinction, satire, warmth, and trust," her genius was dragged in the dust, her flag "liveried o'er with foreign Gold." In such an age "NOT TO BE CORRUPTED IS THE SHAME." All England worshiped cheats, whores, thieves, and fools. " 'Tis avarice, all ambition is no more." This degenerate set of men were the "last of Britons"; a people so depraved could not survive.[42]

There was one possible salvation: a Patriot King. Bolingbroke had fired the imagination of Pope with the essay he had written in 1739 and had left with the poet. Pope agreed with Bolingbroke that only a great man near or on the throne could save a people too corrupted to reform themselves. Only such a man could save the people from their own vices and follies and bring them back to the reign of honesty and virtue. In 1740, Pope put into verse the themes of Bolingbroke's *Patriot King*. It is a little known fragment of a poem, published only in 1797, which illustrates both Pope's involvement in the Opposition and the spirit and intent of Bolingbroke's essay. *The Idea of a Patriot King* is sadly distorted when read in the perspective of some possible use or role in the later eighteenth century. It must be read in terms of 1739 and the prevailing nostalgia in that year for the Elizabethan past. *The Patriot*

*King* is no blueprint for despotism or absolute Stuart government, but is simply a plea for a Machiavellian great man—Frederick, Prince of Wales—who, in repudiating Walpole and Georgian England, would restore the England of the past, a virtuous and properly ordered England. Bolingbroke's dream had become Pope's.

> Alas! on one alone our all relies,
> Let him be honest, and he must be wise;
> Let him no trifler from his [father's] school,
> Nor like his [father's] [father] still a [fool,]
> Be but a man! unministered, alone,
> And free at once the senate and the throne;
> Esteem the public love his best supply,
> A king's true glory his integrity;
> Rich with his [Britain] in his [Britain] strong,
> Affect no conquest, but endure no wrong.
> Whatever his religion or his blood,
> His public virtue makes his title good.
> Europe's just balance and our own may stand,
> And one man's honesty redeem the land.[48]

Pope agreed with Bolingbroke's contention that responsibility for the corruption and depravity of their age lay not simply with one man, but more generally with the sinfulness of the new moneyed society that had produced Walpole's power. Immediately after the Bubble, Pope had written to Atterbury describing how England was beset by a proud avarice that had brought down upon it a dramatic rebuke from God.[44] Ferreting out those responsible for this rebuke, Pope turned in his poetry to an assault on Mandeville's assumptions, which he saw as basic to the new order. His *Epistle to Burlington* is ostensibly a simple critique of architectural taste and extravagance in new country homes, and argues that luxury and elegance in art are a departure from the natural, and thus a neoclassical heresy. The poem turns, however, into an attack on squandered wealth, vast expense, and luxury in general. Luxury is a departure from nature and thus not only an abuse of taste, but a danger to the harmony of the natural order. Pope would repudiate Mandeville's praise of profusion and insatiable rapacity, for, in the midst of Timon's luxurious and wasteful banquet, which the satirist curses, the defense is offered, "yet hence the poor are clothed, the hungry fed." But in the poet's view, the prodigal Timon, far from helping the poor with his luxury, has merely defiled the moral character of the commonwealth. The poor are better helped by virtuous and charitable gentlemen like Bathurst and Burlington who improve their soil, and "whose cheerful tenants bless their yearly toil."[45]

In the *Epistle to Bathurst,* Pope offers a more direct attack on the corruption of a moneyed society. The poem reads like a sermon against avarice in which Pope marshals a legion of theological and scriptural references. No longer are luxury and corruption judged simply violations of good taste and the natural order, as in the *Epistle to Burlington* two years earlier; more heinously, the corrupting power of money is now seen as an offense against God. Pope counters the defense of wealth traditionally offered by the dissenter. He insists that wealth is "no grace of heaven or token of the elect" since it is given also to fools and madmen. The poem surveys the Augustan world dominated by avarice and corruption, the latter unleashed by a new "innovation":

> Blest paper credit! last and best supply!
> That lends corruption lighter wings to fly.

Having condemned the practice, the poet shows us the practitioners: a gallery of usurers, jobbers, and South Sea Company directors immortalized by portraits in verse. Money-grubbing Sir Balaam receives the most satiric castigation, in the guise of the archetypal avaricious man of Christian tradition, who, in the New Testament, is described as one who "loved the wages of unrighteousness" (2 Peter 2:15). In the biblical passage Balaam is a gentile seeking to corrupt the Israelites. Pope's use of Balaam suggested to his reader the eighteenth-century money man shunned by the natural Augustan elite, the nobility and landed gentry who observed orthodox Christian teachings on riches and charity.[46]

The poem's answer to Mandeville is offered by both Christian and aristocratic humanism. Pope praises virtuous noblemen like Bathurst and virtuous gentry like the Man of Ross, whose private virtues do lead to public virtues. "Bathurst yet unspoiled by wealth" does not pursue self-interest but because of his aristocratic training is able to overcome his passions and exercise temperance and economy while at the same time enjoying life and the use of riches. The true aristocrat is possessed of that rare classical grace of moving easily between the extremes of the miser and the prodigal. The

Man of Ross, who could well have been the model for Fielding's Squire Allworthy, is a generous soul who spreads charity all around him. He works hard on the soil and has no dealings with evil scriveners and vile attorneys. The poor do not need the venality and luxury of the rich for their support, Pope contends. An enlightened nobility and gentry will see to their welfare because of the precepts of their Christian and humanist values. Public virtue is assured only by such private virtues as charity and honor, not by private vices of luxury, which lead only to the enslavement of England in golden chains. Money, a threat to social stability, is a mechanism which, if effectively used by upstarts, could destroy the positions of power held by the noble Bathurst and the good squire Ross. In Pope's mind, avarice is inextricably linked with proud social climbing—"Avarice, creeping on, Spread like a low-born mist." In an age of greed, "Peeress and Butler share alike the Box."[47]

This is the heart of Pope's antipathy to the moneyed man and the revolution he represents. The new rich threaten the very stability of society with their disdain for the established ranks, ordered in the chain of being. Herein is the essence of a corrupt age. Pope gave the chain of being its principal articulation in the eighteenth century. In his *Essay on Man*, the notion's clearest presentation, he acknowledges his debt to Bolingbroke, "my guide, philosopher, and friend."[48] Pope's image of the chain of being includes the social world as well as the cosmos. The principle of assigned place and rank that holds for angels, men, insects, and pebbles also applies to the various degrees of men. Like Swift's sermon *On Mutual Subjection*, Pope's *Essay* pictures the social world as one great *concors discordia* in which harmony results from subordination of men to those above and authority over those below. Pope's political and social assumptions are described in Epistle IV of the *Essay*.

> Order is Heaven's first law; and this confest,
> Some are, and must be, greater than the rest,
> More rich, more wise.[49]

Into such a hierarchical structure come the money men, breaking apart the natural ties of authority and subjection, and usurping the natural function of leadership. Should his reader doubt that it is the moneyed upstarts the poet would indict in satire, Pope uses the language of the stock exchange to describe this proud man reaching above his place!

> What would this man? Now upward will he soar,
> And little less than angel, would be more;
> Now looking downwards, just as grieved appears
> To want the strength of bulls, the fur of bears.[50]

The money man's aspirations involved a corruption ever more catastrophic than the venal society he represented. They implied the destruction of the humanist world view to which Pope subscribed. The money man was upstart, rootless, and rankless; he threatened not only the aristocratic and gentry leadership, but the entire set of cosmic, religious, and social assumptions upon which it was built. The terror that characterized the reaction of Bolingbroke's circle to the new world is now more understandable. They saw their intellectual as well as sociopolitical world crumbling about them. Without degree, there would be perpetual struggle and universal disorder. One break in the great chain could bring a frightening and chaotic state of upheaval. No wonder, then, the Augustan Poet, confronting such a possible nightmare, would heap scorn on those few money men whose failure to keep their place jeopardized the entire order.

> Where, one step broken, the great scale's destroy'd:
> From Nature's chain whatever link you strike,
> Tenth or ten thousandth, breaks the chain alike.
>
> And, if each system in gradation roll
> Alike essential to the amazing Whole,
> The least confusion but in one, not all
> That system only, but the Whole must fall.[51]

Money men were totally corrupt. They were steeped in a sin more heinous than the petty personal sins of most men. They had willfully threatened the universal order by their rejection of their proper subordination to the natural ranks and degrees of leadership. The creature who rebelled against and disobeyed the laws of hierarchy sinned against God.

> In Pride, in reasoning Pride, our error lies;
> All quit their sphere, and rush into the skies . . .
> All this dread ORDER break—for whom? for thee?
> Vile worm!—Oh madness! Pride! Impiety![52]

England stood on the brink of ruin, and Rome's fate awaited her.

Walpole and his order, thought Pope, had not only destroyed the aristocratic and gentry leadership and humanist values, but they had also destroyed England. The gloom of Bolingbroke's group was the only appropriate response to the doom which must inevitably come when proud man tampers with the great chain of being.

> Lo! thy dread Empire, CHAOS! is restored;
> Light dies before thy uncreating word:
> Thy hand, great Anarch! lets the curtain fall;
> And universal darkness buries all.[53]

England did not die, nor did darkness bury all. The supremacy of the traditional ruling class outlived the lamentations of Pope and Bolingbroke. The view of the world that they saw shattered would be revived later in the century, when the prospect of total social revolution made Edmund Burke return to the imagery that Swift, Pope, and Bolingbroke had revived in the eighteenth century. The French Revolution and its more fundamental threat to what Burke called society's little "platoons" made Walpole and the money man seem insignificant. But one cannot discount the terror felt by conservatives in 1733 simply by describing the more widespread and legitimate horror they experienced in 1790.

### JOHN GAY—BEGGARS, GENTRY, AND SOCIETY

The final member of the triumvirate of Augustan wits in Bolingbroke's coterie was John Gay, born of a comfortable gentry family in rural Devonshire. At seventeen, Gay moved to London and made the city his home for the rest of his life.[54] He never forgot his rural Devon and in his writings Augustan humanism has its poetic rejection of urban civilization and its venal corruptions. In Gay, Augustan nostalgia is given geographical roots. Pope, Swift, and Bolingbroke might look to the past; but Utopia for Gay was closer at hand, in the rural Arcadia outside London, where men and life were natural and genuine.

Gay was a charter member of the Opposition. He had been a "Brother" and an early devotee of the Scriblerus Club's efforts to rout knavery and foolishness. His initiation into the Opposition came during his collaboration with Swift and Bolingbroke on *The Examiner*.[55] His closest political friends were William Pulteney and Will Shippen, the Jacobite, who represent the left and right extremes, of the opposition to Walpole—a fact of more than passing interest, given the tendencies inherent in Gay's poetry.

With the possible exception of *Gulliver's Travels*, there is no more devastating political satire in the English language than Gay's major work, *The Beggar's Opera*. The Augustan wits had learned well from Dryden, their spiritual father. Lord Hervey described Walpole and the Court as infuriated at Gay's "theatrical *Crafts-man*,"[56] and Dr. Arbuthnot, writing to Swift in 1729, informed him that according to Court circles the "inoffensive John Gay is now become one of the obstructions to the peace of Europe, the terror of the ministers, the chief author of *The Craftsman* and all seditious pamphlets which have been published against the government."[57] If there were any doubts as to the political intent of the *Opera*, *The Craftsman* laid them to rest on February 17, 1728, when it "complained" that such a play attacking "certain great men" should be allowed to continue. Some thought, it wrote, that Lockit, the "prime minister" of Newgate, was the hero, because he was a very "corpulent and bulky man," who, with his brother Peachum, controlled a gang of thieves and pickpockets; others argued that Macheath, head of a gang of robbers, was the hero, for "he is often called a 'great man.'" There is no doubt that the *Opera* satirized Walpole, but it did much more than this; it indicted an entire age. Beneath the picturesque, ribald energy and humor of the work is the gloom and nostalgia of Bolingbroke's circle.

Gay devoted more of his literature than *The Beggar's Opera* to the Opposition's attack on Walpole and his politics. His second set of *Fables*, written between 1727 and 1732 for the political instruction of the future Duke of Cumberland, was written in the medieval genre of the beast fable, and employed the jackal, leopard, and bee, to suggest satirically that Walpole and his henchmen were somewhat less than men, having acted so immorally as to lose their place in the chain of being. The morals derived from these *Fables* were the stock Opposition attitudes.[58] Good political men were "by neither place nor pension bought, / they spoke and voted as they thought" and were zealous of the public weal and defended its laws. Socially, they were those "whose ancestors served the crown with loyal zeal," whose "virtue prove you greatly born." What a contrast to the realities of the Augustan scene, where Walpole's reign was, on the contrary, built upon the evils of the moneyed society.

> If schemes of lucre haunt his brain,
> projectors swell his greedy train;
> vile brokers ply his private ear
> with jobs of plunder for the year;[59]

It is Mandeville whom Gay seeks most to ridicule. Fable XI directly assaults the philosopher of avarice using the same poetic imagery he had used. If there were any doubt of the relationship between Mandeville's ideas and his age, this poetic rebuttal by Gay makes it clear that they were inextricably bound to Walpole and the new economic order. Gay describes an honest and industrious beehive, in which prosperity and public virtue result from the several bees' practice of private virtues. Reversing Mandeville, Gay places a degenerate and corrupt bee in the hive who "reforms" it by turning the virtuous bees to useless lives of luxury and idleness. Only one lone patriot bee remembers the old days of the hive, and he is soon evicted by the degenerate bees for upholding old traditions of honest toil. The hive, once productive and happy, becomes depraved, corrupt, and moribund. In his description of the one original corrupting bee, Gay lashes out not only at Walpole and Mandeville, but at the larger social vices which he felt they served.

> A bee of cunning, not of parts,
> Luxurious, negligent of arts,
> Rapacious, arrogant and vain,
> Greedy of pow'r, but more of gain,
> Corruption sow'd throughout the hive—
> By petty rogues the great ones thrive.[60]

Gay's poetry reflects another dimension of the Opposition mind in its contrast of the country with the town.[61] His *Rural Sports* and *Polly* describe an idyllic image of rural Arcadia. The King of the noble and innocent rural Indians in *Polly* discovers, while talking with the leader of the city thieves, that people in an urban and commercial civilization have no honest industry and no respect for virtue, wisdom, or honor. "Have you no conscience, have you no shame?" the King asks. Only "of being poor" is the thief's response. The Indian King replies.

How can society subsist with avarice! Ye are but the forms of men. Beasts would thrust you out of their herd upon that account, and men should cast you out for your brutal dispositions.[62]

This confrontation, reminiscent of that between Gulliver and the King of Brobdingnag, repeats the charge so often heard in the Opposition's central organ, *The Craftsman*. Covetous destroyers of the established order were less than men; they were monstrous specimens incapable of inhabiting their God-given place.

Gay, with his *Trivia or the Art of Walking the Streets of London* and the *Beggar's Opera* was, along with Defoe, the great eighteenth-century poet of London. But Gay depicts London as a far less pleasing place than Defoe does. Gay continually contrasts the foibles and corruptions of artificial and venal urban civilization with the simplicity and naturalness of life in the country. Rural man is innocent and honest; urban man is obsessed with greed for money or power. Gay's descriptions of the city emphasize the superfluous and useless jobs of those who cater to luxury and pride, whereas in "the virtuous" countryside the economy and social order tolerate only functional and useful occupations. City man practices deceit and hypocrisy, whereas rural man has common sense, reason, and integrity.

> Long in the noisie town have been immur'd,
> Respir'd its smoak, and all its cares endur'd,
> Where news and politicks divide mankind,
> And schemes of state involve th' uneasie mind;
> Faction embroils the world; and ev'ry Tongue
> Is moved by flatt'ry, or with scandal hung:[63]

A recent student of Gay's social thought regards this fascination with the countryside as derived from Gay's sense of the injustice that resided in the town.[64] Country life, Armens suggests, seemed more egalitarian to Gay, who like Rousseau, is said to have seen there some primitive democratic ideal. It is just as easy to argue, however, that the countryside appealed to Gay because it embodied social order and stratification. In the eighteenth century, the town was the altar upon which the egalitarian worshipped.[65] The traditionalist, appalled at social mobility and loss of distinction in the city, turned, as Gay did, to the rural scene. Rural society was not only functional, honest, and innocent, but also structured. Men knew their place there. In Gay's praise of the innocent rural maid, it was not only her simplicity and frugality that he contrasted favorably with the luxury of the city, but also her acceptance of her place and rank in the social chain of being. Country man and woman were not proud; they were not overreachers. Unlike city people, they posed no threat to the social order.

> What happiness the rural maid attends,
> In cheerful labour while each day she spends!
> She gratefully receives what heav'n has sent,
> And, rich in poverty, enjoys content:
> Her home-spun dress in simple neatness lies,
> And for no glaring equipage she sighs:[66]

Like Goldsmith's, Gay's criticism of the emerging institutions of a commercial urban and bourgeois society is derived not from radical egalitarianism, but from a socially reactionary position. The new civilization threatened to destroy the stable and traditional order of an organic and hierarchical society, rooted in the land.[67] "There Essex, Cecil, Bedford's, Villier's, now no more," laments the poet while walking the London streets in his *Trivia*.[68] In the new order such noble men have been replaced by thieves, pickpockets, and beggars.

*The Beggar's Opera*, Gay's masterpiece, is more than a mere satire on Walpole and Townshend and their patronage of corruption. The play is a parable on the fate of men of quality, which explains, perhaps, why Gay's fellow poet, Defoe, found the opera so morally reprehensible.[69] There are two predominant themes in the opera: the first, and more obvious, deals with the changes in values brought to society by money and its preeminence, exemplified by the image offered of a society made up completely of bees like Mandeville's, who pursue vice and crime. But Gay's satire is double-edged. The band of thieves presents a negative image of the pervasive corruption in society; at the same time, it can be taken to represent former men of quality who have been victimized by social upstarts. Having been reduced to the lowest position on the social ladder, they are now ruled by Lockit and Peachum, men intrinsically less honorable than they.

Gay has much to say in *The Beggar's Opera* on the significance of money, at the root of corrupt London. He depicts a society obsessed with a passion for gain. The whores sell their friend Macheath to Peachum and the police for money; Peachum and his wife want to kill Macheath, the husband of their beloved daughter, Polly, for profit. Lockit proclaims Mandeville's ideal, which rules this society. "Everyone of us preys upon his neighbours." In Gay's presentation, this is an accounting society in which Peachum and Lockit stand over their balances, and tally up the fruits of human self-interest and avarice. The cardinal rule of the society is exposed by the indignant Macheath. "Money well timed and properly applied, will do anything." Bolingbroke had said the same in *A Dissertation upon Parties*: in the world as now constituted, money was the real power.

Gay also uses the gang of thieves headed by Macheath to illustrate the fate of gentry and noblemen of quality in a commercial society. This device makes his evident sympathy and preference for the thieves over Lockit and Peachum more comprehensible. Throughout the opera, Macheath, called "sir" and "noble captain," and the thieves, are described as fine men, gentlemen, and men of honor. Their values are those of men of quality: honor, loyalty, and courage. One of the band exclaims "the world is avaricious and I hate avarice," another "I hate your bank bills." When Gay has one of the gang ask "Why are the laws against us?", it is more than the moan of an oppressed criminal questioning his exclusion from the legal system of his masters; it is also a characteristic theme of gentry discontent, an attack on law and lawyers as agents of the new artificial world brought by financial capitalism, much like the theme Goldsmith would give voice to in his poetry and Swift in his prose. The discontented gentry-thief in the *Opera* speaks out against the law and its role in the new contractual world that has destroyed the natural and genuine world where legal bonds were irrelevant. Gay's intention in the *Opera* is to picture the pathetic depths to which former men of quality have sunk at the hands of such as Lockit and Peachum. How else can the lament of the whore Jenny be understood?

> The gamesters and lawyers are jugglers alike:
> If they meddle, your all is in danger;
> Like gipsies, if once they can finger a souse,
> Your pockets they pick, and they pilfer your house,
> And give your estate to a stranger.

London low life had few houses and even fewer estates! That Gay intends Macheath and the "noble" members of his gang to represent the social revolution of the age satirically is further suggested by his description of their relationship to Peachum. Just as the leadership of the gentry and nobility had been usurped by upstart money men and Walpole, who understood the mysterious workings of the new financial world, so, too, Macheath and his gang were dependent upon Lockit, the Walpole of Gay's *Opera*. Although they are patently more honorable and more virtuous than Lockit and Peachum, and although they should by right be his superiors, Lockit controls their lives and gives them orders. He is leader because he is privy to secrets of the system beyond the grasp of Macheath and the gang. "Business cannot go on without him; he is a man who knows the world, and is a necessary agent to us."[70]

Gay's *Beggar's Opera* can be seen, then, as a central statement of the Opposition argument. On the one hand, in its picture of the army of beggars, whores, and pickpockets organized by Lockit and Peachum, it portrays a corrupt urban society preoccupied with money, a world in which "if you would not be looked upon as a fool, you should never do anything but upon the foot of interest. Those that act otherwise are their own bubbles."[71] On the other hand, Gay has, at the same time and with the same devices, depicted the fate of men of quality in such a venal society and world. The *Opera* is a tale of economic and social injustice, but in Gay's version, the virtues belong not to the poor! Noble and honorable Macheath and his gang, all men of quality, are subordinated, jailed, and put totally at the whim of the organizers and manipulators of the corrupt world, Peachum and Lockit, who are themselves mere upstarts with no quality, honor, or virtue. How truthful Lockit is when he tells Peachum, "You and I . . . are to have a fair trial which of us can overreach the other."[72] The ultimate fate of men of quality, Gay suggests, is to become as venal and corrupt as their new masters. When their fraternal and noble club becomes a band of thieves, then the entire society had been rendered corrupt by the Lockits and Peachums. If there were any doubts about Gay's intention or sympathies, his epilogue sets them to rest. Macheath and his band are indeed the oppressed former ruling class.

[Beggar:] Through the whole piece you may observe such a similitude of manners in high and low life, that it is difficult to determine whether . . . the fine gentlemen imitate the gentlemen of the road, or the gentlemen of the road the fine gentlemen.[73]

*The Beggar's Opera* was, as Hervey said, a true theatrical rendering of Bolingbroke's *Craftsman*. In it, Gay dramatized the central concern of *The Craftsman*—the destruction of the traditional ranks in society that put men of virtue and quality at the mercy of upstarts and overreachers.

LORD LYTTELTON'S *Persian Letters* AND THE ELIZABETHAN MODEL

Lord Hervey said of Lyttelton, who criticized Hervey's king and first minister, that his writings, "were generally borrowed from the commonplace maxims and sentiments of moralists, philosophers, patriots, and poets."[74] Lyttelton's writings were, for the most part, repetitions in more popular terms of the positions set forth by Bolingbroke. But George Lyttelton, secretary to Frederick, Prince of Wales, and the poets' friend, was considered by Walpole's press to be second only to Bolingbroke as a theoretical spokesman for the political and poetic Opposition.[75] He contributed two significant works to the corpus of Augustan and Opposition political thought, his *Considerations Upon the Present State of Affairs at Home and Abroad* (1739) which repeats Bolingbroke's call for a patriot king to rescue the English, and his *Letters from a Persian in England to a Friend at Ispahan*. So great was the success of Montesquieu's *Persian Letters* and so evident was their usefulness as a tool for social criticism, that Lyttelton was able to copy their format and their use once again in *The Craftsman*, and, to produce, in 1735, one of the most popular works of political writing in the reign of George II.

One of the themes in Lyttelton's *Persian Letters*, as in all Opposition writings, was an attack on the new economic order. In most parts of England, the Persian wrote, gentlemen were so racked by taxes "that those who have nothing from the Court can scarce support their families." The only prosperous men he found were those who had money in the funds. All men gamed with pieces of paper which decided "whether he who is now a man of quality shall be a beggar." Other men made sport with the public's money, raising estates by the misery and ruin of the country. The gentry, the Persian found, lay oppressed by the new mechanisms of public credit, false and illusory foundations for a strong state. Selim wrote from England to his friend in Persia:

I have seen them wrapt up in full security upon the flourishing state of public credit, only because they had a prodigious store of paper, which now indeed they circulate as money, but which the first alarm of a calamity, may in an instant make meer paper of again.[76]

Visiting the Royal Exchange, the Persian noted how useful and honorable the merchants were who met there to contribute to the common happiness. In a neighboring alley, however, he found magicians, "masters of the secret art," who, by creating ebbs and flows, destroyed all fortunes but their own. Sometimes, Selim wrote to Mirza, they raised such violent storms as to sink half the wealth of the nation.[77]

Selim's letters also had much to say about English political institutions. The English, he wrote, prided themselves on a mixed government which they claim to have possessed since their Saxon days. This Saxon balance had been threatened, though not destroyed, by the large landholdings of the Crown, Church, and nobility in the medieval period. The Crown, he reports, jealous of the nobility, raised up the Commons in the early Tudor period to be a match for both the Crown and the Lords. Selim informs Mirza that thus it was that the English achieved perfection of government in the late sixteenth century during what they call the golden age of Queen Elizabeth.

> Thou will be surprised to hear that the period when the English nation enjoyed the greatest happiness was under the influence of a woman . . . It was not until the Reign of Queen Elizabeth that this government CAME TO AN EQUAL BALANCE, WHICH IS THE TRUE PERFECTION OF IT.[78]

Under Elizabeth, the Commons' riches secured their independence. Her great skill, the Persian wrote, was to give each power its proper weight, while keeping her own authority entire. "She was the head of a well proportioned body, and supremely directed all its motions." Elizabeth, the model of a patriot monarch, "ruled by no party; therefore, she had no occasion to employ the arts of corruption to attach her subjects to her service, a maxim little known and seldom practiced by her successors."[79]

Like Bolingbroke, Lyttelton's Persian interpreted the constitutional crisis of the seventeenth century as a breakdown in the perfect Elizabethan balance of property and power. James I "endeavored to break the balance of the government by her so wisely fix't." Stuart claims of prerogative threatened the power that commoners had acquired and maintained under the Tudors. The result was a great defensive war waged by the Commons. Charles II and James II, later kings, returned to the bad practices of their Stuart predecessors and destroyed the balance. The Glorious Revolution, however, restored the government to its Saxon and Elizabethan principles. "King James the second lost his crown," Selim informs his friend, "and the nation gave it to their deliverer, the Prince of Orange; the government was settled on . . . the ancient Saxon principles from which it had declined." The story does not end here, Selim reports, for the Elizabethan balance, reestablished in 1688, was again threatened in the eighteenth century, not by prerogative, but by money. The power of the Commons was being undermined by the Crown and the ministers, who were making Parliament dependent on the throne. They were enabled to do this by corruption and the general venality encouraged by the post-Revolutionary economic order. Of the tools used to destroy the traditional order, Selim wrote to Mirza, "many . . . are newly introduced, and so contrary to the genius of the people, that one could hope they might be easily rooted out."[80] The new age, Selim thought, was extravagant and luxurious, and had no regard for frugality or public expense; because hordes of officers were required to collect taxes and administer the funds, the Crown and the minister acquired vast power over and above that gained from their purchase of the Commons.

Like Goldsmith and Gulliver, Lyttelton's Persian denounced the legalism implicit in the new contractual and financial world. More genuine political systems, he contended, lacked the multiplicity of English laws. "In Asia, a few plain words are found sufficient to settle the difference of particulars in a state." The new order was not only a departure from the true constitution of government, but also involved the decline and degeneration of the entire society. With this pessimistic prophecy Selim took leave of his English hosts.

To the constitution of their government alone are attached all those blessings and advantages; should that ever be corrupted or depraved, they must expect to become the most contemptible and most unhappy of mankind . . . I therefore take my leave of my friends here, with this affectionate and most dignified advice; that they should vigilantly watch over their constitution, and guard it by those Bulwarks, which alone are able to secure it justice, vigor, perseverance and frugality.[81]

Lyttelton's writings were, along with the *Patriot King*, at the center of the cult of Elizabeth in the late 1730's. Elizabeth was important for the Opposition not only because her reign appeared the golden age of balance that marked the beginning of gentry power, but also because of developments in the international sphere and the rivalry with Spain. Despite the affair of Jenkins' Ear and small trader demands for a war, Walpole sought accommodation and peace. How better for the Opposition to ridicule his pacifism than to compare it with Elizabeth's earlier treatment of the brazen Spaniard? The political literature of the period, in its attacks on Walpole's convention of 1739, constantly dwelt on this aspect of the Elizabethan Age. Lyttelton called upon the English in retaliation for twenty years of Spanish insult "to seize their Treasures."[82] He invoked memories of Drake, Raleigh, Grenville, and Cumberland to illustrate how a glorious age met Spanish treachery. Walpole's pamphleteers retaliated by attempting to dim the splendor of Elizabeth's achievements, one even suggesting that the Armada would never have been defeated "had not the providence of God by storms and tempests established her safety."[83] H. R. Trevor-Roper's "declining mere gentry" of the seventeenth century, nostalgic for the Spanish plunder of Elizabethan England, almost pale before the explosion of Elizabethan and anti-Spanish feeling among the discontented gentry and city traders in 1739. This popular ground swell got its war in 1742, and with it release for two decades of frustration.[84] The existence of this sentiment makes Bolingbroke's preoccupation in the *Patriot King* with trade, Elizabeth, and Britain's mastery of the sea more understandable, since all of these concerns reached a peak in the year he wrote the essay. Here was yet another reason for Burke to care little for Bolingbroke, whose *Patriot King*, albeit merely circulated among friends, tied him to the pressure that had forced Walpole into war. The events of these years were forever a frightening example to Burke of the hazards created by outside pressure on the independent decisions of reasonable and wise legislators.

Sir Robert was forced into the war by the people who were enflamed to this measure by the most leading politicians, by their own orators and the greatest poets of the time. For that war Pope sang his dying notes. For that war Johnson, in more energetic strains, employed the voice of his early genius . . . The crowd readily followed the politicians for the

233

cry for war which threatened little bloodshed . . . and promised something more solid than glory, plunder . . . When I was very young, a general fashion told me I was to admire some of the writings against that minister [Walpole]; a little more maturity taught me as much to despise them.[85]

Burke was right. The poets did sing the praises of both the war and Bolingbroke's idea of a patriot king. Lyttelton, the literary patron, was the center of this poetic cult of Frederick and the war.[86] Richard Glover, Henry Brooke, David Mallet, and James Thomson wrote poems and plays depicting a corrupt, failing Albion, suffering insults from southern insolents. Their writings contained verse after verse praising Frederick as a patriot restorer of the glorious past. This was the setting in which Thomson and Mallet wrote their "Rule Britannia," Pope his *Seventeen Hundred and Forty,* and Johnson his poems, *London* and *Irene,* which attacked Walpole.[87]

The social and political nostalgia of Bolingbroke's circle expressed itself in political poetry and romantic politics. This group of intellectuals sensed that the social order that had supported them for a century and a half was passing. They responded to the new society that had developed since 1688 with satire, drama, poetry, and political essays. The intellectual center around which these wits gathered was Bolingbroke, whose writings expressed the lamentations of the traditional ruling class and shaped the political mind of the literati. The nostalgia that pervades Bolingbroke's circle is best captured in verse. The poet is Lyttelton's protégé, Thomson, King Edward is Frederick, and the ideas are Bolingbroke's.

> O save our Country, Edward! save a nation,
> The chosen Land, the last Retreat of Freedom,
> Amidst a broken World! Cast back thy view,
> And trace from farthest Times her old Renown.
> . . . Then see all This,
> This Virtue, Wisdom, Toil and Blood of Ages.
> Behold it ready to be lost for ever.
> Behold us almost broken to the Yoke,
> Robbed of our ancient Spirit, sunk in Baseness,
> At home corrupted, and despis'd abroad,
> Behold our Wealth consum'd, those Treasures squander'd,
> That might protect and nourish wholesome Peace,

Or urge a glorious War; on Wretches squander'd,
A venal Crew that plunder and disgrace us.
In this important, this decisive Hour,
On Thee, and Thee alone, our weeping Country
Turns her distressful Eye; to Thee she calls,
And with a helpless Parent's piercing Voice.
Wilt thou not live for Her?[88]

# IX

## The Ambivalence of the Augustan Commonwealthman

The political thought of the Augustan period includes one final set of important writers, the Commonwealthmen. The group has recently been depicted as a progressive, even radical force, who "in varying ways provided a deterrent to complacency, and reminders of the need for improvement and continual adaptation of even good governments to economic and political changes."[1] To oppose corruption, the Cabinet, and the office of Prime Minister is, however, not the same as being progressive; nor, in an age pervaded by the thought of Harrington, is it a sufficient mark of a radical Whig for one to be thought a Harringtonian. In the thought of these Commonwealthmen or "honest Whigs," much of what appears to be opposed to the prevailing thought and mores of the period is really a substantial social and political nostalgia. A great deal of the thought of the Commonwealthmen is tied to gentry discontent and reflects a longing for a return to pre-Revolutionary England. They sought to return to Harrington's dream, his complete dream, the gentry paradise as well as the Rota.

The Commonwealthmen did advocate electoral and colonial reform and increased toleration, in which they looked to the future, but in aligning them with a continuum of reform from Harrington to Price, one should not overlook the extent to which they also reflected the Augustan mood of gloom and resentment at the changes in the economy, politics, and social structure of England.[2] The similarity of the tone of much of their writing to the mood of Bolingbroke's circle is important in helping to account for the ease with which Bolingbroke could be included with these "radical Whigs" in countless invocations by later English and American radicals. It also helps to illustrate the wide base of alienation from the new England that existed among political writers of the period.[3] The Commonwealthmen, then, present two faces to the student of Augustan political thought: one that very much resembles Bolingbroke, and another whose appearance is genuinely liberal tending to radical.

### DR. CHARLES DAVENANT

Dr. Charles Davenant, a member of that remarkable circle of economists and statisticians that flourished in England at the very end of the seventeenth century, has been described by some commentators as a Tory and member of the Tory freetrading circle, or even as a High Church Tory.[4] Others include Davenant in the circle of the Commonwealthmen, basing this description on his writings, which defend old Whigs against modern Whigs, and on his friendship with the third Earl of Shaftesbury.[5] However one labels Davenant, a reading of his political works proves him to be the first major Augustan writer to respond unfavorably to the new age. In his writings are many themes which would be picked up in the next forty years.

At the center of his social thought is a rejection of the post-Revolutionary innovations that uses the very terms in which Defoe had so glorified them. Davenant agreed with Defoe's assertion that they lived in an age of projects, but, his response paralleled the gloom of Swift and Bolingbroke.

War, among the Monsters it engenders in the womb of the state, begets and gives rise to a set of busy, undertaking, ambitious, light and projecting persons, who are then brought upon the stage of business. These, whom peace would have left in their original obscurity, in troublesome times shine forth; but they are like portentous meteors, threatening ruin to the country that is under their malevolent aspect.[6]

The inventors of these pernicious projects charge the income of England with new duties. This "mine of new projects" seemed never to be exhausted because a projecting party of obscure men was bent on raising prodigious fortunes. The gentry, Davenant wrote, suffering unjustly under the long burden of taxes, had been made to pay for the whims of the projectors: the national Bank, the immense debt, large moneyed companies, and stockjobbing. The "inventors and promoters of these projects," the money men and usurers, grew rich at the expense of the land and the labor of the people. The national debt, he wrote, the most pernicious of the projects, divided the country into two ranks of men, the creditors and the debtors. The creditors were the Bank, lenders of all kind, and foreigners; the debtors were the landed men, small merchants, and shopkeepers. One project of the moneyed man which he singled out was paper credit. The projecting party might boast of it, he wrote, but this "imaginary wealth" lulled the nation asleep, while the ready money to carry on business was exported. The projector and his work were threats to the stability of the body politic. "Let the Bank and New companies at no time give visible proofs that they unite their interest and strength against the constitution and liberties of England."[7] Money men, who gave the law and held the rest of the people in their power, were the only beneficiaries of an age of projects.

In Davenant's opinion England was a totally corrupt land. The war and the age of projects had left all ranks of men depraved, and had allowed private men to make fortunes out of the kingdom's treasury. None were even ashamed that they robbed the nation.

The little public spirit that remained among us is, in a manner, quite extinguished. Everyone is upon the Scrape for himself, without any regard to his country; each is cheating, raking and plundering what he can, and in a more profligate degree than ever yet was known. In short this self-interest runs through all our actions and mixes in all our councils.[8]

The most insidious manifestation of this spirit of corruption, he felt, was the bribing of Members of Parliament with pension and place. A servile legislature spelled the doom of free government; wealth and greatness depended upon keeping the legislative power untainted. The commonwealth needed to be ever watchful over its ministers, to see that the members of the legislature were not awed by standing armies, nor seduced by preferments, bribes or pensions. Davenant anticipated, however, an increase in parliamentary corruption, since the projecting party had so distressed the gentry that they would be made to turn to the court and ministry for a livelihood.[9]

Like most of the critics of "corrupt England" in the early eighteenth century, Davenant was fond of antiquity. Not only was his writing, therefore, liberally spiced with classical wisdom, but before him always loomed the model of Rome and its decline. The decline of public spirit among the English, combined with their corruption and profligacy, augured a similar fate. The only way for the English to save themselves was retrenchment, public thrift, and frugality; they should make an example of Roman greatness that, before the decline, took its rise "from the thrift shown in all matters relating to the public." In his *Discourse on the Public Revenue and on the Trade of England,* Davenant included a *Discourse* by Xenophon on the revenue of Athens that had been translated by another of the Commonwealthmen, Walter Moyle.[10] His purpose, Davenant wrote, was to show the public how ancient were the true notions of thrift, and how the treasure of the public could be managed with frugality.

The decline of Rome, and of an unaware England, began with the extinguishing of ancient honor by luxury, ambition, and a careless and profligate reign. Davenant, unlike Mandeville and Defoe, was suspicious of too much foreign trade, because it introduced luxury that depraved, corrupted, and enslaved people, destroying their virtue and simplicity of manners. But it was a necessary evil, to be tolerated so long as it served the advantage and safety of the state rather than the rapacious ambitions of traders. But necessary evil or no, Davenant could not help but admit that "the writer of these papers thinks it is his duty to recommend frugality in the state and he believes it is the wisest and most honest way of enriching the public to make it rich out of its own revenue."[11]

Davenant's image of the ideal constitutional order was that of the apologists for the aristocracy and gentry.

> In the natural body, the head does not walk, the hands digest, or the stomach think, but each member has its proper and separate performances. It is the same in a state well regulated, where all the parts that compose it have their distinct and peculiar functions.[12]

In such a natural and well-regulated state it was not the function of upstart money men to govern. Obscure persons who sought only to build families they did not have and to make their fortunes were not natural leaders of the political community. Such men had a different interest from that of their country. They preferred, wrote Davenant, peace or war only as it affected their Bank, or East India Stock, the interest on their tallies, their Exchequer bills, or their

Bank notes. Such men lacked honor and virtue and pursued only their own interest, not the commonwealth's. They were unfit to be governors. The function of governing the commonwealth rested with the nobility and the gentry, those who were high born, whose virtue put them on a pedestal, and whose wealth put them above private and domestic cares. Such men should devote all their time and thought to the service of the community. The men who helped the monarch govern should have fortunes of their own, courage, eloquence, experience, and "ancestors the people read of every day in the chronicles of past times." In a perfect order, Davenant wrote, neither wealth, nor titles, but only virtue and ability would entitle a man to the honors and employments of his country. In this imperfect world, however, there was but one choice:

> They should endeavor to have places of great honour and high trust filled with persons whose birth, estates, and other circumstances, seem in human probability to set them at least above the common temptations of the world . . . He who has a large estate will not consent to have the laws subverted, which are his firmest security . . . They who are well born will desire to preserve that constitution of which they and their ancestors have always been a part.[13]

Several other interesting contributions to the political thought of the Augustan Age are found in the writings of this political arithmetician and statistician. Davenant, for example, had harsh words for what he saw as the developing institution of the first minister. He called him the "political manager," a man upon whom all eyes were bent, and who gave the first turn in most things. Davenant correctly perceived the fusion of powers implicit in this new office. "In the House they undertake for the Court, and at Court for the House." Things never went well under such a minister. Moreover, a free country should never allow the prince to be engrossed by any one person. Figures in the past who had sought to be ministers without associates had ended up unfortunately. The example of Wolsey should be enough to discourage the phenomenon of a single minister.[14] As their historian has noted, this reaction to the early development of the prime minister was a common reflex among Augustan Commonwealthmen.[15] Davenant's views on representation, however, were similar to the conventional Whig position found in Walpole, Hume, and later, in Burke. The people had no right to dictate to their members; the vulgar, he wrote, should have little role in the political process. Harrington and Sidney, Davenant points out, and all the best of the Republican writers, thought nothing more should be left to the judgment of the common people than the power to assent or dissent. Davenant's description of the representative function of the Member of Parliament is an almost verbatim anticipation of Burke's terminology.

When they enter the House, they are not so much to pursue the interest of this or that borough, as to promote the general interest of England: As indeed when they are assembled all together, not properly representing their respective counties and corporations, but representing the whole kingdom.[16]

Like the other Commonwealthmen, Davenant praised England's gothic constitution. Similarly, he attacked factions. "Faction itself is in its nature, pernicious and produces more fatal mischiefs than foreign war, sickness, famine or any other evil the anger of heaven brings down upon us." His writings, however, contain comments on party more interesting than this traditional attack. He describes, for example, the inevitability of two parties appearing in great assemblies; a country party which loves the country and its liberties, and a court party of mercenary slaves to power. More interesting, because of its less obvious partisanship, is his suggestion that any party in power, although it began as just and mindful of the commonwealth, will be "quite corrupted by prosperity and power," and that the opposition, although it may have been in the wrong at first, will, while it is "out," acquire honor and virtue and thus provide a suitable alternative for the "ins" corrupted by power. The most important of Davenant's insights into the nature of party is his early recognition of the loss since the Revolution of the hitherto significant distinctions between the Whigs and the Tories. "It is hoped these names of distinction are now quite forgotten." New distinctions might arise, however; old Whigs might, as modern Whigs, carry out the old Tory principles. If this occurred, as seemed likely, then the English Constitution would be in mortal danger, for who, he asks, would be suspicious of these modern Whigs, the favorites of the people for having so often preserved England? "No person could be popular enough in Rome to think of subverting its constitution in the purity of the Commonwealth, but Manilius who had saved the capitol."[17]

Davenant's contention that the modern Whig was equivalent to

the old Tory, and the present day Tory to the true Whig, anticipated and perhaps helped shape, the attitude fundamental to Bolingbroke and his Opposition. This argument is most concisely put
in Davenant's dialogue, *The True Picture of a Modern Whig*
(1702),[18] in which Mr. Double, the modern Whig, informs Mr.
Whiglove, the real Whig, of the principles of modern Whiggery.
The first is that this party reaps the advantages from long, bloody,
and expensive wars. The modern Whig, Double contends, is a man
with money in his pockets, which gives him power, however mean
his birth. Mr. Double is himself worth £50,000, although only
fourteen years ago (1688!) he had had no shoes for his feet. The
modern Whig does not rise by virtue, he relates, but by office and the
market; he advocates a standing army, opposes frequent parliaments,
and is in favor of the corrupt dependence of the legislature on the
executive. While the old Whig was frugal, the modern squandered
money and loaded the people with taxes. After listening to this, Mr.
Whiglove asks if there is any way he can prove his conversion to
the modern Whig notions of Mr. Double. "Yes, indeed," answers
Mr. Double,

> In general, detract from and asperse all the men of quality of whom
> there is any appearance that either their high birth, or their great for-
> tunes, or their abilities in matters of government should recommend
> them to the future administration of affairs . . . It is our interest to
> humble the ancient gentry because they know our originals and call us
> upstarts and leeches that are swollen big by sucking up the nation's
> blood.[19]

Double tells Whiglove that modern Whigs stick to the cry of the
Revolution, "Borrow, borrow"; the more you borrow, the more
friends you fix to your side. Create new funds, and all who are
drawn in are with you through any hazard. Double informs Whiglove that, a war being in the offing with France, modern Whigs
would tax the land four or five shillings in the pound and impoverish the gentry, while "our ready money . . . will increase like a
snowball, rolling it about as we intend to do from fund to fund, so
that all the land will be ours, and then most of the elections will be
at our disposals."[20]

Writing in 1702, Davenant prefigured with amazing precision
the contents of much of the later writings of Swift and Bolingbroke. His was a rejection, as bitter as theirs, of the new order in

England with all its economic, social, and political ramifications. They stood together as implacable enemies of Defoe's age of projects. Had not Mr. Double, the modern Whig, told Mr. Whiglove:

For what had become of our party if it had not been for these projects? It is true we have run the nation over head and ears in debt by our funds, and new devices . . . in tallies and the new stocks.[21]

### JOHN TRENCHARD AND THOMAS GORDON: *Cato's Letters*

With the exception of Bolingbroke, the most interesting and significant political writing of the Augustan period came from the two Commonwealthmen, Trenchard and Gordon, who produced *Cato's Letters* in the years immediately after Walpole became first minister. Trenchard, the more distinguished and impressive of the two, was a Member of Parliament from the 1690's to the early 1720's. He and Walter Moyle had, in 1697, written the classic "Commonwealth" attack on William's standing army, and in 1718 and 1719 Trenchard wrote pamphlets for Walpole against Stanhope's Peerage Bill. Trenchard's greatest political achievement was his leadership with Lord Molesworth of the attack in Parliament on Walpole's "screen" of the South Sea Directors in 1720. Collaborating with Thomas Gordon, he wrote weekly letters in what was then an Opposition weekly, *The London Journal,* under the pseudonym, Cato. For a three year period, these letters roamed the entire field of politics, concentrating in an attack on Walpole and the financial order responsible for the great Bubble. Trenchard and Gordon produced another weekly in the early 1720's, the *Independent Whig,* an anticlerical set of papers that popularized the freethinking and deism of other Commonwealthmen such as Toland. Trenchard died in December, 1723, and with his death, Gordon's opposition came to an end. The latter married Trenchard's widow and accepted a place from Walpole as the first commissioner of wine licenses, which he kept to the end of his life in 1751. He joined Walpole's Grub Street stable and in time became the chief of the court writers.[22]

During the period of their collaboration the political writings of Trenchard and Gordon exemplify the ambivalence of the Augustan Commonwealthmen, exhibiting both a radical Whiggism and a nostalgic conservatism that lashes out at the new economic and social order. This dualism, a recurring theme of English radicalism, would reappear among some of the radicals under George III, and again in Cobbett and left wing radicalism later in the nineteenth century. The English political radical has often been socially reactionary, looking to a golden order in the past, a fact which has helped facilitate the recurring aristocratic and radical alliances in English politics. Trenchard and Gordon mark an important landmark in this tradition.

Trenchard's first effort at political writing was his collaboration with Walter Moyle in 1697 on a *History of Standing Armies in England,* in which he cautioned that the standing army, sought by William III and defended by such stalwart Whigs as Somers, would result in slavery. The power of a standing army in the hands of the monarch, added to the tendency of the court to give offices and places to men in Parliament, would upset the balance of power. In this, his earliest writing, Trenchard illustrated his preoccupation with a theme that would persist in all his writings, the precariousness of the delicate balance that inhibits the arbitrary use of power. The standing army and placemen, wrote Trenchard, threaten free government, "for all wise governments endeavour as much as possible to keep the legislative and executive parts asunder, that they may be a check upon one another." The *History of Standing Armies in England* also includes Trenchard's attack on the cabinet system and the suggestion that a militia replace the standing army. It concludes with a plea for frugal public management and for fewer government officers. Trenchard has not yet reached the degree of alienation from his age that would characterize his writings after the Bubble, but even here, in 1697, he longs for that most golden of past eras, which ended when "in the year 1603, died Queen Elizabeth and with her all the virtue of the Plantagenets and the Tudors."[23]

Another work of Trenchard's that merits mention before we turn to *Cato's Letters* is a seldom noted pamphlet of 1720 entitled the *Considerations Upon the State of Our Public Debts,* a despairing diatribe against the new commercial world. The mood of the essay, written in the traumatic year of the Bubble, is that of much of Augustan political writing. England is described as teetering on the edge of decline and inevitable destruction, oppressed by debts and needless officers and salaries. "What has then become of the noble spirit of our illustrious ancestors?" is the cry. Staggering with debt, the country stands prey to usurers and "projects cook'd up by stock-jobbers." Havoc exists in the traditional social structure, and men of great family and great estates are made to worship those who should by right worship them. If the stockjobber left the Alley, where he daily created his new funds and bargains, and went into the country, he would find desperate and mortgaged country gentlemen.

It is possible, too, some of these rusticks may shew a little uneasiness to see those, who but few years since would not have kept on their hats before them, rich now about in coaches and six, with pompous liveries and attendants, maintained out of their estates.[24]

Places and pensions, Trenchard wrote, were being sold at great premium, leaving the entire legislature mercenary and servile. No Tory, Trenchard included in the pamphlet an indictment of the last four years of Anne and her Tory government as both equally corrupt and full of projects. England and the traditional order, Trenchard wrote, could be saved by retrenchment, and "curbing those who will otherwise curb us." Public expenses should be contracted, pensions cut off, exorbitant and useless salaries ended. Every branch of the public revenue and expense should be examined and laid out anew, carefully and frugally.

But the complete salvation of such a corrupt and degenerate nation could be effected only by a popular hero. Trenchard's call to George I in 1720 illustrates the influence of Machiavelli on the Augustans that we see again in Bolingbroke's *Patriot King*. A popular hero would

form a generous and steady resolution to call up all our ancient virtue and restore so great a people to themselves. Almighty God cannot open a larger or more nobler scene to a truly great man for the exercise of his virtues, than to have the honour of restoring and reforming them, which is a glory beyond all the gaudy triumphs of fabulous and imaginary heroes.[25]

Even in its eighteenth-century manifestation, Trenchard and Bolingbroke express the dynamic of populism, which seems inexorably to turn up the great man. Their great man is not the legislator of Helvetius and Bentham who, reforming society and her laws, serves progressive bourgeois and rational objectives. He is more akin to populist heroes like Prince Frederick, Jackson, Bryan, and Poujade, who promise to restore a people to the virtue it has lost, and to return them to a "genuine" order of society in rural Arcadia where there are no banks, and no moneyed men.

Trenchard's most significant work, *Cato's Letters,* has important things to say about gentry discontent; at the same time, it clearly illustrates the radical dimension of the Commonwealthman's political thought. The four-volume collected *Letters* of 1724 assigns its authorship to Trenchard and Gordon "assisted occasionally by Lord Molesworth."[26] In the preface to the collected edition, Gordon, however, admits that most of the work was Trenchard's. This neglected work is indispensable to a proper understanding of political thought in the age of Walpole and Bolingbroke.

Like so much of Augustan writing on politics, one of the overriding themes of *Cato's Letters* is a rejection of the new economic order. *Cato's Letters* were written in the years immediately following the great Bubble, and its tone is vicious and uncompromising. It depicts an England threatened by a conspiracy of companies and stockjobbers, who are "vermin, dregs of human kind, scum of even the vulgar," and "cannibals feeding on the body politic." The moneyed companies, wrote Cato, were new, unshapely, and monstrous members of the state. A project was afoot in Exchange Alley to deliver the nation to the South Sea Company, the Bank of England, and the East India Company. "O Companies, Companies! Ye bane of honesty, and ruin of Trade; the market of jobbers, the harvest of managers, and the tool of knaves and of traitors." The kingdom had been overrun by credit, a "new fangled and fantastical invention" that transformed all subjects to pickpockets and gamesters. Credit and the stocks hawked in the Alley were a new and dangerous kind of property. "Let us try no more projects, no more knavish experiments," pleads Cato. The principal effect of such experimentation had been to upset the ranks of society, a hierarchical order that Cato was so determined to preserve that he condemned the charity-school movement because of the social mobility it encouraged. Like Swift, Cato wrote that education should not place any notions into the heads of those who ought to have pickaxes in their hands. Send the poor to charity school and "they will immediately fancy themselves to be another rank of mankind." Cato was possessed of a social bias that makes it no surprise that for him the gravest of all the evils the new financial order wrought was bringing havoc to the social chain of being. The men of parts and quality, the nobility and gentry, were being made the tools and instruments of knaves, who took over their estates, turned on their natural superiors, and usurped their rightful function of governing.

What Briton, blessed with any Sense of Virtue, or with common Sense; what Englishman, animated with a public Spirit, or with any Spirit, but must burn with Rage and Shame, to behold the Nobles and Gentry of a great Kingdom; Men of Magnanimity, Men of Breeding; Men of understanding, and of Letters; to such Men bowing down, like Joseph's Sheaves, before the Face of a dirty Stock-Jobber, and receiving Laws from Men bred behind Counters, and the Decision of their Fortunes, from Hands still dirty with sweeping shops![27]

Cato is frightened by the "alteration of the balance of our government," signified by the rise of the moneyed power. If the moneyed companies united, he suggests, they would prevail against the Kingdom of England. The ease with which this moneyed interest insinuated itself into Parliament augurs a speedy end to the power of men of landed property. Like Bolingbroke, it is as a student of Harrington that Cato is led to these gloomy insights; the inexorable law of politics is that all who have a share of property have a share of power, because dominion follows property. The tremendous accumulation of this new form of property by the moneyed interest would inevitably lead to their power. The broad balance of landed property upon which the gentry commonwealth rested was being replaced by the concentration of property in a few hands. A tyranny, Cato wrote, was inevitable for England, once this balance was destroyed. Would that England had an agrarian law, he lamented, to preserve the balance, and prevent the emergence of a few men in power. But of what use even, he asks, is an agrarian law in dealing with the property other than land, which has risen to such importance since 1688?[28]

Corrupt England, where government is now a gainful trade, has departed from its original principles and faces decline and extinction. Once again Augustan classicists predicted the demise of English civilization because its citizens were bereft of public spirit and mired in luxury, prodigality, and corruption. Cato quotes Sidney on the incompatibility of riches and virtue and the role that luxury and riches played in the fall of Rome. When the Romans, Cato suggests, valued nothing but money and when only the bribed were advanced to high office, they began to decline. Cicero, Machiavelli and other commentators on the fall of Rome are paraded in the pages of *Cato's Letters,* all to speak the same moral: when vanity, luxury and corruption are the fashion, and men have lost their public spirit, the days of greatness are short. There is hope only if the English learn from the experience of Rome, "Let their virtues and their vices, and the punishment of them, too, be an example to us, and so prevent our miseries from being an example to other nations." Once again, it is the wise Machiavelli who is invoked by the Augustan political writer. Cato repeats the Florentine's prescription for corrupt political systems, a renewal of the constitution and a return to first principles.[29] Such a *ritorno* would take the English back to 1688, to the constitution settled by the Glorious Revolution without the subsequent innovations and projects.

In all that Cato had to say of the new age, he spoke with the same voice as Bolingbroke's Opposition. And Bolingbroke's *Craftsman* was not the least reluctant to quote from this Commonwealthman sheet. Over a two-month period in the summer of 1731, *The Craftsman* used citations from *Cato's Letters* in its weekly assault on Walpole. Bolingbroke was well aware and approved of the nostalgic aspect of Cato's thought. *The Craftsman* wrote of Cato

As our principles of government seem to be generally the same, I have long endeavoured to imitate his manner of writing . . . The object of our complaint is the same, as well as our principles in political affairs. Where he left off I began . . . against the mischievous consequences of venality and corruption.[30]

Although Cato was in agreement with the mainstream of Bolingbroke's dissent he was, however, less concerned with dissociating himself from the political philosophy which lay behind the emerging bourgeois world. Unlike Bolingbroke, Cato did not reject the liberal theory of contract and the origin of the state. His roots were too deeply Whig for him to repudiate Locke. It is here one begins to discover the ambivalence of the Augustan Commonwealthman. Man, wrote Cato, originally in a state of nature, establishes government because of the absence of a common judge, and the consequent lack of security for his property. The government set up by the contract is "a great and honourable trust," in which the governors agree to secure the property and lives of the governed.

Should the government violate this trust, the community can reject their agent and install another. Cato wrote, following Locke, that to be secure and independent in one's property is the end and effect of liberty. There is only this negative meaning to liberty. Participation, fulfillment of one's function and duties, and service to the community play no part in freedom, and the state's function is only to provide the individual with security in which to possess and enjoy the effects of his industry. "The business of government is to protect people in their property," Cato proclaims. The state is a negative protective presence that does not meddle in individuals' lives. In Cato's thought there is a decisive break from paternalistic notions of the state, and humanistic notions of the function of political leadership as tutelage and guidance in virtue or public service. "Let people alone and they will take care of themselves and do it best," is Cato's creed. The state has no interest in the individual or the social order other than as protector of natural rights. Cato's emasculated state is the liberal Utopia. Cato, writing in 1721, is truly liberal and progressive, and, in his rigorous espousal of Locke's basic principles, anticipates even the liberalism of Mill.

> What is it to the magistrate how I wash my hands, or cut my corns, what fashion, or colours I wear, or what notions I entertain, or what gestures I use, or what words I pronounce, when they please me, and do him and my neighbor no hurt?[31]

In accepting Locke's ideas and in his concern for individual rights, Cato is a liberal, but there is also a strain of what is more accurately described as radicalism in *Cato's Letters*. This radicalism appears to run quite contrary to much in the *Letters* that reacts against the new economic age. The ambivalent Commonwealthman had difficulty in nailing down his allegiances. Alongside his lamentations at the passing of the hierarchical world, Cato could also write on one occasion that men were born naturally equal, and possessed equal endowments, and on another, that there was nothing in blood, or title, or place, that put one man above or below another in virtue or ability. Good birth did not preclude folly, lunacy, or crime. The ordinary people often have "natural qualifications equal to their superiors; and there is oftener found a great genius carrying a pitchfork, than carrying a white staff." Moreover, Cato once wrote, "there are not such mighty talents requisite for government," honest affections and common qualifications are sufficient. Plain honesty and common sense govern best, not the subtleties and distinctions of refined understandings or the riches and luxury of the men of parts.[32] This is a very different Cato from the one who ridiculed the dregs with hands dirtied from sweeping. But, it should be noted, he is praising not sensible shopkeepers, but sensible small gentry, the yeoman farmer of radical and populist mythology from Cromwell to Jackson.

Cato is not always so optimistic as in these assumptions of the general distribution of common sense and honesty, or in his belief in a universal natural law and reason. In some of the *Letters,* man is described as mired in self-love and malice, seeking only the gratification of his own insatiable passions. In this more pessimistic strain, Cato assigns a positive function to law as essential and necessary for the restraint of man's base and evil nature.[33] Convinced of this susceptibility and corruptibility of man, Cato is led to a discussion of power, and why and how it must be curbed and checked. What emerges is a statement of constitutionalism that is the most significant theoretical element in Cato's political thought.

If, as is generally held, the central ideal of modern constitutionalism is the checking and restraining of power, then *Cato's Letters* is one of its earliest and most explicit expressions.[34] Cato is preoccupied with the need to restrain power and the power holder for, "unlimited power is so wild and monstrous a thing." The need to check power is imperative because man's passions, boundless and insatiable, are terrible when not controlled. He is never sated with riches, satisfied with power, or tired of honors. If his lust is generally mild then the possession of power alters and vitiates his heart and enlarges his desires to an unnatural size. "Considering what sort of creature man is, it is scarce possible to put him under too many restraints, when he is possessed of great power."[35] Pessimism, it would seem, whether Christian or Stoic in origin, is a necessary prerequisite of constitutional theory.

Cato rejects the medieval notion that the magistrate, accountable to none but God, ought to know no other restraint, and that the only restraint upon him should be that of natural law. "This reasoning is as frivolous as it is wicked." Power without control appertains to God alone "and no man ought to be trusted with what no man is equal to." The only effective restraints are institutional, "checks and restraints appointed and expressed in the constitution itself." Abuse of power, Cato suggests, is too grievous a situation to be left to chance or to the humors of the man in authority. "All should proceed by fixed and stated rules . . . and this is the constitution." Here in *Cato's Letters* is a fully developed constitutional theory emphasizing fixed and definite constitutional limitations on government and its leaders. A people is considered free only when its magistrates are confined within the bounds set them by the people.[36]

Fixed constitutional rules are not the only way to restrain and check power effectively. Another tool is the mixed constitution. Men being men, Cato writes, will soon seek to usurp the fortune and liberty of others, and to enlarge their own power. Liberty can be preserved, however, by the establishment of a perpetual struggle between the branches of government, to "make the several parts of it control and counterpoise one another, and so keep all within their proper bounds." The magistrates, the people, and the Senate, Cato suggests, in zealously guarding their own interests, check and restrain the overreaching of one another. Another check on power is the frequent elections of the people's deputies who will not abuse their power if they must be mindful of the need to be returned to power by the people. "Fear and selfish considerations can keep men within any reasonable bounds." His use of base interests to check the abuse of power, itself a grim reality of human nature, has Cato describing the checks and balance of a free government in terms striking in their anticipation of the constitutional theory of Madison (expressed in no. 10 and especially no. 51 of the *Federalist Papers*).

> But the power and sovereignty of magistrates in free countries was so qualified, and so divided into different channels, and committed to the discretion of so many different men, with different interests and views, that the majority of them could seldom or never find their account in betraying their trust in fundamental instances. Their emulation, envy, fear, or interest, always made them spies and checks upon one another.[37]

*Cato's Letters* mark an important advance in the history of constitutional thought. Written after the Revolution and the apparent eclipse of royal power under the first Hanoverian, their concern is not primarily the restraint of the monarch's power, but the checking and restraining of Parliament and ministers. Because of this redirection of constitutional thought, it is easy to appreciate the possible influence of *Cato's Letters* on a theorist like Madison, more concerned with checking and restraining legislatures than monarchs.[38]

### ROBERT MOLESWORTH, WALTER MOYLE, AND JOHN TOLAND

At the center of the Commonwealth circle stood Robert, Lord Molesworth, in his day, "the most widely quoted and probably most influential among the liberal Whigs."[39] A friend and correspondent of Shaftesbury's, Molesworth gathered around him a circle that included such distinguished radical writers as Moyle, Toland, Anthony Collins, Trenchard, and Gordon. His most noticeable achievement in thirty years as Member of Parliament was vigorous criticism of the South Sea Company directors after the Bubble that led his contemporaries to associate him with *Cato's Letters,* and their vicious attacks on the vile jobbers. His most important political work, *Principles of a Real Whig* (or *Essay on Parties*), originally appeared as a preface to his translation of Francis Hotman's *Franco-Gallia* in 1711.[40] In this short essay, Molesworth set out to describe all those positions "which amount to a commonwealthman," a name of which he would forever be proud.[41]

The first fundamental for this "real Whig," he writes, is a commitment to the mixed gothic constitution of three estates, with the legislature found in all three estates and the executive in the monarch.[42] This was a concern of his throughout his life and writings. In 1694 he had written a book on recent Danish history in which he praised the form of government spread by the Goths and Vandals in all parts of Europe. In Denmark, unfortunately, the balance had recently been upset, and since 1660 the kings had been absolute and arbitrary. He wrote the book, he informs the reader, so that the English would be mindful of the Danish experience and treasure and preserve their own gothic government the more.[43] This same concern prompted Molesworth to translate Hotman's *Franco-Gallia* and append his own *Principles.* He gave the English Hotman's work, then being revived in the Parlement resurgence in France, to teach them the value of their own mixed government and the misery that followed the loss of it. Hotman's praise of the just mixture of all three kinds of government, his invocation of Plato, Aristotle, Polybius, and Cicero in his defense, would, hopefully, prompt the English to preserve their own gothic government, which alone insured true liberty.[44]

On this battle waged in France by the Parlements, the Walpole and Bolingbroke camps split again, *The Craftsman* seeing the position of the Parlements of Paris as a noble defense of ancient rights and privileges, and *The London Journal* cautioning that the claims of the Parlements seemed to be prompted more by a desire for their own power, than for any ancient constitution. Once again the Commonwealthman and Bolingbroke were of the same opinion.[45]

A second fundamental principle of the real Whig, as Molesworth described him in his *Principles,* was a belief in the necessity for frequent parliaments. Triennial parliaments were better than septennial, but annual parliaments better still. Such frequent renewals would remove more often from its midst all members with offices, employments, or pensions from the Crown, and would free Parliament from unconstitutional dependence on the Court. Molesworth also favored Parliamentary reform, approving the end of representation for places as desolate as Old Sarum. "Certainly a waste or a desert has no right to be represented." The deputies of such constituencies, he suggested, should be transferred to more populous and wealthier areas. The "real Whig" also stood unalterably opposed to a standing army. The Commonwealthman preferred a militia, armed and trained, to a professional army so tempting to tyrants.[46]

In his listing of these principles of a real Whig, Molesworth said nothing that would not fit in Bolingbroke's Opposition, and includes much that would fit, even the proposal for parliamentary reform, which was advocated in *The Craftsman* and in Lyttelton's *Persian Letters.* Molesworth includes in this list of real Whig principles, written in 1711, approval of Bolingbroke's Landed Qualification Act. The moneyed man and the banker, writes Molesworth, cannot serve his country for he has no "competent, visible landed estate." The representative in Parliament must have landed property, a fixed and permanent interest in England's soil, "not those fleeting ones, which may be sent beyond the sea by Bills of Exchange by every Pacquet-Boat."[47]

The similarity with the views of Bolingbroke's circle holds despite Molesworth's contention in his *Principles* that "a true Whig is not afraid of the name of a Commonwealthman because so many people who know not what it means run it down," a statement often quoted to illustrate the Augustan Commonwealthman's sense that he is the bearer of the Republican tradition of Harrington and Sidney.[48] This, however, was not entirely the case, as the rest of Molesworth's statement makes quite clear. The Commonwealthman may well differ here from Walpole Whigs, but as much because of his nostalgia for the Tudor age as because of his seventeenth-century radicalism. When the entire quotation from the *Principles of a Real Whig* is read, it becomes clear why Walpole's attack on Bolingbroke might appear to be an attack on the Commonwealthman. On certain fundamentals they thought very much alike.

A True Whig is not afraid of the name of a Commonwealthman, because so many foolish people, who know not what it means, run it down: the anarchy and confusion which these nations fell into near sixty years ago, and which was falsely called a Commonwealth, frightening them out of the true construction of the word. But Queen Elizabeth, and many others of our best Princes, were not scrupulous of calling our Government a Commonwealth, even in their solemn speeches to Parliament. And indeed if it be not one, I cannot tell by what name properly to call it: For, where in the very frame of the Constitution, the good of the whole is taken care of by the whole (as it is in our case) the having a King or Queen at the head of it, alters not the case; and the softening of it by calling it a limited monarchy, seems a kind of contradiction in terms, invented to please some weak and doubting persons.[49]

Of the entire Augustan Commonwealthman circle, Walter Moyle was both the most Harringtonian and (what follows naturally) the most classical. He did not write much. He collaborated with Trenchard on the history of standing armies, and his writing includes an essay on Roman government, and another on Lycurgus and the Spartan constitution.[50] Written in 1698, these essays were not published until five years after his death, in the significant year 1726. Moyle played an important role in shaping the classical bent of Augustan political thought and its preoccupation with Rome's fate as a model for England's. He also passed on to the Augustans the Harringtonian tools with which to understand political change.

The image of government that pervades Moyle's thought is the same as that found in Harrington and other seventeenth-century Harringtonian Commonwealthmen like Henry Neville. Their preoccupation with the proper balance and distribution of power was derived not from any organic notion of the body politic, but from a rational technical image of government that describes power in strictly mechanistic terms. Moyle insisted that "number, weight and measure" were important in the political world and that the distribution of power into branches of government that checked one another "composed as it were one great machine."[51] The imprint of the Newtonian revolution is clearly seen in the mechanistic phraseology of Augustan Commonwealthman thought. In their *History of Standing Armies,* Moyle and Trenchard spoke of government as "a mere piece of clock work," and in *Cato's Letters,* Trenchard completed the description by envisioning government as a mechanism with "springs and wheels" and "peculiar motions of balance and equilibrium."[52]

For Moyle, the spring and wheel upon which the machine of government turned was the balance of property, which, specifically in land, "is the only standing foundation of dominion . . . the true center of power." The successive revolutions in the Roman government from its monarchic origins to an aristocracy and then to a democracy and back again into a monarchy were occasioned as "the balance of lands vary'd from one order to another."[53] The cycle of generation and corruption of states is the same as that described by Polybius and Machiavelli. Moyle is critical, however, of their nonstructural analysis of this cycle. He uses against Polybius, the founder of this view, the argument Harrington had made against his idol, Machiavelli. Harrington's critique of Machiavelli's excessively moral interpretation of Rome's decline, recently stressed by Harrington scholars,[54] was both recognized and repeated by Moyle, Harrington's Augustan disciple, in his discussion of the cyclical decline and regeneration of governments.

> The succession of these changes Polybius knew from experience, but not from their true natural causes; for he plainly derives these alterations from moral reasons, such as vice and corruptions, the oppression and tyranny of their governors, which made the people impatient of the yoke, and fond of new forms; and not from the change of the only true ground and foundation of power, property.[55]

The balance of power, and the shift of orders of government to follow property, is as definite a law of politics as the natural laws of the physical world—"the needle in the compass shifts its point just as the great magnet in the earth changes its place." This iron law confirmed by the experience of all ages and all governments, was "irrefutably demonstrated by the great Harrington in his *Oceana*." In his essay on Spartan government, Moyle even credits Lycurgus, as had Harrington, with the equal divisions of the lands to insure what the moderns call the balance of power; "but it was ancient prudence taught us the thing."[56]

Moyle's use of Harrington's ideas illustrates the easy Augustan identification of the principles of the balance of power and mixed government with basic questions of property and social structure. Changes in the balance of government did not come simply from actions of statesmen, not even from such great men as Walpole, but resulted from changes in the holdings of property. This assumption among Augustans of an economic and social foundation to the political ideas of the balance and separation of powers is most clearly seen in the thought of Bolingbroke. In both Moyle and Bolingbroke, however, Harrington's insight is vitiated by a final moral prescription. What, after all, is a Harringtonian to do when he disapproves of structural change? He can only turn to the vague hope of moral reform. The Machiavellian is at least consistent. The ruin of the English commonwealth can be prevented only by its being returned to its first principles, pleads Moyle. Like Bolingbroke, in other words, Moyle flees Harrington's structural diagnosis and ends with a prescription of moral invocation. He cites Cicero and Machiavelli who had written that commonwealths cannot subsist unless frequently renewed; human nature introduces corruption into the soundest of constitutions. The great age of Sparta passed, wrote Moyle, because the stern and thrifty Spartans succumbed to the love of money, and covetousness and the tendency to ease and pleasure overcame their private integrity and public spirit. Pride and avarice, supported by riches, push governments so far from virtue that they "will sink in glory, and fall to ruin."[57]

The decision to publish his works in 1726, five years after his death, was a judicious one; his Augustan readers could easily enough read into his discussion of antiquity an implied criticism of English politics.[58] What they found in Moyle was not very different from what they could read in *The Craftsman*, founded that same year. It is Moyle, concluding his study of the Spartans, who wrote the following, not Bolingbroke:

In Lacedaemon the distinct function and different power of each branch of the government was well known, and therefore it was as well known among them, when an encroachment and invasion was made by the one, upon the inherent Rights and inseparable privileges of the other. I should be glad we could say the same thing of our own government here in England.[59]

The final member of this circle of Augustan Commonwealthmen is the great deist, John Toland, whose fame rests primarily on his free-thinking religious works, the most famous of which, *Christianity Not Mysterious*, was published in 1696. A protégé of Molesworth and Shaftesbury, editor and biographer of Harrington's works, Toland, too, was concerned with politics. In 1695, he wrote his *Danger of Mercenary Parliaments*, and in 1701 his longest work, *The Art of Governing by Parties*. In the reign of Anne he wrote the *Memorial of the State of England* (1705) and, under George I, *The State Anatomy of Great Britain* (1717), the ostensible purpose of which was to inform a foreign minister assigned to the English Court about the nature of English politics. Like the other Commonwealthmen, Toland was not simply a radical or progressive Whig whose spiritual home was the radical Commonwealth of the seventeenth century; his thought is as ambivalent as his colleagues' and as impossible to fit into a single pattern.

Toland's longest political work was devoted to an attack on that plague which had overrun England, the pernicious distinctions of party, faction, and cabal. Their major evil was in rendering the government so unsteady that no one knew whether what may be allowed by those in power today may not be disallowed by those in power tomorrow. In all good governments, divisions should be carefully avoided. A king should never head a party, he wrote, but he should be the common father of all his people. Governing by parties is governing by tricks, and all parties should join together in nonpartisan government.[60]

If Toland sounds here like the later Bolingbroke, his views by 1717, were identical with those held by Walpole ten years later. In his *State Anatomy*, addressed to the hypothetical foreign minister, Toland stressed the impossibility of party alliances, because English parties were too far apart. Party government, Whig party government, was, he now insisted, essential for the preservation of the ancient constitution. The king owed personal obligations to the Whigs, and as the best patriots, they were the party most fit for him to consult. The Tories were thoughtless and brutal, not to be trusted or preferred. There was no mistaking these two parties. Unlike most of his contemporaries, Toland, at this point, agreed with the view, later held by Walpole, that party differences had not vanished and were, in fact, inevitable. "Men may change and words may change, but principles never . . . The Whig will no more be reckoned a Tory than a Tory will pass for a Whig," declared Toland.[61]

Toland's views on parliamentary reform were, however, not those of the Establishment Whig. Here he sided with the Commonwealth-man and Opposition thought in general. Parliament should be annual; under- and non-populated boroughs (such as Old Sarum) should lose the privilege of sending members to Parliament; new members should be sent from towns "grown to considerable riches and extent."[62] This need for parliamentary reapportionment also concerned Rapin de Thoyras. In his *Dissertation Concerning Whigs and Tories*, Rapin made a great deal of the inequities of parliamentary representation, writing, "it is at present no small abuse that hamlets, consisting perhaps of about four or five thatched houses, should have as much power in Parliament as the greatest cities in the Kingdom."[63]

Like most Augustans, Toland praised England's mixed government, in which each of the three branches had "a mutual check and balance on one another." A commonwealth was just such a mixed form of government, deemed so perfect by the ancients. Being editor of Harrington's works did not prevent Toland, however, from criticizing those who sought to turn England's perfect government of 1701 into a commonwealth, since "one can never make it more a commonwealth than it is already." Toland, like Molesworth, tended to understate any link of the Augustan Commonwealthman with the seventeenth-century Commonwealth.

> The several factions who usurped the government and maintained themselves by military force before the Restoration, assumed the title of a Commonwealth, tho' they were the farthest imaginable from the thing. The people, who smarted under their tyranny, abolished the very name ever after.[64]

For Commonwealthmen like Toland and Molesworth, a commonwealth had connotations other than simply those of seventeenth-century radicalism. In his *Anatomy of British Government*, Toland informs his foreign minister that it is impossible to find in England "one single commonwealthman," in the sense of one who favors aristocracy or democracy, or the sovereignty of Parliament, exclusive of all royal government. The English monarchy was, in fact, the best form of a commonwealth. Toland proceeded to explain to the foreigner what was really meant by a commonwealth, and his definition, like Molesworth's, is clearly not far removed from the Opposition thought of Bolingbroke and his circle.

> As for the word Commonwealth, which is the common-weal or good, whenever we use it about our government, we take it only in this sense; just as the word Republican in Latin is a general word for all free governments, of which we believe ours to be best. This is the sense in which King James I called himself the great servant of the Commonwealth; and in which Sir Thomas Smith, secretary of state to more than one of our princes, entitles his account of the English government, the Commonwealth of England.[65]

What worried Toland most about the English commonwealth was the fate of the mixed constitution at the hands of widespread parliamentary corruption. In his *Danger of Mercenary Parliaments*, he sounded a theme heard again and again in Augustan thought. Since 1688, he wrote, misfortune had flowed from the corruption overspreading both the Court and Parliament. "'Tis this that has changed the very natures of Englishmen," making valiant, eloquent, and honest men cowardly, dumb, and villainous. The age was one of wretched degeneracy.[66] In their attack on placemen and parliamentary corruption, the Commonwealthman and Bolingbroke's Opposition were both, it seems, being true to old Whig principles.

Toland was as concerned about upstarts and moneyed men as any non-establishment Whig thinker of the period. Governors, he suggested, should be not mean, moneyed, or obscure men, but rather should be chosen from among the people of better rank who had a great stake in the country. In 1701, the Commonwealthman Toland, called for the Landed Qualification Bill championed and passed in 1711 by Swift and Bolingbroke. Money men should not sit in Parliament, he wrote, only men with considerable landed estate who "have a firm pledge in England to answer for their behaviour." Moneyed men can "remove their effects into another country in four-and-twenty hours, and follow themselves the next night." The moneyed man was, in Toland's view, "but a traveller in an inn."[67] The idea is familiar. Bolingbroke would merely change the imagery; the moneyed man was, for him, a passenger on a ship. The Commonwealthman Toland, shared, in these respects, the views of the reactionary Tory gentry and intellectuals. Such, inevitably, was the fate of a Harringtonian in the early eighteenth century. To be a convinced Harringtonian in the face of the social and economic revolution after 1688 was to be more often than not a social reactionary. The gentry utopia seemed a thing of the past.

Toland's political views were ambivalent as were those of all the Augustan Commonwealthmen. There is in their thought a progressive and radical defense of minority rights, of toleration, of Irish freedom, of free trade. But as Swift's dedication to Irish liberation and opposition to English tyranny does not define him as a progressive and libertarian alone, so the Commonwealthmen were not solely great landmarks in the history of English libertarian thought.[68] Their writings indicate a more complex position, part of which involved a basic inability to come to terms with the new England, and its social and economic changes. In this mood, like the Tory intellectuals, they fled to the past, to Harrington's seventeenth-century gentry utopia or even beyond, to the commonwealth of Elizabeth, Smith, or Elyot.[69]

# Conclusion: Toward a Reassessment of Bolingbroke

Chesterfield wrote to his son in 1752, "Lord Bolingbroke joined all the politeness, the manners and the grace of a courtier, to the solidity of a statesman, and to the learning of a pedant. He was *omnis homo*."[1] Much earlier, Swift had written to Stella, "I think Mr. St. John the greatest young man I ever knew; with his wit, capacity, beauty, quickness of comprehension, good learning and excellent taste, the best orator in the House of Commons."[2] After Bolingbroke's disgrace in 1715, Swift wrote that Bolingbroke's mind "was adorned with the choicest gifts that God hath yet thought fit to bestow upon the children of men."[3] Voltaire, at the feet of Bolingbroke in the 1720's, saw in him "all the learning of his country and all the politeness of ours. This man who has been all his life in pleasure and business, has however, found time for learning everything and retaining everything."[4] At a later stage in Bolingbroke's career, Pope wrote to Swift, "Nothing can depress his [Bolingbroke's] genius. Whatever befalls him, he will still be the greatest man in the world, either in his own time, or with posterity."[5] To Richardson, the artist who had painted Bolingbroke, Pope wrote, "posterity will, through the means of that portrait, see the man whom it will for ages honour, vindicate and applaud, when envy is no more, and when the sons shall blush their fathers were his foes!"[6]

Yet he was also damned by his contemporaries. Walpole's *Daily Courant* of June 8, 1732, wrote: "Thus so much of this most detestable traytor and ingrate since Judas, who has not yet swung on the gallows—which that he may soon do, God, of his infinite mercy to these kingdoms, grant."[7] And, Pope's prediction notwithstanding, the son of Bolingbroke's greatest foe did not blush. Horace Walpole wrote to Horace Mann that "we have discovered that he [Bolingbroke] was the worst man and the worst writer in the world . . .

nay I don't know whether my father won't become a rubric martyr for having been persecuted by him."[8] "Who now reads Bolingbroke, who ever read him through?" asked Burke, a question repeated in the twentieth century by G. D. H. Cole who asks even more emphatically, "Who reads, who can endure to read Bolingbroke now?"[9]

Some have read Bolingbroke, and even read him through. John Adams wrote to Jefferson in 1813 that he had "read him through more than five times in his life." Upon reading *A Dissertation upon Parties*, Adams exclaimed, "This is a jewel, there is nothing so profound, correct, and perfect on the subject of government, in the English or any other language."[10] Jefferson recommended that Bolingbroke's writings should be in the library of every well-read gentleman.[11] There have also been, as noted in the introduction, some who in recent years have been equally enthusiastic about Bolingbroke's writings on government. But, with these few exceptions, his political writings have fared poorly in assessments from modern observers. Sir Charles G. Robertson wrote in 1947 in the English Historical Association's monograph on Bolingbroke that, "he really has no place in the political and philosophical thought of his age, his contribution fades out completely, nor had he either the knowledge or the scholarship."[12] The late Carlton Hayes explains that "a great deal of solemn drivel has been written about Henry St. John, perhaps because he wrote a great deal of more or less solemn drivel himself."[13] This judgment is seconded by Archibald Foord, who labels Bolingbroke's political writings "high flown metapolitics."[14] The assessment of Harold Laski perhaps best sums up this consensus found among students of politics and political thought in the eighteenth century.

> Nor has he [Bolingbroke] any enthusiasm save that of bitter partisanship. He hated Walpole, and his political writings are, at bottom, no more than an attempt to generalize his animosity . . . his opinions are no more than a mask for ambition born of hate . . . He had evolved a theory of politics than which nothing so clearly displays the bankruptcy of the time.[15]

One strain of modern interpretation does insist, however, that there is in Bolingbroke's writings more than mere personal spite and ambition. In what is really a revival of the reading of Bolingbroke in Burke's *Vindication of Natural Society*, A. O. Aldridge and H. M. Mansfield, Jr., insist that Bolingbroke is an exemplary Enlightenment political philosopher, hostile to irrationality and prejudice and bent on reshaping the world by reason. In the words of Aldridge, "Bolingbroke is relatively cold and completely rational. He carries his convictions to their logical conclusions and makes no compromises with tradition or sentiment."[16] This common interpretation of Bolingbroke by Burke, Aldridge and Mansfield is striking because it runs directly contrary to one of the persistent strains of Bolingbroke interpretation that sees Bolingbroke as a pillar of the English Tory tradition.

This Tory reading of Bolingbroke began with Disraeli, who credited Bolingbroke with being the founder of the modern Tory party, with purging it of Jacobite tendencies, and with restoring it to both respectability and true Tory principles.[17] A long line of Tory writers have echoed Disraeli's beatification of Bolingbroke. His most sympathetic biographers, Walter Sichel and Sir Charles Petrie, express this "romantic Tory" interpretation, as does Richard Faber.[18] Keith Feiling invoked Bolingbroke's ideas as a source for true Conservatism.[19] F. J. C. Hearnshaw wrote that, along with Burke and Disraeli, Bolingbroke was "a supreme exponent of Conservatism."[20] According to Maurice Wood, "Bolingbroke stated the Tory case as it had never been stated, and the echoes of that supreme presentation still ring down the centuries."[21] Sir Geoffrey Butler and his nephew, R. A. Butler, place Bolingbroke with Burke, Disraeli, and Salisbury as the cornerstones of the Tory tradition. R. A. Butler has advanced the ideas of Bolingbroke at a recent Conservative Party conference.[22] Though Burke might dissent, Bolingbroke seems to occupy a secure niche in the Tory pantheon.

To label Bolingbroke an important figure in the English conservative tradition implies that such a tradition exists and, moreover, that it goes back to the early eighteenth century. One vigorous opponent of such a view was Lord Hugh Cecil, who argued, in his brilliant little book, that English conservatism was born with the French Revolution, when men had to choose to be for or against Jacobitism.[23] Against this opinion there can be amassed, of course, the long line of Tories mentioned above, as well as American scholars who describe an older and continuous English conservative tradition.[24] Some of Bolingbroke's Tory commentators insist that Bolingbroke played an important role in establishing the continuity of Tory practice and organization; but such claims must overcome the powerful critique that Namier and his students have made of those who read nineteenth-century notions of party organization back into the eighteenth century. But what of Bolingbroke's ideas? Surely they must fit the many long lists of conservative principles that have, from time to time, been offered.[25] His Tory worshippers, Wood, Hearnshaw, Sichel, Feiling, Faber, and Butler, answer yes. This, they suggest, is why Bolingbroke is a great conservative thinker. But a reading of Bolingbroke's political writings does not disclose such a complete affiliation with traditional conservative doctrines, and with good reason. He was no Burke, and most of the catalogues of conservative principles are merely listings of the essential elements of Burke's theory. Much closer, in fact, to this "conservative creed" are the truly skeptical and pessimistic political ideas of the great trimmer, the Marquis of Halifax.[26]

If he is not a conservative in organizational terms or in terms of the creed, perhaps, Bolingbroke should be removed from the clutches of the Tories who write of him with such great fondness. Better yet, it might be worthwhile to reject entirely the metaphysics shared by Sir William Gilbert and Karl Marx that depict mankind inevitably divided between the conservative and the liberal. One can reject this metaphysical assumption, however, and still regard Bolingbroke as a conservative; just as it is possible to hold that, although his political ideas do not match Burke's, he was a conservative in the context of the Augustan period and its political thought.[27] His is very much the "primitive conservatism" that Mannheim points to as the first stage in the shift of conservative ideology from mere traditionalism to self-conscious conservatism.[28]

The "primitive conservative" Bolingbroke experienced the beginning of a challenge to the old order. This order, not yet behind him, was an integral part of his life; it was not yet only a memory. His defense of an aristocratic England was an intensified experience of something he still possessed but felt himself in great danger of losing. It is of paramount significance that this idealized order was not yet totally lost. Because this order was not merely an object of reflection, he was not led to the introspection of romantic conservatism. His conservatism bears the stamp of thought before the French Revolution. He praised the good old days, but he was still within the perimeter of the Enlightenment; sober, practical, and rational. He experienced no sudden shock, no sudden recognition that the old aristocratic institutions were a thing of the past. Such shocks would come later and would lead conservatives to weave daydreams and to engage in mere speculation. Bolingbroke lived in an age when the old order, though challenged, still seemed appropriate and possible, when men could do more than dream; they could deliberately set about to maintain the aristocratic ideal against the challenge of liberalism. Bolingbroke was a reactive conservative who sought to defend the old order when it was first attacked by the liberalism of Locke and the financial innovations of the early eighteenth century, which would usher in the bourgeois age. He could be both the aristocratic conservative and the Enlightenment philosopher, because defending the old order in Augustan England required no leap from sensory data. The old order was there to be seen, to be experienced and, if men only followed the advice of Bolingbroke, Swift, and Pope, it was there to be preserved.

# Notes

---

# Index

# Notes

INTRODUCTION: BOLINGBROKE, POLITICAL THOUGHT, AND THE
AUGUSTAN AGE

1. IX *Parliamentary History,* 471-472.

2. T. B. Macaulay, *Essays and Lays* (London, 1888), pp. 263-264.

3. John Morley, *Life of Walpole* (London, 1889), p. 78.

4. Leslie Stephen, *History of English Thought in the Eighteenth Century,* 2 vols. (New York, 1962), I, 149-51; II, 144.

5. C. G. Robertson, *Bolingbroke* (London, 1947), p. 13.

6. Caroline Robbins, *The Eighteenth-Century Commonwealthman* (Cambridge, Mass., 1959).

7. J. H. Plumb, *Sir Robert Walpole,* 2 vols. (Boston, 1956), II, 311. See also *The Spectator,* 15 September 1961, for Plumb's review article on Robert Shackleton's *Montesquieu* where he praises Bolingbroke's brilliance and "mock profundity."

8. H. N. Fieldhouse, "Bolingbroke and the Idea of Non-Party Government," *History* 23 (June 1938); Kurt Kluxen, *Das Problem der Politischen Opposition* (Freiburg, 1956); Harvey Mansfield, Jr., *Statesmanship and Party Government* (Chicago, 1965).

9. Robert Shackleton, "Montesquieu, Bolingbroke and the Separation of Powers," *French Studies* 3 (January 1949) and *Montesquieu: A Critical Biography* (Oxford, 1961); J. H. Burns, "Bolingbroke and the Concept of Constitutional Government," *Political Studies* 10 (October 1962); Jeffrey Hart, *Viscount Bolingbroke: Tory Humanist* (London, 1966).

10. See, for examples, the discussions in J. J. Maquet, *The Sociology of Knowledge* (Boston, 1951); Judith Shklar, *Political Theory and Ideology* (New York, 1966); Karl Mannheim, *Ideology and Utopia* (New York, 1940); J. S. Runcek, "A History of the Concept of Ideology," *Journal of the History of Ideas* 5 (June 1944); Arne Naess, *Democracy, Ideology and Objectivity* (Oslo, 1956), pp. 141-234.

11. Karl Mannheim, *Essays on Sociology and Social Psychology* (New York, 1953), pp. 74-79.

12. Lucy Sutherland, "The City of London in Eighteenth-Century Politics," in *Essays Presented to Sir Lewis Namier* (London, 1956); John Brooke, "Party in the Eighteenth Century," in *Silver Renaissance Essays in Eighteenth-Century English History* (London, 1961); Archibald Foord, *His Majesty's Opposition* (Oxford, 1964).

13. Sutherland, "The City of London," p. 58.

14. The disciples of Namier have little use for Burke or Bolingbroke. The opposition of *The Craftsman* and the Rockinghams is of little interest to them in terms of ideas. Robert Walcott acknowledges this grievance of non-Namierites. "It is this cavalier brushing aside of the writings of Burke and Bolingbroke that is at the root

of much of the criticism of the Namier school" ("Sir Lewis Considered—Considered," *Journal of British Studies* 3 [May 1964], 90). He and other disciples of Namier see this writing and nearly all political writing of the century as mere "cant." Burke is not the concern here. What this book hopes to illustrate is that there is more than mere cant in Bolingbroke's writings, more than unprincipled opposition from ambitious outsiders. His party and his opposition, it is suggested, were structured by a set of ideas, an ideology in both the conventional and Marxist sense of the term.

15. This "stylistic conservatism" is conceivably a recurring attitude in British politics. Bolingbroke's super-refinement and preoccupation with how men act in politics could be seen in Shaftesbury's writings as well as in the contemporary writings of Michael Oakshott. Throughout the Tory tradition has lingered this obsession with the artful performance as opposed to the policy produced. In this vein it is interesting to note that the two most recent interpretive studies of Bolingbroke's political thought, though differing widely in substance, have the common feature of their author's political sentiments, both Professors Hart and Mansfield being figures of the intellectual right in America.

CHAPTER I. THE "ANTI-MINISTER": THE POLITICAL CAREER AND
WRITINGS OF LORD BOLINGBROKE

1. This chapter is not intended to present a biography of Bolingbroke, only a discussion of the relationship between his political writings and the events of his career. The following list of Bolingbroke's biographers may be consulted for the facts of his life. They are, however, often far from reliable. David Mallett, *Life of Bolingbroke* (London, 1754); Oliver Goldsmith, *Life of Bolingbroke,* added to ninth edition of *A Dissertation upon Parties* (London, 1771); Phillipe-Henri, Comte de Grimoard, *La Vie de Bolingbroke,* added to *Lettres Historiques, Politiques et Particulières de Henri St. John, Lord Vicomte Bolingbroke, Depuis 1710 Jusqu'en 1736,* 3 vols. (Paris, 1808), vol. I; G. W. Cooke, *Memoirs of Lord Bolingbroke,* 2 vols. (London, 1835); *Life of Bolingbroke,* in *The Works of Lord Bolingbroke,* 4 vols. (Philadelphia, 1841), vol. I; Thomas Macknight, *Life of Henry St. John, Viscount Bolingbroke* (London, 1863); Robert Harrop, *Bolingbroke: A Political Study and Criticism* (London, 1884); Walter Sichel, *Bolingbroke and His Times,* 2 vols. (London, 1901-1902); Arthur Hassal, *Life of Viscount Bolingbroke* (Oxford, 1915); J. M. Robertson, *Bolingbroke and Walpole* (London, 1919); Sir Charles Petrie, *Bolingbroke* (London, 1937); Paul Baratier, *Lord Bolingbroke et ses Ecrits Politiques* (Lyons, 1939); M. R. Hopkinson, *Married to Mercury* (London, 1936); Sir Douglas Harkness, *Bolingbroke the Man and His Cause* (London, 1957); S. W. Jackman, *Man of Mercury* (London, 1965). For the problems inherent in Bolingbroke's biography, see "What of Bolingbroke?" *Times Literary Supplement,* May 12, 1966. Note also the inadequate treatment in all these biographies of Bolingbroke's schooling, which was in fact at a dissenting academy. For corroboration of this, see Irene Parker, *Dissenting Academies in England* (Cambridge, Eng., 1914), p. 139, and VI *Parliamentary History,* 1350.

2. Bolingbroke, *Works,* I, 117.

3. See Historical Manuscripts Commission, *Portland Mss.,* 10 vols. (London, 1891-1931), V, passim, for Bolingbroke-Harley correspondence and the deferential tone adopted by Bolingbroke.

4. *Letter to Sir William Windham* in Bolingbroke, *Works,* I, 114.

5. *Ibid.,* I, 115.

6. *Ibid.,* I, 115.

7. *Ibid.,* I, 116. Bolingbroke's letters during his four years in office reveal his continued emphasis on the socioeconomics of peace. "Our government is in a consumption, and our vitals are consuming, and we must invariably sink at once." The nation, he wrote, wants peace, "whatever noise may be made about London, by those who find their private account in the universal calamity." "Whenever we shall have got rid of our war, the landed interest will then rise, and the moneyed interest, which is the great support of Whiggism, must of course decline." *Letters and Correspondence Public and Private of the Right Honourable Henry St. John, 1st Viscount Bolingbroke* . . . Gilbert Parke, ed., 4 vols. (London, 1798), I, 113, 264, 428.

8. See *The Prose Works of Jonathan Swift,* T. Scott, ed., 12 vols. (London, 1897-1908), V, 384, for Swift's description of this work and his associates. Bolingbroke's *Letter to the Examiner* (London, 1710) was his first published material on politics.

9. Jonathan Swift, *The Conduct of the Allies* (London, 1711), p. 91ff. Recent evidence has been uncovered justifying Swift's allegations of corruption, for example, Godfrey Davies, "The Seamy Side of Marlborough's War," *Huntington Library Quarterly* 15 (1951-1952).

10. Ian Watt, *The Rise of the Novel* (Berkeley, 1962), pp. 35-60.

11. The flavor of this new and exciting dimension of political life was captured in a tract of the period. The Lord of Hades asks a recently arrived spirit how the party wars of England are carried on. "Pluto: 'What sort of weapons do they use?' Belfagor: 'Pamphlets, sir. You may go into a coffee house and see a table of half an acre's length covered with nothing but tobacco, pipes and pamphlets, and all the seats full of mortals leaning on their elbows, licking in tobacco, lies and laced coffee, and studying for arguments to revile one another with.'" *The Conference on Gregg's Ghost* (London, 1711), p. 11.

12. For details on the founding of the club, see Bolingbroke, *Letters and Correspondence,* I, 150.

13. Jonathan Swift, *Journal to Stella,* Harold Williams, ed., 2 vols. (Oxford, 1948).

14. G. P. Gooch, *Political Thought in England, Bacon to Halifax* (London, 1960), ch. xi.

15. Bolingbroke, *Letters and Correspondence,* II, 416. Such a treaty with France was sought again in 1786 by the Tory Pitt the Younger in Eden's Treaty. Adam Smith is often cited as the source of Pitt's free trade sentiments; no mention is ever made, however, of the possible influence of Bolingbroke, whose similar commitment to the principle could easily have come to Pitt via Bolingbroke's protégé, Pitt the Elder. See J. H. Rose, "British Commercial Treaty of 1786," *English Historical Review* 23 (1908).

16. *The Wentworth Papers, 1705-1739,* J. J. Cartwright, ed. (London, 1883). This comment (21 December 1710) should be seen in the context of the events of 1710.

17. Bolingbroke's contentions have been upheld by the research of H. N. Fieldhouse, who concludes that before the Queen's death, Bolingbroke had no more dealings with the Jacobite Court than any English statesman might normally have had. "He was not before the Queen's death deeply committed. Certainly at that date he had not plunged into the Jacobite scheme headlong and decisively." (H. N. Fieldhouse, "Bolingbroke's Share in the Jacobite Intrigue of 1710-1714," *English Historical Review,* 52 [July, 1937].) On the eve of his flight, despite the fact that he saw the Whigs driving toward civil war, "he had not yet even at that date, committed himself to the Pretender." ("Bolingbroke and d'Iberville Correspondence," *English Historical Review* 52 [October 1937].) See also by the same author, "Oxford,

Bolingbroke and the Pretender's Place of Residence, 1710-1714," *English Historical Review* 52 (April 1937).

18. Edward Hughes, *North Country Life in the Eighteenth Century* (Oxford, 1952), passim.

19. The best printed source of information on Bolingbroke's years in France is still Grimoard's *Lettres Historiques . . . de Henri St. John*. The author would like to thank Mr. George Nadel of the Warburg Institute, London, for his insight into the labyrinthine complexities of Bolingbroke's career and contacts in general, and those in France in particular. Two British scholars at the University of Wales also helped the author to come to terms with this period through their conversation and unpublished works. E. R. Briggs, "The Political Academies of France in the Early Eighteenth Century with Special Reference to the Club de l'Entresol and Its Founder, the Abbé, Pierre Joseph Alary," unpub. diss., Cambridge University, 1931; also D. J. Fletcher, "The Intellectual Relations of Lord Bolingbroke with France," unpub. master's thesis, University College of Wales, 1953. Fletcher has recently published "The Fortunes of Bolingbroke in France in the Eighteenth Century," *Studies on Voltaire and the Eighteenth Century* 47 (1966), pp. 207-232.

20. Paul Baratier, *Lettres inédites de Bolingbroke à Lord Stair 1716-1720* (Lyons, 1939), pp. 39, 48, 93.

21. Bolingbroke, *Works*, I, 177. See also British Museum Add. Mss., 4984A ff. 2-64.

22. H.M.C., *Portland Mss.*, V, 535.

23. For these dealings see Basil Williams, *Stanhope* (Oxford, 1932), pp. 258, 310, 408-409; Grimoard, *Lettres Historiques . . . de Henri St. John*, II, 479; and Paul Baratier, *Lettres inédites de Bolingbroke*, pp. 92-97. Bolingbroke sought the advice of the Abbé Vertot, the distinguished Roman historian.

24. Bolingbroke, *Works*, I, 50.

25. D. J. Fletcher, "The Intellectual Relations of Lord Bolingbroke with France," p. 40; Grimoard, *Lettres Historiques . . . de Henri St. John*, II, 453, contains a familiar reference to Boulainvilliers in a Bolingbroke letter of 1718. Also, see Brook Taylor, *Contemplatio Philosophica* (London, 1793), p. 135. The friendship with Voltaire is evident from the extensive correspondence with and mention of him reproduced in Grimoard. A lively debate has raged for some time now on whether or not Bolingbroke was a significant intellectual influence on the young Voltaire. See, for example, arguing yes: J. C. Collins, *Voltaire, Montesquieu, and Rousseau in England* (London, 1908), pp. 61-62; Leslie Stephen, *History of English Thought in the Eighteenth Century*, 2 vols. (New York, 1962), I, 151; A. S. Hurn, *Voltaire et Bolingbroke: Étude Comparative sur leurs idées philosophiques et religieuses* (Paris, 1915), esp. pp. 109-115. The leading debunker of this alleged influence is N. L. Torrey. See his "Bolingbroke and Voltaire: A Fictitious Influence," *Publications of the Modern Language Association* 42 (1927), 788-797; and *Voltaire and the English Deists* (New Haven, 1930). For recent reassertions of a possible influence, see George Nadel, "Bolingbroke and the Letters on History," *Journal of the History of Ideas* 23 (October-December, 1962), 550; I. H. Brumfitt, *Voltaire Historian* (Cambridge, 1958), pp. 42-45; and Voltaire, *Correspondence,* Thomas Besterman, ed. (Geneva, 1953), I, 245-248. For Voltaire's comments on Bolingbroke, see *Oeuvres,* Louis Moland ed., 52 vols. (Paris, 1877-1885), X, 252; XX, 90; XXXIII, 90; XXXIX, 569, XL, 193.

26. Taylor, *Contemplatio Philosophica*, p. 5.

27. For details of Alary's career, see Briggs, "The Political Academies of France," pp. 16-27.

28. Robert Shackelton, *Montesquieu: A Critical Biography* (Oxford, 1961), p. 63. For Bolingbroke's membership in the group, see Grimoard, *Lettres Historiques . . . de Henri St. John,* III, 191.

29. Rene Louis de Voyer, Marquis d'Argenson, *Journal et Memoire inédits* (Paris, 1859-1867). The best treatment of the Entresol in English is the Briggs dissertation mentioned in note 19. In French there are articles by Lanier: "Le Club de l'Entresol (1723-1731)," *Memoirs de l'Académie des Sciences, des Lettres et des Arts d'Amiens,* 3rd series, VI, 1880; and Paul Janet, "Une Académie politique sous le Cardinal de Fleury," *Seances et Travaux de l'Académie des Sciences Morals et Politiques,* 5th series, IV, 1865.

30. For Montesquieu's membership, see Briggs, "The Political Academies of France," p. 138 and Shackelton, *Montesquieu,* p. 65; for Parlement views, see Briggs, p. 143, and Franklin Ford, *Robe and Sword* (Cambridge, Mass., 1953), p. 232.

31. Alexander Pope, *Correspondence,* G. Sherburn, ed., 5 vols. (Oxford, 1956), III, 349 (Pope to Swift, October 15, 1725).

32. C. B. Realley, *Early Opposition to Sir Robert Walpole* (Lawrence, Kansas, 1931), p. 197.

33. Anthony Ashley Cooper, third Earl of Shaftesbury, *Characteristicks of Men, Manners, Opinions, Times,* J. M. Robinson, ed., 2 vols. (London, 1900), I, 148.

34. Bolingbroke's political partner at the head of the Opposition was William Pulteney, who had recently broken with Walpole. For details of the Walpole-Pulteney breach, see Realley, *Early Opposition to Walpole,* pp. 155-160, and J. H. Plumb's *Sir Robert Walpole,* 2 vols. (Boston, 1956), II, 75, 122. No biography of Pulteney exists; for details of his career, see *The Dictionary of National Biography,* vol. 47, as well as Realley and Plumb. Realley is of the opinion that "from 1725 to 1742 Pulteney was the acknowledged leader of the movement [Opposition]," p. 160. He does not limit this claim to the parliamentary side of the Opposition; yet Boling-broke was certainly regarded by his contemporaries, Whig and Tory, as the driving force behind the Opposition.

35. *Observation on The Craftsman* (London, 1730), p. 11.

36. *The Craftsman* (7 August 1731); *The London Journal* (14 August 1721).

37. *The Daily Gazetteer,* No. 234 (27 March 1736).

38. Samuel Johnson, *The Lives of Most Eminent English Poets,* 4 vols. (London, 1783), IV, 337. See also Goldsmith, *Life of Bolingbroke,* p. 67. *The Craftsman* was directed by Bolingbroke for ten years, but it did not die in 1735 when he left; it survived as a relatively unimportant journal until 1750.

39. Lawrence Hanson, *Government and the Press 1695-1763* (Oxford, 1936), pp. 85, 108.

40. Cholmondeley Mss. (Cambridge University Library), item 73.

41. Hanson, *Government and the Press,* p. 108.

42. Plumb, *Sir Robert Walpole,* II, 141.

43. There is a serious problem involved in determining the authorship of indi-vidual essays in *The Craftsman.* They were unsigned and the only possible clue to the writer was an initial that appeared at the end of the essay in their bound reprints. Since all the published essays of Bolingbroke that originally appeared in *The Crafts-man* were signed "O," it has been traditional to identify that letter with Bolingbroke. But there is no agreement on whether all "O"'s in *The Craftsman* signify his essays. There is also no agreement on the authors to whom the other initials (C, N, D, R, A) belong. Contemporary opinion inclined to Bolingbroke and William

Pulteney as the two main authors, with occasional contributions from Nicholas Amhurst, the nominal editor. Lord John Hervey, *Some Materials Towards Memoirs of the Reign of George II,* Romney Sedgwick, ed., 3 vols. (London, 1931), I, 203; Montesquieu, *Oeuvres,* André Masson, ed., 3 vols. (Paris, 1950-1955), III, 285; H.M.C., *Portland Mss.,* VII, 473; Historical Manuscripts Commission, *Egmont Mss.,* 2 vols. (London, 1905-1909), II, 147; Thomas Newton, "Auobiography" in *Works,* 3 vols. (London, 1782), I, 71-72. Only Walter Sichel, of the many who have written on Bolingbroke, has tackled the problem of *The Craftsman's* authorship. He rejected the eighteenth-century view on the tripartite authorship and detected in *The Craftsman* the additional pens of Swift, Arbuthnot, Pope, Gay, and Chesterfield (*Bolingbroke and His Times,* II, 236-254). Sichel's speculations on authorship, like so much else of his biography, are hopelessly confused and inaccurate, as, for example, when he attributes articles to gentlemen long after their deaths. These shortcomings have been clarified by Giles Barber of the Bodleian Library in a recent bibliographical dissertation on Bolingbroke ("A Bibliography of Henry St. John, Viscount Bolingbroke, unpub. diss. Oxford, 1963). Barber rejects Sichel's claims (echoed, by the way, in such an otherwise responsible book as John Loftis, *Politics and Drama in Augustan England* [Oxford, 1963], p. 95) and repeats the traditional view of the three authors. He adds that there were three other authors (corresponding to the three remaining letters) whose identities must remain a mystery. I have myself indulged in the game of "initialmanship," the intricacies of which are spared the reader of this book. (See Isaac Kramnick, "Lord Bolingbroke: Political Thought in the Augustan Age," unpub. diss., Harvard University, 1965.) The conclusions of this inquiry point to the irrelevance of such a search. All the essays in the journal reflect the stamp of Bolingbroke's ideas. It is beyond question that Bolingbroke wrote some of the essays, but in terms of their ideas he could well have been the author of them all. There is a unity of ideas in *The Craftsman* during these ten years which reflects the hegemony of one mind—Bolingbroke's. It is not crucial that some of the ideas cannot be assigned with certainty. It is still Bolingbroke's *Craftsman.*

44. *The Craftsman,* no. 1 (6 December 1726); also repeated in no. 285 (18 December 1731). The name has, not unexpectedly, led to a certain amount of confusion. The preface to the French translation in 1737 informed the reader that it had considered as possible translations of the title, "l'homme du métier" or "l'homme du peuple." It was left in English, *Le Craftsman* (Paris, 1737), preface, viii. In a similar vein, Mr. Barber of the Bodleian Library, tells of a communication from a Polish scholar seeking information on this early proletarian paper. It is conceivable that the name chosen for the journal is a memory from Bolingbroke's past. In the early 1720's a pamphlet appeared with the title *The Craftsman: A Sermon or Paraphrase Upon Several Verses of the Nineteenth Chapter of the Acts of the Apostle: Composed in the Style of the Late Daniel Burgess.* It appears that a traditional theme of Mr. Burgess, the childhood tutor of Bolingbroke, was that priests were craftsmen, using craft to amass their power and wealth.

45. *Correspondence of Jonathan Swift,* F. E. Ball, ed., 6 vols. (London, 1910-1914), II, 89.

46. VIII *Parliamentary History,* 533.

47. *The Craftsman,* no. 172 (18 October 1729).

48. *Ibid.,* no. 36 (19 April 1727); no. 92 (7 April 1728).

49. *Ibid.,* no. 55 (22 June 1727). Shaftesbury commented on the monster vogue in 1710 with little sympathy for its satiric value. "Monsters and monster lands were never more in request; and we may often see a philosopher, or a wit, run a tale-

gathering in those idle deserts as familiarly as the silliest woman or merest boy." *Characteristicks,* I, 225.

50. *The Craftsman,* no. 62 (9 September 1727); no. 98 (18 May 1728); no. 141 (15 March 1729); no. 168 (20 September 1729); no. 159 (9 July 1729).

51. *Ibid.,* no. 6 (23 December 1726).

52. *The Examiner,* no. 14 (9 November 1710).

53. For evil minister Sejanus, see *The Craftsman,* no. 115, 153. For the Russian minister Menzikoff, see no. 75. For Wolsey, see no. 8, no. 23, no. 72, no. 84, no. 107, no. 136. For Buckingham, see no. 44, no. 139, no. 298. For Danby, see no. 111.

54. *The Craftsman,* no. 16 (27 January 1727), and Bolingbroke, *Works,* I, 236-240.

55. *The Craftsman,* no. 297 (25 March 1732).

56. *Ibid.,* nos. 44, 197.

57. *The Craftsman* (London, 1737); (reprint), "Dedication to the People of England," VIII, iii; nos. 330-335. It is not in the least surprising that Walpole sought to suppress *The Craftsman.* In its first four years, eight writs were served on the paper, the first coming immediately after no. 16, "The First Vision of Camilick." The printer, Franklin, was arrested and tried several times and found not guilty (State Papers Domestic, Criminal Correspondence, Public Records Office, LXXXI-LXXXIII). He finally landed in jail in 1731, and was fined £100 and given a year's imprisonment. Justice was apparently not jeopardized by the presence among the jurors of one Mr. Thomas Skerrit, father-in-law of Mr. Walpole (H.M.C., *Egmont Mss.,* I, 198).

58. The essays appeared in *The Craftsman* on and off from no. 218 (5 September 1730) to no. 255 (22 May 1731); in Bolingbroke, *Works,* they are found in I, 292-455.

59. Herbert Butterfield, *The Englishman and His History* (Cambridge, Eng., 1944), p. 2.

60. Bolingbroke, *Works,* I, 408.

61. *Ibid.,* I, 385.

62. In *The Craftsman,* the *Dissertation* ran from nos. 382-396 (27 October 1733 until 2 February 1734) and from nos. 436-443 (9 September 1734 to 28 December 1734). In its entirety, it appears in *Works,* II, 5-171. The *Dissertation* was translated into French in 1739 by Etienne de Silhouette (1709-1767), close friend and admirer of Bolingbroke. M. de Silhouette, who had visited England in 1731, and resided with Bolingbroke, wrote in 1736 a history of the glorious reign of Elizabeth. It appears that he was also influenced by Bolingbroke's financial writings, for when Silhouette became Controleur General des Finances in March 1759, he sought to implement Bolingbroke's injunctions against luxury and financiers by reducing the number of unproductive pension holders. He was singularly ineffective and fell from office eight months later. M. de Silhouette's only lasting claim to fame other than his translation of and friendship with Bolingbroke is the legacy of his name. So hated were his financial measures that he was savagely ridiculed by cutouts which showed merely the outlines of individuals. These outlines of bodies, *portraits à la Silhouette,* indicated to what extent the Controleur General had reduced the individual and his wealth. See the *Nouvelle Biographie General.*

63. Bolingbroke, *Works,* II, 84.

64. *Ibid.,* II, 93.

65. *Ibid.,* II, 114.

66. *Ibid.,* II, 163.

67. *Ibid.,* II, 159, 165-166, 610.

68. Among these is an attack on luxury, *The Craftsman*, nos. 29, and 131, which berates the vogue for Italian music in England as enervating and feminizing. There is also an attack on bribery and corruption in general, *The Craftsman*, no. 406. Walpole is defamed in "On Good and Bad Ministers," *The Craftsman*, no. 154. The description of constitutional changes since the Revolution is found in "On the Power of the Prince and Freedom of the People," *The Craftsman*, no. 371 and in "Of the Constitution of Great Britain," *The Craftsman*, no. 375.

69. *The Craftsman*, nos. 324, 325, 326 (16, 23, and 30 September 1732). Bolingbroke may have had in mind the similar attack on Pericles found in Plato's *Gorgias*.

70. *The London Journal*, no. 693 (7 October 1732). *Daily Courant* (10 October 1732).

71. *The Craftsman*, no. 402 (16 March 1734).

72. For a vivid description of Walpole's tactics, see Plumb's *Sir Robert Walpole*, II, 305-308.

73. IX *Parliamentary History*, 471-472.

74. British Museum Add. Mss., 34146 (Bolingbroke Family Papers), f/93.

75. Fletcher, "The Intellectual Relations of Lord Bolingbroke with France," pp. 103ff; William Coxe, *Memoirs of the Life and Administration of Sir Robert Walpole*, 3 vols. (London, 1798), III, 337.

76. Coxe, *Memoirs of Walpole*, II, 338; III, 318, 494.

77. Bolingbroke, *Works*, II, 352-371. The letter is addressed to Lord Cornbury.

78. Benjamin Disraeli, *Vindication of the English Constitution* (London, 1839), passim.

79. Bolingbroke, *Works*, II, 363-364.

80. *Marchmont Papers*, G. H. Rose, ed., 3 vols. (London, 1831), II, 188-189; Coxe, *Memoirs of Walpole*, III, 522.

81. George Young, *Poor Fred, the People's Prince* (Oxford, 1939), is the best history of the Prince's circle. For the literary dimension of the circle, see M. H. Cable's "Idea of a Patriot King in the Propaganda of the Opposition to Walpole," *Philological Quarterly* 18 (January 1939).

82. Though written in 1738 or early 1739, *The Idea of a Patriot King* was not published for ten years and then only reluctantly. The tale surrounding its publication is one of the more interesting associated with the classics of political thought. It is not clear precisely when, but at some time, either in 1739 or when he returned for short visits in 1742 and 1743, Bolingbroke left the manuscript of *The Idea of a Patriot King* with his dear friend Pope, instructing him that it was not for publication. After Pope's death in 1744, Bolingbroke, one of the poet's literary executors, uncovered some fifteen hundred copies of an edition of *The Idea of a Patriot King* that Pope had printed. Pope had also made minor changes in the text. Infuriated at this violation of his wishes, Bolingbroke had the fifteen hundred copies destroyed, but for two copies, which he retained himself (*Marchmont Papers*, II, 338-339). He was apparently successful in keeping the manuscript from becoming public until January 1749, when the first of three abstracts of the work appeared in *The London Magazine*. Preferring that if they had to appear, they be in his own text, Bolingbroke reluctantly authorized the definitive edition of *The Idea of a Patriot King*, which finally appeared ten years after it was written. The author has compared the Pope text in the British Museum with the published version, and very little, if anything of substance was changed. For a similar finding, see F. E. Ratchford, "Pope and the Patriot King," *University of Texas Bulletin*, Studies in English (1926), 157-177.

83. Bolingbroke, *Works*, II, 126, 372-430. *The Complete Works of George Savile, first Marquess of Halifax*, Walter Raleigh, ed. (Oxford, 1912), p. 54; "Monarchy is like'd by the people, for the bells and the tinsel, the outward pomp and gilding, and there must be milk for Babes, since the greatest part of mankind are, and ever will be included in that list."

84. Bolingbroke, *Works*, II, 429.

85. "Rule Britannia" was heard for the first time in a musical drama, *The Masque of Alfred*, written by Thomson and Mallet (friend and literary executor of Boling-broke) and held before Frederick in August 1740. *Memoirs and Correspondence of George, Lord Lyttelton*, Robert Phillimore, ed., 2 vols. (London, 1845), I, 160.

86. Coxe, *Memoirs of Walpole*, I, 160.

87. *Marchmont Papers*, II, 182.

88. *Ibid.*, II, 273, 282.

89. *Ibid.*, II, 350, 360, 367; Historical Manuscripts Commission, *Denbigh Mss.*, 5 vols. (London, 1874-1911), I, 118.

90. Bolingbroke, *Works*, II, 439-462.

91. *Ibid.*, II, 443.

92. *Ibid.*, II, 451, 458; Swift, *Correspondence*, IV, 250-251.

93. Horace Walpole, *Letters to Sir Horace Mann*, 2 vols. (London, 1833), II, 86, and James Boswell, *Life of Johnson*, 5 vols. (London, 1889), I, 218.

94. Edmund Burke, *Reflections on the Revolution in France* in *Works*, 12 vols. (London, 1887), III, 349.


## CHAPTER II. WALPOLE AND THE NEW ECONOMIC ORDER

1. Most analysts tend to see the period they study as characterized by revolutionary economic developments. J. H. Hexter has aptly cautioned against this excessive zeal. ("Myth of the Middle Class in Tudor England," *Reappraisals in History* [Evanston, Ill., 1962], pp. 70ff.) "Why," he asks, "does each one think his era is entitled to be called revolutionary?" (p. 81). To accept the testimony of contemporaries is to find that men always lament that things have changed, that the previous age was different and better, that the social order is threatened by new men. In this latter respect the recurring Augustan lament sounds very much like the resentment in the Tudor Age against the low-born bureaucrats manning the centralizing monarchy. All of this well-intentioned caution does not detract, however, from the real novelty of the economic change which occurred in the years 1690-1740.

2. Daniel Defoe, *An Essay Upon the Public Credit being an Enquiry How the Public Credit Comes to Depend Upon the Change of the Ministry or the Dissolution of Parliaments* (London, 1710), p. 6. This tract was written for Harley, to help prevent the expected run on credit when the Tories replaced the Bank-backed Whigs. Defoe went on in the tract to calm the fears of the moneyed community. There was no need, he assured them, to sell their tallies or to discount their exchequer bills.

3. Note the title of a 1676 pamphlet: *The Mystery of the New Fashioned Goldsmith or Bankers* (London, 1676).

Some sources for the early history of English banking are: R. D. Richards, *Early History of Banking in England* (London, 1929); Ephraim Lipson, *Economic History of England,* 3 vols. (London, 1947), vol. III; W. R. Bisschop, *Rise of the London Money Market 1640-1828* (London, 1910); John Clapham, *The Bank of England: A History,* 2 vols. (Cambridge, Eng., 1944); J. B. Martin, *The Grasshopper on Lombard Street* (London, 1892); Charles Wright and C. Ernest Fayles, *A History of Lloyds* (London, 1908).

4. See Clarendon's famous statement on the importance of goldsmiths under Oliver Cromwell, *Life of Edward, Earl of Clarendon,* 3 vols. (London, 1827), III, 7.

5. Bisschop, *Rise of the London Money Market,* p. 72.

6. The scrivener was another pioneer of the English banking system (Lipson, *Economic History of England,* III, 228, and Richards, *Early History of Banking in England,* pp. 15-16). By craft a professional penman, scribe or clerk, he figured in the drawing up and writing of bonds, bills obligatory, and contracts. His activity as a clerical intermediary between trade and trader, buyer and seller, lender and borrower, gave him intimate knowledge of the financial and mercantile world. In the sixteenth and seventeenth centuries he came to perform certain functions of banking; he received money and then placed it out at interest. He advanced money for marriage settlements and acted as a financial contact man. As a result he became an important middleman in the estate market of the late seventeenth and early eighteenth century. D. C. Coleman, "London Scriveners and the Estate Market in the late Seventeenth Century," *English Economic Review* 4 (1951), no. 11. Because he arranged sales and mortgages he became a favorite object of gentry resentment. The statute passed against high interest under Anne singled him out as particularly exploitive (*Statutes at Large* XIII, 12 Anne 2.c.16, 119). Note also Charles Davenant, *Political and Commercial Works,* 5 vols. (London, 1771), I, 79. "If these high land taxes are long continued in a country so little given to thrift as ours, the landed men must inevitably be driven into the hands of scriveners." But the banking functions of the scriveners, like the goldsmiths', were doomed by the establishment of the Bank of England.

7. Walter Bagehot, *Lombard Street: A Description of the Money Market* (London, 1873), p. 92.

8. Jonathan Swift, *The History of the Four Last Years of the Queen,* H. Davis, ed. (Oxford, 1951), p. 69.

9. The total of parliamentary grants in 1689 was £184,786; in 1694, £5,830,581; in 1696, £7,961,469. Richards, *Early History of Banking in England,* p. 144.

10. Clapham, *The Bank of England,* I, 10. Most of the subsequent data is from Clapham's masterful study.

11. An exception is the Bank of Sweden, which, founded in 1656, was not only the last of the public banks before England's, but also the smallest and least well-known.

12. William Temple, *The Works of Sir William Temple,* 4 vols. (London, 1814), I, 35.

13. Swift, *History of the Last Four Years of the Queen,* p. 70.

14. Temple, *Works,* I, 36. These statements by Swift and Temple show how current ideas of cultural determinism and relativism were in the generation before Montesquieu.

15. Maurice Cranston, *John Locke: A Biography* (London, 1957), p. 377. Locke took five hundred pounds of the first issue of Bank of England stock.

16. This data is in Clapham, *The Bank of England,* pp. 270ff.

17. Note the title of a tract written in 1748: *A Winter Evening's Conversation in a Club of Jews, Dutchmen, French Refugees and English Stockjobbers at a Noted*

*Coffee House in Change Alley* (London, 1748). This anti-Semitism and anti-foreigner sentiment would reappear in later "populist" phenomena in other countries.

18. B. R. Mitchell, *Abstracts of British Historical Statistics* (Cambridge, 1962), pp. 401-402.

19. These figures are from E. L. Hargraves, *The National Debt* (London, 1930), pp. 23ff.

20. *The Necessity of Lowering Interest and Continuing Taxes* (London, 1750), pp. 15-16.

21. *The Present State of the National Debt with Remarks on the Nature of our Public Funds and the Uses Which a Large National Debt May Be of to a Sole Minister* (London, 1740), p. 20.

22. *An Essay Upon Public Credit* (London, 1740), pp. 9-10.

23. See A. L. Rowse, *The England of Elizabeth* (New York, 1951), p. 111; and W. R. Scott, *Constitution and Finance of English, Scottish, Irish Stock Companies to 1720*, 2 vols. (Cambridge, Eng., 1912).

24. For these figures, see Scott, I, 336, 394, 418, 419, 439.

25. A good discussion of this group is found in G. P. Gooch, *Political Thought in England: Bacon to Halifax* (Oxford, 1915), pp. 178-196. The influence of this group of economists, statisticians, and political arithmeticians on the nascent eighteenth-century study of society is an interesting issue and merits investigation.

26. Between 1660 and 1700, 236 patents for new inventions were issued. Of these 64 were issued in the two years between 1691-1693. K. G. Davies, "Joint Stock Investment in the Late Seventeenth Century," *Economic History Review* 4 (1952), no. 3, 285. See also Scott, *English Stock Companies to 1720*, I, 327.

27. Davies, "Joint Stock Investment in the Late Seventeenth Century," p. 292.

28. R. F. Jones, "The Background of the Attack on Science in the Age of Pope," in *Pope and His Contemporaries: Essays Presented to George Sherburn* (Cambridge, Eng., 1949), pp. 96-113.

29. The obvious exceptions are, of course, Rousseau and Montesquieu. The latter's *Persian Letters* and *Spirit of the Laws* are overtly critical of the projecting spirit.

30. Lucy Sutherland, *East India Company in Eighteenth-Century Politics* (Oxford, 1952) and "City of London in Eighteenth-Century Politics," in *Essays Presented to Sir Lewis Namier* (London, 1956).

31. Sutherland, *East India Company,* p. 25. It is interesting to note that the companies did not subscribe in their corporate capacities, but in the person of the directors, who had their companies' backing. See L. B. Namier, *The Structure of Politics at the Accession of George III* (London, 1929).

32. Charles Duguid, *The Story of the Stock Exchange* (London, 1901).

33. *Cato's Letters,* 4 vols. (London, 1724), I, 8, 16, 24. The vehemence is explained by the year of the original publication, 1721.

34. Sutherland, *East India Company,* pp. 10-11.

35. Duguid, *The Story of the Stock Exchange,* p. 5.

36. *Statutes at Large,* 819 William III, c. 32. See also Duguid, *The Story of the Stock Exchange,* p. 16.

37. See, for example, *A proposal for putting some stop to the extravagant Humour of Stock-Jobbing* (London, 1717), p. 4; also *The Villainy of the Stock-Jobbers Detected* (London, 1701); Duguid, *Story of the Stock Exchange,* p. 19.

38. Daniel Defoe, *A Tour Thro' the Whole Island of Great Britain,* G. D. H. Cole, ed., 2 vols. (London, 1962), I, 336; Sutherland, *East India Company,* p. 29.

39. Historical Manuscripts Commission, *Diary of the First Earl of Egmont,* 3 vols. (London, 1920), (London, 1920-1923), I, 86.

40. Lord John Hervey, *Some Materials Towards Memoirs of the Reign of George II,* Romney Sedgewick, ed., 3 vols. (London, 1931), I, 138. See also Sutherland, *East India Company,* p. 18.

41. Sutherland, *East India Company,* passim; and "City of London," p. 55. Also A. J. Henderson, *London and the National Government, 1721-1742* (Durham, North Carolina, 1945), pp. 11-13; Clapham, "The Bank and the Government, 1697-1764," in *The Bank of England,* I, ii.

42. For details of Gideon's career see Duguid, *The Story of the Stock Exchange,* p. 46ff. Also Lucy Sutherland, "Sampson Gideon: Eighteenth-Century Jewish Financier," *Transactions of the Jewish Historical Society* 17 (1951-1952), 79-90.

43. John Barnard, *Reasons for the Representatives of the People of Great Britain to Take Advantage of the Present Rate of Interest for the More Speedily Lessening the National Debt* (London, 1737), p. 3.

44. Clapham, *The Bank of England,* I, 54, 91, 93.

45. *Some Considerations on Public Credit and the Nature of its Circulating in the Funds . . .* (London, 1733). See also the Opposition response in *The Present State of the National Debt with Remarks on the Nature of our Public Funds . . .* (London, 1740), p. 16. "I know that there is a notion industriously spread, as if the present establishment had no other security for its continuance but the continuance of the public debts, detestable insinuation!"

46. *Some Considerations on Public Credit,* pp. 20-21.

47. *The London Journal,* no. 548 (31 January 1730).

48. J. H. Plumb, *Sir Robert Walpole,* 2 vols. (Boston, 1956), II, 304-309; and Virginia Cowles, *The Great Swindle: The Story of the South Sea Bubble* (London, 1960), 142.

49. *The London Journal,* no. 666 (1 April 1732); *The Daily Gazetteer,* no. 72 (20 September 1735).

50. *The London Journal,* no. 571 (11 July 1730).

51. Described in Sutherland, *East India Company,* p. 29.

52. John Barnard, *Considerations Upon a Proposal for Lowering Interest of all Redeemable Debts to Three Percent* (London, 1737), p. 4.

53. William Coxe, *Memoirs of the Life and Administration of Sir Robert Walpole,* 3 vols. (London, 1798), I, 409.

54. X *Parliamentary History,* 184.

55. VIII *Parliamentary History,* 943-959; *Case of the Salt Duty and Land Tax Offered to the Consideration of Every Freeholder* (London, 1732), p. 103.

56. William Kennedy's *English Taxation 1640-1799* (London, 1913), pp. 64-100, has an excellent discussion of the excise tax and its theoretical assumptions, and of the general position stated above. See John Locke, *Second Treatise on Civil Government,* Peter Laslett, ed. (Cambridge, Eng., 1960), p. 380. "Tis fit everyone who enjoys his share of the protection shall pay out of his estate in proportion for the maintenance of it."

57. C. B. Macpherson, *The Political Theory of Possessive Individualism* (Oxford, 1962).

58. VIII *Parliamentary History,* 1050-1051. See also Wyndham's speech. "Every man ought to pay to the public charge in proportion to the benefit he receives therefrom; a poor man, who has no property, ought not to be charged for the defense of property . . . Liberty may be equally dear to every man, but surely he that has the

largest property ought to contribute most to the public expense." VIII *Parliamentary History*, 953.

## CHAPTER III. BOLINGBROKE AND THE NEW ENGLAND

1. J. H. Plumb, *Sir Robert Walpole*, 2 vols. (Boston, 1956), II, 310.

2. See H. J. Habbakuk's "English Landownership 1680-1740," *English Historical Review* 10 (February 1940). See also his "Marriage Settlements in the Eighteenth Century," *Transactions of the Royal Historical Society,* Fourth Series, 32 (1950); "Daniel Finch, Second Earl of Nottingham, His Home and Estates," *Studies in Social History* (London, 1955); "Long Term Interest Rates and Price of Land in the Seventeenth Century," *English Historical Review* 5 (1952). For a recent assimilation and presentation of Habbakuk's views, see G. E. Mingay, *English Landed Society in the Eighteenth Century* (London, 1963).

3. Habbakuk, "English Landownership," p. 3.

4. Habbakuk's thesis is essential to the Tawney school. Somehow one must get from the seventeenth century, with its decline of greater proprietors and increase in the holdings and numbers of smaller gentry, to the late eighteenth century with its predominantly large holdings (see Mingay). Habbakuk's analysis does just this. It describes the decline of the small squarearchy, the class which had risen in the sixteenth and seventeenth centuries. That Tawney recognized the complementarity of Habbakuk's thesis with his own is indicated by his discussion of it in his famous lecture to the British Academy. "Habbakuk shows that the land-system after 1688 changed. The economic tide which for a century favored disintegration of great estates now it appears turned and ran the other way. Hard hit by war taxation, smaller squires and country gentry whose advance had been the theme of earlier writers were selling out." "Harrington's Interpretation of His Age," *Proceedings of the British Academy* (London, 1941), p. 233.

5. Habbakuk, "Marriage Settlements," p. 19.

6. Habbakuk, "English Landownership," passim. See also W. R. Ward, *English Land Tax in the Eighteenth Century* (Oxford, 1953), p. 10 and passim; and William Kennedy, *English Taxation 1640-1799* (London, 1913). In Ward's book (pp. 50-55), there is a good discussion of the political importance of the local commissioners appointed by the Crown to supervise assessment and collection of the tax.

7. *Statutes at Large,* XIII, 12 Anne Statute 2.C.16 (1713).

8. Edward Hughes, *North Country Life in the Eighteenth Century* (Oxford, 1952), p. xvi.

9. *Considerations on the Necessity of Taxing the Annuities Granted by Parliament and Reducing One-Fifth of the Capital Stock of all Persons Possessed of Five Thousand Pounds or More in the Public Companies, in order to Pay Off the National Debt* (London, 1746), pp. 12-13.

10. *Considerations Upon a Reduction of the Land Tax* (London, 1749), p. 22. Note the similarity of these opinions to those of David Hume.

11. Habbakuk, "English Land Ownership," p. 13; "Daniel Finch," p. 168. See also Plumb, *Sir Robert Walpole*, I, 7, for the fortune made by Chandos while Marlborough's Paymaster. Blenheim was constructed unashamedly at the public expense. It was "a pleasing spectacle to the generosity of the people, being more for their four shillings in the pound than ever yet they saw." Historical Manuscripts Commission, *Portland Mss.,* 10 vols. (London, 1891-1931), IV, 110.

12. H. R. Trevor-Roper, "The Gentry 1540-1640," *Economic History Review Supplement* I. See also by Trevor-Roper, "Country House Radicals, 1590-1640" and "The Social Causes of the Great Rebellion," in *Historical Essays* (London, 1957).

13. J. G. A. Pocock, "Machiavelli, Harrington and English Political Ideologies in the Eighteenth Century," *William and Mary Quarterly* 22 (October 1965), 575.

14. H.M.C., *Portland Mss.,* VIII, 196.

15. John Locke, *Some Considerations of the Consequences of Lowering the Interest and Raising the Value of Money* in *Works,* Edmund Law, ed., 10 vols. (London, 1801), V, 53, 60, 71.

16. *Considerations on the Necessity of Taxing the Annuities,* pp. 13, 17.

17. *The Sentiments of a Great Man Upon Proposals for a General Reduction of Interest to Three Percent* (London, 1751), p. 18. See also John Barnard's *Consideration Upon a Proposal for Lowering the Interest Rate of All the Redeemable Debts to Three Percent . . .* (London, 1737), p. 23. In it Barnard says of those who oppose the reduction, "It is conceivable that those who have made these observations have had in their head Mr. Locke's reasoning against reducing by law interest of money."

18. Locke, *Works,* V, 37.

19. Locke, *Works,* V, 60. The party of the gentry and the small trader would not hesitate to use these statements, however, in their opposition to Walpole's Excise Bill in 1733. David Hume rejected Locke's argument in his essay "Of Taxes." "Why the landed gentleman should be victim of the whole, and should not be able to defend himself as well as others are, I cannot really imagine," *David Hume: Writings on Economics,* Eugene Rotwein, ed. (Madison, 1955), p. 87.

20. This association prompted the lyrical praise of Macaulay. "Never had the world seen the highest practical and the highest speculative abilities united in an alliance so close, so harmonious and so honourable as that which bound Somers, and Montague to Locke and Newton." *Essays and Lays* (London, 1888), p. 472.

21. A discussion of this gentry grievance is found in Ward, *English Land Tax,* p. 42.

22. G. M. Trevelyan, *England Under Queen Anne,* 3 vols. (London, 1934), III, 69-70.

23. Clara Buck and Godfrey Davis, "Letters on Godolphin's Dismissal in 1710," *Huntington Library Quarterly* 3 (1940), 230. James Brydges to George Brydges (17 June 1710). James Brydges subsequently became Lord Chandos.

24. Buck and Davis, "Letters on Godolphin's Dismissal," p. 232.

25. *The Works of Lord Bolingbroke,* 4 vols. (Philadelphia, 1841), I, 116.

26. *The Examiner* (19 April 1711).

27. The description of the Bubble is based on pamphlet and contemporary comment as cited, also the accounts in John Clapham, *The Bank of England: A History,* 2 vols. (Cambridge, Eng., 1944), I, 79-89; Ephraim Lipson, *Economic History of England,* 3 vols. (London, 1947), III, 368ff; W. R. Scott, *English Joint Stock Companies to 1720,* 3 vols. (Cambridge, Eng., 1912), III, 288-363; Virginia Cowles, *The Great Swindle* (London, 1960); and John Carswell, *The South Sea Bubble* (Stanford, 1960).

28. Quoted in Cowles, *The Great Swindle,* 92.

29. *A Letter to a Conscientious Man, Concerning the Use and Abuse of Riches* (London, 1720), p. 3.

30. Charles Duguid, *The Story of the Stock Exchange* (London, 1901).

31. *Applebee's Journal* (14 July 1720); *Exchange Alley: or the Stock-Jobber Turned Gentleman* (London, 1720), p. 34.

32. *Applebee's Journal* (22 October 1720); *The Weekly Journal and Saturday's Post* (10 October 1720).

33. Godfrey Davis and Marion Tinling, "Letters of Henry St. John to James Brydges," *Huntington Library Quarterly* 8 (October 1935), 154.

34. Alexander Pope, *Moral Essays*, Epistle III, lines 135-143. All citations to Pope unless otherwise indicated are to *The Poetical Works of Alexander Pope*, Robert Carruthers, ed., 4 vols. (London, 1854).

35. *An Essay Towards Preventing the Ruin of Great Britain* (London, 1721), pp. 5, 25.

36. *The Craftsman*, no. 228 (8 January 1732); no. 479 (6 September 1735).

37. *Ibid.*, no. 166 (6 September 1729); no. 134 (25 January 1729); no. 304 (29 April 1732).

38. *Ibid.*, no. 19 (10 February 1727); also no. 12 (13 January 1727).

39. *Ibid.*, no. 47 (27 May 1727); no. 480 (8 November 1735); no. 288 (8 January 1732); no. 114 (7 September 1728); no. 71 (11 November 1727).

40. *Ibid.*, no. 71 (11 November 1772); also no. 5 (19 December 1726); and no. 341 (13 January 1733).

41. *Ibid.*, no. 288 (8 January 1732); no. 426 (31 August 1734).

42. *Ibid.*, no. 27 (10 March 1727); no. 21 (17 February 1727); no. 21 (17 February 1727); no. 46 (20 May 1727).

43. Bolingbroke, *Works*, II, 61, 166.

44. Bolingbroke to Chesterfield (no date, circa 1750), British Museum Add. Mss., 4948A, folio 422-425.

45. Bolingbroke, *Works*, II, 65, 355, 333, 356, 234, 373-374; *The Craftsman*, no. 3 (12 December 1726); Bolingbroke, *Works*, I, 474ff; also *The Craftsman*, no. 20 (13 February 1727); no. 99 (25 May 1728).

46. Aristotle, *Politics*, II, ii. "Whenever the chiefs of the state deem anything honorable, the other citizens are sure to follow their examples." Cicero, *De Legibus*, III, 13-14. "The whole state is habitually corrupted by the evil desires and vices of its prominent men." See also Machiavelli's *Discourses*, passim.

47. *The Craftsman*, no. 166 (6 September 1729); no. 178 (29 November 1729).

48. British Museum Add. Mss. 4948A, folio 422-425. Also see *The Craftsman*, nos. 291, 312, 320, in 1732, for attacks on Mandeville.

49. Bolingbroke, *Works*, II, 365.

50. *The Craftsman*, no. 377 (22 September 1733); no. 89 (16 March 1728); no. 29 (17 March 1727); Bolingbroke, *Works*, I, 474ff, "On Luxury" and I, 496ff, "On the Policy of the Athenians."

51. Bolingbroke, *Works*, II, 152; also I, 301 and II, 173-242.

52. *The Craftsman*, no. 124 (16 November 1728); Bolingbroke, *Works*, II, 131, 165, 357, 363, 455. See also II, 152.

53. *The Craftsman*, no. 94 (20 April 1728); no. 456 (29 March 1735).

54. Bolingbroke, *Works*, I, 346, 359, 361, 363; II, 147, 148.

55. *Ibid.*, II, 61, 166.

56. *Ibid.*, II, 158, 159, 163-164, 166.

57. J. G. A. Pocock, "Machiavelli, Harrington, and English Political Ideologies in the Eighteenth Century," passim. For the phrase "gentry paradise," see Judith Shklar, "Ideology Hunting-Case of James Harrington," *American Political Science Review* 53 (September 1959), 68. See also the articles of H. R. Trevor-Roper and

R. H. Tawney; also C. B. Macpherson, *The Political Theory of Possessive Individualism* (Oxford, 1962), pp. 161-194; J. G. A. Pocock, *The Ancient Constitution and the Feudal Law* (Cambridge, Eng., 1954), pp. 129-147.

58. Bolingbroke, *Works*, II, 152.

59. The opposite of a "genuine" political system was usually described as "unnatural" or "bastard." This typology is a recurring motif in his writings. For one of the more explicit references see Bolingbroke's "Freeholders' Political Catechism," *The Craftsman*, no. 377 (22 September 1733); reprinted in Bolingbroke's *Collected Political Tracts* (London, 1748). "Q: 'What means thou by a "genuine" House of Commons?' A: 'One that is the lawful issue of the people, and no bastard.' Q: 'How is a "bastard" House of Commons produced?' A: 'When the people, by terror, corruption, or other indirect means, choose such as they otherwise would not choose.' "

60. Bolingbroke, *Works*, II, 401.

61. Lines 348-352. In light of the recurring temptation to draw parallels between the thought of Bolingbroke's circle who were early critics of English financial capitalism and American populist thinkers, it is interesting to note that "Oliver Goldsmith's classic statement, *The Deserted Village*, became, well over a hundred years later, the unchallenged favorite of American Populist writers and orators." Richard Hofstader, *Age of Reform* (New York, 1956), p. 26.

62. Bolingbroke could have derived his Aristotelian notions of political economy from Harrington, their main English interpreter, or from his own familiarity with Aristotelian and Greek notions of citizenship. J. G. A. Pocock, "Machiavelli, Harrington, and English Political Ideologies in the Eighteenth Century," passim. The argument in this paragraph was suggested by Pocock's excellent article. For the influence of Harrington on Bolingbroke, see, in addition, *Marchmont Papers*, G. H. Rose, ed., 3 vols. (London, 1831), II, 240. The claim by Shklar, "Ideology Hunting," pp. 664-665, and G. P. Gooch, *English Democratic Ideas in the Seventeenth Century* (New York, 1959), pp. 250-251, that Harrington received little notice in the early eighteenth century must be amended. See, for example, Christopher Hill, "James Harrington and the People," *Puritanism and Liberty* (London, 1962), p. 310; Caroline Robbins, *Eighteenth-Century Commonwealthman* (Cambridge, Mass., 1959), passim; and of course the Pocock article.

63. Pocock, "Machiavelli, Harrington and English Political Ideology in the Eighteenth Century," p. 576.

64. Bolingbroke, *Works*, I, 492-493; II, 237, 360ff.

65. *The Craftsman*, no. 9 (2 January 1727); and no. 127 (7 December 1728).

66. *Ibid.*, no. 57 (5 August 1727); no. 184 (10 January 1730); no. 419 (13 July 1731); no. 151 (24 May 1729); no. 158 (12 July 1729).

67. William Pulteney, *An Humble Address* (London, 1734), p. 11.

68. See Giuseppe Giarizzo, *David Hume* (Turin, 1962), pp. 87ff for a discussion of the impact of the Jacobite 1745 on Hume and his decisive turn to Toryism.

69. David Hume, "Of Public Credit," in *David Hume: Writings on Economics*, pp. 98-99. For a general discussion of the similarities between Hume's conception of politics and the economy and Bolingbroke's see Giarizzo, *David Hume*, pp. 69-70, 71, 74. For Hume's dislike of stockjobbers and financiers, see pp. 60, 94-95; his anger at the debt, taxation, and the power of public finance, p. 50; his attacks on projects, pp. 50, 95.

CHAPTER IV. BOLINGBROKE ON NATURAL LAW, SOCIETY, AND THE ORIGINS OF GOVERNMENT

1. Bolingbroke, *The Works of Lord Bolingbroke,* 4 vols. (Philadelphia, 1841), IV, 119ff, 406.

2. *Ibid.,* III, 50, 52, 66, 76, 103-104, 121, 124, 129, 135, 290, 446, 530; IV, 120, 121ff, 141.

3. *Ibid.,* III, 72, 103, 129; IV, 121, 129; see also John Locke, *Essay on Human Understanding* (London, 1879), p. 2.

4. Bolingbroke, *Works,* IV, 145, 147, 150, 168, 175, 179.

5. *Ibid.,* IV, 156; also IV, 171-172.

6. *Ibid.,* IV, 137-138, also III, 106, 397.

7. See Peter Gay, *Voltaire's Politics* (Princeton, 1959), pp. 343-346, and Robert Shackleton, *Montesquieu: A Critical Biography* (Oxford, 1961), pp. 244-265.

8. Bolingbroke, *Works,* III, 396; IV, 147, 176, 180, 242, 246.

9. See Edmund Burke, *Vindication of Natural Society* (London, 1757). This reading of Bolingbroke has been given in recent years by A. O. Aldridge, "Shaftesbury and Bolingbroke," *Philological Quarterly* 31 (January 1952), 16. Burke's image of Bolingbroke the radical philosopher has been repeated again by Harvey M. Mansfield, Jr. in his *Statesmanship and Party Government* (Chicago, 1965) where it is argued that Bolingbroke sought to reduce all governments to rational first principles and to remove all trace of prejudice and prescription. See also for a similar but less developed view of Bolingbroke, J. C. Weston, Jr., "The Ironic Purpose of Burke's Vindication Vindicated," *Journal of the History of Ideas* 29 (June 1958). The heart of Burke's and later expressions of this interpretation of Bolingbroke is a projection of Bolingbroke's religious views into radical political ideas. Deism need not, however, be associated with political radicalism; indeed, the early deists Shaftesbury and Bolingbroke had distinctly aristocratic outlooks. In its early stages when its Stoic roots were most exposed deism was a most appropriate aristocratic religion. Bolingbroke, it should be added, warned against the very identification of religion and political ideas that Burke attributed to him. *Works,* III, 397.

10. Bolingbroke, *Works,* IV, 243, 246; see also II, 365, 381. "For no human institution can arrive at perfection, and that the most that human wisdom can do, is to procure the same or greater good, at the expense of less evil." See IV, 243, 290, 364.

11. *Ibid.,* IV, 145; also IV, 167.

12. Anthony Ashley Cooper, third Earl of Shaftesbury, *Characteristicks of Men, Manners, Opinions, Times,* J. M. Robinson, ed., 2 vols. (London, 1900). That Shaftesbury intended Hobbes and Locke to be the recipients of this criticism is made clear in his unpublished papers. See *The Life, Unpublished Letters and Philosophical Regimen of Anthony, Earl of Shaftesbury, Author of the Characteristicks,* Benjamin Rand, ed., 2 vols. (London, 1900), pp. 403-404; 414-416; Shaftesbury, *Characteristicks,* I, 74; II, 83.

13. *Ibid.,* I, 72-73; II, 79.

14. For the complexities of Bolingbroke's intellectual debt to Shaftesbury see its passing mention in Robinson's editorial comments in *Characteristicks,* II, 260-262. See also Aldridge, "Shaftesbury and Bolingbroke," which deals primarily with a comparison of their deist positions.

15. Bolingbroke, *Works,* IV, 187; see also IV, 164-165, 369.

16. Alexander Pope, *Essay on Man,* Epistle III, lines 317-318.

17. Shaftesbury, *Characteristicks,* I, 79-80. Bolingbroke, *Works,* III, 399; see also Bolingbroke, *Reflections on Innate Principles* (Paris, 1754).

18. Bolingbroke, *Works,* IV, 103, 181, 185, 194.

19. *Ibid.,* IV, 146, 150, 228.

20. *Ibid.,* IV, 129. While Bolingbroke is no Filmer it should be evident, however, that Bolingbroke has learned much from Filmer's mentor, Jean Bodin.

21. *Ibid.,* IV, 187, 189, 194. Though his emphasis is very different it is not clear that Locke meant anything drastically different than the heads of families. He might consider sons, if they were of age, but certainly not women or servants, to be part of the contract.

22. *Ibid.,* IV, 189, 190; for both Lycurgus and Aristotle.

23. *Ibid.,* III, 223. Bolingbroke's discussion never returns to his suggestion that war and conquest were the original source of political authority. He here suggests that the first kings were philosophical legislators as if he had never made the earlier point. See also *Works,* III, 228, 231; IV, 191, 194, 214.

24. *Ibid.,* IV, 193-194.

25. Of course Locke shared some of these views. In their discussions of natural law itself, Bolingbroke and Locke held quite similar views.

26. Bolingbroke, *Works,* IV, 194, 195-198.

27. *Ibid.,* IV, 196.

28. Shaftesbury had claimed that Locke's state of nature was distasteful because it accepted Hobbes' political theory. Locke had seen morality operative in the state of nature, but he denied the innate ideas basic to Shaftesbury's Platonic defense of an innate moral sense. What is more, Locke based the origin of civil society on the ethical value of self-interest (Shaftesbury, *The Life, Unpublished Letters . . . ,* p. 404). Shaftesbury reasoned that at heart Locke must really agree with Hobbes. They must both accept self-interest and, he adds mistakenly, believe that morality originates in civil authority. Shaftesbury's argument sounds much like the argument of the contemporary Strausian school. For recognition of this see Jason Aronson, "Shaftesbury on Locke," *American Political Science Review* 53 (December 1959). According to the arguments of this book, Bolingbroke could very well be the penultimate Strausian hero, if one agrees with him and shares his values. To defend his social and political attitudes has not been our concern. For such an effort from the Strausian perspective, see Jeffrey Hart, *Viscount Bolingbroke, Tory Humanist* (London, 1966), passim.

29. Bolingbroke, *Works,* IV, 195-196. See A. P. d'Entreves, *Natural Law* (London, 1951), pp. 48-64; and Leo Straus, *Natural Right and History* (Chicago, 1953), passim; Bolingbroke, *Works,* IV, 197-199. See Mansfield, *Statesmanship and Party Government,* pp. 244-245 for the contrary suggestion that Bolingbroke shared the belief in natural rights.

30. Bolingbroke, *Works,* IV, 197-198.

31. *Ibid.,* II, 456. This statement could just as easily have come from the pen of Rousseau, who did not believe in paternal authority, subordination and rank; radical and conservative critiques of the liberal world view can sometimes speak the same language.

32. *Ibid.,* II, 85, 116-117; 390-392; IV, 189.

33. *Ibid.,* I, 396-397. See also the similarity with sixteenth-century Spanish-Jesuit

theories of contract in Bernice Hamilton, *Political Thought in Sixteenth Century Spain* (Oxford, 1963), p. 3, n.2.

34. The *Vindicae Contra Tyrannos* emphasized the legitimacy of resisting princely threats to the true church; it also stressed that only the aristocracy should resist the unChristian acts of princes. See J. W. Allen, *Political Thought in the Sixteenth Century* (New York, 1960), pp. 314-330. Bolingbroke, so familiar with the "thèse nobilaire" writings and sentiment in his French period, was probably familiar with the *Vindicae*, which interestingly enough was first published in England in 1581 and revived again in a printing of 1689.

35. Arthur O. Lovejoy, *The Great Chain of Being: A Study of the History of an Idea* (Cambridge, Mass., 1936) and E. M. W. Tillyard, *Elizabethan World Picture* (New York, 1956); Thomas Elyot, *The Governor*, Everyman Edition (London, 1962).

36. Bolingbroke, *Works*, IV, 320-345.

37. *Ibid.*, IV, 339.

38. *Ibid.*, IV, 363.

39. *Ibid.*

40. Bolingbroke throughout this discussion attributes to Locke equalitarian views which, if pressed, Locke would not defend. Locke's writings on education, for example, suggest that he, too, expected the upper classes (even perhaps the landed classes) to do the governing.

41. Bolingbroke, *Works*, II, 90, 355, III, 222. The Renaissance humanist's utilization of the chain of being also led to similar political conclusions. See, for example, the sentiments of Sir Thomas Elyot, which read very much like Bolingbroke: "So in this world they which excel others in this influence of understanding . . . ought to be set in a more high place than the residue, where they may see and also be seen, that by the beams of their excellent wit, showed through the glass of authority, others of inferior understanding may be directed to the way of virtue and commodious living . . . A ploughman or carter shall make but a feeble answer to an ambassador. Also a weaver or fuller should be an unmeet captain of an army, or in any other office of a governor. Wherefore, to conclude, it is only a public weal, where like as God hath disposed the said influence of understanding, is also appointed degrees and places according to the excellency thereof" (Elyot, *The Governor*, pp. 4-5). The roots of Tory ruling-class notions go at least as far back as the Platonism of Renaissance humanists like Elyot and of Augustan humanists like Bolingbroke.

42. Bolingbroke, *Works*, III, 224. See David Hume, *Theory of Politics*, Frederick Watkins, ed. (Edinburgh, 1951), p. xviii. Bolingbroke's philosophical essays were not published until after his death in 1754, but they were written originally as letters to Pope, which would date them at least before 1744, the date of Pope's death.

43. Bolingbroke, *Works*, II, 190-299; III, 374-375; IV, 151. Bolingbroke wrote to Swift in 1721 to dissuade him from "talking sense and trying to do good to the rabble." Had Swift not yet realized, Bolingbroke asked, of the public that "this monstrous beast has passions to be moved, but no reason to be appealed to." Plain truth, he added, would influence only a few men in a nation but millions can be led by the nose (*Correspondence of Jonathan Swift*, F. E. Ball, ed., 6 vols. [London, 1910-1914], III, 89 [21 July 1721]). For similar aristocratic distinctions, see Shaftesbury, *Characteristicks*, I, 265.

44. Bolingbroke, *Works*, II, 353-355. The political and sociological roots of such claims are clear to at least one modern student of society who writes "the *je ne sais quoi* element in politics, which can be acquired only through long experience, and

which reveals itself as a rule only to those who for many generations have shared in political leadership, is intended to justify government by an aristocratic class." Karl Mannheim, *Ideology and Utopia* (New York, 1936), p. 120.

45. Bolingbroke, *Works*, III, 223-224, 487. John Locke, *Letters on Toleration* (London, 1765), pp. 2-37.

46. Bolingbroke, *Works*, III, 487.

47. *The Daily Gazetteer*, no. 120 (15 November 1735).

48. See Leonard Krieger, *The Politics of Discretion* (Chicago, 1965), pp. 92, 113, 142, 221.

49. Shaftesbury, *Characteristicks*, I, 73.

50. Charles Leslie, *The Finishing Stroke, Being a Vindication of the Patriarchal Scheme of Government* (London, 1711); *The Rehearsal, A View of the Times, Their Principles and Practice*, 4 vols. (London, 1708-1709); "A short account of the original of government," in *The New Association of Those Called Moderate Churchmen with the Modern Whigs and Fanatics to Undermine and Blow up the Present Church and Government* (London, 1703), Part III. I am indebted to Mr. John Dunn of King's College, Cambridge, for bringing this aspect of Leslie's thought to my attention.

51. Charles Leslie, "A short account," p. 4.

52. Charles Leslie, *The Finishing Stroke*, pp. 87, 164-165; "A short account," p. 14.

53. Bolingbroke, *Works*, II, 27.

54. T. B. Macaulay, *Essays and Lays* (London, 1888), p. 436. See also F. I. Herriot, *Sir William Temple on the Origins and Nature of Governments* (Baltimore, 1893) for an equally uncomplimentary reading of the essay. Bolingbroke had certainly read Temple's Essays, see his *Works*, I, 512; II, 64.

55. *The Works of Sir William Temple*, 4 vols. (London, 1814), I, 9-10.

56. *Ibid.*, I, 18.

57. *Ibid.*, I, 11, 18, 21.

58. *Ibid.*, I, 24.

## CHAPTER V. WALPOLE ON POLITICS AND THE ENGLISH CONSTITUTION

1. Basil Williams, *The Whig Supremacy* (Oxford, 1962), p. 75. The estimate of nonjurors for 1720 was 20,000. See also J. H. Plumb, *Sir Robert Walpole*, 2 vols. (Boston, 1956), I, 1, 72. The fascinating tale of the coming of political stability to England has been told with great clarity and insight by J. H. Plumb in his Ford lectures, given at Oxford in 1965. See his *Origins of Political Stability: England 1675-1725* (Boston, 1967).

2. *The Craftsman*, no. 58 (12 August 1727).

3. This analysis is generally that offered by Plumb, *Sir Robert Walpole*, II, 92-93, 172, 327-328. Sir Lewis Namier in his *England in the Age of the American Revolution* (London, 1956), is the father of this view of the Walpole-Pelham system; that is, if one discounts the analysis offered by Bolingbroke and his Opposition. Namier prefers the term "Government party" to Plumb's later "Treasury party." See also the excellent discussion of the system Walpole created in Betty Kemp's *King and Commons 1660-1833* (London, 1959).

4. *The Craftsman*, no. 56 (29 July 1727).

5. *Ibid.*, no. 414 (8 June 1734).

6. *Ibid.*, no. 381 (20 October 1733).

7. British Museum Add. Mss. 32857, f. 553 (Holderness to Newcastle); also B. E. Carter, *Office of Prime Minister* (Princeton, 1956), p. 24. George I had more than a smattering of English and all his ministers, including Walpole, could speak the King's natural language, French (Plumb, *Sir Robert Walpole*, I, 71).

8. Quoted in M. T. Blauvelt, *The Development of Cabinet Government in England* (New York, 1902), p. 173; see also Williams, *The Whig Supremacy*, p. 35.

9. *Grub Street Journal*, no. 152 (23 November 1732).

10. *The Craftsman*, no. 22 (20 February 1727).

11. *Ibid.*, no. 196 (4 April 1730); also no. 46 (20 May 1727).

12. William Coxe, *Memoirs of the Life and Administration of Sir Robert Walpole*, 3 vols. (London, 1798), III, 465.

13. Plumb, *Sir Robert Walpole*, I, 216, 362; and II, 310, 312; but see also I, 21, for a description of Walpole's father's extensive library. For an eighteenth-century appreciation of Walpole that corresponds closely with Plumb's, see Philip Yorke, *Walpoliana* (London, 1783), written by the son of Walpole's colleague, Hardwicke. See p. 16, "his mind perhaps was not very elevated, nor his accomplishments very extensive."

14. *The Correspondence of Jonathan Swift*, F. E. Ball, ed., 6 vols. (London, 1910-1914), III, 388.

15. *A Further Report from the Committee of Secrecy Appointed To Enquire into the Conduct of Robert, Earl of Oxford, during the last Ten Years* (London, 1742), appendix xiii. See also Lawrence Hanson, "The Government Press," in *Government and the Press 1695-1763* (Oxford, 1936); and Plumb, *Sir Robert Walpole*, II, 314-315.

16. *Essay upon the Taste and Writings of the Present Times* (London, 1728), p. 45. "I have often thought that the author of *The London Journal* is a much more dangerous enemy to the present ministry, which he (good man) endeavors to defend, than any other of our public writers. His encomiums upon them are generally so unfortunately flat and dull, that one can't help suspecting that he is sneering at them."

17. *The Craftsman*, no. 265 (31 July 1731).

18. Hanson, *Government and the Press*, p. 112.

19. Alexander Pope, *The Dunciad*, Book II, lines 319-320.

20. Lord John Hervey, *Some Materials Towards Memoirs of the Reign of George III*, Romney Sedgewick, ed., 3 vols. (London, 1931), I, 263.

21. *The London Journal*, no. 689 (9 September 1732) and no. 706 (6 January 1733). For this presentation of Locke's ideas see also no. 689, no. 575, and no. 605.

22. Thomas Gordon, *Essay on Government* (London, 1747), p. 18. Gordon came to Walpole's employment after his collaboration with John Trenchard in the highly successful anti-Walpole *Cato's Letters*. See below.

23. *The London Journal*, no. 689 (9 September 1732); no. 605 (6 March 1731).

24. Caroline Robbins, *The Eighteenth-Century Commonwealthman* (Cambridge, Mass., 1959), p. 5.

25. *The London Journal*, no. 694 (14 October 1732).

26. *The London Journal*, no. 592 (5 December 1730); cf. also no. 723 and *The Daily Courant* (28 August 1731).

27. *A Full and True Account of the Strange and Miraculous Conversion of the Tories in Great Britain by the Preaching of Caleb d'Anvers, Prophet and Apostle to these Nations* (London, 1734), p. 9.

28. T. B. Macaulay, *Essays and Lays* (London, 1888), p. 239. The application of this law to practice has implied for Whig observers a perpetual conflict between the

two parties which represent these tendencies. "After 1688 the rule of England by the contest of the two parties was begun in earnest" (G. M. Trevelyan, *England Under the Stuarts* [London, 1960], p. 488). Perhaps the most extreme statement of this Whig view is found in W. A. Abbot, "Origins of English Political Parties," *American Historical Review* 24 (1918-1919), 602. In all fairness, one should note that Tory historians before Namier, such as Keith Feiling, also assume that the two parties were founded in the reign of Charles II, and that from this origin they persisted with little change until modern times (*History of the Tory Party* [Oxford, 1924]). It should also be noted, however, that Sir William Gilbert's maxim has been questioned by Herbert Butterfield, who writes that "in every Englishman there is hidden something of a Whig that seems to tug at the heart strings," *The Englishman and His History* (Cambridge, Eng., 1944), p. 73.

29. *The London Journal*, no. 777 (18 May 1734).

30. *Ibid.*, no. 786 (20 July 1734).

31. Edmund Burke, *An Appeal from the New to the Old Whigs*, in *Works*, 12 vols. (Boston, 1866-1867), IV, 107. The Rockingham Whigs could not possibly find corruption in Walpole's administration or under the first two Georges, for it was an innovation of George III and his Tory ministers.

32. See Plumb, *Sir Robert Walpole*, II, 307.

33. *The London Journal*, no. 606 (13 March 1731); no. 783 (29 June 1734); no. 799 (19 October 1734). See Kemp, *King and Commons*, pp. 52ff, for the history, number, and effect of Place bills.

34. *The London Journal*, no. 558 (11 April 1730); no. 770 (30 March 1734).

35. *The Case of the Opposition Stated Between the Craftsman and the People* (London, 1731), p. 13.

36. *The Free Briton*, no. 128 (11 May 1732).

37. *The London Journal*, no. 768 (16 March 1734); no. 581 (19 September 1730). See Kemp, *King and Commons*, p. 879, for a discussion of the validity of Walpole's claim.

38. *The London Journal*, no. 744 (29 September 1733).

39. David Hume, "Of the Independence of Parliaments," in *Hume's Theory of Politics*, Frederick Watkins, ed. (Edinburgh, 1951), p. 160. Walpole's writers must be added to Miss Kemp's list—which includes Hume, Paley, and the author of the letter to Lord Norton—of those who saw the importance of patronage to the balance of government (*King and Commons*, pp. 88-89).

40. IX *Parliamentary History*, 473.

41. *The Craftsman*, no. 208 (27 June 1730).

42. *The London Journal*, no. 558 (11 April 1730); cf. also no. 570, no. 571, no. 581, no. 765.

43. *The London Journal*, no. 726 (26 May 1733); no. 581 (19 September 1730).

44. *Ibid.*, no. 758 (5 January 1734); no. 726 (26 May 1733).

45. John Locke, *Second Treatise of Civil Government*, Peter Laslett, ed. (Cambridge, Eng., 1960), paragraphs 222, 430.

46. *The London Journal*, no. 758 (5 January 1734); no. 726 (6 May 1733).

47. "Were the members obliged to receive instructions from their constituents, like the Dutch deputies, this would entirely alter the case . . . [It] would introduce a total alteration in our government and would soon reduce it to a pure Republic . . . Let us cherish and improve our ancient government as much as possible without encouraging a passion for such novelties." David Hume, "Of the First Principle of Government," *Hume's Theory of Politics*, pp. 151-152. Walpole's views on representa-

tion were not unique in the Augustan period. Note, for example, the yearly comment on the representative's duties in Chamberlayne's *Present State of Great Britain,* cited in Kemp, *King and Commons,* p. 43.

48. George Lyttelton, *Letters from a Persian in England to a Friend at Ispahan* (London, 1739), lix, 179.

49. See J. G. A. Pocock, *The Ancient Constitution and the Feudal Law* (Cambridge, Eng., 1957). Much of this discussion is based on that excellent study. See also Butterfield's *The Englishman and His History,* and D. C. Douglas, *English Scholars* (London, 1951).

50. For Spelman, see Pocock, *Ancient Constitution,* 92-115; for the antiquarian circle in general, see Douglas, *English Scholars.*

51. Quoted in Pocock, *Ancient Constitution,* p. 194.

52. See Pocock, *Ancient Constitution,* pp. 209, 226, 231; Butterfield, *The Englishman and His History,* p. 78; Douglas, *English Scholars,* pp. 355-369. Pocock has changed his mind on this, and now points to the Walpole-Bolingbroke confrontation. See his "Machiavelli, Harrington and English Political Ideologies in the Eighteenth Century," *William and Mary Quarterly* 22 (October 1965), 578-579.

53. Pocock, *Ancient Constitution,* pp. 226, 231.

54. *The Works of Lord Bolingbroke,* 4 vols. (Philadelphia, 1841), II, 108.

55. The Walpole side in this debate can be found in the following sources. *The London Journal,* no. 575 (8 August 1730); no. 600 (30 January 1731); no. 647 (20 November 1731); no. 740 (1 September 1733); no. 768 (16 March 1734); no. 765 (23 March 1734); *The Daily Gazetteer,* no. 6 (5 July 1735); no. 12 (12 July 1735); no. 18 (19 July 1735); no. 24 (26 July 1735); no. 30 (2 August 1735); no. 42 (16 August 1735); no. 48 (23 August 1735); no. 54 (30 August 1735); no. 64 (11 September 1735); no. 78 (27 September 1735); no. 96 (18 October 1735). Also see John, Lord Hervey, *Ancient and Modern Liberty Stated and Compared* (London, 1734).

56. *The Daily Gazetteer,* no. 48 (23 August 1735); no. 78 (27 September 1735).

57. *The London Journal,* no. 575 (8 August 1730); no. 768 (16 March 1734).

58. *The Daily Gazetteer,* no. 24 (26 July 1735).

59. *The London Journal,* no. 740 (1 September 1733).

60. *Ibid.,* no. 769 (23 March 1734).

61. *Ibid.,* no. 575 (8 August 1730).

62. *The Daily Gazetteer,* no. 12 (12 July 1735).

63. *Ibid.,* no. 12 (12 July 1735); no. 8 (16 July 1735).

64. *The London Journal,* no. 768 (16 March 1734).

65. *Ibid.,* no. 24 (26 July 1735); *The London Journal,* no. 768 (16 March 1734); also *The Daily Gazetteer,* no. 30 (2 August 1735); *The Daily Gazetteer,* no. 30 (2 August 1735).

66. *The London Journal,* no. 769 (23 March 1734); *The Daily Gazetteer,* no. 30 (2 August 1735).

67. Hervey, *Ancient and Modern Liberty,* pp. 14, 23-24; *The London Journal,* no. 600 (30 January 1731).

68. *The Daily Gazetteer,* no. 6 (5 July 1735).

69. *Ibid.,* no. 6 (5 July 1735).

70. *Ibid.,* no. 48 (23 August 1735).

71. G. M. Trevelyan, *A Shortened History of England* (London, 1959), p. 90.

72. For the intellectual sources of Walpole's history, see Isaac Kramnick, "Augustan Politics and English Historiography," *History and Theory* 6 (1967), 33-56,

where it is linked to the positions of the Whig Bishops in the convocation controversy. Some of these bishops, especially Gibson, were close to Walpole in the period
of historical debate with Bolingbroke and *The Craftsman*. It might also be noted,
for what it is worth, that Dr. Brady was a friend of Walpole's father, and actually
saved the life of the younger Walpole. See Plumb, *Sir Robert Walpole*, I, 37.

## CHAPTER VI. BOLINGBROKE ON POLITICS AND THE ENGLISH CONSTITUTION

1. C. C. Weston, *English Constitutional Theory and the House of Lords* (London, 1965), passim.

2. *Ibid.*, pp. 9-43. Note particularly the extensive humanist educational background of these religious writers. See also R. W. K. Hinton, "English Constitutional Theories from Sir John Fortescue to Sir John Eliot," *English Historical Review* 296 (July 1960), and Weston, p. 9, for a discussion of the earlier contributions of Fortescue.

3. Edward Spelman, *A Fragment out of the Sixth Book of Polybius* (London, 1743).

4. J. T. Desaguliers, *The Newtonian System of the World, The Best Model of Government* (London, 1728), pp. iii-iv; 183-184.

5. *The Works of Lord Bolingbroke*, 4 vols. (Philadelphia, 1841), II, 85.

6. See also Thomas Gordon's *Tacitus* (London, 1728).

7. See, for example, Weston, *English Constitutional Theory;* J. W. Gough, *Fundamental Law in English Constitutional History* (Oxford, 1955); Samuel Kliger, *The Goths in England* (Cambridge, 1952) and Felix Rabb, *The English Face of Machiavelli* (London, 1965).

8. Christopher Hill, "The Norman Yoke," *Puritanism and Revolution* (London, 1962), pp. 75-82.

9. Weston, *English Constitutional Theory*, pp. 5, 23.

10. *Cardinal Documents in British History* (Princeton, 1961), pp. 78ff.

11. Weston, *English Constitutional Theory*, p. 142.

12. Francis Atterbury, *Sermons and Discourses on Several Subjects and Occasions*, 4 vols. (London, 1761), I, 263ff.

13. *The Complete Works of George Savile, first Marquess of Halifax*, Walter Raleigh, ed. (Oxford, 1912), pp. 54, 62, 103.

14. For a detailed discussion of this change, see Weston, *English Constitutional Theory*, pp. 29, 87ff. Citing contemporary distinctions, Miss Weston refers to the new theory of mixed government as the theory of "mixed monarchy."

15. Jonathan Swift, *A Discourse on the Contests and Dissensions between the Nobles and Commons in Athens and Rome* (London, 1701).

16. St. John-Trumbull Correspondence (Berkshire Record Office, Reading, England), f/100. J. Dedieu, *Montesquieu et la Tradition Politique Anglaise en France* (Paris, 1909), p. 101, informs us that Mackworth's book, translated into French, had a great vogue in France in the 1720's.

17. Humphrey Mackworth, *A Vindication of the Rights of the Commons of England* (London, 1701), pp. 2-4.

18. James Harrington, *Oceana*, S. B. Liljegren, ed. (Heidelberg, 1924), p. 23. "A commonwealth consists of the Senate proposing, the people resolving and magistracy executing." Aristotle, *Politics*, Ernest Barker, trans. (New York, 1962), Book IV, chaps. 14-17, 188-203.

19. Mackworth, *A Vindication,* p. 24 (also pp. 3, 5).

20. Some of the pamphlets consulted were: *Some Considerations Relating to the Peerage of Great Britain* (London, 1719); *Six Questions Stated and Answered for and Against the Peerage Bill* (London, 1719); *The Constitution Explained in Relation to the Independency of the House of Lords* (London, 1719); *A Supplement to the Paper with a Defense of the Peerage Bill* (London, 1719); *Remarks on a Pamphlet Entitled Thoughts of a Member of the Lower House* (London, 1719); *Farther Reasons Against the Peerage Bill* (London, 1719); *The Thoughts of a Member of the Lower House* (London, 1719); *Some Reflections Upon a Pamphlet Called the Old Whig* (London, 1719). See also the article by E. R. Turner, "The Peerage Bill of 1719," *English Historical Review* 28 (1913).

21. On one of his visits to France, Stanhope asked the exiled Bolingbroke to obtain information on the composition of the Roman Senate for his use in the debate. Bolingbroke, who supported Stanhope's Bill, sought the advice of the Abbé Vertot, the distinguished Roman historian, on Stanhope's question. The information he relayed to Stanhope provided the basis for this atypical classical reference in the debate. Details of this transaction and Stanhope's comments are found in Basil Williams, *Stanhope* (Oxford, 1932), pp. 258, 310, 408-409; Phillipe-Henri, Comte de Grimoard, *Lettres Historiques . . . de Henri St. John,* 3 vols. (Paris, 1808), II, 479, and Paul Baratier, *Lettres inédits de Bolingbroke* (Lyons, 1939), pp. 92-97. The turning point in the debate was no telling classical reference but Walpole's very practical and immediate exploitation of commoners' aspirations to sit some day in the House of Lords. Cf. J. H. Plumb, *Sir Robert Walpole,* 2 vols. (Boston, 1956), I, 280.

22. See for example, *The Thoughts of a Member of the Lower House,* pp. 14-15. Cf. also Weston, *English Constitutional Theory,* pp. 167-173 for a further discussion of constitutional issues that emerged in this controversy.

23. Mackworth, *A Vindication,* p. 71. A recent work by W. B. Gwyn, *The Meaning of the Separation of Powers* (New Orleans, 1965) contains an interesting and accurate description of Bolingbroke's notion of separation of powers, pp. 90-99.

24. Henri See, *Les Ideas Politiques en France au XVIII Siécle* (Paris, 1920), pp. 15, 36. In the eighteenth century both Pope and Mrs. Thrale noted a similar influence; see Joseph Spence's *Anecdotes of Mr. Pope* (London, 1820), p. 169, and *Thraliana,* Katherine C. Balderston, ed., 2 vols. (Oxford, 1951), I, 425. Another claim that Bolingbroke was the teacher of Montesquieu is found in Dedieu, *Montesquieu,* where he writes, "toute la pensée philosophique si profondement revolutionaire de *L'Ésprit Des Lois,* nous la retrouvons pure et claire, dans l'oevre [*The Idea of a Patriot King*] de Milord Bolingbroke," p. 272. Dedieu's contention, a most dubious one, is that Bolingbroke's *Patriot King* was the source of Montesquieu's theory of *ésprit general.*

25. Robert Shackleton, "Montesquieu, Bolingbroke, and the Separation of Powers," *French Studies* 3 (January 1949), and *Montesquieu: A Critical Biography* (Oxford, 1961). Shackleton's argument has been seconded by Kurt Kluxen, *Das Problem der Politischen Opposition* (Freiburg, 1956), pp. 224-227 and John Plamenatz, *Man and Society* 2 vols. (New York, 1963), I, 284. In a review of Shackleton's book in *The Spectator* (15 September 1961), J. H. Plumb agrees with its author that Bolingbroke believed in the separation of the three powers in the state and that "Montesquieu swallowed this wholesale." He does differ from Shackleton, however, in suggesting that Bolingbroke's views were not novel and "already had a long history."

26. Shackleton, "Montesquieu, Bolingbroke," p. 37.

27. Bolingbroke, *Works*, I, 306.
28. *The London Journal* (19 September 1730).
29. Bolingbroke, *Works*, I, 333.
30. Mackworth, *A Vindication*, p. 5.
31. *The Free Briton*, no. 142 (17 August 1732).
32. *The Craftsman*, no. 258 (12 June 1731).
33. C. H. McIlwain, *The Growth of Political Thought in the West* (New York, 1932), p. 101; and Kurt von Fritz, *The Theory of the Mixed Constitution in Antiquity* (New York, 1954), passim. Nicolo Machiavelli, *Discourses on Titus Livius*, Modern Library edition (New York, 1950), I, ii, 115.
34. Bolingbroke, *Works*, I, 296; cited in Shackleton, "Bolingbroke, Montesquieu," p. 36. *The Craftsman*, no. 213 (1 August 1730).
35. Von Fritz, *The Theory of the Mixed Constitution*, pp. 12, 79-81.
36. Harrington, *Oceana*, pp. 185-186; Algernon Sidney, *Works*, Joseph Robertson, ed., 3 vols. (London, 1772), II, xix, 159; III, vi, 298; Anthony Ashley Cooper, third Earl of Shaftesbury, *Characteristicks of Men, Manners, Opinions, Times*, J. M. Robinson, ed., 2 vols. (London, 1900), I, 64. *The London Journal*, no. 726 (26 May 1733).
37. Shackleton's findings have been ingeniously seconded by Giuseppi Giarizzo, who, describing David Hume's reading of *L'Ésprit des Lois*, c. 1749-1750, suggests that Hume learned Bolingbroke's version of the nature of English government from Montesquieu; see *David Hume: Politico e Storico* (Turin, 1962), p. 88.
38. See Franz Neuman's introduction of Hafner edition of Montesquieu's *Spirit of the Laws* (New York, 1949), pp. xix-xxiii; Franklin Ford, *Robe and Sword* (Cambridge, Mass., 1953), pp. 222ff; and Peter Gay, *Voltaire's Politics* (Princeton, 1959).
39. Giarizzo, *David Hume*, p. 104, contends that Bolingbroke's influence on *L'Ésprit des Lois* is visible in more than just Book XI. In particular, he points to Books V, 7; XIII, 14, 15 and 17. He notes as most significant evidence for the claim, Montesquieu's negative reference in XIII, 15, to ministers and projects. But Montesquieu had written of such things in the *Persian Letters*, long before his trip to England and before learning of Bolingbroke's impressions of Walpole. See in particular Letters CXXXVIII, CXXXIX, and CXLVI, for Montesquieu's attack on John Law's Mississippi scheme. His comments indicate the fundamental unity of social and political outlook that he shared with Bolingbroke. Law's crime, he wrote, had been his never-ending projects, new plans and new systems, which resulted in social disorder. People who had been rich six months earlier were now poor, wrote Montesquieu, and those who had had no bread to eat, now burst with wealth. Lackeys were served by their former masters, and, having new fortunes, dared to brag of their lowly birth. The cry heard from these *Persian Letters* is the same frightened one that could be heard from Bolingbroke. "Nobility is ruined!" wrote Montesquieu's Persian. "What disorder in the state! What confusion in rank! I rather approve of everyone's holding firm to the position nature has given him" (Letters CXXXVIII, and CXXXIX). Responsibility for this disorder, the Persian goes on, rests with the minister, Law, who has perverted a once noble and virtuous people. It is he who has filled the body politic with a disease that corrupts its members and creates an insatiable thirst for wealth that diverts them from honest work and noble industry (Letter CXLVI). Montesquieu's attack on John Law could pass for Bolingbroke's later indictment of Robert Walpole. Montesquieu's words in Letter CXLVI of the *Persian Letters* would be heard often in the course of Bolingbroke's opposition. "What greater crime is there than the one a minister commits when he corrupts the

morals of a whole nation, debases the most noble souls, tarnishes the splendor of high office, obscures virtue itself and confounds the highest birth with universal scorn? . . . What will a young generation say when it compares its ancestors' steel with the gold of those to whom they directly owe the light of day?" (Letter CXLVI).

40. D. J. Fletcher, "The Intellectual Relations of Lord Bolingbroke with France," unpub. master's thesis, University College of Wales, 1953, p. 111. At Club de l'Entresol, d'Argenson's "research" dealt with the history of French public law, cf. his *Journal et Memoire inédits,* E.-J. Rathery, ed., 4 vols. (Paris, 1859-1862), I, 97.

41. René Louis de Voyer, Marquis d'Argenson, *Considerations sur le Gouvernement Ancien et Présent de la France* (Amsterdam, 1765).

42. After reading the manuscript of d'Argenson's *Considerations* in 1739, Voltaire wrote to him, "My Dear Sir, I have just finished reading a work which consoles me for the flood of bad books wherewith we are inundated . . . How have you had the courage? You, whose House is as old as M. de Boulainvilliers, to declare so grievously against him and his fiefs? That is the thing I cannot get over; you have divested yourself in favour of the public and the dearest prejudice to which men can cling." Quoted in Arthur Ogle, *The Marquis Argenson* (London, 1893), p. 90. For further discussion of d'Argenson, see Ford, *Robe and Sword,* pp. 230-233; Gay, *Voltaire's Politics,* passim; and See, *Les Ideas Politiques en France an xviii Siecle,* pp. 51-65.

43. D'Argenson, "De L'Angleterre," in *Considerations,* ch. III, pp. 37-43.

44. *Ibid.,* ch. iii. All citations are from this chapter.

45. While visiting England, Montesquieu wrote in his notebooks, "l'argent est ici sourverainement estimé, l'honneur et la vertu peu." *Oeuvres,* 2 vols. (Paris, 1859), II, 472. By 1750, he had written to an acquaintance that corruption in the English government had nearly exhausted the English spirit of liberty, *Pensées et Fragment inédit de Montesquieu* (Bordeaux, 1901), p. 12.

46. Betty Kemp, *King and Commons, 1660-1832* (London, 1959), p. 2.

47. Caroline Robbins, "Discordant Parties—A Study of the Acceptance of Party by Englishmen," *Political Science Quarterly* 78 (1958).

48. Samuel Beer, *British Politics in the Collectivist Age* (New York, 1965), pp. 34-43.

49. Halifax, *Works,* p. 157; see also pp. 160, 182, 225. There is one other objection to parties found in Halifax's writings, seldom mentioned by later writers, but particularly apt to impress Bolingbroke when he contemplated party in the Walpole years. Halifax wrote that, "amongst the many other ill consequences of a stated party, it is none of the least, that it tempteth low and insignificant men to come upon the stage, to expose themselves, and to spoil business." Party distorted an individual's true worth, making unknown or weak men bombastic and pompous through the shelter of their affiliations. Party was thus an agent of political mobility, distorting the natural play of the Senate where true statesmen would emerge because of their own ability and virtue (*Works,* p. 159). Halifax's views on party are particularly interesting in light of Burke's hopes for party government which quite contradicted Halifax's prediction; see Harvey Mansfield, Jr., *Statesmanship and Party Government* (Chicago, 1966), passim.

50. John Toland, *The Danger of Mercenary Parliaments* (London, 1695).

51. *The Works of Sir William Temple,* 4 vols. (London, 1814), III, 34ff; Percival, Lord Egmont, *Faction Detected by the Evidence of the Facts* (London, 1743), pp. 5-6.

52. Shaftesbury, *Characteristicks,* I, 76-77.

53. Toland, *Memorial of the State of England,* p. 44; *State Anatomy,* p. 2; Temple,

*Works,* III, 48; George Lyttelton, *Letters from a Persian in England to a Friend at Ispahan* (London, 1724), pp. lvi, 172-173.

54. Spelman, *A Fragment out of the Sixth Book of Polybius,* p. v. Spelman, like Toland and Temple, is repeating Machiavelli's assessment of faction in ancient Rome, a view usually frowned upon by their Augustan colleagues and revived again in Montesquieu's *Considerations sur le Grandeur et La Décadence* (Amsterdam, 1773), pp. 67-75.

55. Spelman, *A Fragment,* pp. v-ix.

56. One might make a good case for Bolingbroke having anticipated Namier's analysis of eighteenth-century politics. "We are grown into an unanimity about principles of government," he wrote, "which the most sanguine could scarcely have expected, without extravagance" (*Works,* II, 23). He described the struggle for office since 1688 as "in the main for power, not principle" (*Ibid.,* II, 79). He wrote to Windham in 1739, "party has become faction, distinguished no longer by principles, whatever may be represented, but by personal attachments" (William Coxe, *Memoirs of the Life and Administration of Sir Robert Walpole,* 3 vols. [London, 1798], III, 522). The only party division that exists, he suggests, is that of the court and administration on the one hand, and the independent country gentlemen on the other (Works, II, 167-168). See also Lewis Namier, *Monarchy and the Party System* (Oxford, 1952), p. 12. Bolingbroke was not alone among Augustan writers on politics to hold these views. In *Cato's Letters,* Trenchard and Gordon described the same lack of party differences. "Indeed I can't see what we differ about . . . All the grounds of distinction are now at an end, and the honest and wise men of all parties mean the same thing." *Cato's Letters* (London, 1724), no. 79. Bolingbroke, Trenchard, and Gordon would agree, then, with Walcott's understanding of early eighteenth-century party politics (Robert Walcott, *English Politics in the Early Eighteenth Century* [Cambridge, Eng., 1956]). Swift, of course, would violently disagree, at least in his *Examiner* period; see *The Examiner,* no. 31 (8 March 1710). For an attack from the contemporary left on Walcott's development of Namier's ideas, see Michael Foot, *The Pen and the Sword* (London, 1957). J. H. Plumb, no providential Whig historian, still feels that one should not discount the importance of Whig-Tory conflict in the early eighteenth century. In local county politics, families and factions engaged in party strife, he suggests, "because Whig and Tory were names about which factions could crystallize their natural hatred for each other, a hatred which had in some cases lasted for centuries" (*Sir Robert Walpole,* I, 62). In any case, it should also be noted that Bolingbroke also insisted that new ideological differences had sprung up since 1688 as bases for a new and different party division in the community.

57. Bolingbroke, *Works,* I, 114.

58. Robbins, "Discordant Parties," p. 523.

59. Bolingbroke, *Works,* I, 444; II, 78, 410.

60. See, for example, H. N. Fieldhouse, "Bolingbroke and the Idea of Non-Party Government," *History* 23 (1938), and Robbins, "Discordant Parties."

61. Harvey Mansfield, Jr., *Statesmanship and Party Government* (Chicago, 1965).

62. Kluxen, *Das Problem der Politischen Opposition.*

63. See, for example, comments on the book jacket and in the preface.

64. See Kluxen, *Das Problem,* pp. 70-73 and 119 for specific references, although this argument is implicit throughout the book.

65. George Young, *Poor Fred, the People's Prince* (Oxford, 1937). R. A. Butler

invoked the ideas of Bolingbroke at the Tory convention in 1963 (*The Observer* [13 October 1963]).

66. Quintin Hogg, *The Conservative Case* (London, 1959), p. 39.

67. Cited in Beer, *British Politics in the Collectivist Age,* p. 102.

68. Bolingbroke, *Works,* II, 48; II, 435; II, 168.

69. Hugh Cecil, *Conservatism* (London, 1937), pp. 34-35.

70. Bolingbroke, *Works,* II, 404.

71. *Ibid.,* I, 393.

72. *Ibid.,* I, 295; also *The Craftsman,* no. 180 (15 December 1729); no. 213 (1 August 1730); no. 165 (30 August 1729); no. 368 (21 July 1733).

73. Bolingbroke, *Works,* II, 370.

74. XV *Hansard,* 135-149 (Second Series). Hobhouse was addressing the Lords in April 1826. See Robbins, "Discordant Parties," p. 504.

75. Bolingbroke, *Works,* II, 370.

76. *Ibid.*

77. *Ibid.*

78. *Ibid.,* II, 88-89. Professor J. H. Burns in "Bolingbroke and the Concept of Constitutional Government," *Political Studies* 10 (October 1962), is much impressed with this idea of Bolingbroke's, which he considers novel and important for constitutional theory. For a further discussion of Bolingbroke on constitutionalism, see C. H. McIlwain, *Constitutionalism: Ancient and Modern* (Ithaca, 1947), pp. 2-10.

79. Archibald Foord, *His Majesty's Opposition* (Oxford, 1964), p. 150.

80. *Ibid.,* pp. 155-158.

81. *The London Journal,* no. 771 (6 April 1734); no. 633 (11 September 1731); no. 680 (8 July 1732).

82. Bolingbroke, *Works,* II, 365.

83. Percival, Lord Egmont, *Faction Detected by the Evidence of the Facts* (London, 1743).

84. *The New Opposition Compared with the Old in Points and Practice* (London, 1744), pp. 56-57. See also the following: *The Dissertation Discussed or the Last and the Present Opposition Placed in Their True Light* (London, 1743); *A View of the Whole Political Conduct of a Late Eminent Patriot* (London, 1743); *A Defense of the People in a Letter to the Author of Faction Detected* (London, 1744); *Opposition, not Faction, or the Rectitude of the Present Parliamentary Opposition, in Answer to a Late Book Faction Detected* (London, 1743).

85. Herbert Butterfield, *The Statecraft of Machiavelli* (New York, 1962), and Jeffrey Hart, *Viscount Bolingbroke: Tory Humanist* (London, 1966), have commented on this relationship at some length. I tend to see Bolingbroke as less critical of Machiavelli than Butterfield suggests, and certainly less critical than Hart suggests. See also Rabb, *The English Face of Machiavelli,* p. 254, and J. G. A. Pocock, "Machiavelli, Harrington, and English Political Ideologies in the Eighteenth Century," *William and Mary Quarterly* 22 (October 1965), for a discussion of Bolingbroke as a Machiavellian.

86. Rabb, *The English Face of Machiavelli,* passim.

87. *An Essay Towards the Ruin of Great Britain* (London, 1721), pp. 11, 25.

88. *The Constitution Explained in Relation to the Independency of the House of Lords* (London, 1719), pp. 21ff.

89. *The Craftsman,* no. 2 (9 December 1726); no. 174 (1 November 1729).

90. *Ibid.,* no. 431 (5 October 1734). This "scarecrow" interpretation of Machiavelli's *Prince* was revived by radicals later in the century. "This was well understood

by the subtle and comprehensive genius of Machiavel . . . he therefore taught that the vigilance and vengeance of the people must be placed like a flaming sword to guard their rights; and he gave the most salutary and effectual admonitions against unlimited power, by exhibiting the crimes through which it is pursued, the horrors by which it is maintained." *Minutes of the Society for Constitutional Information* (London, 1780), p. 6.

91. *The London Journal,* no. 552 (28 February 1730).

92. Charles Davenant, *The Political and Commercial Works,* 5 vols. (London, 1771), II, 289, 336.

93. *Ibid.,* IV, 395.

94. Walter Moyle, *An Essay upon the Constitution of the Roman Government* (Dublin, 1728), pp. 26-27.

95. *Cato's Letters,* I, 110.

96. John Trenchard, *Some Considerations upon the State of our Public Debts in General and of the Civil List in Particular* (London, 1720), p. 31.

97. Machiavelli, *Discourses on Titus Livius,* Book III, ch. xxv; Book I, chs. xi-xii; Federico Chabod, *Machiavelli and the Renaissance* (London, 1958), p. 55; Machiavelli, *Discourses,* Book I, chs. xvii-xviii; Machiavelli, *Prince,* ch. xii; *Discourses,* Book I, ch. xxi.

98. E. W. Montagu, *Reflections on the Rise and Fall of the Ancient Republics adapted to the Present State of Great Britain* (London, 1759), pp. 376-383.

99. Machiavelli, *Discourses,* Book I, ch. xvii. "No change however great could ever restore Milan and Naples to liberty, because the whole peoples of these states were thoroughly corrupt." For a discussion of native English ideas not derived from Machiavelli on the power of princes to shape and reform public manners, see Gerald Straka, *Anglican Reaction to the Revolution of 1688* (Madison, 1962), pp. 82-83.

100. Machiavelli, *Discourses,* Book I, chs. ii, iv; also Chabod, *Machiavelli and the Renaissance,* pp. 192ff.

101. J. G. A. Pocock, *The Ancient Constitution and the Feudal Law* (Cambridge, 1954), pp. 146ff; and Judith Shklar, "Ideology Hunting—Case of James Harrington," *American Political Science Review* 53 (September, 1959).

102. Bolingbroke, *Works,* II, 393.

103. *Ibid.,* II, 396.

104. David Hume's description of the ideal prince is not unlike Bolingbroke's Patriot King. Hume's prince will protest all divisions in society, he will call to his side all honest and independent men above party, who, in turn, will flock to him. *Essays Moral, Political and Literary,* 2 vols. (London, 1907), I, 115. For specific comparison of these ideas with Bolingbroke's, see Giarizzo, *David Hume,* p. 96.

105. Bolingbroke, *Works,* II, 397.

106. See Felix Gilbert, "The Humanist Concept of the Prince and the Prince of Machiavelli," *Journal of Modern History* 11 (December 1939), and A. H. Gilbert, *Machiavelli's Prince and its Forerunners* (Durham, 1938).

107. Horace Walpole, *Letters of Horace Walpole to Sir Horace Mann,* 2 vols. (London, 1883), II, 17 May 1749. Whether or not George II read or was tutored in the principles of Bolingbroke's major work has recently become a subject of great contention. *Letters from George III to Lord Bute 1756-1766,* Romney Sedgewick, ed. (London, 1939), Introduction, denies this, as does Namier in *England in the Age of the American Revolution* (Cambridge, 1930), pp. 57-75; Mansfield disagrees in "Sir Lewis Namier Considered," *Journal of British Studies* 2 (November 1962), 28-34. See also J. J. Watson, "Parliamentary Procedure as a Key to the

Understanding of Eighteenth-Century Politics," *Burke Newsletter* 3 (1962), 109, and Robert Walcott, "Sir Lewis Considered—Considered," *Journal of British Studies* 2 (May 1964), 85-108. No such doubt exists with respect to young Louis XVI. D'Argenson, in his journal for 1750, wrote, "M. le Dauphin a lu le Patriotisme Anglois de Milord Bolingbroke et en parle avec estime." *Journals et Memoirs,* VI, 152.

108. Herbert Butterfield has described the use made of Bolingbroke by radicals such as James Burgh, John Jebb, and Christopher Wyvill (*George III, Lord North and the People, 1779-1780* [London, 1949]). See also Pocock, "Machiavelli, Harrington" for a discussion of the influence of early eighteenth-century "country language" on later English and American radicals. For specific influence on American thought, see *Pamphlets of the American Revolution,* Bernard Bailyn, ed. (Cambridge, Mass., 1965), Introduction, pp. 9, 24, 32, 50, 77.

109. *London Society for Constitutional Information* (London, 1782), 7 June 1782, pp. 31-33. Swift was also cited by the Society on 28 June 1782 for his reference to annual parliaments in his letter to Pope.

110. *Minutes for 1780,* pp. 9-10.

111. Richard Price, *An Appeal to the Public on the Subject of the National Debt* (London, 1771).

112. There is a final footnote to this radical face of Bolingbroke. There appeared in 1831 an English edition, *The Patriot King and the Essay on the Spirit of Patriotism by Ld. Viscount Bolingbroke incorporated with such Observations as May Render His Lordship's Principles Subservient to Practical Use at this Momentous Crisis of Reform by a Reformed Whig,* which offers the ultimate radical reading of Bolingbroke. The "Reformed Whig" offered the *Patriot King* in 1831 as an argument to justify the proposed Reform Bill. He interrupted the text with comments in which he drew attention to the "similarity" of Bolingbroke's views with those of a most impressive gallery of radical thinkers: Thomas Paine, Horne Tooke, John Cartwright, Rousseau, Helvetius, Robert Owen, William Cobbet, Joseph Hume and Jeremy Bentham. In this light it is interesting to note that the first and most ambitious nineteenth-century biography of Bolingbroke was written in 1835 by G. W. Cooke, a Whig M.P. His biography of Bolingbroke ranks with those of the two Tories, Goldsmith and Sichel, as the most extensive treatments of Bolingbroke's career.

113. Frederick Antal, *Hogarth and His Place in European Art* (London, 1962), passim; H. C. Breeching, *Francis Atterbury* (London, 1909), passim; A. J. Henderson, *London and National Government 1721-42* (Durham, N.C., 1945), passim; Plumb, *Sir Robert Walpole,* II, 107-109.

114. George Lyttelton, *Considerations Upon the Present State of Affairs* (London, 1739), p. 40; and *The Craftsman,* no. 214 (8 August 1730).

115. See May McKisack, *The Fourteenth Century* (vol. V, *Oxford History of England,* Oxford, 1959), pp. 194-199; and Samuel Beer, *British Politics,* pp. 6-7, cited in C. S. Emden, *The People and the Constitution* (Oxford, 1962), p. 19; Gilbert Burnett, *History of My Own Times* (Oxford, 1823), II, 281.

116. Quoted by Emden, *The People and the Constitution,* p. 23. Emden is in error, p. 24, when he attributes these attitudes, so much like Burke's, to *The Craftsman.*

117. *The London Journal,* no. 755 (15 December 1733).

118. Quoted in *The London Journal,* no. 755 (15 December 1733).

119. *The Craftsman,* no. 389 (22 December 1733).

120. *Ibid.,* no. 389 (22 December 1733).

121. *Ibid.,* no. 372 (18 August 1733).

122. Egmont, *Faction Detected,* p. 100. See also, *Seasonable Expostulations with The Worthy Citizens of London, Upon Their late Instructions to Their Representatives* (London, 1742).

123. Egmont, *Faction Detected,* p. 134.

124. *The Daily Gazetteer,* no. 2309 (23 November 1742).

125. Beer, *British Politics,* passim.

126. *Opposition Not Faction* (London, 1743), pp. 33, 42-43.

127. *The Craftsman,* no. 702 (22 December 1739); no. 857 (25 December 1742).

128. See Edmund Burke, *On a Regicide Peace,* in *Works,* 12 vols. (Boston, 1866-1867), V, 288-289.

129. Bolingbroke's *Craftsman,* no. 421 (27 July 1734), had proposed parliamentary reform in terms that suggested the end of representation for uninhabited boroughs like Old Sarum and the increase of representation for cities and counties, a scheme not wholly devoid of partisanship. Similar suggestions for parliamentary reform are found in another Opposition work, Lyttelton's *Persian Letters,* p. 187.

130. Not, of course, to those who adhered to Leveller history which saw all history after the Norman Invasion as bondage; see Christopher Hill, *Puritanism and Revolution* (London, 1962), pp. 75-82.

131. Herbert Butterfield, *The Englishman and His History* (Cambridge, 1944), p. 2.

132. Bolingbroke, *Works,* I, 317-319. As with his views on the origin of government, Bolingbroke here, too, expressed views which could be found in the writings of Sir William Temple. See, for example, Temple's *Works,* III, 199, 377.

133. Bolingbroke, *Works,* I, 360.

134. *The Craftsman,* no. 256 (29 May 1731); see also *The Craftsman,* no. 405 (6 April 1734); no. 447 (25 January 1735); no. 466 (7 June 1735); no. 467 (14 June 1735); no. 470 (5 July 1735); no. 478 (6 September 1735); no. 491 (29 November 1735); no. 493 (13 December 1735); no. 495 (27 December 1735); no. 500 (31 January 1736).

135. *Ibid.,* no. 470 (5 July 1735).

136. *Ibid.,* no. 466 (7 June 1735).

137. The *Argumentum* contended that William had not conquered England, nor had he cancelled and abolished immemorial English law. D. C. Douglas has written that the *Argumentum* was "a book not important save as showing the tendency of a large body of pseudohistorical literature." *English Scholars,* p. 122.

138. *The Craftsman,* no. 466 (7 June 1735); no. 467 (14 June 1735).

139. *Ibid.,* no. 467 (14 June 1735).

140. *Ibid.,* no. 447 (25 January 1735).

141. *Ibid.,* no. 466 (7 June 1735); no. 478 (6 September 1735).

142. H. R. Trevor-Roper, "Hume as a Historian," in *David Hume: A Symposium* (London, 1963), p. 90.

143. Lord John Hervey, *Ancient and Modern Liberty* (London, 1734), pp. 50-51.

144. *The Daily Gazetteer,* no. 64 (11 September 1735). *The Craftsman,* no. 497 (10 January 1736); no. 500 (31 January 1736).

145. To call Hume a Tory historian means much more than simply to find Brady's historical attitudes in his writings. To this extent, then, he differs sharply from the Whig Walpole and his historians. This is clear, for example, in Hume's discussion of the Civil War and the Revolution, where his views would not necessarily be shared by Walpole. What concerns us here, however, is the extent to

which Hume, like Walpole, accepted Brady's interpretation of earlier English history. A reading of Hume's *History of England* reveals that he often did. In the London, 1762 edition, see for example: I, 144ff, on the absence of commoners in the Saxon Witenagemot. See also I, 180-201 on William's conquest and introduction into England of feudal law and institutions. But also note I, 386, and Hume's more favorable attitude to Magna Carta, which is explained by the praise he heaped on the moderate barons, and his wish that the demands of seventeenth-century defenders of freedom had been as moderate. See also I, 397, where Hume agrees with Brady's view of the Norman Parliaments. In II, 46, Hume attributes the "first existence" of the Commons to Leicester's usurpation in 1265. For an excellent discussion of Hume's history see Giarizzo, *David Hume*, pp. 140-270.

146. *The Craftsman*, no. 27 (6 March 1727).

147. Bolingbroke, *Works*, II, 249; II, 461; I, 292-455, passim.

148. Edward Spelman, *A Fragment out of The Sixth Book of Polybius*, p. 91.

149. Hans Kohn, *The Idea of Nationalism* (New York, 1960), pp. 212-215, and Carleton Hayes, "The Philosopher Turned Patriot—Reflections on the Curious Spiritual Adventure of Henry St. John, Ld. Viscount Bolingbroke," *Essays in Intellectual History Dedicated to James Harvey Robinson* (New York, 1929).

150. Hayes, "The Philosopher Turned Patriot," p. 206.

151. Bolingbroke, *Works*, I, 185.

152. The influence of Machiavelli on Bolingbroke's realism and preoccupation with national interest is quite evident. Both Halifax and Bolingbroke were good Tory disciples of Machiavelli's ideas on *raison d'état*.

153. Bolingbroke, *Works*, II, 298; II, 461; *The Craftsman*, no. 234 (26 December 1730); no. 33 (31 March 1727).

154. Bolingbroke, *Works*, I, 385-387.

155. Felix Gilbert, "To the Farewell Address," *William and Mary Quarterly* 1 (1944), third series.

156. Bolingbroke, *Works*, II, 417.

157. *Ibid.*, IV, 203.


CHAPTER VII. DEFOE AND THE LITERATURE OF THE NEW AGE

1. Christopher Hill, *Century of Revolution* (London, 1961), p. 4.

2. See J. H. Randall, *Making of the Modern Mind* (Boston, 1927), p. 253.

3. Daniel Defoe, *A Tour Thro' the Whole Island of Great Britain*, G. D. H. Cole, ed., 2 vols. (London, 1962), I, xiii.

4. Information on Defoe's service for Walpole is found in J. R. Moore, *Daniel Defoe, Citizen of the Modern World* (Chicago, 1958), pp. 207-212, 257, 320; and A. J. Henderson, *London and the National Government 1721-1742* (Durham, 1945), p. 54. Also, see J. H. Plumb, *Sir Robert Walpole*, 2 vols. (Boston, 1956), I, 30, and Lawrence Hanson, *Government and the Press 1695-1763* (Oxford, 1936), pp. 101ff, and William Lee, *Daniel Defoe, His Life and Recently Discovered Writings*, 3 vols. (London, 1869), I, xi-xii.

5. Caroline Robbins, in her "Discordant Parties—A Study of the Acceptance of Party by Englishmen," *Political Science Quarterly* 73 (1958), suggests that articles by Defoe in *Applebee's Journal* (18 and 25 May 1723) entitled "Discordant Parties, Sometimes the Safety of States," illustrate an acceptance and defense of parties. This is understandable given Walpole's (his employer's) own acceptance of parties.

6. For a different interpretation of Defoe, see Lucy Sutherland, "The City of

London in Eighteenth Century Politics," in *Essays Presented to Sir Lewis Namier* (London, 1956), p. 61, in which it is suggested that Defoe was the Opposition's poet.

7. A. L. Smith, "English Political Philosophy in the Seventeenth and Eighteenth Centuries." *Cambridge Modern History* (Cambridge, 1934), VI, 816.

8. Daniel Defoe, *The Review*, A. W. Secord, ed., Facsimile Text Society edition, 22 vols. (New York, 1938), III, 430a, 431a.

9. *Juro Divino* (London, 1706), Book II, p. 3, line 5; Introduction, p. 1, lines 1-4.

10. *Ibid.*, III, 10. Hobbes' influence on Defoe's thought is discussed in Maximilian Novak's excellent study, *Defoe and the Nature of Man* (Oxford, 1963), pp. 18-20, 25-26, 34-35. See also Novak's interesting treatment of Defoe's economic themes in his *Economics and the Fiction of Daniel Defoe* (Berkeley, 1962).

11. Cited in Lee, *Daniel Defoe*, III, 346; *Juro Divino*, Book IV, p. 74, lines 19-20.

12. Brian Fitzgerald, *Defoe: A Study in Conflict* (London, 1954), p. 47. See also Henry E. Jackson, *Robinson Crusoe: Social Engineer* (New York, 1922), of which the subtitle reads, "How the Discovery of Robinson Crusoe Solves the Labor Problem and Opens the Path to Industrial Peace."

13. Daniel Defoe, *An Essay on Projects* (London, 1697), pp. 4, 15, 29.

14. *Ibid.*, p. xii.

15. Moore, *Daniel Defoe*, pp. 283-285.

16. *Ibid.*, p. 290.

17. For details on Defoe's role in the South Sea project, see Lee, *Daniel Defoe*, I, 179ff; Moore, *Daniel Defoe*, pp. 293ff; Historical Manuscripts Commission, *Portland Mss.*, 10 vols. (London, 1891-1931), V, 51, 58-61; and Virginia Cowles, *The Great Swindle* (London, 1960), pp. 24-27.

18. Max Weber, *The Protestant Ethic and the Spirit of Capitalism* (New York, 1958), p. 48.

19. David Hume held views very similar to Bolingbroke's on projectors and the projecting spirit. See Giuseppi Giarizzo, *David Hume: Politico e Storico* (Turin, 1962), pp. 50, 95.

20. For an example of such an attack, see John Tutchin, *The Foreigners* (London, 1701).

21. *The Review*, III, 6-7; V, 406-407.

22. Ian Watt, *The Rise of the Novel* (Berkeley, 1962), passim; and J. F. Ross, *Swift and Defoe: A Study in Relationship* (Berkeley, 1941), passim.

23. Defoe, *A Tour Thro' the Whole Island of Great Britain*, I, 173-176. Defoe was probably referring to Pope's *Windsor Forest*, which has a rhapsody on the Thames at the end of the poem. In this early work, Pope did dwell on the Thames as a symbol of Peace and Commerce but in the symbolic image-laden rhetoric of neo-classical canons. Pope's concern in the poem is less with commercial greatness than with England's representation of the greatness of human civilization and the triumph of order and harmony. See T. R. Edwards, *This Dark Estate: A Reading of Pope* (Berkeley, 1963), pp. 7-9.

24. See Novak, *Defoe and the Nature of Man*, p. 13, for a discussion of Defoe's rejection of the idea of the chain of being implicit in the theory of cosmic plenitude. See also Defoe's *Review* (23 January 1711) in which he talks of credit and financial institutions in the terminology used by proponents of the social chain of being. "See the dependence of one part upon another and how credit fastens every link in the chain."

25. William P. Trent, *Daniel Defoe: How to Know Him* (Indianapolis, 1916), p. 3.

26. Daniel Defoe, *Roxanna*, George Aitken, ed., 2 vols. (London, 1895), I, 193-194.

27. Daniel Defoe, *Complete English Gentleman*, Karl D. Bulbring, ed. (London, 1890), p. 257.

28. Defoe, *A Tour Thro' the Whole Island of Great Britain*, I, 15; *Complete English Tradesman*, 2 vols. (London, 1732), I, 244-245; *Plan for English Commerce* (Oxford, 1928), p. 28; *Complete English Gentleman*, pp. 98, 187, 197, 230, 257.

29. Defoe, *Complete English Gentleman*, p. 18; *Complete English Tradesman*, I, 246; II, 150-151.

30. A good discussion of the "conservative" tendencies of this aspect of the neo-classical canon is found in John Loftis, *Politics of Drama in Augustan England* (Oxford, 1963), pp. 41ff., and in the same author's *Comedy and Society: Congreve to Fielding* (Stanford, 1957), pp. 42ff.

31. Loftis, *Comedy and Society*, pp. 44ff.

32. Loftis, *Politics of Drama*, pp. 42, 125.

33. *The Spectator* (London, 1797), I, 12 (March 2, 1710).

34. Richard Steele, *The Conscious Lovers* in *Bell's British Theatre*, 19 vols. (London, 1780), IV, 53.

35. Cited in Loftis, *Comedy and Society*, p. 88.

36. E. G. Halevy, *The Growth of Philosophical Radicalism* (Boston, 1955), pp. 15-16; and editor's introduction, passim in Bernard Mandeville, *Fable of the Bees*, F. B. Kaye, ed., 2 vols. (Oxford, 1924). All the Mandeville citations are from this edition.

37. Norman Rosenberg, "Mandeville and Laissez-Faire," *Journal of the History of Ideas* 24 (April-June, 1963); Mandeville, *Fable of the Bees*, I, cxxxix; editor's introduction to Adam Smith, *Wealth of Nations*, E. Cannon, ed., 2 vols. (London, 1904), I, xlvi. For the mercantilist Mandeville, see Eli Hecksher's *Mercantilism*, 2 vols. (London, 1955), II, 290; and Jacob Viner, *Long View and the Short* (Glencoe, Ill., 1958), p. 341. This problem of interpretation is no less a problem with Defoe; see Novak, "Defoe the Mercantilist," in *Economics and Fiction of Daniel Defoe*.

38. Mandeville, *Fable of the Bees*, I, 17-37.

39. John M. Mitchell, "Bernard Mandeville," *The Encyclopedia Britannica*, 11th ed. (New York, 1911), XVII, 560.

40. See *Pecuniae Obedieunt Omnia—Money Masters All Things* (1648); Ned Ward, *The Miracles Performed by Money* (1695); *The Character of a Covetous Citizen or a Ready Way to Get Riches* (1702) and *To That Celebrated Idol Mammon, Chief Governor of Men's Consciences and Both Spiritual and Temporal Lord of all Christendom* (1709). The first poem could have served as the immediate inspiration for Mandeville; it describes the money market as a giant beehive swarming with avaricious bees. Another product of the school was the anonymous *The Cheating Age Found Out—When Knaves Were Most in Fashion* (1705) which describes money's corrupting effect on a staggering total of 170 different members of society.

41. Mandeville, *Fable of the Bees*, I, 20, 24, 26, 27, 32, 35, 36.

42. See John Dennis, *An Essay Upon Public Spirit, Being a Satire in Prose Upon the Manners and Luxuries of the Times* (London, 1711). See also Jonathan Swift, *The History of the Last Four Years of the Queen*, H. Davis, ed. (Oxford, 1951).

43. Mandeville had easy access to high Whig circles. His patron, Thomas Parker (First Earl of Maccesfield), Lord Chancellor from 1718 to 1725, apparently learned much from his protégé's writings. In 1725, he was impeached for taking bribes and

selling offices. Mandeville wrote a pamphlet for the Whigs in 1714, *Mischiefs that Ought Justly to be Apprehended from a Whig Government,* which followed the straightforward Whig doctrines—Hanoverian, against the High Church, and in favor of greater toleration. This paled in significance, however, beside his great attack on the Tories published in 1714.

44. Mandeville, *Fable of the Bees,* I, 10, 43, 104-107, 124, 134.

45. *Ibid.,* I, 4-5, 122.

46. *The Craftsman,* nos. 291, 312, 320 (29 January, 24 June, 19 August 1732).

NOTES TO CHAPTER VIII. THE NOSTALGIA OF THE AUGUSTAN POETS

1. Horace Walpole, *Letters of Horace Walpole to Sir Horace Mann,* 2 vols. (London, 1833), II, 102. See also *The Weekly Journal* (27 April 1728) for a poem satirizing Swift, Pope, Gay, Pulteney, and *The Craftsman.* "These four in strict alliance/ Most bravely did defiance/ To virtue, sense and science/ And who but reads must praise em."

2. *The Correspondence of Jonathan Swift,* F. E. Ball, ed., 6 vols. (London, 1910-1914), II, 497-498.

3. Swift, *Correspondence,* III, 259.

4. Swift's epitaph, which he composed himself, reads in English: "He has gone where savage indignation can lacerate his breast no more."

5. Jonathan Swift, *Gulliver's Travels* (Edinburgh, 1814), p. 172.

6. Swift, *Correspondence,* III, 296.

7. *Ibid.,* 120-121.

8. For Bolingbroke's views, see St. John—Trumbull Correspondence (Berkshire Record Office, Reading, England), f/95-22, June 1701. Bolingbroke to Trumbull, ". . . it is whether the Commons shall suffer the Lords to break through all the rules of reason, all the constitution of Parliament."

9. Jonathan Swift, *A Discourse on the Contests and Dissension Between the Nobles and Commons in Athens and Rome* (London, 1701), pp. 196-199. Students of political thought have tended to pass by this early piece of Swift's propaganda, although one German scholar imputes to it the first full statement of the separation of powers on which Montesquieu would build his theory. Harry Jannsen, *Montesquieu's Theorie von der Dreiteilung der Gewalten in Staate* (Gotha, 1878), p. 7. See also Jonathan Swift, *Abstract of the History of England* in *The Prose Works of Jonathan Swift,* T. Scott, ed., 12 vols. (London, 1897-1908), X, 226-227, where he denies that the Goths ever had tripartite government. They had two estates, he argued; the nobility and the military chief alone made up the government. James Harrington, *Oceana,* S. B. Liljegren, ed. (Heidelberg, 1924), pp. 23-25.

10. Swift, *A Discourse,* pp. 209-217; 230.

11. Swift, *Gulliver's Travels,* p. 180. See also Z. S. Fink, "Political Theory in Gulliver's Travels," *English Literary History* 14 (June 1947). See also Book III and Gulliver's description of the Struldbruggs which shows how corruption inevitably steals into the world, and the various revolutions of state and empire are explained by the degeneracy of human nature.

12. Swift, *A Discourse,* pp. 232-234; *The Examiner,* no. 31 (8 March 1710); no. 33 (22 March 1710); no. 43 (31 May 1711); see also Irvin Ehrenpresis, "Swift on Liberty," *Journal of the History of Ideas* 13 (April 1954); *Gulliver's Travels,* pp. 65; 241; 175.

13. *The Examiner*, no. 13 (2 November 1710).

14. Jonathan Swift, *The History of the Four Last Years of the Queen*, H. Davis, ed. (Oxford, 1951), pp. 68-69; and *The Conduct of the Allies* (London, 1711), p. 10.

15. *The Examiner*, no. 13 (2 November 1710); *Gulliver's Travels*, pp. 71, 133.

16. Swift, *Gulliver's Travels*, pp. 168-169; *The Examiner*, no. 34 (29 March 1711); no. 44 (7 June 1711).

17. *Ibid.*, no. 31 (8 March 1710) for an attack on schemers in politics.

18. See R. F. Jones, "The Background of the Attack on Science in the Age of Pope," in *Pope and His Contemporaries: Essays Presented to George Sherburn* (Cambridge, Eng., 1949), pp. 96-113.

19. Arthur E. Case, *Four Essays on Gulliver's Travels* (Princeton, 1945), chs. iii and iv.

20. Jonathan Swift, *Sermons and Irish Tracts*, H. Davis, ed. (Oxford, 1948), pp. 282ff. See also *Gulliver's Travels*, pp. 227-248, and Case, *Four Essays*, pp. 87-89, for a discussion of Munodi's ruined mill as an allegory for the South Sea Bubble.

21. Swift, *Gulliver's Travels*, pp. 225-226.

22. Swift, *Correspondence*, IV, 135, 273; V, 143.

23. Swift, *Sermons and Irish Tracts*, p. 233.

24. Swift, *Gulliver's Travels*, pp. 255-257, 171, 325-330.

25. *Ibid.*, pp. 260, 322-324, 346.

26. See Swift's attack on corrupt lawyers, *Gulliver's Travels*, pp. 319-322. Also in the tradition of the poets who attacked luxury, he attacks corrupt doctors (pp. 325-327) and corrupt clergy (p. 171). The attack on lawyers is, of course, not unique to Bolingbroke's circle or to gentry discontent in the early eighteenth century. It is a staple ingredient in English political and literary thought from the Levellers to Bentham. It is the nature of its significance to Bolingbroke's circle that is stressed here.

27. Swift, *Gulliver's Travels*, p. 261.

28. It is usually Pope's versification of this idea that is cited to show its prevalence among Augustan thinkers. Even S. H. Monk, who argues for the presence of such ideas in Swift, chooses to cite its articulation by Pope; see "Pride of Lemuel Gulliver," *Sewanee Review* (Winter 1955). Richard Quintana, *Swift: An Introduction* (Oxford, 1954), p. 174, does, however, specifically cite Swift's *Sermons*.

29. Arthur Lovejoy, *The Great Chain of Being* (Cambridge, Mass., 1936). See Thomas Elyot, *The Governor*, Everyman Edition (London, 1962), pp. 3-4. "Behold also the order that God hath put generally in all his creatures, beginning at the most inferior or base, and ascending upward . . . so that in everything is order and without order may be nothing stable or permanent, and it may not be called order except it do contain in it degrees, high and base, ascending to the merit or estimation of the thing that is ordered."

30. Swift, *Sermons and Irish Tracts*, p. 142.

31. *Ibid.*, pp. 174, 186; *Gulliver's Travels*, pp. 79-80, 259.

32. *The Prose Works of Jonathan Swift*, IV, 214-215; see also Louis Landa, "Jonathan Swift and Charity," *Journal of English and Germanic Philology* 44 (October 1945).

33. *The Examiner*, no. 38 (26 April 1711); no. 14 (9 November 1710).

34. Swift, *Gulliver's Travels*, pp. 49-51.

35. See, for example, Thomas More, *Utopia* (London, 1551).

36. *The Examiner*, no. 40 (10 May 1711).

37. Alexander Pope, *Essay on Man*, Epistle II, lines 3-4, 7-9.

38. Swift, *Gulliver's Travels,* pp. 377-378.

39. Swift, *Correspondence,* II, 175.

40. George Lyttelton, *Memoirs and Correspondence,* R. Phillimore, ed., 2 vols. (London, 1845), I, 181-182.

41. Alexander Pope, *The Dunciad,* Book IV, lines 597-605.

42. Alexander Pope, *Epilogue to the Satires,* Dialogue I, lines 64-65, 152-156, 160, 247.

43. Alexander Pope, "One Thousand Seven Hundred and Thirty-Eight," in *The Works of Alexander Pope,* W. Elvin and W. J. Courthope, eds., 8 vols. (London, 1871-1889), III, 500. The words in square brackets are editorial suggestions; the poem is incomplete.

44. *The Correspondence of Alexander Pope,* G. Sherburn, ed., 5 vols. (Oxford, 1956), II, 53.

45. Alexander Pope, *Epistle to Richard Boyle, Earl of Burlington* (1731), line 183.

46. Alexander Pope, *Epistle to Bathurst,* lines 39-40; 340-400. See the recent edition by E. R. Wasserman, ed. (Baltimore, 1960), especially page 43 of the introduction for views of a similar nature on Balaam.

47. Alexander Pope, *Epistle to Bathurst,* lines 137-140, 220-230.

48. Most observers since the early eighteenth century have accepted both Bolingbroke and Pope on face value in their many assertions that Bolingbroke's thought is the basis for the *Essay.* In the extensive correspondence between Swift, Pope, and Bolingbroke, it is made abundantly clear that in the early 1730's Pope was learning his social, political, and metaphysical views from Bolingbroke. Despite this wealth of "proof," Maynard Mack denies Bolingbroke's influence in his Twickenham edition of the *Essay on Man* (London, 1950). He goes so far as to suggest that the influence is the other way. Mack, however, places too much reliance on Bolingbroke's failure to publish the *Philosophical Fragments* until later in his life; the letters between the two attest that conversations were the source of the influence. Professor Mack also magnifies areas of difference and overlooks the much greater similarity in the core of ideas. Finally, his revision is based on the belief that Bolingbroke was simply not so well-read or great a thinker as to have imparted this philosophy to Pope. He may not have been a great thinker, but we now know more of his French years and the great concern with scholarship he showed in those years. Bolingbroke was familiar with the work of Montaigne, Charron, and the English Renaissance, the very influences that Mack suggests operated directly on Pope. See Swift, *Correspondence,* IV, 197-198, 250-251; V, 92; also Joseph Spence, *Anecdotes* (London, 1820), p. 114, and *The Works of Lord Bolingbroke,* 4 vols. (Philadelphia, 1841), II, 350.

49. Alexander Pope, *Essay on Man,* Epistle IV, lines 49-52.

50. *Ibid.,* Epistle I, lines 173-176. The historian of the English stock market, Charles Duguid, writes that the terms "bear and bull" were already in use in the second decade of the eighteenth century, and can be found in two plays of the period, C. Johnson's *Country Lasses* (1714) and Colley Cibber's *The Refusal or Ladies Philosophy* (1720). In 1761, Horace Walpole wrote to Mann on the activity of the stockbrokers in London, ". . . do you know what a Bull and Bear and a lame duck are? Nay, nor I either; I am only certain they are neither animal nor fowl, but are extremely interested in the new subscription." Cited, *The Story of the Stock Exchange* (London, 1901), pp. 55-56.

51. Alexander Pope, *Essay on Man,* Epistle I, lines 244-250.

52. *Ibid.,* Epistle I, lines 123-124, 257-258.

53. Alexander Pope, *The Dunciad*, Book IV, lines 653-656.

54. For biographical information on Gay, see W. H. Irving, *John Gay: Favourite of the Wits* (Durham, N.C., 1940).

55. Of all the intellectuals opposed to Walpole, Gay was hit hardest by the Bubble, a fact that helps to explain the zeal with which he pursued the Opposition line in the 1720's.

56. Lord John Hervey, *Memoirs*, Romney Sedgewick, ed., rev. ed. (London, 1963), p. 20.

57. Swift, *Correspondence*, IV, 73.

58. It cannot be held, as does Sven H. Armens (*John Gay: Social Critic* [New York, 1954], p. 190), that Bolingbroke's *Patriot King* determined what few commonplace views on politics Gay had in the 1720's. The *Patriot King* was not conceived until well into the 1730's, and Gay was dead by 1732.

59. John Gay, *Fables*, A. Dobson, ed. (London, 1884), pp. 142-143, 199.

60. *Ibid.*, p. 196.

61. Equally significant in this respect is, of course, Fielding. He is not discussed here because he was only tangentially related to Bolingbroke's circle, through Lyttelton. His social and political views, however, were certainly close to those of the Opposition; see, for example, George Sherburn, "Fielding's Social Outlook," *Philological Quarterly* 35 (1956) and John Loftis, *Politics of Drama in Augustan England* (Oxford, 1963), pp. 113-122.

62. John Gay, *Polly* (London, 1729), Act III.

63. John Gay, *Rural Sports* (London, 1731), 11, 11-16.

64. Armens, *John Gay: Social Critic,* passim. Also see John Loftis, *Comedy and Society: Congreve to Fielding* (Stanford, 1957), p. 109.

65. There is a strong strain of rural radicalism and primitive egalitarianism in English thought which manifested itself in medieval peasant discontent and millenarium movements. In the seventeenth century this strain could be found in Anabaptist and Digger thought. Granted, then, that this tradition exists in England; but Gay's pastoral thought does not fit into such a framework. His fascination with the countryside is much more a reflection of aristocratic than egalitarian values, and is clearly related to the moral idealizing associated with the conventions of pastoral poetry, an aristocratic genre.

66. Gay, *Rural Sports,* pp. 409-412, 419-420.

67. The question might now be asked, what if anything does this reveal about Brecht's use of Gay? Is the nostalgic longing for a world before capitalism, characteristic of so much of romantic left-wing thought, at work in his writings, and to what extent does this make his choice of Gay's *Beggar's Opera* more meaningful?

68. John Gay, *Trivia* (London, 1731), pp. 489-490.

69. John Gay, *The Beggar's Opera*, Everyman Edition (London, 1946), p. xii.

70. John Gay, *The Beggar's Opera* (London, 1773), pp. 94, 99.

71. *Ibid.*, p. 113.

72. *Ibid.*, p. 115.

73. *Ibid.*, p. 130.

74. Hervey, *Memoirs*, p. 78.

75. *The Daily Gazetteer,* throughout 1737 and 1738, especially 20 February 1739. For material on Lyttelton's career, see Rosemary Davis, *The Good Lord Lyttelton* (Bethlehem, Pa., 1939); Lyttelton, *Correspondence*; and George Young, *Poor Fred: The People's Prince* (Oxford, 1937).

76. George Lyttelton, *Letters from a Persian in England to a Friend at Ispahan*

(London, 1734), Letter vi, p. 15; see also Letter cxxvii, p. 236. Note the relevance of the former letter to the suggestion above on the interpretation of *The Beggar's Opera.*

77. *Ibid.,* pp. xliii, 137.

78. *Ibid.,* pp. lxii, 187.

79. *Ibid.,* p. 189; George Lyttelton, *Ministerial Prejudices in Favor of the Convention, Examined and Answered* (London, 1739), p. 18.

80. Lyttelton, *Persian Letters,* Letter lxiii, pp. 191-193; Letter lxxxvi, p. 252.

81. *Ibid.,* p. lxxvii, 225.

82. Lyttelton, *Ministerial Prejudices,* p. 22.

83. *Popular Prejudices Against the Treaty with Spain Examined and Answered* (London, 1739), pp. 7-8.

84. Richard Pares, *War and Trade in the West Indies 1739-1763* (Oxford, 1936), passim.

85. Edmund Burke, *On a Regicide Peace,* in *Works,* 12 vols. (Boston, 1866-1867), V, 288-289.

86. For an excellent study of this aspect of Augustan writing, see M. H. Cable, "Idea of a Patriot King in the Propaganda of the Opposition to Walpole 1735-1739," *Philological Quarterly* 18 (January 1939), 119-130.

87. See Donald J. Green, *The Politics of Samuel Johnson* (New Haven, 1960), pp. 74-85.

88. James Thomson, *Edward and Eleonora* (London, 1739), pp. 20-21.

## CHAPTER IX. THE AMBIVALENCE OF THE AUGUSTAN COMMONWEALTHMAN

1. Caroline Robbins, *The Eighteenth-Century Commonwealthman* (Cambridge, Mass., 1959), p. 133. See also Z. S. Fink, *The Classical Republicans* (Evanston, Ill., 1945), and J. G. A. Pocock, "Machiavelli, Harrington, and English Political Ideologies in the Eighteenth Century," *William and Mary Quarterly* 22 (October 1965).

2. This is noted by Pocock in his William and Mary article.

3. Walpole, nevertheless, saw the opposition to his order as only Bolingbroke's circle. When in 1734 his *London Journal* wrote that "a Whig out of power, ever since the Revolution hath been a kind of state enthusiast, his head is turned with dreaming of a rotation of power from Harrington's *Oceana,* Plato's *Commonwealth,* Sir Thomas More's *Utopia* and other visionary schemes of government," it intended no establishment Whig critique of clandestine radical, "real Whigs," or Commonwealthmen. This quotation, part of the frontispiece to Miss Robbins' history of the Commonwealthman, is actually part of Walpole's press' continuous attack on *The Craftsman,* and Bolingbroke's Opposition. *The London Journal* continually blasted the Opposition in the 1730's as republican and utopian. The writings of the Augustan Commonwealthmen, on the other hand, are seldom mentioned in the weekly articles of Walpole's press. The issue of *The London Journal* (no. 787, 27 July 1734), quoted by Miss Robbins, is no exception; it was directed at Bolingbroke and William Pulteney, not at Molesworth, Toland, or Moyle. See also *The Daily Courant* of 11 March 1731, writing of the "dangerous Republican principles which *The Craftsman* had lately tended among us"; see also Lord John Hervey, *Conduct of the Opposition and the Tendency of Modern Patriots* (London, 1734) and its attack on Bolingbroke's Opposition because of its "chimerical Whig principles as are imbibed from Eutopian [sic] speculation," p. 37.

4. G. P. Gooch, *Political Thought in England, Bacon to Halifax* (London, 1960), p. 188; and J. R. Moore, *Daniel Defoe* (Chicago, 1958), passim.

5. Robbins, *The Eighteenth-Century Commonwealthman*, pp. 94-95, and Pocock, "Machiavelli, Harrington."

6. Charles Davenant, *Works*, 5 vols. (London, 1771), I, 319.

7. *Ibid.*, II, 296-297; III, 327-329.

8. *Ibid.*, III, 301.

9. *Ibid.*, II, 300, 308; III, 301.

10. *Ibid.*, I, 300ff; III, 30.

11. *Ibid.*, II, 289, cf. II, 275.

12. *Ibid.*, V, 22.

13. *Ibid.*, II, 341, 366-368, III, 301; V, 52.

14. *Ibid.*, II, 12; V, 33.

15. Robbins, *The Eighteenth-Century Commonwealthman*, passim.

16. Davenant, *Works*, IV, 292.

17. *Ibid.*, I, 181, 439; II, 304-305, 330-331; III, 59-63; IV, 309, 317-318, 340; V, 57.

18. *Ibid.*, IV, 130-264.

19. *Ibid.*, IV, 179, 208.

20. *Ibid.*, IV, 215.

21. *Ibid.*, IV, 146. With his characteristic penetration, J. G. A. Pocock has noted, in passing, the common qualities in Davenant and Bolingbroke's ideas. He places them quite rightly in the midst of what he calls the "country" attitude to politics. ("Machiavelli, Harrington," passim.) This is due to a great extent, as he claims, and as I hope is substantiated here, to the central importance of Harrington to both thinkers. I would, however, dissent from one small part of Pocock's discussion of Davenant, the contention that Davenant's *Essay Upon Ways and Means* (1695) indicates his abandonment of country principles and acceptance of the new economic and political order. *The True Picture of a Modern Whig*, after all, came some seven years later; moreover, the *Essay* itself is replete with characteristic Davenant "country" notions (e.g., pp. 110, 111, 156, 160). Nor is there any acceptance of the standing army in the *Essay*. There is merely the recognition that since wars were won by money, England had to raise money for some time, and that this needed to be done more equitably.

22. Thomas Gordon has been saved from obscurity by Pope's verse: *Epilogue to the Satires*, Dialogue I. "Twill only be thought/ The great man [Walpole] never offered you a groat/ There's honest Tacitus [Gordon] once talked as big,/ But is he now an independent Whig?" One of Gordon's works for Walpole was a lengthy introduction to his translation of Tacitus (London, 1728) in which he wed history and Walpole propaganda. For details on Trenchard and Gordon, see Robbins, *The Eighteenth-Century Commonwealthman*, pp. 116-125, and especially C. B. Realley, *The London Journal and its Authors* (University of Kansas, 1935), 2-35.

23. John Trenchard and Walter Moyle, *History of Standing Armies in England*, 2 ed. (London, 1739), vii, 12.

24. John Trenchard, *Some Consideration upon the State of our Public Debts in General, and of the Civil List in Particular* (London, 1720), pp. 6-7, 15 (British Museum catalogue No. 1093, d. 40). Trenchard's views on the Bubble and the new financial projects contained in this pamphlet are to be found in an expanded form in *Cato's Letters*. What is significant is the compactness with which they are found in this writing of 1720.

25. *Ibid.*, pp. 10, 28-29, 31.

26. All the citations from *Cato's Letters* are from the London edition of 1724.

27. *Cato's Letters*, I, 12, 24, 47, 58-59, 146, 189-190; III, 181, 182, 314; IV, 96, 246-247, 297-298.

28. *Ibid.*, I, 12, 117; III, 120, 177, 178 (for Agrarian law), 181-182.

29. *Ibid.*, I, 123; see also I, 110-111, 119, 139-140, 145, 204-206, 211, 306; III, 265-266.

30. *The Craftsman*, no. 268 (21 August 1731). References to Cato are found in *The Craftsman*, no. 267-292 of that summer. Walpole's press was not pleased with *The Craftsman's* use of a Whig journal; see *The London Journal* and *The Daily Courant* in August and September 1731. One interesting sidelight on the extent of *The Craftsman's* borrowing from *Cato's Letters* is the earlier appearance in *Cato's Letters* (II, 262-263; IV, 314-317), of similarly distorted historical accounts of Periclean corruption and venality.

31. *Cato's Letters*, II, 76; also I, 98-99, 304; II, 51, 80, 150; III, 296-307.

32. *Ibid.*, I, 181-182; II, 275, 280.

33. *Ibid.*, II, 234-241, 266-268; III, 209-210; IV, 4.

34. For this view of constitutionalism, see C. J. Friedrich, *Constitutional Government and Democracy* (Boston, 1950), p. 26, and C. H. McIlwain, *Constitutionalism: Ancient and Modern* (Ithaca, 1947).

35. *Cato's Letters*, I, 262, 266; II, 67; III, 326.

36. *Ibid.*, I, 197, 268-270; II, 41; III, 326-327.

37. *Ibid.*, II, 66-67, 173-175; III, 58-59, 70. For the American popularity and reception of Trenchard and Gordon and *Cato's Letters*, see *The Independent Reflector*, M. Klein, ed. (Cambridge, Mass., 1963), pp. 21-22. "*Cato* and the *Independent Whig* achieved a phenomenal popularity in the American colonies." Clinton Rossiter, *Seedtime of the Republic* (New York, 1953), p. 141, writes that Gordon and Trenchard were cited more often than Locke in colonial America. See also *Pamphlets of the American Revolution*, Bernard Bailyn, ed. (Cambridge, Mass., 1965).

38. Another possible influence of *Cato's Letters* is on Montesquieu. Robert Shackleton makes a strong case for Montesquieu's learning the evil of power and the need to check it from Bolingbroke. He also informs, however, that Montesquieu had read *Cato's Letters*, in which there is, as we have seen, this much more striking presentation of the checking and balancing argument (*Montesquieu: A Critical Biography* [Oxford, 1961], p. 292).

39. Robbins, *The Eighteenth-Century Commonwealthman*, p. 92.

40. The work was reprinted in *The Memoirs of John Ker* (London, 1726), pp. 191-221; citations here are from this 1726 reprint.

41. Molesworth, *Principles of a Real Whig* (London, 1711), pp. 220-221.

42. *Ibid.*, p. 192.

43. Robert Molesworth, *An Account of Denmark as It Was in 1692* (London, 1694).

44. Francis Hotman, *Franco-Gallia* (London, 1711). "Translated by the author of the Account of Denmark," p. ii; see Chapter X, pp. 63-77, for Hotman's description of "the form and constitution of the Franco-Gallican Government," and the very relevant praise of mixed government.

45. *The Craftsman*, no. 316, 322 (22 July and 2 September 1732); *The London Journal*, no. 690 (16 September 1732).

46. Molesworth, *Principles of a Real Whig*, pp. 202, 210, 212.

47. *Ibid.*, p. 205.

48. See, for example, Robbins, *The Eighteenth-Century Commonwealthman*, p. 3. This is a frontispiece quotation as well as the opening line of the book.

49. Molesworth, *Principles of a Real Whig*, pp. 192-193; in the Preface to the 1721 edition of *Franco-Gallia* the quotation appears on p. viii.

50. Walter Moyle, *The Political Works*, 2 ed. (Dublin, 1728).

51. *Ibid.*, p. 175.

52. Trenchard and Moyle, *History of Standing Armies*, p. i. *Cato's Letters*, III, 119-120.

53. Moyle, *Works*, pp. 29, 52-54.

54. Judith Shklar, "Ideology Hunting-Case of James Harrington," *American Political Science Review* 53 (September, 1959); and J. G. A. Pocock, *Ancient Constitution and Feudal Laws* (Cambridge, 1954), pp. 129-147.

55. Moyle, *Works*, p. 53.

56. *Ibid.*, p. 54.

57. *Ibid.*, pp. 96-99, 169-170.

58. Robbins, *The Eighteenth-Century Commonwealthman*, p. 107.

59. Moyle, *Works*, p. 177.

60. John Toland, *The Art of Governing by Parties* (London, 1701), pp. 7, 9-10, 41-43.

61. John Toland, *The State Anatomy of Great Britain* (London, 1717), pp. 14-18.

62. Toland, *Art of Governing*, pp. 70-71, 75-77.

63. Rapin de Thoyras, *A Dissertation Concerning the Whigs and Tories*, found in *The Memoirs of John Ker*, pp. 67-191.

64. Toland, *Art of Governing*, p. 34; see pp. 32-34 for the above citations.

65. Toland, *The State Anatomy*, pp. 10-11; also pp. 8-9, 13. Toland goes so far here as to describe Elizabeth as "the gloriousest figure of any monarch in Europe," p. 12.

66. John Toland, *The Danger of Mercenary Parliaments* (London, 1695), pp. 3-5.

67. Toland, *Art of Governing*, pp. 100; 165-166.

68. Robbins, *The Eighteenth-Century Commonwealthman*, p. 125. See in light of these comments the recent *English Libertarian Heritage: From the Writings of John Trenchard and Thomas Gordon*, David L. Jacobson, ed. (Indianapolis, 1965).

69. And even beyond this, in many cases to antiquity.

## CONCLUSION: TOWARD A REASSESSMENT OF BOLINGBROKE

1. Philip Dormer Stanhope, Earl of Chesterfield, *Letters to His Son* (London, 1744), I, 73.

2. Jonathan Swift, *Journal to Stella*, H. Williams, ed., 2 vols. (Oxford, 1948).

3. Jonathan Swift, *History of the Last Four Years of the Queen*, H. Davis, ed. (London, 1952), p. 135.

4. Voltaire, *Oeuvres*, Louis Moland, ed., 52 vols. (Paris, 1877-1885), X, 252.

5. *The Correspondence of Jonathan Swift*, F. E. Ball, ed., 6 vols. (London, 1910-1914), V, 305 (Pope to Swift).

6. Cited in *Life of Bolingbroke* in *The Works of Lord Bolingbroke*, 4 vols. (Philadelphia, 1841), I, 80.

7. *Daily Courant* (8 June 1732).

8. Horace Walpole, *Letters to Sir Horace Mann*, 2 vols. (London, 1833), II, 86.

9. Edmund Burke, *Reflection on the Revolution in France* in *Works*, 12 vols. (London, 1887), III, 349; G. D. H. Cole, *Politics and Literature* (London, 1929), p. 87.

10. Zoltan Haraszti, *John Adams and the Prophets of Progress* (Cambridge, Mass., 1952), pp. 51, 54.

11. *The Papers of Thomas Jefferson,* Julian P. Boyd, ed. (Princeton, 1950), I, 374 (Jefferson to Skipworth, "A Virginia Gentleman's Library").

12. C. G. Robertson, *Bolingbroke* (London, 1947), p. 13.

13. C. J. H. Hayes, "The Philosopher Turned Patriot," *Essay in Intellectual History Dedicated to J. H. Robinson* (New York, 1929), p. 189.

14. Archibald Foord, *His Majesty's Opposition* (Oxford, 1964), p. 142.

15. Harold Laski, *Political Thought in England—Locke to Bentham* (London, 1920), pp. 86, 90.

16. A. O. Aldridge, "Shaftesbury and Bolingbroke," *Philological Quarterly* 31 (January 1952), 16.

17. See Benjamin Disraeli, *Vindication of the British Constitution* (London, 1839).

18. See Walter Sichel, *Bolingbroke and His Times* (London, 1901-1902); Charles Petrie, *Bolingbroke* (London, 1937); and Richard Faber, *Beaconsfield and Bolingbroke* (London, 1961).

19. Keith Feiling, *What Is Conservatism?* (London, 1920), p. 35.

20. F. J. C. Hearnshaw, *Conservatism in England* (London, 1933), p. 154.

21. Maurice Wood, *A History of the Tory Party* (London, 1924), p. 178.

22. See Geoffrey Butler, *The Tory Tradition, Bolingbroke, Burke, Disraeli, and Salisbury* (London, 1957). This book was written and first published in 1914. It was reprinted by the Conservative Political Centre in 1957 with a new preface by R. A. Butler, the nephew of Sir Geoffrey Butler (*The Observer* [13 October 1963], p. 1). "Butler's Tory Program for People." Mr. Butler spoke of the Tory's traditional use of the state for the people. "We have used the power of the state since Bolingbroke, long before the Socialists were ever thought of."

23. Hugh Cecil, *Conservatism* (London, 1937), pp. 44, 118, 248ff.

24. See, for example, Harvey Glickman, "Toryness of English Conservatism," *Journal of British Studies* 1 (November 1961); S. H. Beer, *British Politics in the Collectivist Age* (New York, 1965); Sheldon Wolin, "Richard Hooker and English Conservatism," *Western Political Quarterly* 6 (March 1953), 28-47; "Hume and Conservatism," *American Political Science Review* 48 (December 1954); Samuel Huntington, "Conservatism as an Ideology," *American Political Science Review* 51 (June 1957).

25. See Hearnshaw, *Conservatism in England,* pp. 22ff, twelve principles of conservatism; Russell Kirk, *The Conservative Mind* (Chicago, 1953), pp. 7-8, has "six canons of conservative thought"; Clinton Rossiter has twenty-two principles of the Conservative tradition, *Conservatism in America* (New York, 1962), pp. 65-66; Hugh Cecil, *Conservatism,* pp. 48ff has six; Quintin Hogg, *The Conservative Case* (London, 1959), pp. 19-175, has seventeen "basic Conservative ideas"; Samuel Huntington, "Conservatism as an Ideology," p. 456, has "six major components of the Conservative creed."

26. See *The Complete Works of George Saville, first Marquess of Halifax,* Walter Raleigh, ed. (Oxford, 1912), pp. 50-51, 53, 63, 67, 209, 244; also Herbert Butterfield, *The Englishman and His History* (Cambridge, 1944), pp. 88ff; and G. P. Gooch, *Political Thought in England: Bacon to Halifax* (London, 1960), pp. 141-156.

27. A model of various kinds of conservative thought has recently been suggested in which three ideal varieties are isolated; aristocratic, autonomous, and situational (Samuel Huntington). Aristocratic conservatism, it is suggested, is the ideology of the aristocratic and agrarian reaction to the rise of liberalism and the middle class.

By definition, it is limited to a particular class and a particular time. Autonomous conservatism is the set of ideas and beliefs usually listed as "the conservative creed" unrelated to any one group or one era. Situational conservatism, then, is simply the defense of existing values and existing institutions whenever they are challenged, and whatever they may be. Burke, Huntington contends, could not have ascribed to the first, since he shared some of the emerging liberal values. He was, to be sure, principal author of the "creed"; but first and foremost he was a defender of existing institutions against challenge from any quarter. Bolingbroke, on the other hand, may not have shared the same creed of autonomous conservatism, but he was, we contend, a "situational" conservative par excellence. His entire corpus of political writings can be read in political terms as a defense of existing institutions and values in reaction to alleged departures from them effected by Walpole and the new order of post-Revolutionary England. Moreover, Bolingbroke was also an aristocratic conservative. One may question Huntington's exclusion of Burke from this category, but Bolingbroke is unmistakably a conservative on this score as well.

28. Karl Mannheim, "Conservative Thought," *Essays on Sociology and Social Psychology* (New York, 1953), p. 115.

# Index

# Index

# Index

# Index

# HARVARD POLITICAL STUDIES

\*Out of print

\*John Fairfield Sly. *Town Government in Massachusetts (1620-1930)*. 1930.

\*Hugh Langdon Elsbree. *Interstate Transmission of Electric Power: A Study in the Conflict of State and Federal Jurisdictions*. 1931.

\*Benjamin Fletcher Wright, Jr. *American Interpretations of Natural Law*. 1931.

\*Payson S. Wild, Jr. *Sanctions and Treaty Enforcement*. 1934.

\*William P. Maddox. *Foreign Relations in British Labour Politics*. 1934.

\*George C. S. Benson. *Administration of the Civil Service in Massachusetts, with Special Reference to State Control of City Civil Service*. 1935.

\*Merle Fainsod. *International Socialism and the World War*. 1935.

John Day Larkin. *The President's Control of the Tariff*. 1936.

\*E. Pendleton Herring. *Federal Commissioners: A Study of Their Careers and Qualifications*. 1936.

\*John Thurston. *Government Proprietary Corporations in the English-Speaking Countries*. 1937.

Mario Einaudi. *The Physiocratic Doctrine of Judicial Control*. 1938.

\*Frederick Mundell Watkins. *The Failure of Constitutional Emergency Powers under the German Republic*. 1939.

\*G. Griffith Johnson, Jr. *The Treasury and Monetary Policy, 1933-1938*. 1939.

\*Arnold Brecht and Comstock Glaser. *The Art and Technique of Administration in German Ministries*. 1940.

\*Oliver Garceau. *The Political Life of the American Medical Association*. 1941.

\*Ralph F. Bischoff. *Nazi Conquest through German Culture*. 1942.

Charles R. Cherington. *The Regulation of Railroad Abandonments*. 1948.

\*Samuel H. Beer. *The City of Reason*. 1949.

\*Herman Miles Somers. *Presidential Agency: The Office of War Mobilization and Reconversion*. 1950.

\*Adam B. Ulam. *Philosophical Foundations of English Socialism*. 1951.

\*Morton Robert Godine. *The Labor Problem in the Public Service: A Study in Political Pluralism*. 1951.

\*Arthur Maass. *Muddy Waters: The Army Engineers and the Nation's Rivers*. 1951.

\*Robert Green McCloskey. *American Conservatism in the Age of Enterprise: A Study of William Graham Sumner, Stephen J. Field, and Andrew Carnegie*. 1951.

\*Inis L. Claude, Jr. *National Minorities: An International Problem*. 1955.

\*Joseph Cornwall Palamountain, Jr. *The Politics of Distribution*. 1955.

\*Herbert J. Spiro. *The Politics of German Codetermination*. 1958.

Harry Eckstein. *The English Health Service: Its Origin, Structure, and Achievements*. 1958.

Richard F. Fenno, Jr. *The President's Cabinet: An Analysis in the Period from Wilson to Eisenhower*. 1959.

Nadav Safran. *Egypt in Search of Political Community: An Analysis of the Intellectual and Political Evolution of Egypt*. 1961.

Paul E. Sigmund. *Nicholas of Cusa and Medieval Political Thought*. 1963.

Sanford A. Lakoff. *Equality in Political Philosophy*. 1964.

Charles T. Goodsell. *Administration of a Revolution: Executive Reform in Puerto Rico under Governor Tugwell*. 1965.

Martha Derthick. *The National Guard in Politics*. 1965.

Bruce L. R. Smith. *The RAND Corporation: Case Study of a Nonprofit Advisory Corporation*. 1966.

David R. Mayhew. *Party Loyalty among Congressmen: The Difference between Democrats and Republicans, 1947-1962*. 1966.

Isaac Kramnick. *Bolingbroke and His Circle: The Politics of Nostalgia in the Age of Walpole*. 1968.